CRUISIN'

CAR CULTURE IN AMERICA

Michael Karl Witzel and Kent Bash

Lowe & B. Hould
Publishers

This edition published in 1999 by Lowe and B. Hould, an imprint of Borders, Inc., 515 East Liberty, Ann Arbor, MI 48104. Lowe & B. Hould Publishers is a trademark of Borders Properties, Inc.

Previously published in 1994, 1996, and 1997 by MBI Publishing Company, 729 Prospect Avenue, PO Box 1, Osceola, WI 54020-0001 USA

The information in this book is true and complete to the best of our knowledge. All recommendations are made without any guarantee on the part of the author or Publisher, who also disclaim any liability incurred in connection with the use of this data or specific details.

We recognize that some words, model names and designations, for example, mentioned herein are the property of the trademark holder. We use them for identification purposes only. This is not an official publication.

Library of Congress Cataloging-in-Publication Data Available

ISBN 0681-46068-7

On the front cover: Classic American cruisers, a split-window Corvette and a Shelby Cobra, tear down Route 66 in this painting by noted automotive artist Kent Bash. *Image courtesy George Cross and Sons, Pomona Swap Meet*

On the frontispiece: Car club plaques allowed cruisers to quickly identify street rivals. *Kent Bash*

On the title page: A speeding pack of muscle machines hauls down Detroit's Woodward Avenue, one of America's classic cruising strips. In the sixties and seventies, Woodward was home to endless street racing. *© 1997 Tom Shaw/Musclecar Review Magazine*

On the back cover: Top: What road trip would be complete without a burger and fries accompanied by some rock and roll courtesy of a tableside jukebox? *Michael Karl Witzel* Center: Route 66 is *the* American highway. In its heyday this mythic paved ribbon, running from Chicago to Los Angeles, played host to millions of travelers treating them to an endless array of roadside attractions. *Michael Karl Witzel* Bottom: Once Americans got in their cars and on the road, they just wanted to keep moving. Speedy drive-ins with curbside service helped them achieve that goal. *National Archives*

Printed in Hong Kong

Contents

Dedication

This book is in memory of Dave Wallen and dedicated to East Belknap Avenue, a once-vibrant cruising strip located deep in the heart of Haltom City, Texas. During the waning years of the seventies, I imagined that this linear representation of the American dream could be conquered with relative ease—as long as one possessed a cool car, a full tank of gas, and a blaring eight-track tape deck.

From its unofficial starting point at the sprawling complex of buildings that once housed Haltom High, it rolled right past a hodgepodge of "we tote the note" used car lots, commercial sales outlets, and third-rate motels. Within the first tenths of this miracle mile, the Belknap drive-in and its buffalo-bedecked screen (my alma mater's football mascot) announced its presence as *the* place for entertainment, socialization, and back-seat romance. At one time, I even worked there, flipping burgers and popping corn.

As the crossroads of Highway 377 zipped past, the asphalt followed a bead into the more urban section of town. There, the cacophony of wholesale and retail continued. Restaurants that were just beginning to steal the thunder from curb service stops became the unofficial landmarks: a vintage Arby's wearing multicolored cowboy hat neon and a Weinerschnitzel sporting a high-pitched roof. I reserved my unsophisticated palate for more basic car food, however: greasy cheeseburgers, fries, and a Coke.

With a languorous speed limit of just 30 miles per hour, Belknap straightened and sauntered past a Clownburger drive-in on the left and Griff's burger bar to the right. One and a half miles and four stoplights later, the ribbon of pavement unfurled a shameless path through a crazy jungle of juke joints, sleazy strip clubs, liquor stores, barbecue stands, greasy spoon cafes, second-hand furniture outlets, vacuum cleaner repair shops, and an ample assortment of porcelain-clad gasoline stations (I was awarded a pair of speeding tickets along this unforgettable stretch).

Beyond this illuminated mayhem of roadside commerce, bathed in the warm rays of flickering neon and the mournful sounds of a twanging pedal steel guitar (country and western music ruled in this part of town), the two-lane corridor dipped, curved, and slipped gracefully into the darkness. Overhead, a discordant highway overpass and its steady din of traffic marked the gateway to downtown Fort Worth and its deserted side streets. Here, a 180-degree turn was indicated to get back to the action. The busy cruisin' strip was over; East Belknap had run its course.

The Haltom City, Texas, cruising strip known as East Belknap Street was the driving destination of choice during the sixties and seventies. Today, it's just an alternate route heading into downtown Fort Worth. *Mike Witzel*

Foreword

I wish I had a dollar for every mile I cruised in my lifetime. If I did, I could retire and spend the rest of my days wrenching on hot rods and going on rod runs. No doubt about it, I've driven millions of miles going nowhere and doing nothing special. Sounds crazy, but that's what cruising is all about: driving for the fun of it. Showing off your car, looking for races, or better yet, looking for girls, was all a part of the action.

Egos were big during the fifties and sixties, and if you were cool and had a nice car, you had to cruise around your high school in the morning and after school to show it off. Despite the fact that I lived less than 100 yards away from my high school, I drove there in my car anyway just to "make the scene." It was an adolescent ritual that everyone followed.

I was fortunate enough to own two nice cars at the time, and they were both pretty well known by the entire school. In one of these, we would cruise to the high school football games on Friday nights. When we saw a good-looking girl walking to the game we would "shoot her a rev" to get her attention. It worked every time. Then, if her response was favorable, we would pick her up and give her a ride, or we would try to locate her at the game or the sock hop that was held after the game.

We also cruised the local hot spots around town. One of the most action-packed was King's Ice Cream Parlor. The location was a great one, right in a shopping center that had a record shop and a movie theater. Since all the local kids hung around the ice cream store and record shop, it was a natural place for cruising. Most of the girls that hung out there were hoping some fellow with a nice car would want to meet them. The cute ones were very, very successful; I can vouch for that.

Drive-in restaurants were also perfect places for cruising. In the southern California area, Bob's Big Boys were the top spots. Most of the kids who lived in the northern areas of the San Fernando Valley, a Los Angeles suburb, cruised Bob's Big Boy in San Fernando. Although every weeknight it was loaded with cars, on the weekends it was extremely busy. This particular Bob's had two lines you could get your car into: one for a parking spot that had car service and another just for cruising through!

Some of the nicest cars would cruise through, go around the block, and cruise through again. This could go on well into the night. It was like a revolving car show. The Bob's Big Boy in the town of Van Nuys was even better: At this location, a seemingly endless stream of hot rods and customs cruised through the lanes, and seldom did you see the same one. The line of cars that were waiting for service or cruising stretched out for a good number of blocks. At the busiest times, it wasn't at all unusual to be in line for an hour or more just to pick up a hamburger!

It sounds simple, but there was much more to cruising than just driving your car through a restaurant parking lot. There were unwritten rules you had to obey. First of all, you had to be cool doing it. If you owned a hardtop, all the windows had to be rolled down and the radio or Muntz four-track stereo had to be full blast. At the same time, you had to sit low in the seat. If it was a convertible, the top had to be down. If you were cruising through a drive-in after dark, your headlights had to be turned off the minute you got in the cruise line. If you were driving a custom, hubcaps were fine if they were Fiestas, spinners, Caddies, Moons, or chrome wheels with baldies, but if you were driving a stocker, the hubcaps had to come off (before leaving home), because otherwise everyone would accuse you of driving "Daddy's car."

A "good" cruiser never sat at its stock height either. In the early sixties, your car had to be low. After the muscle cars came out, it became acceptable to raise your car a little, just as the Super Stock racers of the era did. You also needed a dual exhaust setup with glasspack mufflers, so your car sounded really tough. If you were a member of a car club, the plaque had to be prominently displayed.

When you cruised through a restaurant, it had to be done very slowly, and you had to check everyone out while you were doing it. Some of the really cool custom guys even cruised with their shades on at night. If you were cruising with your girlfriend, she had to be sitting right next to you, even if that meant that she had to sit on the console! If you didn't follow the rules, everyone would know you were a novice cruiser. Not cool.

Many of these rules applied to cruising Van Nuys Boulevard, the ultimate cruising strip in the San Fernando Valley. This was one of many streets in southern California crowded with kids cruising and having a good time. Hawthorne Boulevard was another favorite in the South Bay area, and Whittier Boulevard was also a popular cruising strip. And there were countless others. People cruised these boulevards for a host of reasons, but the obvious ones were to check out the cool cars, show off your car, and try to get into races. Ultimately, though, most guys and gals cruised for social reasons.

Young fellows cruised for chicks, and the gals looked for guys. Cruising provided a chance to meet people who didn't go to your high school. Friday and Saturday night were hot, but Wednesday night was known as "girl's night" and the boulevard was packed. For a cover story, girls would inform their parents that they were going to a "girl's club meeting." Later, after the meeting, they went cruising! As they arrived, the guys were already there waiting to "pick up on them."

Here are the basics of the ritual: You cruise onto Van Nuys Boulevard, ending up in one group of traffic. If you spotted a carful of girls, you then tried to wind your way through cars until you were right next to them. If they looked good, you would strike up a conversation and make plans to meet them at Bob's Big Boy, or another location. Most of the time these "meetings" took place in front of the Praisewater Funeral Parlor, the only section of boulevard that wasn't lined with shops; it was more like a small park and became the favorite meeting area. If you didn't like any of the girls in your group of cars, you would cruise around the block one more time and join another group of cars to start the search all over again.

Some of the races run on the boulevard started the same way, except the flirtatious exchange was replaced by some guy making a sarcastic remark about your car. The manly thing to do was "blow his doors off." But most of the cool guys wouldn't choose-off another car on the boulevard; they would go to the parking lot where street racers hung out. That's where the real racing action was taking place, for money. Guys who tried to start races out on the boulevard were usually high school nerds driving Daddy's car for the night.

Ah, the good ol' days. We were all having fun with cars and really didn't have a care in the world. Without a doubt, it would be fun to relive those days. Unfortunately, all of it changed during the mid-sixties, and it hasn't been the same since. For those who would like to take a trip into the past and experience that way it was, *Cruisin'* provides a comprehensive look at how cruising evolved, the cruising heydays of the fifties, the muscle car influence of the sixties, a look at contemporary boulevard action, and a prediction of what the future holds for cruising. Read on and learn all about it. Me? I'm gonna turn up the radio, lay a patch of rubber, and cruise off into the sunset.

—Jeff Tann, editor, *Rod & Custom*

Acknowledgments

Thank you to all of the car nuts, gearheads, grease monkeys, automaniacs, customizers, hot rodders, shade-tree mechanics, and motoring maniacs who assisted with time, advice, knowledge, and materials. The top eliminators: Howard Ande, Bill Aufman, Jerry Bryant, Steph Butler, Martin Cable, Frank and Sondra Campbell, Randy Chadd, Pat Chappel, Eunice Christianson, Gil Clayton, Dan Daniels, Joseph DeRenzo, Michael Dregni, Albert Doumar, Fred Dupuis, Peggy Dusman, Sue Elliott-Sink, Wolfgang Fanth, Tic and Kay Featherstone, Mike Fennel, Howard Frank, Robert Genat, Robin Genat, Margaret Gifford, Scott Guildner, Serena Gomez, Mike Goyda, Shellee Graham, Frederick B. Group, Tab Guildner, Richard Hailey, Mark Hamilton, Dan Harlow, John Hutinett, Joan Johnson, Parker Jones, Dave King, Max Klaus, Gary and Diane Lick, Derek Looney, Harold Looney, Joe Loprino, Ron Main, Cliff Maxwell, Jerry McClanahan, Bill and Cindy McClung, Duncan McIntyre, Richard Mclay, Mike and Cindy Morgan, Bill Norton, Tom Otis, Brett Parker, Clare Patterson Jr., Dalton Patterson, Steve Perrault, Louis Persat, Wes Pieper, Ed Potthoff, Don Preziosi, Mike Rascoe, Halvin "Jackrabbit" Releg, David Rodarte, Ted Roen, Jerry and Linda Rogers, Mel Santee, Perry Schafer, Tom Shaw, Robert Sigmon, Charles F. Smith, Andy Southard, Gary Spaniol, Larry Spaniol, Mel Spaniol, Harry Sperl, Alice C. Stewart, Mel Strong, Jeff Tann, Clark "Crewcut" Taylor, Paul Taylor, George and Beverly Tibbs, Jeff Tinsley, Bud Toye, Cheryl Travers, Charles Vandreason, A. J. Vogel, Dave Wallen, Mike Wallen, "Slim" Waters, J. Frank Webster, Steven Weiss, Anthoula White, Jerry White, John White, June Wian, Tim Wisemann, Joe Van Witsen, Gyvel Young-Witzel, Brock Yates, and Hervez Zapata. Finally, a special thank you goes out to all the organizations that assisted with various photographic images and research, including Applied Images Inc., American Automobile Manufacturers Association, American Petroleum Institute, Automotive Hall of Fame, Burbank Historical Society, Chevron Inc., Circa Research and Reference, George Cross and Sons, Inc., C. W. Moss Auto Parts, the Library of Congress, Dallas Public Library, Detroit Public Library National Automotive History Collection, Douglas Photographic, Henry Ford Museum and Greenfield Village, the National Archives, Personality Photos, Phillips Petroleum Company, Security Pacific National Bank Photograph Collection of the Los Angeles Public Library, Steak n' Shake Inc., University of Louisville Photographic Archives, and the University of Southern California Library Whittington Collection.

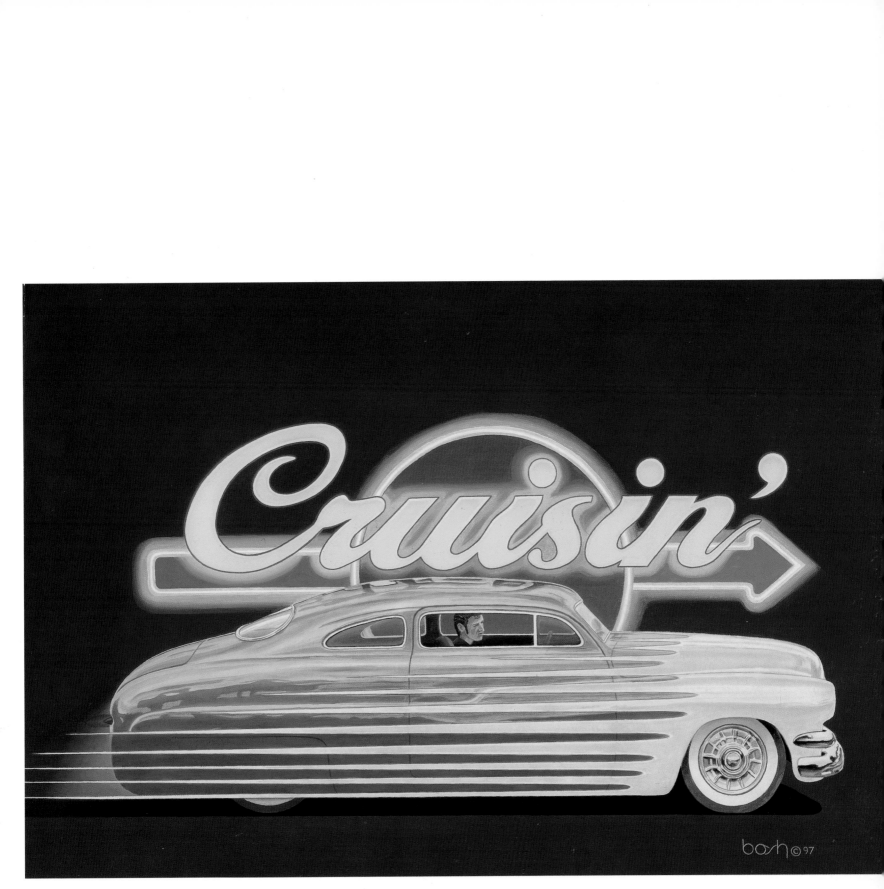

Introduction

I Feel the Need for Speed

The urge for vehicular movement begins young; the influences that guide our subconscious toward "automotive frenzy" are first encountered in our youth. During this formative period, our minds take in a vast variety of stimuli, analyze the information, and store it for retrieval at some later date.

It's no wonder children can't wait to get their feet on the accelerator pedal! Since the early days of the wheel, mobile contraptions have colored a baby's first trips into the outside world. After successfully entering the world, attendants wheel the infant from the delivery room on a gurney, where it is most likely placed in a basket mounted atop four tiny wheels. Some might argue that the first fuzzy images a child sees are the happy, smiling faces of parents, but there's no denying the influence of the dizzying blur of ceiling and lamp fixtures whizzing past the baby's eyes as it makes the rounds from delivery room to newborn ward.

Once the child is transported home, the introduction to vehicular movement is further reinforced. The car trip home becomes the first pleasing experience of mobility. As Dad takes the automobile up to speed, the engine begins to hum, and the gentle rocking motion over the roadbed mimics the environment within the womb. Enclosed in the vehicle's protective shell, the child lies face up staring at a headliner and dome lamp as an entirely new world rushes past the windows.

Within days, parents treat the new arrival to a host of adventures, by means of a variety of wheeled contraptions. First comes the standard baby carriage. The fledgling gearhead lies recumbent in a kind of open coach—a roadster if you will—guided by its parents. Much like a hot rodder running along the dry lake beds, the child cruises along the sidewalk, safely tucked in and wearing a knit-weave crash helmet and a woolen-

blanket safety belt. A parent's firm grasp on the handlebar is the only brake to stop its forward movement.

But while the baby becomes the center of attention for friends and relatives, the carriage often takes on as much significance as the newborn itself. Always on public parade and demonstration, this simple child transporter becomes the outward indication of the parents' prosperity, social standing, style, and personality. The infant's "ride" functions as the predecessor for all four-wheeled status to follow, whether the tiny passenger is aware of it or not. Long before we utter the word *car*, the competition for speed and beauty has begun.

Parents who earn a decent wage can afford the luxury of pushing little junior down the avenue in the finest of perambulators. Automotive-like features such as a landau roof, convertible top, removable sunshade, rubber tires, ball-bearing hubs, spoke wheels, adjustable undercarriage, parking brake, chrome-plated trim, tufted upholstery, removable mattress, and a spring-cushioned suspension are some of the extras that leave budget baby carriages in the dust. Coincidentally, most of these features translate to the automobiles of later years.

In the final analysis, it's our parents who unknowingly prepare us for the attack of "automania" that occurs during adolescence. There's a good chance our folks have dragged, dropped, and driven us in almost every kind of rolling contraption while we were still very young. We are completely powerless to resist the draw of internal combustion and movement. By the teenage years, the wheel has become another extension of our body, and we are ready to assume ownership of mobility and embrace it fully. It's time to cruise.

Hot rod rides enjoyed for a nickel were perhaps some of the first automotive experiences children remember. Unlike a smooth riding car, these rides—with their exaggerated movements and sound effects—provided a fertile base for the imagination to form its own opinions about speed and motion. Even at such an early age, the desire for a better street machine begins. No doubt this toddler is pointing at a better ride just down the midway of this Pine Brook, New Jersey, auction market. *Author portrait/courtesy Karl Witzel*

Directly and indirectly, children are taught the wonders of the automobile from the time of birth. In the imaginations of the young, it's quite easy to turn a home-built go-cart into a full-house street machine. Today, as it always was, this is the seed behind the entire hot rod movement. *Kent Bash*

13

America's Heyday for Hot Rods

Forming the Obsession for Cruising

"I remember my older brothers buying their first car together when I was around six or seven years old. It was the early fifties, and there was this guy living up the street who had an old automobile—I think it was a Nash or a Willys—sitting there on the curbside near his house. It sat there gathering dust for a few years, just begging for a new owner. Hot for the road and for girls, my two brothers were destined to buy it.

Dangerously close to the legal driving age and eager to get behind the wheel, my brother Gary walked down and talked to the guy about the possibility of him selling his relic (it hadn't been fired up in years). At first, the man wasn't keen on the idea, and he started bragging about how he would eventually fix the thing up. Little did the guy know that this was precisely the plan my brother had—sort of.

Fortunately, the neighbor changed his mind and agreed to sell the old clunker. The asking price was a grand total of 10 bucks. My brothers pooled their cash, and after a handful of dollar bills were exchanged, they became the proud owners of their very first set of wheels. Excited by the prospect of cruising around town in their new prize, they pushed the bomb home. There in our driveway, they began work on reviving the dead engine with a devotion that bordered on mania.

As it turned out, it took a lot of tinkering and tweaking to get that baby running. What's worse, the junker didn't even have floorboards in the back seat. No big deal—they just patched the holes by welding in a few pieces of scrap metal! Jury-rigged repairs were the standard of the day. No other option existed really. There simply weren't many places for a gearhead to pick up resto parts such as fenders or interior trim. To fix up a ride and personalize it, you picked up a few more cheap wrecks as donor cars and towed them home. Stuff was removed from one car and added to another. If the pieces you needed didn't match up with your jalopy, they were just cut to fit!

In those days, kids didn't have access to store-bought parts, aftermarket goodies, or other repros. During the fifties, guys like my brothers, who were wigged out on cars and had a burning desire to bolt together their very own hot rod, relied on good old-fashioned American ingenuity to get rolling. The fact that a guy was broke and unable to buy parts wasn't a handicap at all. Lack of money was the mother of all invention and creativity."

—Kent Bash

Throughout the decades, the businesses involved with the repair and modification of automobiles have provided the fertile breeding grounds for all manner of hot rods and custom cars. Since materials and equipment were readily available, shop down time was put to good use, resulting in lookers like the flamed 1932 Ford Roadster and gleaming 1951 Mercury shown in this scene. *Kent Bash*

Chapter One

A M E R I C A ' S cruise craze reached a frenzy during the fifties and, like a juggernaut on wheels, kept right on rolling. Postwar society regarded the modern-day, motorized equivalent of the horse-drawn carriage a necessary element of every person's life—a gadget essential for all manner of employment, travel, and recreation. The prosperity that followed World War II created an exceedingly amicable climate for cars, and the automobile transcended its more obvious uses and rose from the streets to become a distinct part of American culture.

The cult of the American teenager and the culture of the automobile were racing toward each other at high speed—head on. When they finally collided in the streets, motorists felt the impact nationwide, and before all was said and done, the sounds of squealing tires and rumbling mufflers reverberated from coast to coast.

Both the auto and the automobilist were changing. Kids were snapping up old cars, tinkering with the engines to make them go faster, reshaping the bodies to make them look sportier, and reworking suspensions to achieve an altered ride. No longer an afterthought, paint became a dramatic way to display one's style. Motoring the drives of Detroit and the lanes of Los Angeles, one could witness the metamorphosis: Cruisers reworked their cars to reflect the changing attitudes of a new generation. Suddenly, the accepted standards of mechanics and design were being rewritten as a new form of vehicular jazz. High

By 1925, three out of every four cars in America were being purchased on the installment plan. More and more people could get in on the American dream and with little or no money down look as if they were doing better than they actually were. At the same time, the popularity of golf surged, and it seemed everyone was taking up the sport and putting on the outward appearance of prosperity. Car makers responded with a roadster revival to lure this sporty crowd into showrooms. Later, these two-door convertibles would become the body style favored most by America's first hot rodders. *From the collections of the Texas/Dallas History and Archives Division, Dallas Public Library*

notes were being hit across America and the virtuosos of the genre coined a new phrase to describe their driving passions: *hot rod*. Christened by the collective consciousness of a nation and baptized with mechanic's sweat, a new variation of the automobile was born that all at once was loose, wild, hip, and racy.

According to the late Dean Batchelor, automotive journalist extraordinaire and author of *The American Hot Rod*, "any production vehicle which has been modified to provide more performance" may be classified as a hot rod. Though that defined hot rods in the early years, it might be more inclusive to say that a hot rod is any engine-dominated vehicle that breaks accepted rules and invents new ones. Forty years ago, that's precisely what returning servicemen were doing. Landing in the shore cities of California, they returned with practical, hands-on experience in the disciplines of aircraft design and engineering. Unlike shade-tree mechanics who understood only the functional basics of cars, these ex-servicemen possessed valuable experience in the design principles that made it all work. To their credit, they applied the knowledge to the creation of automobiles.

Because of the proliferation of good roads, a year-round mild climate, and the vast availability of second-hand cars, California quickly became the number one breeding ground for these future hot rodders. In light of the fact that California led the rest of the nation in the ratio of population to motor vehicle registrations, it wasn't extraordinary that the West Coast became the hot bed of American automotive activity. As far back as 1929, the statistics were already raising eyebrows: For every two and one-third residents, one motor vehicle was wheeling down the street! When the automobile manufacturing industry compared this ratio to the national average, they categorized the California market as the "bottomless pit" of automotive sales!

Although hot rod historians acknowledge that the modification of cars and their engines probably occurred around the same time nationwide, it was the Golden State that nurtured the movement into a full-blown obsession and made it a cultural phenomenon. As experimentation with modified vehicles took place, California operators made plans to serve all the smoking, sputtering hoards motoring down the pike. Car-oriented

businesses of all types sprang up: In 1929, Harry Carpenter built a series of drive-in restaurants in Los Angeles and before too long, it seemed that everyone thought of eating and driving as the same thing. Drive-in shopping centers sprouted, along with drive-in theaters, drive-in dry cleaners, drive-in banks, and even drive-in car washes. By the time hot rods gained notoriety during the fifties, roadside businesses provided the self-sustaining loop: Additional cars created more commerce, and additional commerce created more cars.

Without a doubt, all of those heaps and hot rods clogging the streets made the notion of cruising around in a car difficult to ignore. Plus, the image of the decadent hot rodder leaving a trail of madness and mayhem in his wake was just the ticket for those young people wishing to stir up the

The 1950s was a great time to be a kid and a great time to learn about the joys of owning an automobile. In America's sprawling suburban settlements (like the one that sprouted in California's San Fernando Valley), streets and sidewalks were busy with all sorts of vehicular activity. Foot-powered bicycles, tricycles, and scooters vied for space as pedal cars like this fetching police cruiser (driven by future street cruiser Mike Wallen) zipped along the sidewalks in search of automotive fun and adventure. It's ironic that the same kids would one day be pulled over by the cops while cruising. ©1997 Dave Wallen

In 1928, the nation was high on the automobile and every available hour of leisure time was spent in pursuit of activities within vehicles. This "human hood ornament" pose is a perfect example of the giddiness of the era. Pictured here is actress Sally Blane, a player for Paramount pictures. The vintage ride is an Oldsmobile Landau sedan. *The Automotive Hall of Fame*

older set's emotions. In September 1955, actor James Dean personified the defiance felt by an entire generation of teens and aptly portrayed the rebellion in film. Although the establishment didn't know it then, *Rebel Without a Cause* marked a turning point in the hot rod movement, with the doomed misfit Dean cast as the speed-loving, drag-racing, chicken-playing troublemaker. At long last, the hot rodders-turned-juvenile-delinquents had their poster boy.

In an uncanny twist that became automotive irony, Dean met his untimely death three days before producers released the movie. While driving his Porsche 550 Spyder on Highway 46 near Paso Robles, California, another vehicle crossed his path on a wide curve and the two crashed—with fatal results. In the frenzy of posthumous adulation that

A MONOGRAM PICTURE
with
JAMES LYDON

Baker · Gil Stratton, Jr. Gloria Winters · Myron Healy

duced by JERRY THOMAS · Directed by Lewis D. Collins Screenplay by Dan Ullman

"Spindizzies," or toy racing vehicles that employed miniature internal combustion engines to make them go, were one of the more exciting types of car toys for children who grew up during the twenties and thirties. Without a doubt, toys like these set young imaginations to wonder what it would be like to drive at high speeds in a real car. *Courtesy Jerry Bryant*

followed, teenagers began to covet the freedom and mobility afforded by the motor vehicle more than ever before—whether their parents approved of the idea or not. The car, and especially the hot rod, was crazy, sexy, and cool.

To be fair, impressionable adolescents of the era had no choice over their drive-in destiny: A seemingly endless parade of billboards, magazine advertisements, radio programs, television commercials, and popular films assailed the senses with automotive propaganda. In mainstream periodicals such as *Life* and the *Saturday Evening Post*, one couldn't turn more than a few pages before catching sight of a gleaming new machine. Oil companies sponsored the latest radio and television programs, and shows like the *Texaco Star*

Theater promoted gasoline consumption. The gas station attendant became a friendly assistant, one who filled your car with the fuel needed to motor out to the local drive-in theater or movie palace. There, virtually every motion picture featured a combination of new cars and hot rods.

By the time Dwight D. Eisenhower signed the American Highway Act of 1956, teenagers were hypnotized by automobiles and the allure of driving. Everyone was. As work on more than 40,000 miles of modern, concrete, four-lane "limited-access" highways began, America's adolescents desperately clutched at the wheel to log as many miles as they possibly could. Indoctrinated by more than 15 years of training in baby carriages, strollers, tricycles, bicycles, pedal cars, and the various "motor toys" of childhood, there was no way to deny them a place behind the wheel.

Since the early 1900s, American family photo albums and personal scrap books have been characterized by happy images of people sitting in their automobiles or standing somewhere near them. However, no documentation of the long journey to one's automotive independence can be complete without a snapshot of Junior and his first motoring machine, the pedal car. The teenage years—and the hot rod yearning that they inevitably bring—are waiting only a few miles down the road. *Courtesy John Hutinett*

Going on a cruise with the entire family was one of the main leisure activities for the nuclear family of the 1950s. The car provided the means to get wherever Mom and Dad wanted to take us—whether that was on a vacation, a trip to Grandma's house, or down to the local shopping center. *Courtesy American Automobile Manufacturers Association*

The following text appears within the image:

HOT ROD 5¢ **BUBBLE GUM**

22 **Spec Sheet**

HOT ROD DICTIONARY

QUARTER—quarter mile

RAIL JOB—an all-out dragster, because its frame is made from thin tubing.

TRAPS—area at end of strip where speed and elapsed time are measured.

WIPED OUT—to h...

...get your complete HOT ... ...heck offer on back of wrapp...

SERIES 1 NUMBE...

GET MORE OUTS' PICTURES EVER' ...test HOT ROD - DRAGSTER ... 7"x10" Full color pin-up HOT ROD maga...

GET YOUR COPY VORITE NEWS D ...nd $3.25 by check or mo 10 month trial subsc... HOT ROD MAG ...EPT. BGL 5954 HOLLY LOS ANGELES, CALI...

...D DICTIONARY

HOT ROD DICTIONARY

...and 5 Hot Rod Bubble Gum wrappers for your HOT ROD DICTIONARY to: HOT ROD DICTIONARY P. O. BOX 2838 MEMPHIS, TENN. 38102

DONRUSS CO., MFR., MEMPHIS, TENN. MADE AND PRINTED IN U.S. GUM BASE, SUGARS, CORN SYRUP, NATURAL AND ARTIFICIAL FLAVOR AND U.S. CERTIFIED COLOR. CONTENTS 1 SLAB BUBBLE GUM AN... PICTURE CARDS. © B.L.W.

The culture of the hot rod had such a pervasive effect on the popular culture of America during the fifties and sixties that all sorts of products took advantage of the theme. In addition to a wad of chewing gum, kids got great trading cards of neat rods and a lot of inside info on the back. *Courtesy Mike & Cheryl Goyda*

Regardless of race, color, creed, or social standing, this unceasing urge to "go mobile" became a universal phenomenon among our nation's young people (it remains so today). "When I was a kid I just couldn't wait to get my driver's license," reminisced Jeff Tann, editor of *Rod & Custom* magazine. "I bought my first car, a Model A Ford, when I was 14 years old and

would sometimes sneak it out when my parents weren't home. I would cruise the 'A' on the local back streets of my neighborhood and check out all the other hot cars in the area. In the process, I met a lot of older guys who told me about all the great cruising spots they'd been to. When I was finally old enough to get my driver's license, I already knew where all the best cruising places were, and naturally I had to visit each and every one."

Not surprisingly, Tann's cruising experience is not unique. Most males who grew up during the fifties succumbed to the siren song of the internal combustion engine, and some even decided to make it their life's work. Even as early as the thirties, more progressive high schools across the nation had added to their curricula a new type of industrial arts course known as "auto shop." Initially viewed as an elective intended to train those individuals without plans for college, it proved to be a salvation for countless kids who harbored childhood dreams of building a car that looked hot and ran fast. Kids enrolled in droves just so they could get their hands on some *real* tools, like hydraulic hoists and other tools of the trade

Contrary to popular belief, auto shop enrollees weren't dumb. While some lacked the patience for "book learnin'," many proved their mettle in the mechanical arts, and for them auto shop became a place where they could learn practical, tangible skills and get immediate feedback from their efforts. Young men (and a few women) worked with their hands and mastered the techniques required to construct hot rods of their own design. Engines, exhausts, body panels, and bumpers became the outlet for excess energy. Future gearheads and drag racers spent time rebuilding carburetors and packing their fingernails full of grease while high school socialites (more commonly referred to as "soshes") crammed for college entrance exams and memorized algebraic equations.

Present-day hot rodding enthusiast and restorer Wolfgang Fanth was one of those hot rod hopefuls. "When I was goin' to high school back in '54, hot rods were the one thing I dreamed about most . . . next to girls," he claimed. "I practically lived in the garage of our school's shop, and so did a lot of other guys. One May afternoon, I dozed off under a 1932 Ford heap I was fixin' up and woke to find that all the lights had been turned out. Everyone had split! I ended up stayin' all night until I got the gearbox I was workin' on put back together." For parents and teachers, it was incidents like these that defined the teenagers' strong points of view when it came to their cars.

Of course, there was whole a lot more behind the car fetish than just the hankering to waste after-school hours avoiding homework and zigzagging aimlessly around town. The obsession for motors and cars took root in the compulsion to make contact with the opposite sex! As envied as they were, those spoiled preppies whose parents

Future hot rodder Mel Spaniol taking the first steps to building a Model A roadster in the growing bedroom community of Woodland Hills, California, circa 1954. After the work was completed, the vehicle was hand painted with a brush, the young hot rodder's tool of choice when it came to affordable paint jobs. *Courtesy Mel Spaniol*

Mel and Gary Spaniol, two brothers and fellow hot rodders who knew a good deal when they saw one. The 1935 Willys in the background was the first car they bought, purchased from a neighbor down the street when Gary turned 16. This was the age of the $10 car, a carefree time when wheels could be picked up on the cheap, and no one imagined that a car would one day cost as much as a house. *Courtesy Gary Spaniol*

Most kids who grew up in the postwar era didn't have a lot of money, and the cars they built were sometimes never finished. At cruise nights, cruisers like Fifties Dan, spark the memory and remind those who drive today's ultimate cruisers of their hot rod roots: primer paint jobs, blanket seat covers, missing parts, and engines that were constantly being repaired and overhauled. *Kent Bash*

Hidden away in garages and barns and owned by little old ladies and crusty old curmudgeons, hot rod stock like this 1930 Model A awaited discovery by budding cruisers in small towns across the land. Before these cars became collectibles, hot rodders found little trouble and little expense in talking their owners out of them. Doing all of the work required to make them over into a hot street machine was the hard part. *Kent Bash*

had the resources to purchase the newest model Chevrolet convertible for their offspring knew the score; without a doubt, a cool car was a prerequisite to get girls and to get laid. If that car was a racy, sexy hot rod, one had a good shot. So car owners became aware of the numero uno reason for cruising: Driving an awesome automobile was the most effective way to attract females and keep their interest—far from the prying eyes of parents and other adult authority figures. While parked out on Lover's Lane, the "submarine races" at the lake, or right in the parking lot of the town's drive-in movie theater, the automobile provided the young and the restless a portable, private compartment to act out the tentative night moves of youth.

At the same time, the car and all of its wonderful trappings supplied a ready outlet to vent the effervescent emotions of the teen. That's where the hot rod came in. While at the controls of a boss heap, drivers expressed sexual and aggressive urges by stomping down on the accelerator pedal. The result? Instant power and immediate gratification. Furthermore, the car provided rambunctious juveniles a highly visible way to rebel against their elders (both at school and home) and even enabled the unpopular fringe to show off among peers.

The simple possession of an automobile imbued the American teen with more than just ownership status. The automobile was a magic carpet ride that promised to fulfill every fantasy. The simple acts of sliding a key into the ignition, turning over the engine, and pulling out into traffic, allowed young adults to transform themselves into something that they weren't, to mimic the personalities of their heroes, or build an entirely new legend of their own choosing.

Abandoned by their original owners, future hot rods and custom automobiles began their second lives in America's junkyard. Although it's acknowledged by scholars that fifties "assemblage" artist John Chamberlain first used the scrap of junked cars as sculpture material for his three-dimensional artwork, cruisers would be happy to inform you that it was the clique of unruly hot rodders, the clans of customizers, and the cool lowriders who first rearranged the discards of America's scrap heaps into meaningful, motorized art. *Mike Witzel*

As a birthplace for hot rods, this Wisconsin garage was just like countless other automotive shops strewn across American during the thirties. In places like these, motor mechanics had all of the tools necessary to create the fast, cool cars that existed only in their imaginations. Mechanics working in shops like this ushered in a dramatic new automotive era. *©1997 Dave Wallen*

For parents, age 13 is when the trouble usually began. It had all started out quite harmlessly with father allowing junior to "steer" the car when he was just a toddler. Over the years, this innocuous activity developed into a constant wailing to control the wheel. By the age of 15 or 16, overly anxious teenagers were officially ready to learn how to drive and parents instructed them on how to do it. From the driveway and beyond, unschooled drivers had to endure frantic yelling, horrific contortions of the face, screams to "put on the brakes,"

and crazed howls of fear to "slow down!" For the sake of cars and cruising, they persevered. When a student driver was finally ready to go down to the motor vehicle department to take the driving test and win his or her learner's permit, it was a grand occasion indeed—exceeding the importance of birthdays, Christmas, and all the other holidays in between. With both the written and the physical driving test passed, all the waiting was over. Once kids gained possession of the signed slip of paper from the testing officer's pad, the joys of the automobile became readily accessible. Hot rod hell was keeping a back burner stoked and ready for all new arrivals. The only remaining activity was finding access to a car—any car!

Unfortunately, borrowing mother and father's stodgy four-door sedan, pickup truck, or Woody left many socially conscious kids wanting more. Since buying a new vehicle was almost always out of

the question (for the average kid), so-called "used cars" became a teen's first automotive purchase. There were a lot to choose from, since Detroit had sold 6,326,528 brand-spanking new cars in 1950 alone! During the decade of dazzle, General Motors rolled out 26,215,080 shiny new machines restyled to reflect the optimism of the era. By then, America's motor market was ready, willing, and able to buy, and it wasn't long before soaring tail fins, gleaming chrome, and wide whites took up driveway space. Finally, those worn-out flivvers that saw motorists through the lean years of gas rationing and conservation joined the funeral march to the scrap heap. At last, old motoring stock became freed up—allowing every grease monkey to construct a hot rod and go cruisin'.

With little pomp and ceremony, the mid-forties ushered in the age of the jalopy. By 1948, there were well over 8,000 scrap and junk wholesalers selling and parting out defunct cars in the United States! Somewhere, out there—waiting for resurrection—were the battered hulks of long-forgotten sedans, touring coupes, and roadsters. Stacked high amid the mud and weeds, America's youthful

En route to the Pacific, World War II servicemen shipping out for duty passed through southern California. When they returned from overseas, they brought back a variety of talents in mechanics. After they settled in the region, it didn't take long for these skills to be transmuted to cars. Across driveways, mechanics shared information with their neighbors. Fathers passed down car knowledge to their progeny, as if it were a family history to be revered. Similarly, the groups of teens huddled around drive-in restaurants passed on auto wisdom to all who would listen. Eventually, even schools began holding classes in "auto shop." *John Collier, Library of Congress*

car nuts rescued them from the acetylene torch and car crusher. Along the roadways less traveled, junkyards overflowed with the rusting remnants of forlorn Fords, memorable Mercurys, derelict DeSotos, and crunched Cadillacs—all were excellent pickings for prospective car builders eager to find their diamond in the rust. While in the establishment's view the junkyard was a cemetery for discarded clunkers, young people knew better. For them, the junkyard was a place of promise, the nursery for hot rods, and the primordial soup from which all the great motoring machines to come would soon be born.

So, with learner's permit in pocket or driver's license clutched tightly in hand, the youth of the late forties and early fifties ventured off in search of an acceptable vehicle. As they delivered the newfound prize to its home and dragged it up on the suburban housing tract like a beached whale, mothers peered out from their kitchen windows and fretted about the grease tracks while fathers wrung their hands over the blocked driveway. One-time bomber plant riveter (and mother) Eunice Christianson recalled those days with marked trepidation: "My son Johnny was eat up with that hot rod thing. I'll never forget the day he came home all covered with dirt and grease and oh, so happy as a lark. He was just grinning from ear to ear, beaming over the jalopy he and his friends had just bought at the junkyard 'cross town. My, oh my, the driveway was ruined after that, and my husband had no end of trouble trying to keep the mess from spreading! Until John joined the service, I can't remember one time when there wasn't an old beat-up wreck out there dripping grease all over the place." Drunk with the thoughts of gearshifts, gasoline, and girls spinning

around in their heads, proud Johnnys all over the country were digging into their toolboxes—oblivious to the reactions of disbelief.

All across America, would-be mechanics raised hoods and rolled up their shirt sleeves. The youthful segment of car culture had begun the great experiment. Inspired by the same muses that once guided the coachbuilders of the automobile's golden age, they proceeded to imagine, conceive, and eventually (if they could find all of the parts) construct what they thought a really "neat" car should be. With a couple of years of formal training in the technical arts of the automobile (and some didn't have that), it was nothing more than an overwhelming feeling of self-determination, a few heartbeats of hopeful talent, and plain blind luck that aided their haste to become mobile.

Never mind that the heaps and hot rods that rumbled, lurched, and sputtered forth from the depths of suburban garages, filling stations, and back alleys of America were the direct opposite of the factory-assembled standard. Even though these homemade cars never attained the refinement of mass-produced vehicles, they were by no means less attractive in the mind's eye of those who built

Although these days it's become more difficult, discovering a Model T Touring Car like this rusting relic was the genesis for many a hot rod project in the fifties and sixties. To the uninitiated, this useless hulk may have looked like just so much scrap metal. But to a hot rodder, it was a precious find that only required some hard work and ingenuity to transform it into a prized possession. *Kent Bash*

During the forties and fifties, the 1928–1931 Model A Roadster was one of the most accessible and affordable vehicles to use when one was thinking of building a hot rod. For a teenager who desired to go mobile, all it took was a few visits to the local junkyard to uncover treasures that had been dreamed of for so long. More often that not, the vehicle created would only be a shadow of what one might own 30 years later. *Kent Bash*

them. To their creators, achieving the ultimate car design wasn't the point. More important was the perception that claptrap jalopies could be as liberating, captivating, and magnificent as the finest factory-assembled car. With that realization, builders laid down one of the important creeds of cruising for generations of motorheads to come: You really don't need a pot of money to put together a really bitchin' hod rod. When it comes to the hop-up built from the ground up, teamwork, industriousness, and a little ingenuity go a long way in beating out the big money.

As the urge to build rods spread from the California coast to the rest of the United States, certain vintage models rose to prominence among hot rodders. During the formative years of the movement, enthusiasts cruising the fringes didn't get excited about two-door coupes and four-door sedans. It was those inexpensive, lightweight roadsters stamped out by the Ford Motor Company (in great numbers) that cruisers chose. Originally intended for the sporty set, the jaunty roadster became a protean base for the hot rodder's speedy aspirations. It was lightweight (important for racing), small, and had a four-cylinder engine that almost anyone could rework. For a brief time in hot rod history, it came to define the whole era of the $10 car.

But while the Model T and its four-cylinder "mill" dominated the rodding arena for years, the Model A eventually came to define the hobby's look. When it debuted in 1928, 788,572 units made it to the streets in the first year! The reasons for its popularity were many. Engineers had incorporated 20 years of improvements into its design and it contained 5,580 new parts! Standards that motorists admired in the energetic T went to a new level. New additions

In limbo, a 1927 Model T body rests on a 1932 Ford Frame. Not every hot rod project started by young cruisers managed to make it to the streets. When building a hot rod back in the fifties, money was often in short supply and more than a few cruising dreams were put on permanent hold. *Kent Bash*

For the teenager bent on building a hot rod or street machine, under the hood is where most of their time was spent (when not cruising). Short on funds but long on enthusiasm, young car builders often exhibit an unusually long attention span when it comes to tinkering with automobiles. Is it any wonder that high school auto shop was such a popular course of study? © *1997 Dave Wallen*

included hydraulic shocks, four-wheel brakes, a gasoline gauge, and an automatic windshield wiper. Under the hood, a redesign of all moving parts and major components made the car's mechanical workings much more substantial. Plus, expanded engine bore and stroke added a boost in performance, providing 40 horsepower from the factory.

As speed freaks of the Depression years clamored to see what kind of power they could extract from the revamped four-cylinder, Ford engineers worked on an entirely new powerplant for the line. After four years of research, groundbreaking manufacturing processes allowed technicians to cast an eight-cylinder engine block as one piece. Henry Ford released this revolutionary valve-in-block "flathead" for the 1932 model year. With just a few modifications, this mill would become the reigning favorite of hot rodders during the coming decades.

In a letter dated April 10, 1933, infamous bank robber Clyde Champion Barrow related his great satisfaction with the product to Henry Ford: "I have driven Fords exclusively when I could get away with one . . .," he penned. "For sustained speed and freedom from trouble the Ford has got ever [*sic*] other car skinned and even if my business hasn't been strictly legal it don't hurt anything [*sic*] to tell you what a fine car you got in the V-8."

To placate the loyal customers who helped the Ford company grow during the early years of the Model T and the Model A, Ford introduced the Model B at the same time the flathead rolled out. Although it used the same basic body and trim work as the V-8 variation, the Model B featured an upgraded version of the Model A's four-cylinder engine under the hood (with 10 extra horsepower to

The ever-present "jalopy" was a common sight during the formative years of the cruising obsession. During the twenties and thirties, worn out flivvers like this one could be seen in almost any town and on almost any street. Teenagers everywhere were sowing their wild oats via the automobile. *Courtesy Karl Witzel*

One of the more long-lived hot rod styles is the "highboy," typified by a 1932 (or earlier) fenderless body that's mounted atop the frame. In comparison, the "lowboy" features a body shell that is *lowered* over the frame by channeling (the floor is cut out and raised). This classic beauty was captured at a cruise along Route 66, the Mother Road. ©1997 Robert Genat

Seen parked in front of the Wigwam Village Motel (made famous along Route 66), this cool purple hot rod (a 1929 roadster highboy) is a graphic example of the classy, simple, sublime hot rods that have become so popular among today's cruisers and hot rodders. *Kent Bash/car owned by Bud Toye*

Unlike the ordinary motorist who accepted the fact that his or her automobile should have the same brand of engine as the body, hot rodders and customizers harbored no such preconceived notions. Depending on one's preference, Chevrolets might have had Ford engines or vice versa. Here, a 1932 Ford body and chassis provides a snug home for a powerful Chevrolet engine. *Kent Bash*

In towns throughout America, the motorized youth of the twenties discovered the joys of car ownership and—as they once did in pedal cars—took to it with unrestricted glee. Long before the idea of the hot rod was crystallized in a defined term, open roadsters were adopted as jaunty chariots of freedom for the energetic high school and college crowd. In the days of old it was quite fashionable to paint catchy slogans on the side of one's jalopy—a faint foreshadowing of the all-out craze to customize (with paint and bodywork) that would materialize in the later decades. *Marion Post Wolcott, Library of Congress*

its credit). Bolstered with heavy-duty rod bearings, oil pressure supplied to the main bearings, and a counterbalanced crankshaft, the reliable four-banger had more bite than ever. To its credit, all of the bolt-on "speed equipment" that was compatible with the first Model A engines worked with this new model as well! Nevertheless, this was not the model that later achieved hot rod greatness.

For aesthetic reasons, the 1932 V-8 flathead Ford (roadsters, phaetons, sedans, and three- and five-window coupes) broke ahead of the pack and leaped the quarter-mile stretch to finish as the hot rodder's main machines during the fifties. Although the subtle details were not readily discernible by those outside of the car hobby, the 1932 became prized by hot rod enthusiasts for its looks. In contrast to the Model A, it flaunted a more graceful grille and, according to many, had improved lines. Company designers managed to better integrate the fenders and the hood with the body—attaining a

more pleasant-looking passenger carriage. "There's not one thing that you can put your finger on that makes the '32 a favorite," said Kent Bash. "The whole design of the car just works!"

Because of the numeral *2* in its model year, a hot rod made from this mass-produced series of cars became known in car circles as a "deuce." At that time, people often used the term deuce (or "devil" as Webster's defines it) as a cuss word when expressing anger. Since the aesthetics that were evolving to define the looks of a hot rod were taking on a rather devilish look themselves, the nickname proved to be more than a slang term for members in-the-know. The American hot rod was definitely the devil incarnate. How else would one describe a car that had a chopped top, no fenders, fat rear tires, angled rake, no bumpers, exposed engine, and flames painted on the side?

During the early years of motoring it was all the rage to tie foxtails to the rear-view mirror, paint humorous slogans on the body side panels, and maybe even mount a novelty hood ornament; but the naive trends that defined accessories during the twenties and thirties were no longer fashionable after the war. Although arriving at high school football games sitting in the rumble seat wearing a funny straw hat and thick beaver coat might have been "23 skidoo" for dear old Dad, practices seen as scandalous 20 years prior became the hokum of present day. For the postwar teenager, everyday life was getting faster and more complicated. As a byproduct of progress, "kicks" were getting more difficult to find. The hot rod—or modified car—provided thrills with an amplified version of horseplay that spelled fun for almost every adolescent.

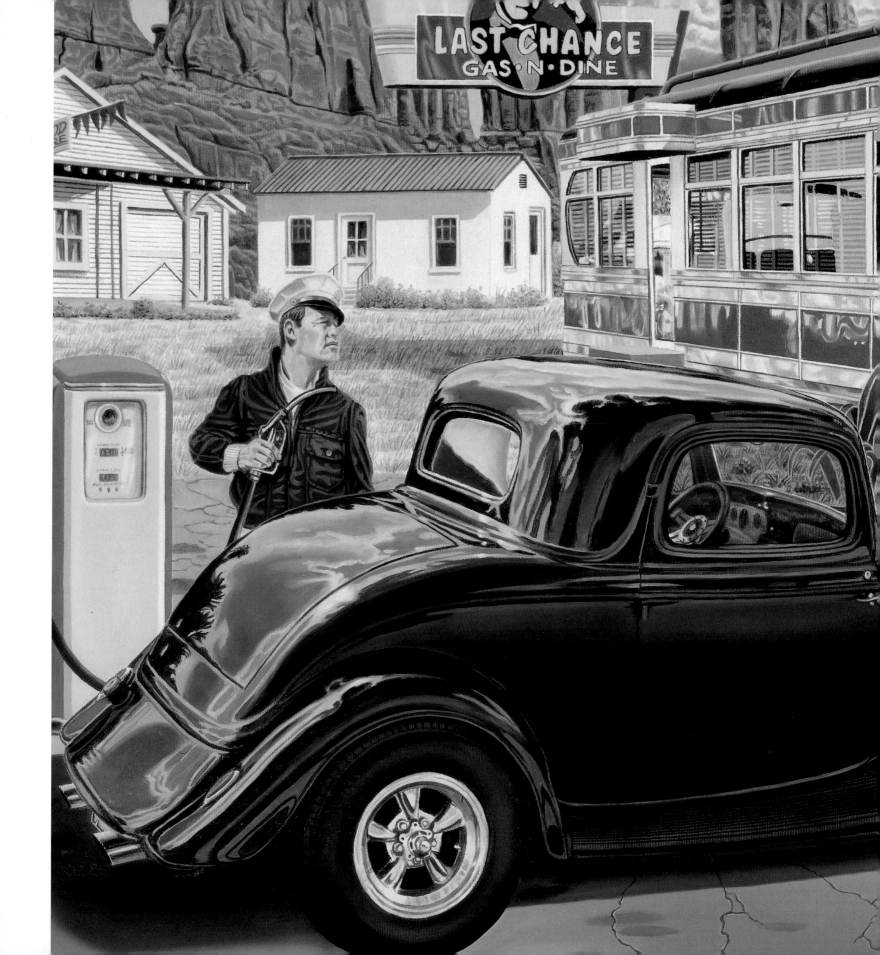

Historically, the diner has been an East Coast phenomenon, but on occasion, one may be seen in more remote parts of the country. The driver of a 1934 Ford three-window coupe running American mag wheels and 1939 Ford taillights (with the popular teardrop shape) stops at this Western dream for gasoline, a cup of Java, and maybe even a cup of chili. *Kent Bash*

THE DEUCE COUPES
THE SHUT DOWNS

WITH MY BABY ★ 36 THREE WINDOW COUPE
TWO FASTEST CARS ★ BODY BY FISHER
TURN HER ON, BUDDY

STARTERS NIGHTMARE ★ OIL ON THE TRACK
GOIN, GOIN, GONE ★ GOGGLES GOT A HOLE IN IT
DEUCE COUPE

With songs like "Goggles Got a Hole in It," the fifties album by the Deuce Coupes was a resounding favorite of the hot rod and custom crowd. The only problem with owning the album was that it couldn't be played in the car. Cassette decks and compact discs were the talk of science-fiction. *Courtesy Mike & Cheryl Goyda*

High-performance cars added a whole new arena of misbehavior for cruisers to indulge in. It was bad enough when cruisers created noise, harassed commuters, instigated traffic accidents, and ran rampant over public and private property; but when they tired of these shenanigans, they turned their wild wheels into instruments of sport! Behind the wheel of a hot rod, drivers issued spur-of-the-moment racing challenges to "opponents" with relative ease. Cruisers acted on racing offers while waiting at the traffic light, fill-ing up a tank at the corner gas station, or getting a bite to eat at the drive-in restaurant. From there, two wild-eyed teenagers floored it and shifted through the gears, putting both life and limb in jeopardy (of themselves and others) in a conspicuous attempt to affirm their driving skills, technical aptitude, and creativity.

At the finish line, the battle for supremacy yield-ed only one clear winner, harking back to the early days of civilization when hunter-gatherers showed their power by way of the hunt and battles with com-peting clans. The temporary flush of victory felt after a race or the feeling of dominance gained by owning a nifty heap was all part of the prize. Call it bravado, cajones, guts, or just blame it on an overabundance of testosterone—the fact was that the hot rod came into being because of the age-old instincts that spur boys to compete and prove themselves. As true today as it was in the past, the force behind the hot rod movement was the American male's need to display his prowess by way of the automobile.

Of course, automobiles and hot rods weren't just the domain of boys. There were some girls who liked hot rods and hot cars, too. During the fifties, so-called "B" movies with evocative titles such as *Dragstrip Girl* and *Hot Rod Girl* quickly stereotyped these car-crazy gals as wild vixens who were "Hell on wheels . . . fired up for any thrill!" Evocative movie posters depicted these "crazy kids . . . living to a wild rock 'n roll beat!" as jiggling blonde bombshells dressed in trampy, skin-tight dresses and sweaters. As their boyfriends raced for supremacy at the local drag strip, they pranced around in high heels with their skirts hiked up way too high and their breasts jostling out of control. Not surprisingly, most parents of the time were mortified by the shameless images being portrayed, and they circled the wagons against the evil hot rodders.

To counter this youthful braggadocio and keep it from going off the rails, a groundswell of opposition formed against all of the racing, cruising, carousing, and crashing that gave hot rods so much bad press. Along with the police and local government, parents became the most vocal adversaries of the hot rod menace and discouraged (or forbade) kids from even building hot rods. To them, rodding was a waste of gas and a quick path to trouble. Religious leaders agreed with the analysis and, in due time, rallied against the excesses of cruising: One prominent preacher who was traveling with a motorcycle daredevil show during the heyday denounced the revelry as "a fast track to Hell." He went on to proclaim that if an accident didn't snuff out your life, eternal damnation would condemn you by way of "the immoral practices indulged in in the back seat"

Although most of the police, parents, and Bible-thumpers who opposed hot rods and fast cars didn't even tune into the same top-40 radio stations as their adversaries, the tension between the old and new generations was manifest in song by 1955. That year, Charlie Ryan and the Timberline Riders debuted a rock and roll

tune called *Hot Rod Lincoln* (Ryan really owned a 12-cylinder Lincoln). In the song, a kid driving a Model A passes cars "like they were standing still" out on Grapevine Hill and then proceeds to blow a Ford and Mercury right off the road. Later, he passes a Cadillac sedan and a new race begins. This time, the hot rod kid develops engine trouble and the cops pull him over. In the final words of the song, the point of view shifts from the racer to the parent who laments, "Son, you're gonna drive me to drinkin' if you don't stop drivin' that hot rod Lincoln." Summarizing the establishment's basic attitude toward fast driving and cruising, the tag line proved to be a somewhat prophetic statement.

Unfortunately, cruising forced many parents to hit the bottle for relaxation. By that time, the hot rod—and the myriad forms of car culture that it had spawned—had contaminated the hearts and minds of youth from coast to coast. The establishment's troubles were just beginning. Over the next 20 years, teenagers would take over Main Street, invade the drive-in restaurants, affect our native tongue, change the course of automotive design, create new rolling art forms, make love in the back seat, do battle with the law, build bigger engines, create a new racing motor sport, waste more gasoline, and have no end of fun doing it all. The best—or worst—of America's cruising craze was yet to come!

In a 1957 issue of *Life* magazine, cruiser Norm Grabowsky and his $8,000 rod were featured in an article about hot rodding. The combination of polished chrome, flamed paint job, "skull" shifter knob, and drive-in food tray somehow caught the imaginations of kids all across the nation. After the tabloid hit the racks, everyone went nuts over his car, including the producers of the television series *77 Sunset Strip*. In the program, Edd "Kookie" Byrnes was to be a carhop who owned the beautiful roadster. Of course, television exposure caused even more people to desire one of those beautiful roadsters and "Grabowskyitus" spread over the highways and byways. A reproduction of the famed "Kookie" car is shown here. *Courtesy Gary Lick*

Cruising the Main Street Strip

Myth and Mayhem Along the Urban Boulevard

"When Friday night finally rolled around, my friends and I hit the roads with a vengeance! It was a wild mix of cars, girls, drive-ins, bowling alleys, racing, rock and roll music, and all of the other pastimes kids growing up during the early sixties loved. The circuit we picked out for cruising was a particular favorite: This night was the one reserved for taking in the sights and sounds found along the mother of all American cruisin' strips, California's Van Nuys Boulevard.

To start the fun we cruised to the teenage hub of activity, the San Fernando Bob's Big Boy drive-in restaurant. From there, we followed the trail of neon lights all the way down Sepulveda Boulevard and hooked a left onto Parthenea to connect up with the bustling Van Nuys strip. The next stop we made was Oscar's Drive-in, a roadside hangout where they fixed a really good triple-deck hamburger and a spot where a bunch of "greasers" always hung out. While this drive-in wasn't as well known in the area as Bob's, the parking lot was always packed with cars. We didn't stay there long, slowing down just long enough to check out the action.

Once we finished the cruising loop through Oscar's lot, we continued rolling south along the main artery of Van Nuys and past all the major businesses. Sometimes, we hung left at Victory and stopped at Cupid's walk-up for a hot dog. Eventually, we ended up at a second Bob's Big Boy drive-in and queued up in a snaking line to get a parking place for curb service. During the long wait, there was ample opportunity to listen to rock and roll music on the car radio, check out the chicks, other hot rodders, and anything else that was interesting.

On the final leg of our Friday night cruise, we drove out to the Toluca Lake Bob's Big Boy. With no thoughts of resting, we drove hard into the night, cruising to the Colorado Boulevard Bob's in Glendale, California. Still eager to run through a few more of the drive-ins, we doubled back to Hollywood and made the obligatory drive-by at the famous curb stand known as Tiny Naylor's. Satisfied that we had hit all of the major hot spots, we slipped down Sunset Strip and returned to the spot where it all began: the Van Nuys Bob's. By then, we were pretty much inebriated with images of hot rods and cool customs dancing in our heads and were ready to call it a night."

—*Kent Bash*

During the height of the cruising craze, scenes like this one were a common sight. Back then, marques like Lexus and Infinity didn't even exist and automobiles like the 1958 Chevrolet Impala and Corvette ruled the street when it came to good looks and class. In the days when hamburgers were made with 100 percent ground beef and milkshakes were mixed up with real ice cream, the accepted aesthetics of the automobile were different. *Kent Bash*

Chapter Two

SINCE the beginning of the automotive age, American children have welcomed any and all invitations to hop into the front seat of the family car. No tricycle, bicycle, or pedal car could compare with the real-life thrills experienced while Mom and Dad were at the wheel. Lacking all thoughts of commuting to work, car payments, insurance and repair bills, the automotive journeys of youth were always an unspoiled pleasure. More important than the destination, the ride was the focus. Among these many-splendored trips taken in the motorcar, the outing glorified as the "Sunday drive" was often the most memorable—and adored—of childhood.

Unfortunately, those innocent automotive adventures of childhood don't last forever. Advancing maturity causes us to change our priorities. By the teenage years, raging hormones bring on an awareness of "self." Suddenly, those once carefree attitudes of childhood become clouded with self-conscious thoughts. As a negative side-effect, the compulsion to sustain a presentable image (constantly) begins to distort the personality. Impressing the reigning teen peer group becomes the most important activity in life. Being seen by one's friends while seated in the back of Mom's old Windsor Town and Country station wagon becomes a major embarrassment—a bittersweet reminder of our toddling years on training wheels. Really, there was only one way to portray an image of cool and sustain it: own your own automobile.

Main Street provided the central corridor for the cruiser and became the strip where much of the automotive action took place. During the fifties, Saturday nights were reserved for the motorized activities of youth and the downtown strip became the "conspicuous gauntlet" for cruising one's car. This sign was spied right off of old Route 66 in Luther, Oklahoma. *Mike Witzel*

"I was really fortunate," explained Clare Patterson, now an avid cruiser and owner of a Cool Mint custom 1955 Chevrolet coupe. "Since we lived out on a farm in Augusta, Kansas, my dad said that I needed a car to get to school! During my freshman and sophomore years I put over 60,000 miles on my '50 Chevy convertible. During that time, we lived only 6 miles from town! On my 1954 Ford (it had only 17,000 miles on it when I bought it), I racked up 110,000 miles during my junior and senior years. . . . My dad just could not understand how I put so many miles on that car!" For cruisers like Patterson who came of age during the fifties, there were many good reasons to turn over the odometer numbers by cruising around.

In those days, the motorized art of looking cool was the top priority. While slung low into the seat, donning a pair of dark Wayfarers (with a pack of Camels rolled up in your shirt sleeve), one hand firmly grasping the suicide knob, and the right foot planted nervously on the gas pedal, there were so many exciting places to go and so many good reasons to go there alone. The high school sock hop or the Friday night football game played across town (and the wild festivities that often followed) were not events one wished to be taxied to! Furthermore, "parking" for a romantic evening or taking in a movie at the drive-in theater (with a date) didn't lend itself to Mama chaperoning in the front seat, either. For those under legal drinking age, it proved difficult to explain why they needed a ride to the liquor store or to the seedy honky-tonk where friends were gathering to catch the latest rockabilly band. Besides, how could a boy salvage his reputation after the fastest guy in town laid down a challenge to race while Mom was behind the wheel?

For these reasons and a glovebox crammed full of a thousand more, America's inventive teenagers formulated a new type of motoring trip to replace the weekend outings once enjoyed with

the family. Although the motorcar was still the method of conveyance, there were a few distinct differences: Instead of being used as a medium for keeping the family together, the car became a personal, private compartment for socialization, amusement, and escape. Automobiles provided teenagers with a self-contained environment that went wherever the action was taking place—whether it was on the move or standing still!

The central street of any American city (large or small) became the most exciting stretch of blacktop. This was the traffic lane known as Main Street, a corridor that hosted the myriad activities of cruising.

Until freeways became the corridors for commuters and travelers alike, the commercial avenues of transportation criss-crossed their way through the center of town. Often, Main Street became part of a major thoroughfare, and consequently, it was packed with businesses attempting to reap the bounty of commerce. After high-speed highways like this one in Los Angeles (1949) were built, many towns were bypassed and the action on Main died. The mega-mall and shopping center on the outskirts of town began a slow takeover. *Library of Congress*

In the far and distant days before the advent of the shopping mall, Main Street was the place where it all happened for the cruiser. On one stretch of centrally located street, one could take care of all the business of living and at the same time find various forms of entertainment. Of course, the car provided the means to get there and to make it all happen. It was only a natural progression for teenagers and young adults (with cars) to adopt it as cruising heaven. ©1997 Dave Wallen

As would be expected, the Main Street that was seen during the day was different than the Main Street that materialized after dusk. When the sun dipped below the horizon and traffic lights took prominence, the strip was transformed. Like clockwork, the authority figures that ran their shops behind the panes of glass locked the doors and doused the lights. When the neon twists of streetside signs flickered to life, the traffic lanes were reborn. Like ravenous ants vacating their hive, four-wheeled creations of every make, model, and description streamed in to get a chance to run the conspicuous gauntlet. ©1997 Dave Wallen

Long before the advent of the shopping mall, Main Street was where the people congregated to conduct the transactions of life. At its starting point, where the rows of houses changed into commercial structures, the filling station occupied a place of prominence. There, car nuts hung out, pumped gas, and gave birth to hot rods (for fifties teens, landing a job as a station attendant was a major coup). Further

down the sidewalk where the parking meters sprouted, townspeople patronized the butcher, baker, and green grocer. Along the way, the red-white-and-blue barber pole was a familiar sight. Anyone who desired a flattop, ducktail, or pompadour took a chair there. Clothing and shoe stores lined the strip, too—along with five-and-dimes like Ben Franklin and Woolworth's. Inside these emporiums, soda fountains and lunch counters beckoned customers of all ages to sample burgers, fries, pop, and malted milkshakes. At the opposite end of Main, the new car dealership was the place of dreams. Through panes of glass, a fantasy world of chrome and lacquer taunted shoppers with the promise of shiny new cars. For young people, everything along Main spoke of prosperity.

Since local residents had to visit Main at one time or another, cruisers driving slowly from one end of the strip to the other would likely see someone that they knew, or wanted to know. After dark, when the stores closed and all of the shoppers had gone home, the atmosphere for automotive carousing became electrified: Flashing light bulbs, neon lights, blinking traffic signals, and glaring street lamps transformed the commercial corridor

into a brightly lit automotive stage. Like colorful, strutting peacocks, cruisers arrived from all points to brave the conspicuous gauntlet.

As a diverse cast of car characters vied for an opportunity to appear on the linear stage, the Main Street venue provided a common ground where both similar and dissimilar car groups could meet and rub bumpers. Everyone was there: greasers, gearheads, socialites, athletes, bookworms, and troublemakers. All comers took their

turns with equal enthusiasm. This was no longer the Main Street that Sinclair Lewis wrote about in his sentimental novel of the same name during the twenties. Now, the gaslights blazed as bright neon and the horse-drawn carriage was replaced by the power of the piston. Main Street had become more than just a place to buy goods. It was now a place to have a good time.

While the merchants locked their doors and parents peered out their windows in anticipation

California's famous Pan Pacific auditorium (now defunct) provides an appropriate Art Deco backdrop for two chrome-bedecked 1959 Dodges and a 1956 Corvette. Ever since the first cars were designed, body styling and commercial architecture have followed similar courses. When art deco was in vogue, car bodies followed the cues of industrial designers and featured rounded shapes and elaborate embellishments. Later, when the architecture along Main Street became more angular, automobiles shared the form. *Kent Bash*

pants jumped out from the car! In a "musical chairs" fashion, participants ran around the vehicle in circles until all the players got back in the car through another door. When the light turned green, the "Chinese Fire Drill" was over and the player who ended up in the driver's seat slipped it into gear and sped away. On a more sinister note, some teens adored nothing better than a really gory practical joke, including the old standby where a bloody rubber arm poked out of the trunk. What did the cruiser do in this scenario to raise eyebrows? He drove around town asking for directions to the nearest lake!

Without thinking, some cruisers engaged in the creation of even more hard-core mischief and mayhem. "We would drive off of the road at night with the lights turned off, just to see how far we could go until we ran off of the road," explains Paul Taylor, publisher of *Route 66* magazine. "We played chicken a lot! When another car was coming down the road,

of trouble, cruisers wrote a new chapter on having fun in the streets. Most of it was pretty tame stuff: While parading up and down Main, kids found recreation in ogling pedestrians, harassing shoppers, yelling to friends, and making a general nuisance of themselves. When traffic was heavy, the kids packed their cars full and when they stopped for a light, all the doors flung open as the occu-

we drove down the same side that they were approaching, until the last minute. Eventually, one of the cars had to give up, and hopefully it was the other guy. We even played it out on the highway, running farmers off the road until they drove into the woods or down into a ditch!" Where were the kids getting the ideas for these unbelievable antics? While a good part of it was born of youth's innate creativity, most of the blame pointed to the moviemakers in Hollywood. Classic "out of control" flicks like *Running Wild* and *Hot Rods to Hell* were some of the influential primers behind the unsavory behavior.

But there was more. When cruisers weren't causing accidents, kids who were getting their kicks in cars engaged in all sorts of other malicious fun. While waiting at an intersection for the light to change, it was great sport to have someone sneak out of the car and deflate the rear tires of the motorist waiting ahead. Occasionally, the vehicle vandalism bordered on the silly: Having a windshield creamed by roving marauders who were carrying cans of shaving cream was common. In times of boredom, a well-positioned potato stuck up the muffler of some unsuspecting Joe's automobile (usually the school principal or some other authority figure) was just the ticket to create a few moments of laughter.

Embarrassing others was a great hobby for the car-crazy kid, too. In that department, "mooning" was an effective way to turn blue-haired grandmas' faces red and make girls scream. By pulling down their pants (or hiking up their skirts) and pressing their bare buttocks against the car window or thrusting them out into the open air, rebellious teenagers could embarrass their victims with great aplomb. The message to rival cruisers passing by: "Kiss my ass!"

Whether or not acts of malice or juvenile pranks defined the cruisin' trip, the destination was universal for most all of the participants. A majority of the Friday night tours taken in an automobile shot straight through a city's heart. In a driving "loop" that extended for miles from the north and south poles of Main Street, the meandering paths that defined the cruising circuits changed according to individual taste. Drive-ins, diners, and ice cream stands defined both shape and direction. To ensure maximum exposure, participants piloted their cars between the most visible landmarks—saving the slow roll along the downtown strip for last. The cruisers who drove the entire loop turned a quick 180, powershifted through the gears, and repeated the exhibition—until the gas, money, or night ran out. Since fuel was an unbelievably cheap commodity, cruisers fed their craving continuously. Well into the wee hours, the kids just kept coming back for more!

California's Ventura Freeway became one of the world's most traveled freeways during the 1970s. As a superhighway that followed the mountains and separated the San Fernando Valley from the beach areas, it became one of the main thoroughfares for West Coast cruisers commuting to work and play. For the cruiser, it was a vital link to all of the many feeder roads where the drive-ins (and fun) could be found. *Kent Bash*

Historically, small town gasoline stations like this extant example in Yoder, Kansas, were the hub of mechanical activity when it came to teenagers and their hot rods. While working there pumping gas, it seemed there was always time to put in a few extra hours on one's own machine. *Mike Witzel*

Parked at a circa 1937 gasoline filling station on the outskirts of town, this Ford five-window coupe and its lovely occupant make an order for gasoline and service. During the early days of pleasure cruising, the act of taking a car to the gasoline station was part of the fun of driving. Attendants in those days wiped the windows, checked the oil, and really took care of the customer. Today's cruisers can only look forward to self-service. *From the collections of Henry Ford Museum and Greenfield Village*

There was good reason for the attraction to the bright lights and excitement of the cruising loops: the goal was to meet members of the opposite sex. Main Street was one big singles bar, and naturally the male of the species flocked there in great numbers. With their hopes inflated by excess hormones, teenage boys who were old enough to pilot two tons of glass and sheet metal—but still too immature to figure out what a woman really wanted in a man—prowled the streets of this two-lane social club with the sole intent of "getting lucky." On a typical Saturday night in America, most of the young bucks who lacked dates but had

cars were trying almost every trick in the cruising book to win over girls and get them to hop into their chariots. And during the revved-up heyday of cruising, they put on quite a show.

Making a racket gained favor as an effective technique for the cruisers who wanted to call attention to themselves. While one waited at the stoplight, cranking up the radio volume was almost an instinctive reaction—especially if girls pulled up in the other lane. When rock and roll anthems like Elvis' *Heartbreak Hotel* or Jerry Lee Lewis' *Great Balls of Fire* seared the airwaves, there was no controlling the volume level. Revving up the Cherry Bombs (a glass-pack muffler)

Getting a job at a gas station during the teenage years was almost as great as dating the prom queen. With all of the mechanic's tools and other equipment available, the corner gas station at the end of Main Street became a virtual nursery for hot rods. In California, Michigan, Texas, New York, and all points in between, street machines of every description emerged from garages to do battle in the streets. With a cool car, one didn't need to be the most popular person in town or have the best looks; a jet-black, 1935 Ford three-window coupe with a chopped top and Halibrand wheels was really all that was needed to get a date with the gal of your dreams. *Kent Bash*

49

and pouring on the power until the car almost red-lined (also used at the drag strip to warm tires prior to a run) a smoky "burnout" came in second.

For older people watching from the sidewalk, the "display" activities of cruising were nothing less than infuriating. The only ones who appreciated the effect of pumping the gas pedal (to make a car surge to and fro), jerking the wheel left and right to create a wild "ride," or tapping the brakes at regular intervals to bring on a "staccato movement," were the participants themselves.

In spite of the male "machismo" that ran roughshod over the streets, having a good time while cruising wasn't only the domain of boys exercising their libidos. Cindy Morgan, a current cruiser with the Heart of Texas Street Machines (she explores the strips of the Lone Star state with husband Mike in a 1959 Pontiac Star-Chief) handily dispels the myth: "My very, very first car was a '66 Volkswagen, and we used to do like everybody else did and see how many people we could pile into it. Usually, we would have at least six or eight girls stuffed into a little Volkswagen drivin' around town, of course, tryin' to see how we could pick up the boys and everything!" From today's perspective, it was mostly harmless fun, since average girls of the age guarded reputations as important assets. So-called "good girls" seldom hopped into the back seat of the first deuce coupe to drive by, just because it had a dreamy paint job and chromed wheels. The reality of the situation was that finding a new flame while cruising wasn't that easy. Protected by the automotive shell, neither party pulled over and put it into park unless the amorous feelings were mutual.

There were a few select places where mixed crowds could mingle outside of the car safely, however. The drive-in restaurant was one of them. Main Street provided the primo place for people to show off their automobiles when moving; the drive-ins provided the best place to display motor vehicles when stopped. As the universal dating, meeting, and gathering spot for the many types of

Main Street denizens of Ellensburg, Washington, once had Wipple's gas station to cruise into when the gas gauge dropped toward the empty mark. In cities and towns all across the country, the scene was the same: At each end of the main traffic route, gas stations of every brand vied for cruisers and commuters alike. *Mike Witzel*

to make the statement, "Look at me, I'm here, I'm cool, and I'm really loud" was another standard practice. "We used to speed up at the big hill right before Main. As we came over the hump, we let up on the gas pedal to get the mufflers a rumblin'," mused Clark "Crewcut" Taylor, now the operator of a small exhaust repair shop in the West. "These days, making muffler noise is a long forgotten art. Nowadays, it's the loud, rap music and those amplified stereo radio systems with those subwoofer things and all that get the looks!"

Besides creating noise, there were other ways to gain the attention of bystanders. Since the car equaled self-image, boys proved the mechanical prowess of their hot rod by laying a "scratch," or long patch of tire rubber on the road. By stomping the brake pedal

At the turn of the century, the Coca-Cola Company promoted its syrup throughout the South with posters and point-of-purchase items that depicted people in their carriages being served by waiters. These runners were often employed by pharmacies of the age to carry out refreshing beverages to people waiting patiently in their horse-drawn coaches. Out of this practice came the drive-in restaurants and the legions of young men and women who cruised there in great numbers to get a drink. *Courtesy Coca-Cola Company/author's collection*

Unlike the average restaurant that concentrated its culinary craft on serious sit-down clientele, the Texas Pig Stands catered to car lovers who wished to remain inside their vehicles. At circular units like this example in Beaumont, Texas, dining away from home was both convenient and fun. Hot rod and custom car crowds especially liked the open-air atmosphere of the carhop service, and by the end of the fifties the drive-in became the hangout of choice for everyone who had access to a set of wheels. *Courtesy the Texas Pig Stands Inc.*

cruisers clogging the streets, drive-ins were at the height of popularity during the fifties and reigned as the preferred hangout until the mid-sixties.

Along with Main Street, drive-ins unified the cruise, providing those "shooting the loop" with convenient way stations with easy access and refreshment. Enthralled by the flamboyant carhops, the neon tubing, and the zesty food, the youthful sector of America's car crowd reacted to the atmosphere of the drive-in restaurant with overwhelming approval. Without walls and the various rules of

Drive-ins, diners, and coffee shops are all geared to serving people who arrive in cars. Before there were motor vehicles, restaurants were located in the downtown area—usually along Main Street—where the customers could get to them easily. As Americans became ever more mobile, dining establishments located themselves on the outskirts of Main Street where land was cheap and they could throw down a couple of acres of asphalt for parking. Shown are a 1957 Chevrolet Nomad station wagon, 1958 De Soto, 1957 Oldsmobile, and a 1958 Plymouth. *Kent Bash, courtesy George Cross and Sons Inc./Pomona Swap Meet*

behavior that accompany them, the atmosphere at America's curbside eateries was unrestricted. Everything took place out in the open. There was a lot of frenzied action, jumpin' music, a diversity of people, and a minimum number of parents. As an added bonus, the drive-in was a fantastic place to flaunt a car when attempting to make new acquaintances. For those competitive types, it was a handy place to issue race challenges.

Bud Toye, a present-day aficionado of highboy hot rods and owner of The Toye Corporation (a manufacturer of intelligent building systems), still gets a twinkle in his eye when he talks about the drive-in days of his youth: "Very often you would end up with a new date. By the end of the night, the date that you brought with you might have disappeared. People who were not going steady were just cruising around, and sometimes there would be an exchange set up. You didn't always take the same girl home you showed up with! On Monday morning, when you went back to school, you rearranged your social priorities because every

continued on page 56

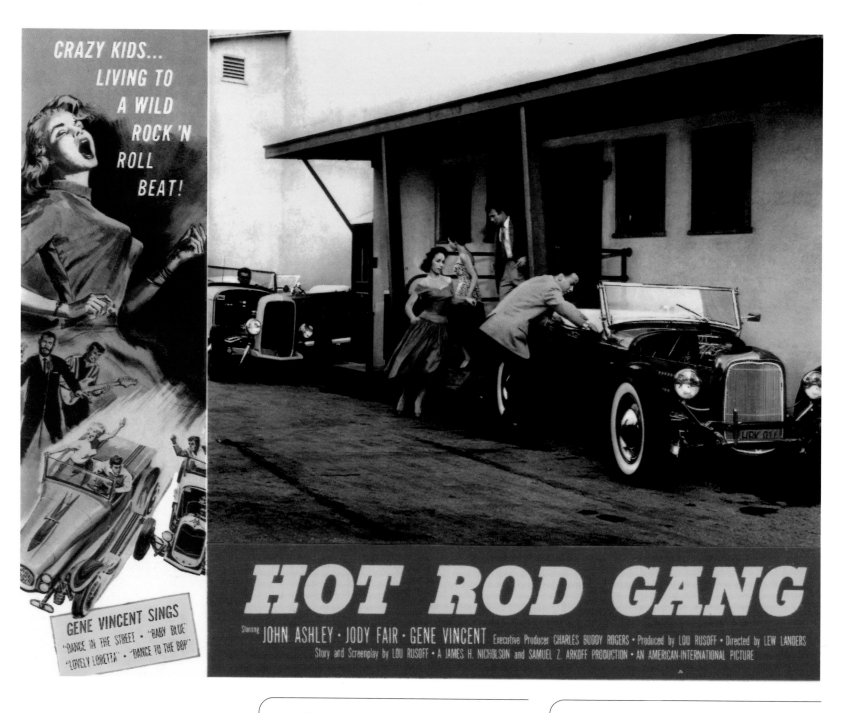

CRAZY KIDS... LIVING TO A WILD ROCK 'N ROLL BEAT!

GENE VINCENT SINGS "DANCE IN THE STREET" • "BABY BLUE" "LOVELY LORETTA" • "DANCE TO THE BOP"

HOT ROD GANG

Starring JOHN ASHLEY • JODY FAIR • GENE VINCENT Executive Producer CHARLES BUDDY ROGERS • Produced by LOU RUSOFF • Directed by LEW LANDERS

Story and Screenplay by LOU RUSOFF • A JAMES H. NICHOLSON and SAMUEL Z. ARKOFF PRODUCTION • AN AMERICAN-INTERNATIONAL PICTURE

One of the great fears of the 50s parent was the hot rod gang—crazy kids who lived to a wild rock and roll beat and had no respect for authority or the everyday rules of society. Many thought that the hot rod was a direct conduit to hell and did all they could to stop its proliferation in the streets. ©1958 American International Pictures/Courtesy Mike & Cheryl Goyda

During the 1970s, Increase Records came out with a series of cool nostalgia albums based on the cruisin' and music themes. On each of the nine records (from the cruising golden years of 1955 through 1963), chart toppers from the past rekindled the memories of fun in the streets. Famous disc jockeys from around the country were featured on each of the installments, lending a sense of excitement to the series. Mike Witzel Collection

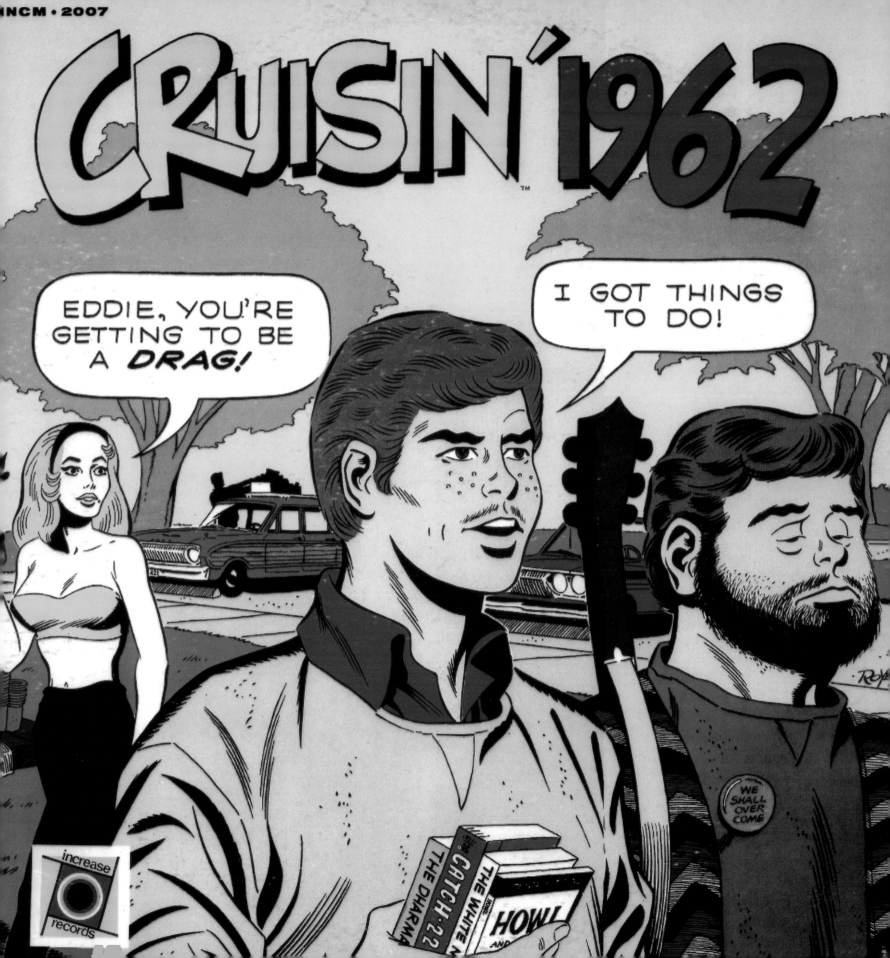

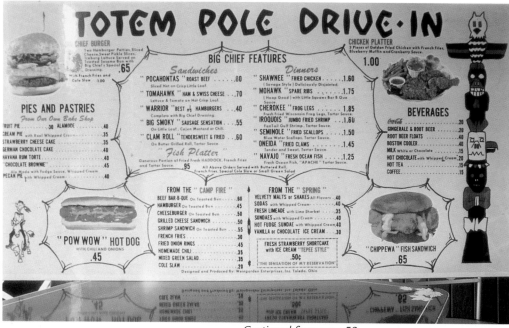

Continued from page 53

Friday night, you fell in love. Not many relationships survived the weekend!" Without a doubt, the American drive-in restaurant was an important catalyst for making and breaking relationships during the cruisin' heyday.

Unfortunately, the success of the drive-in as a meeting and mating place was one of the main factors that contributed to its decline. By the mid-sixties, kids began parking their hopped-up roadsters and low-slung customs and hanging out all night—jamming the service lanes and barring customers that actually *bought* food. Suddenly, the cacophony of revving engines and rock and roll music became unbearable. By then, the illegal racing was flagrant with races run right out in the open. As the excessive alcohol and drug use inflamed the rage of juvenile delinquents, fights broke out regularly. All across America, lawmakers jumped into action and instituted new rules to regulate the motorized free-for-all.

Unfortunately, the fears of parents and educators were coming true: Dick and Jane had grown up and the car was the instrument of their moral corruption! In 1964, San Bernardino, California, attempted to turn the tide when the city enacted ordinance number 2594. Forced by law, drive-in owners posted the regulation at their eateries with multiple signs. Soon, rambunctious teens found placards with this greeting: "Absolutely no loud or excessive motor noises permitted, operation of the radio at a loud volume level, spinning of wheels, cruising! No loitering, no disorderly conduct, threats, altercations! This will be rigidly enforced by Police Order! Thank You!" For the hooligans who chose to ignore the warnings, the reward was a misdemeanor charge with a hefty $500 fine. In the effort to quell the festivities, some proprietors experimented with a less confrontational approach and used tactics such as controlled-access entry gates, pass-through tokens, and lot patrols.

Located at 1205 South Woodward, the Totem Pole Drive-In was a much-loved fixture along Detroit's Woodward Avenue and anchor of the South end of the strip. Its "Heap Good Food" (and the double-deck burger made of two 1/8-pound patties and flavored with a unique sauce) was once a landmark. Mildred Hund bought the business in 1954 and ran the operation through the cruising years of the fifties, until the lease finally ran out during the seventies. For cruisers, the food and fun there are now a fond memory. ©1997 Tom Shaw/Musclecar Review Magazine

When drive-in restaurants began replacing carhops with intercom devices such as these, overhead canopies were used to mount the new gadgets. Today, the Sonic drive-in chain uses units like these in addition to human carhops. This classic was found in Eldorado, Kansas. *Mike Witzel*

The drive-in and cruising situation became so inflamed that by 1967 *Drive-In Restaurant* magazine carried "Ordinance Roundup" as a regular feature. That same year, a crowd of 75 to 100 teenagers converged at the McDonald's Drive-In located at Whittier Boulevard in California and took it over. According to the report, they all came, parked, hung out, and made no effort to leave! To counter the teen invasion, manager Arnand Duncan had already been closing the doors on Monday afternoons "to keep the kids from ruining his business." Duncan hired police guards to enforce a no-loitering rule that required patrons to buy their food, eat it, and move out in 20 minutes. The days of cruisers hanging out at Mel's or the Pig Stand while nursing a Coke or malt were over. Cruising would never be the same again.

At drive-ins like this classic programmatic example, street races were planned, and challenges were made—a tailor-made environment for the hot rodder of the 1950s. It was also a great place for custom car builders and hot rodders to hang out and compare notes about how they built their cars, such as the 1957 Chevrolet on the right and the 1950 Mercury (with a chopped top) on the left. *Kent Bash*

The Healthcamp Drive-In is a modern-day drive-in eatery that's a favorite with cruisers in Waco, Texas. A car club that calls itself "The Heart of Texas Street Machines" has adopted the eatery (located on the famous traffic circle) as their favorite destination. Years ago, places like this one defined the points along the many cruising circuits that fanned out on each end of Main. *Mike Witzel*

Out on the streets, the police ticketed the merrymakers who continued to cruise for speeding, street racing, using improper equipment, having too many people stuffed in a car, noisy headers, loitering at businesses, littering, and vandalism. To some, it seemed that the cops dreamed up charges at the spur of the moment. In Detroit, Michigan, a city known for its cars and its cruising, the aimless habit of recreational driving became a serious moving violation that carried point penalties. In 1960, an amendment to the city's official Traffic Ordinance specified "that no automobile operator shall attempt to drive through or upon any driveway in restaurant driveways [sic] or parking lots for purposes other than those for which they were constructed."

Fortunately, there were other places to drive besides Main Street and the service lanes of drive-ins. While the die-hard cruisers were haunting restaurants on the loop, couples were finding their entertainment in places with dimmer lighting. With many of the same characteristics that made the curb service

Woodward Avenue was the Indianapolis for street racers. The legend of this notorious strip began in 1805 when Michigan was still a territory and the internal combustion engine not even a gleam in the eyes of inventors. That year, the entire city was consumed by a stable fire and plans were made to replot the streets. Using the layout of Washington, D.C., as a model, Judge Augustus Woodward was coordinating the rebuilding when he got the idea to rename Detroit's old fur trading route (known as Saginaw Trail) after himself. By the time auto experimenter Charles Brady King drove his primitive motorized horse buggy down the avenue in 1896, the name was one of many that described identical corridors. But this carriage route proved itself to be no ordinary street. By 1928, it had matured into an eight-lane thoroughfare, swelled by the traffic that rolled in and out of Detroit's great car-making machine. ©1997 Tom Shaw/Musclecar Review Magazine

restaurant so immensely popular, the drive-in theater (an outdoor format for viewing movies patented by Richard Milton Hollingshead in 1933) became a secondary destination for the teen on wheels. During the fifties, the admission was affordable and the parking plentiful. Snack bars overflowed with cheap popcorn and soda pop. Unlike the movie houses that occupied a place on Main Street, the audience could watch a movie in complete privacy, choosing to focus their attention on the flickering screen or the person sitting next to them.

After World War II, the number of drive-in theaters boomed from a low of 102 outlets to well over 1,000. By 1949, the drive-in had become the

bastion of the second rate, "B" movie and remained so until the end of its days. No program aired on the tiny television tubes of the period could compare with the larger-than-life epics being projected on the big outdoor screens. Art imitated life in film after film as a barrage of hot rod and juvenile delinquent exploitation titles (featuring fast cars and fast women) exploded onto the scene. When the mania for flying saucers gripped the nation, weird tales of other worlds and aliens grabbed drive-in viewers by the throat and never let go. Science-fiction became all the rage and cruisers flocked to the nearest "ozoner" to watch favorite actor Steve McQueen battle a shapeless

Around midnight, Woodward ripped. It was quitting time for second-shift assembly line workers and a fresh batch of street machines headed for the avenue. Some of these contestants were rogues with bad reputations, while others were just "factory teams" who liked nothing better than mixing it up in the streets. During the day, they walked the halls of corporate America, but at night they prowled Main Street in the name of market research. While these racing forays were unauthorized by the company, street lore has it that John DeLorean and his colleagues regularly cruised the GTO prototype out on Woodward to test it under street conditions. Today, a McDonald's on Woodward pays tribute to those days with a display of classic street machines. *Howard Ande ©1997*

alien life form in *The Blob*. As teenagers in their cars watched with morbid fascination, the *Devil Girl from Mars* landed and the robot monster *Kronos* trampled everything in its path!

On dates, in groups, alone, or to meet friends, kids cruised out to grand drive-in installations like California's Asuza. To save on the cost of admission, stuffing friends into the trunk became one of the most memorable pastimes. Initially, the ploy worked. Still, the cost-cutting trick was an easy one to spot, as the overloaded trunk caused the rear springs to sink and cars to sit unusually low. Later, a few theaters charged admission to cover a full carload and the practice ended.

By the sixties, though, there were much more serious developments to worry about. Teens were adding hard liquor and drugs like marijuana to their cigarette habit. Adolescents and young adults

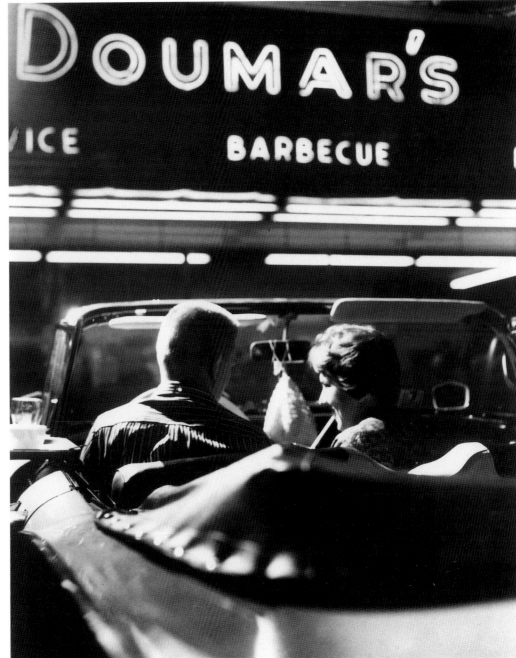

indulged themselves in the evil habits of the day and staged impromptu parties in the parking lot of the local drive-in. Of course, the revelry was all in the name of a good cause: hanging out.

By providing a tailor-made arrangement to accommodate the sexual experimentation of adolescents, drive-ins indulged young lovers in the areas that counted: low lighting, free parking, and a lack

of adult supervision. For teens with other activities in mind, films were nothing more than mood lighting that provided something to watch while waiting in line at the grill. While owners across the country denied the drive-in's reputation as a "passion pit," people knew that kids with cars were really going there to make out. Try as they might, owners were impotent when it came to controlling what paying customers did in their cars. How could they? Technical matters occupied the projectionist. The ushers were barely adults themselves. At the concession stand, the cooks didn't make enough money to

Anyone who has ever taken a cruise down Route 66 remembers the journey. As a two-lane corridor with a character all its own, a drive down this "great diagonal highway" has always been a trip in itself. For on this two-lane ribbon of asphalt, the ride was often much more important than the destination—especially if the vehicle used to get there was the Chevrolet Corvette. *Mike Witzel/Corvette accessories courtesy Mid America Designs*

The car radio was—and still is—a major part of the cruising scene. Over the AM airwaves, future teenage idols sang of drag-racing, dancing, and romance against a background of electric guitars and pounding drums. From chromed slits in the dashboard, the music of a new generation made its way into the hearts and minds of youthful car culture. As shown by this classic 1946 Ford business coupe, the car radio became an integral part of the dashboard design by the end of the forties and, as a result, a major selling point when the time came to purchase a new vehicle. *Mike Witzel/Ford courtesy Dalton Patterson*

oversee the crowd's conduct. Like it or not, almost everything that the parents feared would happen at the drive-in theater did—including holding hands, nuzzling, cuddling, necking, petting, and yes, sometimes even illicit lovemaking.

In 1956, Dr. Evelyn Duvall acknowledged the existence of these back seat escapades in a school textbook when she wrote that "the automobile had definitely changed courtship." She was right

on the money. As easily as it had become a salon for food and a saloon for drink, young lovebirds transformed the car into a portable bed chamber! Since it was the most accommodating place for cruisers to pull down the sheets, venturing out to the drive-in emerged as yet another rite of passage for America's youth.

By the fifties, the average size of a car seat exceeded the dimensions of the standard sofa. Many had the capability of being removed from the

Located on Victory Boulevard in Van Nuys, California, this popular cruising destination was a veritable movie hot spot during the fifties. Unfortunately, man's obsession with tearing down the vestiges of the past to build anew has rendered this classic example of the outdoor theater extinct. The bulldozer and the wrecking ball were the last attractions that played here, turning a parking lot that was once filled with memories into just another space for a shopping center. ©1997 Mike Wallen

During the 1960s, the remaining drive-in theaters still scattered across the United States were managing to hold their own. Although attendance was dropping every year, it would take another decade before the boom in outdoor entertainment became a total bust. By the end of the eighties, watching a movie in a car was no longer a favorite pastime for most motorists. *Courtesy American Automobile Manufacturers Association*

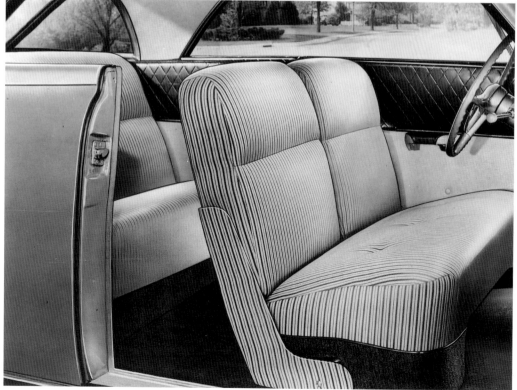

The 1952 Studebaker provided the occupants of the front seat and the back seat ample room to pursue the types of nocturnal cruising activities that were defining the emerging American car culture of the fifties. *Courtesy of the Automotive Hall of Fame*

The Van Nuys Drive-In Theater used to be the primary destination for teenagers who desired a movie and some privacy. Back in the fifties, it was *the* place for entertainment in the California city of Van Nuys, and it remained so for decades. Sadly, this portrait of a 1940 Ford Deluxe Coupe remains as only a reminder of the site; the ozoner was bulldozed a few years ago and part of the area's cruising heritage was lost forever. *Kent Bash*

car completely! Whenever the urge struck, lovers unlatched the seats and laid them out to provide a ready-made bed for "camping." Perhaps the most dramatic example of convertible comfort was the big boat introduced by Nash in 1949. Marketed to families who took highway vacations, its twin fold-down seating arrangement transformed the beast into a rolling boudoir! Custom-built for couples eager to trip the light fantastic, it was one car that parents rarely loaned to children—especially if they planned on cruising. "I knew exactly what was going on at the drive-in," recalls Mrs. A. C. Stewart, a former ticket-taker and usher, now a great-grandmother. "I saw firsthand the goings-on. My kids were never allowed to go without a suitable chaperone . . ."

Fortunately, the love-struck cruisers who overstepped the boundaries of decency at the drive-in theater had other options for parking. There were more secluded locations to consider, including the "submarine races" held out at the lake and the many places called Lover's Lane, Mulholland Drive, or the Point. In the back seat of a car, many a lad or lass found their thrill up on the same "Blueberry Hill" that Fats Domino was singing about. It was all part of the cruising agenda: Once a girl or guy became a willing passenger, trying to get them out to a romantic roadside hideaway later in the evening was all part of the game. When both of the partners agreed, it was off to join other lovebirds at the local make-out spots (usually on the outskirts of town where the view was good—as if anyone wanted to take in the "view" through the steamed-up windows). Still, despite all entreaties, it didn't always work out for some. Guys who struck out with their companions and didn't take "no" for an answer resorted to using the oldest tricks in the book: engine trouble or running out of gas.

Cruisers who wished to take their girls parking across state boundaries had to resist this temptation. There was one good reason: The Mann Act, a law originated in 1910 as the "White Slave Traffic Act," called for penalties to be levied against any person who knowingly persuaded (or even caused to be persuaded) any girl under age 18 from any state to any other state, with the intent that she be induced to engage in "debauchery." Cruisers who took dates to juke joints out of state (and were stupid enough to have sex with them against their will) faced harsh felony charges, along with a fine of up to $10,000, and a term of imprisonment not exceeding five years!

Despite a plethora of ordinances and denouncements, many of the nation's cruisers took the new rules in stride and openly defied the will of the establishment. The urge to drive free and unfettered was just too strong to resist. Kids were hardwired to the automobile and had gasoline in their blood. Cruising was their favorite form of automotive recreation and an activity that no one with a car could ignore or deny.

By the time that duck-walking guitar man Chuck Berry released the tune *No Particular Place to Go* in 1964, the countless feeder roads and lesser-traveled traffic spurs that defined the nation's growing motorways joined Main Street and, suddenly, cruising occurred just about everywhere. Sure, the ride had no real destination, but who gave a hoot? Teenagers were discovering for themselves the wonders of the automobile and were feeling absolutely no shame about "cruisin' and playin' the radio," even if they just drove around in circles and had "no particular place to go!"

LORI · JOHN · CHUCK
ELSON · SMITH · CONNORS
nd introducing ROXANNE ARLEN · MARK ANDREWS
h FRANK J. GORSHIN · CAROLYN KEARNEY · ED REIDER · DEL ERICKSON
Directed by LESLIE MARTINSON · Produced by NORMAN HERMAN
Executive Producer DAVID T. YOKOSEKI
Original Screenplay by JOHN McGREEVEY
Released by

Addicted to Speed and Horsepower

When the Cruisers Craved Street Racing

"My first car was a 1937 Ford sedan that I picked up in 1959 for the modest payout of 40 bucks. Even though it wasn't any kind of a record breaker in the speed department, it ran great. My second was a 1938 Buick coupe with a straight-eight engine that I bought for $50. By that time, I was an experienced cruiser and was ready for some get-up-and-go. So I pulled the tired straight-eight engine that came stock and dropped in a Cadillac flathead! Even though the '48 motor was a lot heavier, it more than made up for its weight difference with the extra power it turned out.

A fenderless 1934 Ford arrives on the scene with a stereotypical cruiser of the fifties era (complete with ducktail 'doo and white T-shirt) at the wheel. The primer gray vehicle is a 1937 Willys sedan, and the yellow machine a 1940 Ford Deluxe Coupe. Looks like a challenge to race will soon be issued here, something that occurred often at the drive-in diner. *Kent Bash*

That was good, because most of the kids that I went to school with were addicted to cars, hot rods, and going fast. Back then, we didn't have video games to play and we didn't spend hours staring at a computer screen. We got our kicks by getting our hands dirty with motor oil, gasoline, and all the other stuff that keeps a car going. Cars were part of our personality, and to us, they meant everything. When we weren't in class, we were out in the streets checking out other fast cars to see what guys were doing to make them run better and figuring out how we could do the same. We spent a lot of time scrounging around the local junkyards looking for small-block Chevy motors and other car parts.

With all of the speed equipment that was becoming available, the small-block Chevy could be refitted with a three-two manifold or even an Iskenderian cam. If you had access to a small machine shop, you could mill the heads to pick up more compression. After just a few basic changes, you could drop one of these "mills" into a vintage Model A chassis and have yourself a pretty hot car. For the guys I cruised the strip with, nothing was more bitchin' than owning a light-weight car with a big eight-cylinder engine, flames painted on the sides of the hood, a stick shift topped off with a small piston head or a menacing skull knob, and cool wheels!

Unfortunately, when muscle cars began showing up at the many cruising circuits of the sixties, the scene began to change. Any guy who could afford to buy himself a new or used one had himself a powerful street machine right off the dealer's parking lot.

By the seventies, it didn't take a lot of imagination or tinkering to build a cool street rod and, of course, the hard-core hot rodder resented this. Now, almost anybody without car know-how could slap down a few bucks for a fast car, challenge you to a race the next day, and beat your pants off. Yeah, there were lots of crazy drivers and lots of smashed muscle cars. Gearheads like us hung out at the wrecking yards just so we could get the first crack at salvaging the motors and trannys to put into our own hot rods!"
—*Kent Bash*

Chapter Three

FOR teenage lads of the forties and fifties, building a hot rod was just about the most counterculture activity one could indulge in—short of robbing gas stations and purse-snatching. When cocooned by the chrome and steel armor of a hot rod, young boys could amplify their personality and improve upon their identity. While driving a souped-up car, the average adolescent assumed an attitude—bashful boys became braver, and careful kids turned careless. Even the meek, mild-mannered Clark Kent types got a chance to play four-wheeled Superman. All it took to gain possession of these strange new powers was to own a powerful heap. All the better if it was fast and could win a few races.

During the hop-up heyday that defined the postwar era, the hot rod became a metaphor for the sexual prowess of the American male and the race a means to prove it. Rambunctious hot rodders who were eager to make a name for themselves challenged others who were driving similar cars to meet them, and then try to beat them. Although street racing had been around since the days of the first horseless carriages, never before were the conditions so right for illegal, one-on-one racing in the streets. Gas was cheap and used cars (that provided fodder for race rods) were affordable. Leisure time was abundant. Impressionable motorheads avoided street gangs (other than car clubs), and when violent clashes took place, seldom were Saturday night specials used to settle

California's Foothill Boulevard, better known as Route 66, was a microcosm of the cruising ideal during the mid-1950s. Everything one could think of that smacks of nostalgia could be found along this stretch of street, including automotive dealerships, drive-in restaurants, coffee shops, and more. Along this well-traveled route, the car was king. At intersections like this one, racing challenges were issued around the clock. ©1997 Dave Wallen

them. Rodders raised in the back seat and weaned on high-octane fuel were more creative: Racing slicks, tuned headers, and a floor-mounted stick shift were the cruiser's dueling weapons. The smooth pavement of the public streets was the preferred place to shoot it out.

Unofficially, the two-lane tango of cruising began during the impetuous years of the Roaring Twenties. While careful car owners stayed within the posted limits, a small clique of wealthy car enthusiasts got the idea to drive their Duesenbergs out to the dry lake beds north of Los Angeles, California, just to see how fast they could go. Ostracized from everyday corridors of travel, these early pioneers of speed realized that locations like Muroc Dry Lake offered acres of the unobstructed space they needed to test the limits of high-speed cruising, without fear of being thrown in jail by the local constable. Without admission charges and no one to monitor them, a single standard emerged: no rules! Four-wheeled adventurers who liked to take their cars to the outer edge and beyond were left to their own devices.

While affluent car jockeys attempted to do things that no one else even dared doing with their cars, so-called normal automobile owners observed from the sidelines in awe, never suspect-ing that someday their kids would try similar feats out in the streets. But as the years passed, the unexpected did happen: The high-speed dance with death turned from an occasional oddity into a regular hobby. Cars were becoming affordable, and soon it was the Model T that saw lake bed action. The interest became intense. By the mid-thirties, dry lake beds became the premiere place for organized speed trials for the everyman.

"Tinkering with race cars and dinking around with motors was a kick back in those days," recalled Halvin "the Jackrabbit" Releg, a retired, one-time dry lakes racer and speed equipment salesman (who claims welding frames for various rods took up 20 years of his life). "When I was a senior [in high school], I burned up most of my extra time working on hot rods, building them up from junk

HONK!
CUSTOM CARS • HOT RODS

WHY a HOT IGNITION?
By Ak Miller

MAY 1953
25c

• SPARKLING CUSTOMS • UNIQUE HOT RODS
• MECHANICAL and CONSTRUCTION DETAILS

After the rusting wrecks of $10 cars were dragged from the junk heaps back to suburbia, the driveway became the hot rodder's domain for repair work. The vehicle receiving a close inspection in this scene is a 1932 roadster; to the left is a 1934 Ford Phaeton, and on the street sits a Model A sedan of 1928 vintage. For some unlucky parents, scenes like this were a never-ending nightmare of spilled oil, rusted parts, and uncompleted car projects. Not all hot rod wannabees were as industrious as this crew. *Kent Bash*

scrap and stuff and figurin' out how to fit the pieces and parts together. Heck, my pals and I took every chance we could to cruise our cars to the flats to run 'em. Going fast was almost better than sex! We loved speed and had no problem gettin' our jollies without drugs!"

In those fledgling days of dry lakes racing, the top speed of a car determined its standing among other contestants. As a result, clocking, or timing a racer's rate of travel between marked points became the defining activity. In a heat known as a "match run," cars lined up with similar machines to race. But that's where the similarities ended: Unlike the lap races held at oval tracks, vehicles sped across the cracked mud in a straight line without turning. After accelerating to a rolling start, the one vehicle that made the fastest elapsed time between measuring posts became the winner. Spectators and participants loved all the action, even though it was a loud, dirty, and highly dangerous pastime.

To the mixed reactions of participants, a group called the Southern California Timing Association (SCTA) organized in 1937. All of a sudden, rules and regulations began encroaching on the once open and carefree contests! Timed match runs were no more and classes grouped cars according to their type. In an effort to nix the dust created when multiple vehicles ran, new guidelines specified that only two cars at a time could compete against one another. While they waited to make their run, a few participants took inspiration from the fresh format and began to stage their own heats. There were a few minor

Oval track racing was very popular in the forties and fifties. While some hopped-up cars were built for the street and others for the drags, track racers liked nothing better than wheeling around a dirt circle in pursuit of the checkered flag. Shown here is a 1933 Ford three-window coupe with a flathead engine. *Courtesy John White*

changes in the way the heat runs were operated versus top-speed runs. The timing aspect wasn't so important, even though races ran in a straight line. Instead of a rolling start, cars took off from a standstill. Now, whoever crossed the finish line first claimed the win. Because the main technique

The pre-1937 Jalopies that were raced on oval tracks were usually stripped of their soft tops, lending an odd look to the event. When racing at night, it wasn't uncommon to catch glare from the lights and be distracted from the action. What happened next was something the spectators knew could happen at any given moment: accidents, wrecks, and rollovers. Along with winning, it was all part of the show. *Courtesy John White*

Bob Johnson and Rueben Thrash raced jalopies at the Veterans Stadium in Long Beach, California, during the mid-fifties. In stark contrast to the big-money racing events that are held today, it was a "kinder and gentler" time. Back then, the cars were simple, the tracks were made of dirt, people were friendly, and competition was largely just for the fun of it. *Courtesy John White*

Ironically, the cruisers that regularly caroused the commercial passageway called Main (like this Fort Worth, Texas, strip) seldom stopped anywhere along its length to conduct business. For those motoring around in menacing hot rods and cool customs, remaining static for too long was a practice tantamount to heresy. Almost always, a street machine that was at rest resulted in its driver being made to shell out more money, answer to a higher authority, explain intentions, or heed lectures on how to behave. In the long run, it was less confrontational to remain in motion and to slow the car only when hangouts that catered to young people were passed. *Mike Witzel*

for victory was to gain quick acceleration by dragging in low gear as long as possible, the event became known as a "drag race."

Jazzed by the uninhibited aura of drag racing, West Coast car fanatics who called themselves "hopup" artists began flocking to Muroc and El Mirage dry lakes to "run what you brung." Often, the enthusiasm waned when the occasional weekend racer realized that the blowing dust, glaring sun, and baking 100-

By the end of World War II, half of America's 26 million automobiles were 10 years old. To meet the rising demand for new vehicles, the Detroit automotive machine churned out new models, producing as many cars in the span of five years that had been plying the roadways before the war. Suddenly, used cars were available everywhere. The surplus of vehicles became the prime stock for hot rodders and customizers to express their art. Here, a maroon 1932 Ford roadster, a blue 1936 Ford three-window coupe, and a 1937 Chevy are on display. Later, when muscle cars roared out of the factories, dealers like this one sold ready-made street machines to a willing market. *Kent Bash*

Speed shops became the primary location for hot rodders to buy the parts and equipment needed to hop up their rides. Some of the early suppliers of specialty parts started in the teens and the business blossomed into a major industry by the 1950s. Today, speed parts are everywhere and even the car parts outfit down at the local strip mall carries a certain amount of custom wheels and other accessories that at one time would have been regarded as specialty items. *Mike Witzel*

degree temperatures weren't always conducive to a fun time. While dyed-in-the-wool time trial participants and their entourages had no problem enduring the conditions, the spectators had a hard go of it. By that time, the drag racing sideshow was splintering off into its own unique category. For the complete expression of the quirky new sport, locations that were better suited to hold races and boosters of the growing racing hobby began looking elsewhere.

The timing was just right, since a smattering of ready-made racing strips in the southern

When the craze for hot rodding was at its peak during the fifties, club jackets and T shirts emblazoned with the name of one's car club were extremely popular garb. At a glance, car nuts could identify their competitors at the track, while giving each individual a sense of group membership and camaraderie. Today, these items of attire are hot collectibles. *Mike Witzel/jackets courtesy Mike and Cheryl Goyda*

California area were just waiting for reclamation. Faster than you could fill a gas tank and clip the nozzle back onto the pump, the abandoned aircraft runways left over after World War II became the new locations for drag racing competition. Behind Newport Bay in the city of Santa Ana, C. J. Hart discovered a quiet little airfield and turned it into one of drag racing's classic venues. Offering

10 percent of the take right off the top, he struck a deal with the airport's manager to rent out one of the unused runways every Sunday morning. The track opened in the fall of 1950 and the sounds of drag racing reverberated across the tarmac—drowning out the propellers of the little planes taxiing nearby. Soon, quarter-mile racing strips that featured specially built facilities appeared in

places like Pamona and Fontana and from there, opened across America.

Even so, hot rodders faced growing opposition from the establishment. Alarmed by the growing amount of street racing, police organizations and the popular press began working the media propaganda machine in hopes of turning public sentiment against the hot rodders. It was the distinct wish of the powers-that-be to ban all hot rods from the roadways.

Concerned about the tide of opposition that was rising against the hot rod hobby, Wally Parks, then the general manager of the Southern California Timing Association, joined forces with Robert E. Petersen of Hollywood Publicity Associates. Together, they had a brainstorm to

stage a hot rod extravaganza at the Los Angeles Armory that would show Joe Public that the average hot rodder was much more than a lawbreaking juvenile delinquent. Some big name Hollywood stars were recruited to attend the pair's souped-up soiree, and as a direct consequence a respectable number of radio, television, and newspaper reporters followed.

However, it was the hot rodders and their gleaming creations that ultimately stole the limelight from the Tinsel Town celebrities. By providing potent examples of ingenious automotive engineering, unlimited creativity, and endless imagination, they managed to make the promotional gala a resounding success. The proof was more than just a few superficial accolades printed in the papers. After the event, even the National Safety Council abandoned its negative attitude towards hot rodding. As hard as it was to believe, the

A gleaming black, flamed fenderless Ford with "big n' little" tires, a blacked-out radiator grille, and fully chromed engine (complete with a blower) strikes a rather sinister-looking pose at a favorite car gathering in Augusta, Kansas. Just looking fast was an important asset to all street racers. *Mike Witzel*

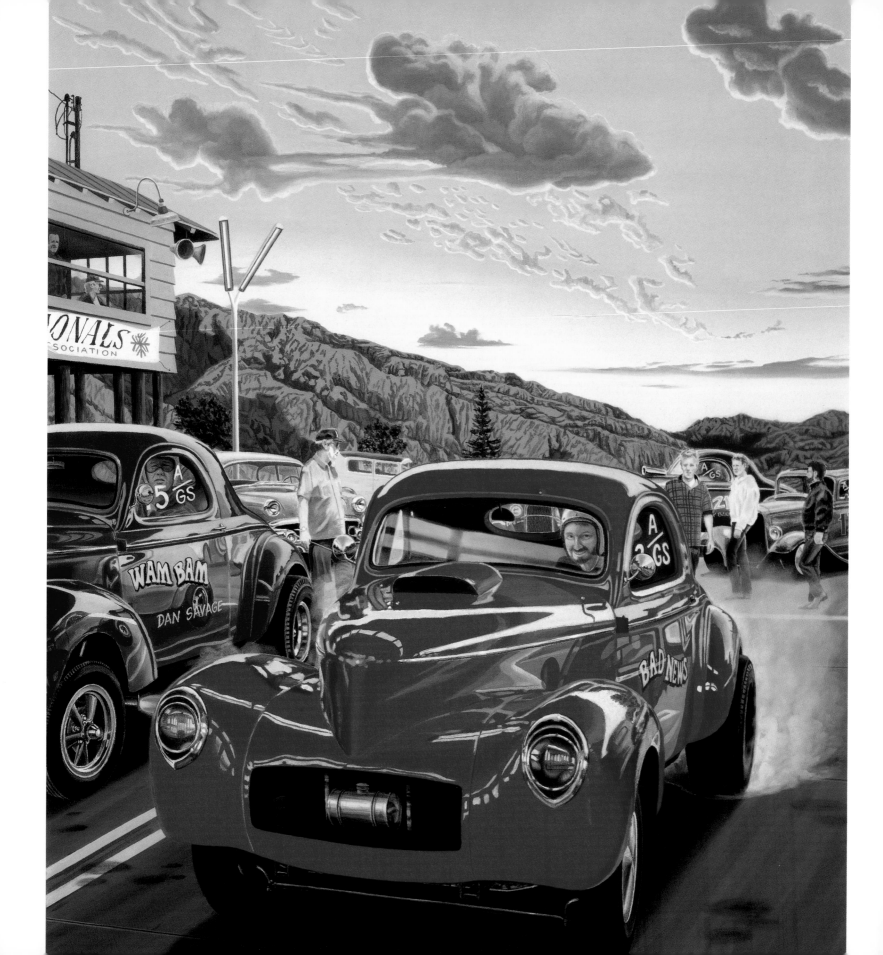

Roaring off the line at the drags, this 1940 Willys depicts the dawn of the hot rod gasser era. After cars were grouped by the NHRA according to classes, the gassers allowed average guys to race cars without having to compete against the big money. Unlike other popular hot rod fodder that was running short, the Willys could be readily found in junkyards, and it didn't take long for hot rodders to discover their magic. They were small and lightweight—a great choice for drag racing duty. *Kent Bash*

Southern California Timing Association was asked to become a member! Supercharged by the development and the groundswell of acceptance that followed, Petersen went on to produce *Hot Rod* magazine with Parks joining as the publication's editor in 1948.

But that was only the beginning of respectability for the hot rod realm. In 1951, The National Hot Rod Association was formed under the leadership of Wally Parks and went on to promote and popularize drag racing nationwide. Under the aegis of the NHRA, a promotional caravan called the Safety Safari (with a full Chrondek timing outfit) toured the country to recruit new racers and fans. In addition to introducing a new generation to the many wonders of the hot rod, this portable drag strip showed police that hot rodders were aware—and concerned—about safety.

Structured hot rod events gained respect and it wasn't long before the general public had drag racing rituals like the National Championships and the Winternationals to attend every year. By 1956, the sport boasted over 130 legal drag racing strips in the United States with more than 100,000 hot rods reported to be cruising the highways and byways. That year, a staggering 2.5 million spectators turned out to watch the drags! With the 1956 speed record set at 166 miles per hour, the public interest in this former fringe activity was electrified. Meanwhile, former illegal street racers were lured to the sport, and hot rod clubs around the nation claimed that they were signing up some 1,500 new members each month!

Speeding off towards the future, drag racing was destined to go totally "commercial." Soon, specialized dragsters, or "rail jobs" that looked nothing like the vehicles that had pioneered the

sport appeared at the strips. In place of brakes, remote-release parachutes assumed the job of slowing a racer's considerable momentum. Engines swelled in size and began sucking in exotic mixtures of explosive fuels. Rear wheels fattened as front tires took a cue from the bicycle. In the end, it was no longer a man driving the machine—the machine drove the man.

Attracted more to the smell of money than the strong odor of race fuel, corporate America caught wind of the phenomenon, and before too long big money flooded into drag racing. Within a few brief years, the inevitable sponsorships and commercialism that followed completely changed the racing scene. By the time America had accomplished its first manned exploration of the moon, the only unregulated, spur-of-the-moment hot rod activities that remained were taking place on the asphalt of America's streets.

Despite advances made in civilizing the hot rod animal, unsanctioned speed runs enjoyed by cruisers remained a disturbing reality—even in the cities that were lucky enough to have lawful racing

This one-time gasser has been made over into an attention-getting street rod. Here, it's parked at the Canoga Park Bob's Big Boy Cruise Night prior to closing. Now, this former drive-in dining location has been converted into just another chain restaurant. While cruise nights and carousing are over, the cruisers are still allowed to visit. *Kent Bash*

The 1932 Ford three-window coupe in the fenderless high-boy configuration was—and still is—an extremely popular style of hot rod. Like the custom coach builders of motoring's early years, the teenagers growing up in automotive America developed tricks and techniques that rivaled the expertise of the finest craftsmen. The chopped top, as exemplified in this whimsical scene, became one of the more prominent modifications. First used by the dry lakebed racers to decrease air resistance, it was retained for its cool visual effect when the racing activities moved onto the streets. The car in this scene is a real-life model owned by famed car culture artist Robert Williams. *Kent Bash*

In its day, the Greer, Black, and Prudhomme Top Fuel was the most winning dragster in the history of drag racing. As indicated by this classic machine, dragster engines were first positioned in front of the drivers. After racer Don Garlits nearly blew his foot off in a racing disaster, he was the first to build a successful dragster with the engine positioned behind the driver. Others saw the logic and followed suit until it became a standard. *Courtesy Gary Lick*

outlets. In 1947, the movie *Devil On Wheels* had brought a new awareness of the speed problem to God-fearing citizens: In the film, a young boy named Mickey slaps together his first hot rod, and then uses it to make racing challenges out along the back roads. Without a doubt, impressionable teens in the audience were eager to jump in their own machines and give 'er the gun. "Problem was, everybody wanted to go fast in a souped hot rod," lamented amateur drag racer Hervez Zapata. "We dug the racing thing so much that we couldn't always hold out for the drag strip to open up. Besides, most of the dudes with bad cars wanted to show them off where other people—I guess girls—could see them do crazy stuff. Taking a rod way out to race them legally in the boonies wasn't always first choice. The street was real fun!" To the chagrin of society's rulemakers, the nation's hot rodding subculture became so inebriated with cars and competition that they had to find places to race—even when the legal strips closed!

As a rather unfortunate side effect of the lack of large numbers of drag strips, cruisers embraced

During the heyday of racing during the fifties and sixties, drag strips and tracks across America were the places where car nuts got their chance to show their stuff. As part of the reward, cars were plastered with cool window decals obtained from the racing venues and were worn like a badge of honor in the streets. *Mike Witzel/Decals Courtesy Steve Perrault collection*

the paved thoroughfares that poured out all across America and made them the destination for recreational racing. There was good reason, since the conditions in the streets were optimal. There weren't any major bumps to contend with, rocks to dodge, or big obstacles to endanger the path of reckless drivers (if one didn't count all of the other cars). For the hot rod rowdy who liked nothing better than seeing how fast his car could go, the message was clear: Not only were these improved roads and highways great locations to go cruising, they were also perfect racing venues. Who cared if it was an illegal activity?

After sundown, secluded hideaways became impromptu meeting places where many of the car clubs conducted illegal drag racing. Not surprisingly, cruisers in California were the most imaginative, and locations like the concrete drainage basin of the Los Angeles River became top spots for clandestine hot rod action. There were hundreds of others prized by the growing street mob, including the smooth roads without cross-traffic like Sepulveda Boulevard. The remote cut of asphalt that ran by the Van Norman Dam and reservoir was a big draw, as was the ribbon of Foothill Boulevard (Route 66) that unfurled past the Santa Anita horse track in Arcadia. Mines Field (an airstrip that later became Los Angeles International Airport) brought to mind a favorite nearby strip called Lincoln Boulevard. Close by in El Monte, illegal racing scarred Peck Road. Still, the best run of all was over in Burbank. Just west of the city limits, Glen Oaks Boulevard boasted an ideal location: Burbank cops didn't have authority across the city boundary, and the Los Angeles squad cars had to come out all the way from the Van Nuys substation!

But whether it was a public traffic strip on the East Coast, a secluded back road on the West Coast, or any of myriad roadways in between, the story was pretty much the same: Street race riffraff wanted nothing to do with civility. This was a style without established guidelines where participants made up the protocol as they went. Hot rod heathens cruising the strip scoffed at traffic laws, snickered at speed limits, and thumbed their noses at authority. A large part of the illegal street racing mystique was disregarding (and breaking) normal traffic laws. "Engaging in a speed contest" became the phrase most feared by street racers, and police regularly chased down the daredevils to issue them a ticket.

Sometimes, things got serious with real bullets fired! At a "cruise night" held in 1996 in New England, an outspoken New Yorker (who preferred to remain anonymous) described a frightening incident that forever changed his outlook on unlawful cruising. "Uh, huh, we took some lead once and let me tell 'ya, it wasn't fun. It all started when we was dragging our favorite strip under this

Cruising the strip was never an unregulated activity. Police patrols were always on hand to keep street racers in check and limit the activities of overexuberant youth. With the widespread addition of the two-way transceiver during the fifties, keeping in touch with nearby squad cars (and central dispatch) made it easy for the boys in blue to nab teenage speeders and other lawbreakers. *From the collections of the Texas/Dallas History and Archives Division, Dallas Public Library*

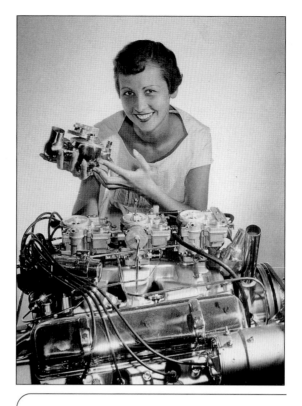

Model Marrlyn Kwast cradles the carb that furnished fuel for the "one-lung," 7-horsepower engine mounted in the Olds curved dash runabout, produced from 1900 to 1905. Shown below is the 1957 Oldsmobile J-2 "Rocket Engine." With three dual carburetors that provided some 300 horsepower, power-packed motors like this one became the basis for the hot rodding hobby and the reason speeds kept rising. *The Automotive Hall of Fame*

freeway overpass out on Long Island and got busted by the cops. My buddy and I already had 16 tickets between us so we made a run for it in my T. Rounding a turn to ditch 'em on some side streets that we knew by heart, we heard a few slugs whiz by us and we almost wet our pants. Later, we found one of 'em stuck in the turtle!"

Guns were only one deterrent to the street racers. Alarmed by the growing popularity of the illicit "sport," both the police and popular press worked to turn public sentiment against the sort of delinquents who liked to race. As early as the mid-forties, the National Safety Council teamed up with the Hearst Newspaper chain to implement a publicity campaign calling for a ban on automotive racing—both in the streets *and* on the track.

More trouble came in 1945 when California lawmakers introduced Assembly Bill No. 408. Simply put, the statute demanded that "every motor vehicle shall be equipped with four fenders and mudguards." Among rodders who liked to cut the wheel shields off their heaps, the news was unwelcome. Bill 910 followed suit with more dictatorial, if not unconstitutional, words: "No equipment shall be installed upon a motor when it is used to propel a motor vehicle, which is designed to increase the horsepower of the motor above that which it had at the time it was manufactured." Translation: no hopped up engines!

In practice, not one of these actions created the roadblock that was necessary to bar the shortcut to hell's highway. The hot rod race had become a part of America's streets, and the government agencies were impotent when it came to capping the craze. The only recourse was to deal with the problem on a family level. And so, Mama, Papa, Grandma, and Grandpa all attempted to warn Junior of the dangers of driving an overpowered, underbraked street machine with reckless abandon. Of course, the warnings fell on deaf ears. As had been the case since the beginning of the automotive age, teenagers with cars imagined that they were invincible and immune to hazards. Street-racing addicts didn't want to hear of the risks and thought it better to blindly follow the muse of speed, often with dire consequences.

Sadly, this was one time when the old fogies of America were dead right. In the hands of the inexperienced driver, a fast car was like a stick of dynamite with a short fuse. With just a little spark, it could blow up in your face and wrap itself around a telephone pole or roll topsy-turvy through a roadside ditch. That's exactly what happened in one of the most famous hot rod mishaps of the thirties. As the story goes, Phil Weiand (a noted designer and manufacturer of automotive speed equipment) was driving his hopped-up Model T Ford with a friend. He was driving at a rather high speed when he encountered a sharp curve and decided to go for it. Despite Weiand's

confidence, his pal in the passenger seat had doubts about the successful execution of the turn. He panicked, yanking the parking brake handle in reaction. Tragically, the roadster flipped out of control with both occupants thrown out. The accident left Weiand a paraplegic.

Competitive driving left many cars incapacitated as well, as a penchant for street racing resulted in a lot of expensive wear and tear on a vehicle's mechanical components. If a rookie driver applied too much power at the wrong time or shifted incorrectly, the excessive rpm could blow an engine.

With its race-bred pedigree, the 426 Hemi threw considerable excitement into the muscle car arena when it was unleashed on the street in 1964 (it was immediately banned from racing). To get the Hemi homologated for NASCAR, Dodge had to make the engine a regular production option for its regular vehicle line-up. Before long, it could be found in such normally staid cars as the 1966 Plymouth Satellite shown here. However, it reached its full potential when it powered muscle cars like the Dodge Charger and Plymouth Roadrunner. *Kent Bash*

Jackrabbit starts ragged out the clutch or tranny and quick stops burned up brakes. Tires were another major casualty of fast cruising, burning rubber, and hard cornering. Van Nuys, California, auto shop teacher David Rodarte recalled the mechanical failures. During the sixties, he discovered the meaning of being stranded when he blew out the driveshaft on his 1965 Galaxy. "I hit third gear at about 110 miles per hour . . . twisted off the output shaft, rolled it up a hill and then down into my friend's front yard! He lived in the projects, so I paid his little brother to sleep in the car while I walked home to get a truck so I could tow it back. As a matter of fact, it's one of the pieces I show off to my auto shop students—that old output shaft all twisted off from the four-speed, with the driveshaft yoke still attached to it!"

Since street racing could commence at the spur of the moment, challengers had the most luck if they maintained their vehicles in top condition. In the days of tail fins and two-tone, all it took to arrange a racing heat was a chance encounter of

two hot cars at a traffic signal, stop sign, or country crossroads. After both drivers eyeballed each other's car, a deadpan nod signaled that the race was on. From there, two complete strangers with nothing in common but four tires and a modified motor entered into a game that allowed only one winner.

This archetype of racing in the public traffic corridors came to life in the seventies motion picture *American Graffiti*. In one of the more memorable scenes, the local street champ slips along Main Street in a yellow deuce coupe when he's confronted by a stranger piloting a sinister black, hopped-up 1955

Chevrolet. Of course, the local hero agrees to take on the out-of-town invader, and the pair meet at an illegal drag racing location on the edge of town. As Wolfman Jack howls on the radio in the background, they roar into the dawn and discover that the old master's rod ain't as fast as it used to be. In a twist of fate, the Chevy flips over and crashes, allowing the local paladin to hold his title—for the moment. As was true on the legal strips, someone faster was always waiting on the sidelines to speed by and grab your crown.

For the street racers who wanted more than a quick pickup, the local drive-in restaurant became the place to camp out with your hot rod. By the end of the fifties, numerous car clubs and lone-wolf cruisers had transformed America's hamburger stands into street racing staging areas. No longer was the drive-in serving stall used to eat food! Much to the concern of owners trying to make a buck, curb stands became a great place for youths to park a hot rod, display it, and tinker with the engine while waiting for the next challenger to

come along. While one munched on an order of french fries or sucked down a milkshake, it was easy to arrange illegal match-ups for later in the evening. Eventually, the drive-in scene became so crazy that some participants towed their hot rods out on trailers and parked them across the street! For these guys, drag racing was serious business. All of the time and money used to tune and trick out a car demanded a reward with some sort of prize—namely, tangible personal property.

At the time, the legal drag racing strips of the day often awarded little trophies to the winners. With that fact in mind, street racers wanted their bonus as well. Many racers who already had a number of notches carved in their belt became bored with the simple contest of one-upmanship and began looking for new ways to raise the thrill level. To increase the risk and heighten fun, they staged a fair amount of "boulevard brawling" to win material possessions like cigarettes, leather jackets,

Two muscle cars, Dodge and Pontiac, face off against each other out in the streets of Detroit. During the 1970s, confrontations like this one were a nightly occurrence along Woodward Avenue. Today, the one-time street racing venue is mostly quiet and high-speed cruising is strictly prohibited. ©1997 Tom Shaw/Musclecar Review Magazine

The running joke among cruisers has always been that if you want to find a cop, just head to the local doughnut shop. During the sixties, the doughnut shop offered hot rodders, hippies, customizers, lowriders, bikers, and even the law a no-man's land that was free from hassle. At the same service counter, a diverse range of individuals could enjoy a cup of coffee and a glazed doughnut. Even so, this wasn't the place to burn rubber. *Kent Bash*

mag wheels, whiskey, speed equipment, switch-blades, and seat covers. On rare occasions, girls were the racer's bounty! Most racing was for cold hard cash where winner took all (unless you were driving against a townie, it was best to have a neutral third party hold the green). Sometimes, street rodders raced head-to-head for pink slips, the postwar equivalent of today's car titles. Whoever won took ownership of the other rodder's car—and its speed secrets.

This combo of cars and high-stakes betting was a risky proposition at best. Unless you knew for certain that you drove the "fastest set of wheels in town," it was unwise to put up title to your little deuce coupe when you were racing an unknown challenger. With all the races being run for real scratch, there were more than a few clever hustlers haunting the streets. These crafty guys drove cars known as "sleepers," vehicles that looked like a decrepit dog on the outside yet had all the workings of a thoroughbred on the inside. "I bit off a little more than I could chew back in 1958," groaned Seattlite Parker Jones, relating the story of how his 1957 Chevy once got stomped by a 1932 highboy with primer. "These days, as a commercial insurance underwriter, I'm a helluva lot more aware of risks than I was during the fifties. I never would have agreed to race that guy who rolled into the Aurora A & W with that ragged old heap had I known what was hiding underneath his hood! It's a good thing we were only racing for a twenty!"

In the same vein of deception, there were a few "posers" who just liked the *idea* of street racing and the benefits it promised. Dean Batchelor in his book *The American Hot Rod* related the ploy such posers would use to fool onlookers into thinking they owned a souped-up car. First, they wheeled into the drive-in lot and parked in a prominent spot. Then, they pulled the hand brake, depressed the clutch, and threw the transmission into second gear. Next, they turned the ignition key off as they removed their foot from the clutch pedal! With the ignition disconnected, the clutch dragged up against the fly-wheel, causing the motor to stop turning. Since the racers in the know were well aware that mills with high compression (and extra power) had light fly-wheels, those that stopped right after the ignition cut off were most likely modified. Peers who watched from the sidelines became duped into believing that the car was a hot one and that the driver was waiting for the next race (it never came).

By the 1960s, differentiating between the real racers and posers became even more complicated. To the delight of enthusiasts, the stock production vehicles made in America began to change. What had begun 10 years earlier as a skirmish among U.S. automakers to build modern, eight-cylinder, overhead-valve motors ended in an industrywide battle for more horsepower and cubic inches! For consumers, the war of automotive supremacy was a dream come true: Many of the performance specs written by hot rod buffs in the back alleys and garages became a part of Detroit's mass-production repertoire. At last, the establishment had acknowledged that cars weren't just a mere practical means of transportation. As legions of street racers and cruisers had tried to demonstrate for so many years, the car was a great gadget for recreation and sport!

In the new decade Pontiac chief engineer John DeLorean introduced a new type of hybrid automobile that combined cool looks and power in one hot package. Taking inspiration from the cadre of illegal street racers shredding the asphalt on Detroit's Woodward Boulevard, DeLorean and his engineers yanked the four-banger from the Tempest model and dropped in a 389-cubic-inch V-8 as replacement. At the same time, they stiffened the suspension and added heavy-duty brakes. Intrigued by the flash of the Italian sports car scene, he "borrowed" Ferrari's exotic-sounding "Gran Turismo Omologato" name from its racing 250 and lifted the lead letters to make his own memorable model name in 1964: GTO. With a mystique all their own, 60,000 Pontiac GTOs thundered out of the factory and onto America's streets. The youth market responded favorably to the $2,500 price tag. Within two years, DeLorean's performance vision became Detroit's best-selling muscle car.

By the time Ronny and the Daytonas debuted their musical homage *Little GTO* in 1964, all of Detroit's automobile manufacturers were developing their own muscles. Shortly thereafter, baby boomers who could afford the monthly payments were snapping up fast-sounding names such as Mustang, Barracuda, Charger, Road Runner, and Camaro. At last, carmakers were assembling fully warranted versions of the passenger coupe, sports car, and hot rod all rolled into one fast, unified package. The new configuration looked to be so popular that even the *Little Old Lady from Pasadena* drove a brand new shiny red Super-Stock Dodge.

Power cruisers knew the Beach Boys' lyrics by heart: "She drives real fast and she drives real hard, she's a terror out on Colorado Boulevard. . . ." With dual exhausts, powerful engines, and four-on-the-floor transmissions, muscle cars were definitely a hit.

Suddenly, production-line racers outnumbered homemade hot rods at the illegal racing venues. Now, it was hot rods against muscle cars, old values versus new. The philosophical concerns about cars became a dividing line between participants: Was a homemade street rod the only way to go? Was a financed purchase from the local car dealer another way to get a racer? The questions were moot. By the mid-sixties, most of the hot rodding purists had gone into hibernation. The war in Vietnam played a big part, since a lot of shade-tree mechanics and hot rodders shipped out overseas. Reduced to dreaming of rods and customs that might have been, departing servicemen passed the ignition keys on to their little brothers. Within the first week, wrecks claimed many cars. More wore out from too much use and a lack of maintenance. Parents sold off the rest after Johnny failed to come marching home again.

Of the hot rods that managed to survive the turmoil of the times, many became so radically modified for dragstrip racing and speed trials that legal cruising on the public streets was out of the question. A victim of continual upgrading, some of the best sported chrome and other expensive goodies and were dressed to the nines. Now, they were far too valuable for casual, everyday cruising in the streets. With their rarity increasing daily, many classic rods headed for static exhibition on the

continued on page 97

NEXT: A scurrilous pack of muscle machines taking over the streets was at one time the bane of Detroit's cops and citizens. Out along the neon-bathed miles of Woodward Avenue, dozens of racing match-ups could be made within the span of an hour. All one had to do was cruise the strip and look for them. When one encountered an able-looking competitor in traffic, the two cars lined up and went for it until traffic congestion or stop lights caused one or the other to break off. In the realm of street racing, there was nothing like it. ©1997 Tom Shaw/Musclecar Review Magazine

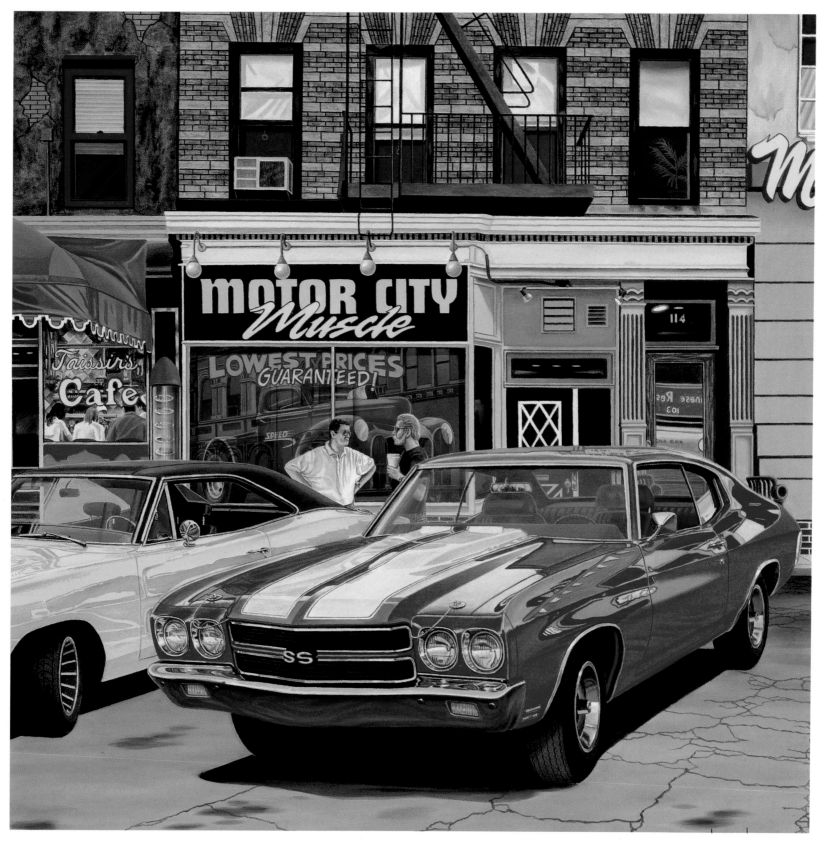

Detroit, Michigan, became the capital of street racing during the sixties and gained national notoriety for Woodward Avenue. On any given night, muscle cars like this 1969 Dodge Charger and 1970 Chevelle Super Sport 396 could be found doing battle on the streets of the "Motor City." *Kent Bash*

Continued from page 93

custom show car circuit—never to be taken out into traffic again! For the time being, the hot rod traditions begun so many years ago were on hold.

In the meantime, muscle cars took over the spotlight and by their mere presence, caused more than a few streets to achieve the status of street racing legend. In Motor City Detroit, Michigan, Woodward Avenue ascended to the throne as the undisputed king of America's illegal dragstrips. In September 1967, writer Brock Yates acknowledged this royal lineage of drag racing in *Car and Driver* magazine, dubbing Woodward Avenue the "street racing capital of the world." Almost 30 years later, *Musclecar Review* magazine editor Tom Shaw reiterated the bold claim in his article, "The Kings of Woodward Avenue." His words tell it all: "There were hot streets in most every town in America, but there was only one Woodward, and the Woodward experience was unlike any other. It was frats versus greasers, north versus south, east versus west, club versus club, GM versus Mopar versus Ford, man versus man, man versus woman, and man versus himself. I'll tell you what Woodward was—it was a real-life movie we all starred in. Too bad nobody made it, because it would have blown *American Graffiti* in the weeds."

As exciting as the ambiance was for car nuts, the authorities didn't much appreciate the no-holds-barred carnival atmosphere of illegal, unchecked street racing on Woodward! By the mid-seventies, serious plans to curtail the fun were being implemented. The first blow was an ordinance that banned customers from car-hopping, or leaving their cars on foot while parked at an eatery. To guarantee against the building of new hangouts, the city fathers outlawed drive-ins! About that time, the police also cracked down on racing: Minor traffic violations like a "display of speed" or rolling a yellow resulted in hefty fines. After realizing that illegal racing provided big revenues, cops began handing out traffic tickets like advertising circulars! Street racers headed for the pits—hit in the wallet where it hurt the most. Competition in public was no longer economically viable and the circuit returned to commuters.

After the mass exodus, the fantasy of driving a muscle car began to shed a lot of its star dust. In 1969, all the illusions shattered when insurance agents nationwide read a report published in *The Reflector* (an insurance industry magazine). "What's Behind the Surcharge" showed that so-called muscle cars would comprise just 6 percent of the total car market for the coming year. Despite this, researchers pointed to the fact that vehicles with engines over 300 horsepower would be responsible for 56 percent more monetary losses than ordinary passenger vehicles! Categorizing America's muscle machines as "overpowered," both the Nationwide and State Farm insurance companies planned to institute a 25 to 50 percent surcharge on the insurance purchased to cover these so-called death machines. Now, performance cars had a price on their heads.

Two years later, the chase thriller *Vanishing Point* debuted at America's drive-in theaters and paid a farewell tribute to the era of powerful cars. In the film, actor Barry Newman starred as Kowalski, one of the "last American heroes," a car delivery driver intent on winning a bet regarding his arrival time after taking a supercharged white Dodge Challenger cross country. In spite of the smashed roadblocks and the trail of mayhem left in his wake, the white knight's final "run" became an ironic allegory for the demise of the muscle car.

Even fearless Kowalski couldn't outrun hungry insurance companies and greedy oil men. In October 1973, an embargo on all petroleum shipments made to the United States began. The next day, the Organization of Petroleum Exporting Countries (OPEC) decided to raise crude prices by a shocking 70 percent! Overnight, gas prices doubled to more than $1 per gallon. Long lines, gas rationing plans, and overheated tempers followed. Forced out by economics and killjoy authorities, American street racing, the muscle car, and wasting gas ground to a halt.

Strutting Their Stuff on the Street

America's Automotive Exhibitionists

"Creating an identity by way of one's automobile is a personal thing. For some, it's the fancy aftermarket goodies, expensive custom bodywork, and the act of displaying that prosperity out on the streets. For others, it's the fun that can be had by doing all of the work yourself and learning a variety of crafts along the way, while enjoying the camaraderie of friends. This scenario of friends helping out friends is what I remember best from hot rodding's heyday in the fifties. It's still important today.

I know about cutting corners when building cars because I saw my brother Mel paint his first hot rod all by himself. It was a nice, Model A roadster with no fenders and a '48 flathead engine. As a teenager slaving away to earn some money at the local Burger Bar flipping burgers, he really couldn't save up the extra cash he needed for a good paint job. So, he decided to take the simplest route and do a homemade job right in our driveway.

After deciding on a color, he picked up the paint he needed from a local paint supply shop, then stopped at the hardware store to pick up a brush. He sanded and prepped the car as best he could and carefully applied a few coats of paint to build up the thickness. When all of the layers finally dried, he finish-sanded the body to smooth out the brush marks and then rubbed it out with plenty of elbow grease until it shone. The crazy thing was, I couldn't really tell any difference between his work and a high-dollar, spray-painted job! From my limited perspective of youth and inexperience, it was one of the keenest paint jobs that I had ever seen. To me, it sparkled with professionalism.

But that wasn't the only thing he did to make his rod unique. The homemade scheme of decorating and customizing continued on the inside of Mel's car. For quick and simple seat covers, he bought a really cool Indian blanket and threw it over the worn seat covers and rips. It might sound like a tacky method when compared to the elaborate upholstery work that's done today— but back then, a lot of cruisers used blankets to make their cars more comfortable. In a pinch, even green Army blankets did the trick.

It all goes back to the same thing: During the early days of hot rods and custom cars, the simple fact that a guy owned a car and had the freedom to go wherever he wanted to go was a lot more important than having the ultimate engine, flame job, interior, or wheels. Besides, once you had the money and could go out and buy all those goodies, a little bit of the magic was lost. Unjaded, it was the dreaming of things to come that mattered the most."
—*Kent Bash*

A set of personalized cruising compartments: a 1932 Ford Roadster and 1949 Oldsmobile Rocket 88, parked at Barkie's famous roadside hot dog stand on West Washington Boulevard in Los Angeles. In 1951, one year before Oldsmobile introduced this brand new, streamlined, Hydra-Matic, eight-cylinder dream machine, Jackie Brenston with His Delta Cats came out with the song Rocket 88, a rock and roll tune that could well have served as an anthem for the custom creed. As a pickup machine, how could an ordinary hot rod compare when one considered the plush seats, comfortable ride, and styling of the first "rocket" engine Olds? The song's hook promised cruisers the world: "You women have heard of jalopies, you've heard the noise they make, well let me introduce you to my rocket 88, . . . baby we'll ride in style." In the world of cars, cruising, and picking up chicks, the custom was king. *Kent Bash*

UP from the rubble of the gasoline-gobbling muscle car era rose a movement to resurrect the dormant hot rod arts of the forties and fifties. As America witnessed the effects of the sexual revolution and the disco descent of rock and roll, the mavens of customized car shows and other exhibitions broke with convention and started taking their show-quality roadsters, coupes, and convertibles out on the asphalt in ever-increasing numbers. Cruising was back!

Driving and displaying their precious cars in public so that other people could see them, loyalists in California took it upon themselves to spread the gospel of cruising up and down the West Coast and then across the continent—re-energizing all of the backsliders across America. Organized motoring clubs like the San Francisco Bay Area Roadsters and Los Angeles Roadsters were at the forefront of the revved-up revival. Taking to the streets whenever and wherever they could, these reborn cruisers sought to disprove the exaggerated reports of the hot rodder's demise!

As American rodders rediscovered their roots, a wave of publicity primed the car crowd's interest. Major motoring magazines like *Hot Rod*, *Car Craft*, and *Street Rodder* began touting the rod and custom formats with renewed vigor. To widen interest, the pundits considered "new" ideas: Could mass-produced, affordable cars (made during the fifties) be considered a starting point for traditional custom projects? The hobby was ripe for expansion, and

With radically restyled taillights, this late-forties Chevrolet custom exemplifies some of the custom work executed during the fifties. Back then, many car builders did extensive rework in areas like the headlights and taillights but left the rest of the car pretty much untouched. *Kent Bash/car courtesy George Killger*

cruising activities began to blossom. "Rod runs" were the newest rage and every type of car under the sun was welcome. "It used to be that only certain cars were thought of as customs but now, many more may be thought about when building a custom car," explained Max Klaus, a cruiser from Germany who makes regular trips to the states to drive the length of Route 66. "In the United States, the group that is called Kustom Kemps of America limits the custom cars to body styles that were stamped out between 1936 and 1964. 'Kemp' was used to refer to cars back during the fifties, it was a beatnik slang word."

In 1970, the good folks at *Rod & Custom* magazine (one of the more vocal periodicals that supported the pastime) sponsored what became the first important national gathering for the hobby. A farmer's field in Peoria, Illinois, was the point of convergence for the highly publicized motoring meet. From all corners of the map, more than 600 hairy hot rods and curvy customs cruised out to America's Heartland. Those who were lucky enough to attend this Woodstock of wheels reveled in the real, motorized sounds of "heavy metal" and witnessed for themselves that the interest in building personalized cars was still goin' strong. Better still, it appeared that the denizens of America's drive-in culture were returning once more to the main core of the cruising philosophy: Driving the strip in an attention-getting vehicle was a helluva lot of fun!

As hot rods made their reappearance, the attitudes toward cruising and cars were changing dramatically. Once a pastime, drag racing had evolved into a big-money, professional sport with corporate sponsors and wide appeal. With the counterculture image somewhat watered down, many cruisers became jaded to the idea of street racing. More important, all of the classic cars that lived through the Vietnam years were worth a lot more money than they used to be. Risking a car crash to prove yourself to another reckless rodder was stupid! Older, wiser, and married with children, former risk-takers now had homes, full-time jobs, and mortgage payments. Sadly, a few had to sell their cars. "With a baby on the way, I didn't have a choice. I had to sell my first roadster,"

Junkyards, salvage sellers, and dumps were the point of birth for many of the classic road machines of the forties, fifties, and sixties. True, new car dealers had some of the best cars in town, but cars built with sweat and imagination were always cooler. *Mike Witzel*

The Pele was a car developed by the Kaiser Aluminum Company during the fifties as an answer to the durable body shell. Body panels were made of stamped aluminum sheet with enameled finish, with side trim of brushed and gold-colored anodized aluminum. Bumpers, roof rails, and the top roof panel were all of aluminum. Wraparound glass was used extensively. During the postwar years, automakers began dreaming up—and building—features that were previously only in the minds of customizers. *Courtesy of the Automotive Hall of Fame*

In the fifties, cruising over the horizon were the automotive attributes Speed and Beauty, a set of parents that would bear a car-crazed America a wondrous new offspring. From the dream factories of Detroit, fabulous concept cars came off the drawing boards and captured the public's attention at car shows and other demonstrations. Some, like General Motor's famed Golden Rocket, were far too extravagant and customized for their time, and as a result, the models never made it into full-scale production. *Courtesy of the Automotive Hall of Fame*

moaned Charles Vandreason, attendee of a recent cruise event near Rancho Cucamonga, California. "If I could have had it my way, I would have kept that car and figured some other way of gettin' up some money. I love my kids, but I will never forget that old Lincoln heap or find another one quite like it!"

With wild-eyed competition no longer the main interest of garage-bound enthusiasts, the hopped-up, slicked out street rod became just another expensive plaything in the adult toy box. Not even the hot rod's racing roots could negate its taming. This was a considerable change from decades past, when the sole intent of America's

backyard car builders was to emphasize *speed* over *looks*. During the hurly-burly days of time trials, competitors knew the drill: You had to eliminate parts if they didn't make a car go any faster! To minimize weight, racers removed nonessentials like the trim, mirrors, running boards, door handles, fenders, and the hood ornaments. To decrease wind resistance, roofs were "chopped" and bodies "channeled" (to allow the body to sit lower on the frame). Later, when the racing rabble roared into the streets, car builders continued the speed-inspired styling techniques largely out of habit. By that time, America's hot rods were beginning to look a lot less like the racing machines that they

Imagine the Chevrolet Corvette completely customized with a mild Jetsons influence and a touch of the hot rodder's art thrown in for good measure. It happened in this fifties concept version of a Corvette, a rather outlandish idea that, fortunately, never saw life on the streets. *Courtesy of the Automotive Hall of Fame*

off the *ride* and turn the *cars* into the competition. It was the visual aspect of cruising that was important, so there wasn't any need to prove mechanical ability. Instead of dancing around the streets to find opponents, those in the custom club drove leisurely down the Main, moving slow enough to see onlooker reactions. For them, speeding tickets were rare. Citations for "impeding traffic" were more likely.

Nevertheless, the customizers still had to prove their status within their own group. Playing to a street-side audience was an important ritual for owners of customized machines, just as participating in a street race was for those infatuated with hot rods. For automotive exhibitionists, the quest for perfection showed a single-minded, manic fervor. Who cared about the horsepower of the engine, the displacement of the piston, or number of carburetors? It was the outside window dressings that transformed an ordinary, clunky coupe into a cool car, and as a result, it was these image-shaping elements that held priority over engine and mechanical work. To elicit a favorable response from the peanut gallery along the Main Street sidewalk, a car's upholstery, exterior paint, and wheel coverings demanded top billing.

After World War II, it was the same self-conscious attitude that led custom car artists to follow America's hot rodders to the junkyards. There, they found that most of the second-hand motoring stock was all but gone. The throng of hop-up hounds bent on building racing roadsters and fast street rods had already snatched up most of the smaller, lightweight cars. Even so, the shortage wasn't a big problem, since the end-product made by the custom crowd relied on the cars that were available—namely, the enclosed vehicles manufactured during the late thirties and early forties that were ill-suited for drag racing. If one

The car radio evolved to become such a dominant part of the automotive experience during the forties and fifties that industry visionaries came up with all sorts of gadgets that would make the cars of the future more entertaining. Forget the theater or drive-in movie; the ordinary dashboard radio would be superseded by the television and back-seat viewing of one's favorite programs would become an integral part of cruising. Only in America. *National Automotive History Collection, Detroit Public Library*

originally started out as. More and more, these insolent chariots resembled the automobiles known as "customs."

The stylistic evolution was important to the cruising hobby, as the Main Street strip was obviously more suited toward the display of cars than it was racing. For the pastime of cruising to gain a wide audience from all types of car owners, it had to lose some of the negative associations linked with hard-core hot rodding. Custom cars and their emphasis on style would go a long way in convincing skeptics that cruising wasn't a disruptive activity. At the same time, a heated clan rivalry between America's customizers and hot rodders had been simmering since the glory days of water bags and hood ornaments. It was an age-old conflict: The hot rodder liked to go fast and turn every run into some sort of competition, while customizers liked to take it slow and easy. Hot rod fans were big on motors, mechanics, and parts that equaled speed. In contrast, the customizer's "thing" was to show

This highly reflective and customized Ford is chopped, channeled, and sectioned with a pancaked hood. The headlights are frenched and the body is so low that the height of the entire car only comes up to your waist. It was this type of car that attracted the attention of the cruisers and crowds. *Kent Bash*

Decked out with massive flame work, minimurals, and running a Chevy drivetrain, this 1949 Mercury is a great example of a mild custom. In the spirit of the great American customizers, who often come up with cool-sounding names like *Chezoom*, *Cadzilla*, and so on, this custom creation is called *Mercula*. *Kent Bash/car courtesy Dave King*

The massive whales made between the years 1949 and 1951 under the Mercury marque became prized commodities for the cruiser and customizer (it was somewhat ironic that these slow cruisin' favorites took the same name of the mythical god of speed). These babies were real driving cars—big, brash, bulbous—with curves in all the right places! *©1997 Andy Southard*

desired to lighten up these heavy cars, there wasn't a good way to cut away parts without making the body look ridiculous. With the integrated bodies these cars wore, the rakish stance of the stripped hot rod just didn't work.

None of this mattered to the customizer. Cruisers fell in love with the bigger, more stylish cars for the comfortable ride and massive visual presence they afforded. As a creative canvas, a few models became hands-down favorites, most notably the 1936 Ford. With a curvaceous design that diverged from models of previous years, it encouraged the customizer's creativity and just begged for extra body modifications and restyling. A few years down the road, the massive whales made by Mercury between the years 1940 and 1951 became prized commodities, too (it was ironic that these slow cruisin' favorites had the same name as the mythical god of speed). These were real driving cars—big, brash, bulbous—with curves in all the right places. Perfectly suited for recreational cruising, customizers adored them.

Automotive author/photographer and long-time Mercury lover Andy Southard remains one of the brand's loyal followers. "I had a 1940 Mercury coupe 'stocker' when I was going to high school," he reminisced. "This was in 1949. I sold it and then had another car, a '49 Ford. Then, I always used to think, Why did I sell my Mercury? I loved it so much that I decided someday I would get another one. Well time went on—40-some years—and I was able to buy this '40 Mercury that I have now! I had a friend of mine who does bodywork, Tom Cutino, do all the customizing. He chopped the top, molded the fenders, and put in electric openers in the doors and the trunk. He installed a 350 Chevrolet engine with an automatic transmission, and, as the style of the period was in 1949, teardrop fender skirts. Underneath, it's all brand new, but by outward appearances, it's the same customized Mercury that you would have seen on the strip during the forties."

With life-long devotees like this, the Mercury brand attained a marked measure of popularity

Architect Mies Van Der Rohe once stated that "God is in the details." While he didn't have automobiles in mind when he uttered these words, it certainly would be true for many custom cars and hot rods. For the automotive aficionado, the simple routing of spark plug wires could turn into an expression of art, and the finishing touches in an engine compartment can be as important as the body. ©1997 Robert Genat

An original, far out paint job is one feature of an automobile that's guaranteed to get attention out in the streets. Hot rodders, lowriders, and customizers all regard the paint job as an important part of the cruising scene. *Mike Witzel*

A 302 Ford mill fitted into a searing red roadster body is a beautiful combination. In the realm of hot-rodding, there's nothing quite like the gleam of a polished engine set against the high-gloss finish of a deep pigment paint job. Who says that speed and beauty can't be combined in one machine? *Kent Bash*

A lowered "resto rod" running Centerline wheels, this 1937 Chevy Coupe is a popular hot rod look. Throughout the years, manufacturers have turned out body styles that were nice enough to leave stock. For those who desire an extra touch, a modern drivetrain and flashy paint job are all that is needed to customize cars like this. *Kent Bash*

among cruisers. Eventually, it was the brand that came to mind whenever someone uttered "customs and cruising" in the same breath. It became such a notorious part of drive-in lore that in 1976, the Steve Miller Band acknowledged the following with a rendition of K. C. Johnson's *Mercury Blues*. One particular verse of the old standard confirmed the babe-pulling power of a tricked-out Merc: "You know that gal I love, I stole her from a friend, fool got lucky stole her back again. Because she knowed he had a Mercury, cruise up and down this road, up and down this road. Well, she knowed he had a Mercury, and she cruise up and down this road." Whether stock or custom, the Mercury had the ephemeral quality that attracted members of the opposite sex.

Despite the numerous songs being written about their romantic qualities, the oversized highway cars like the Fords and Mercurys didn't gain a reputation as love machines. In fact, custom cars became known as "lead sleds!" Despite the somewhat negative connotation, it was a good description, since many cruisers will tell you that the nickname originated from the early coach workers and auto body repairmen who first used molten lead to fill body imperfections and smooth out welds, today, bodywork is done with the plastic filler Bondo. As it happened, custom fans borrowed the regimen during the forties and fifties and used it to shape body contours, patch small dents, and to level connecting seams. Adding weight became a known side-effect of building a custom.

Not everyone saw this added weight as an asset. Like a straight man who waits for his punch line, customizers and their overloaded rides frequently became the butt of jokes whenever jealous hot rodders were around. Those who preferred to "go over show" used the term to denigrate the custom owner every chance they could. "One time on Sepulveda Boulevard, a hot rodder pointed in the direction of my hood and inquired if I had my mama's sewing machine mounted in there," recalled Tim Wisemann, a present-day custom car fan and occasional California cruiser. "I felt like socking him in the mouth, but I took it for what it was, just another jealous comment from a guy that wouldn't know what style was if it hit him right between the eyes." Most of the sarcastic jibes fell on deaf ears, because ardent custom fans didn't give them much credence. They were too busy building a motorized Disneyland for themselves that provided the maximum cruising experience.

The process of turning an ordinary car into a custom was rarely as easy as slapping on new accessories. More often than not, it took a lot of hard work and patience to transform an automobile into the ultimate cruising coach. The changes ran the gamut from minor cosmetic fixes to major bodywork. Car guys (and some gals) referred to simple refinements as mild and extensive reworks as wild. In the mild category, the customizer handy with tools often modified the suspension or cut the coils to make the car hug the asphalt. (At first, customizers dropped the rear and the front remained high.) With a nip here and a tuck there, the body got a face-lift with subtle changes. Maybe it was the sloping line of a fender that changed or, possibly, the crease of the hood. Perhaps it was the way the door panel connected with the rest of the body. And why not hide the gas filler neck in the trunk or employ a few other unexpected tricks? Nothing was off limits! The extent and complexity of rework depended on the fantasy that came alive in the mind's eye of the customizer and his or her ability.

When deciding what changes to make, it didn't take a rocket scientist to figure out what looked cool and what didn't. If one chopped the car's roof or channeled the body, the ride fell on the wild side of custom. Occasionally, cruisers crafted new body segments for this type of vehicle from scratch and replaced the original fenders, hoods,

or rear quarter panels. Swapping nice parts from completely different brands was an acceptable practice, too. Cruisers exchanged bumpers and front grilles like library books. Occasionally, minor surgery allowed the wheel cutouts to conform more perfectly with the circumference of the tires. Custom guys referred to these modified wheel openings as "radiused."

When a custom owner wanted to go beyond the norm and make a bold statement to boot, the automobile was "sectioned." This severe technique was no job for an amateur bodyman, however,

since it called for the careful removal of all excess material around the horizontal axis of the vehicle! If done right, the creation was reborn from the custom shop as a flatter, more sinister version of the original car. "Say you take three inches out of the car, you don't actually do it on all the panels in the same spot," explained Scott Guildner, a prominent Van Nuys, California, customizer. "You might cut the door in the middle and the quarter panel down at the bottom—whatever area is flattest and most vertical. If you do it on an angled area you

This custom Mercury is not really what it seems to be. At a glance, it appears that the curve above the lake pipe is outfitted with an accent of chrome. Closer examination reveals the customizer's secret: The polished metal is actually a skillful application of paint! With custom cars, nothing should be taken for granted. *Kent Bash*

113

Tom Otis, or "Quickdraw" as his business card describes him, spends his days crafting hot rods, spraying paint, and applying pinstriping. Here, the maestro is seen applying the finishing touches to his 1932 Ford Roadster. Whether it's done to a custom car or a hot rod, pinstriping provides the finishing touch needed to make an automobile stand out. *Kent Bash*

Anyone who has taken a shop class in high school knows that the central creed of surface finishing is sanding, sanding, and finally—more sanding. Here Jeff Tann's 1936 Ford is getting the full treatment. *Kent Bash*

may have problems. When you bring the part down, it might not match up. Either way, it's a lot of work!"

Naturally, customizers came up with their own terms for some of these body modifications, adding their own page of slang to the American cruising dictionary. Many of these descriptions are still in use today, and new ones are still being invented. If a car was "nosed," it didn't have hood emblems or ornaments to detract from the streamlined look. At the tail end, a "decked" trunk showed no sign of placards or mounting holes. Enthusiasts filled, sanded, and painted over them. On each body side, "shaved" door panels had nothing to do with the grooming habits of the cruiser. Among customizers, it referred to the fact that no door handles showed. Like all of the other techniques used to make the body as smooth as possible, it added an extra touch that set a car apart from the crowd. To access the car, one reached inside the window or used remote-controlled, electrical solenoids to activate the latches. Custom cruisers figured out other ways to get noticed. Among the most widely used effects were frenched headlight and taillight housings. This sexy-sounding technique allowed for the installation of the lamp lenses from the rear, in an alluring, recessed manner, without trim.

Wheels were a big deal, too. Where the hot rod might be outfitted with "big 'n littles" (small wheels mounted in the front and large ones in the back) both wild and mild customs could have no less than whitewall tires all the way around. Often, fender skirts covered up most of the rear wheels, adding to the look of the laminar flow. Despite the hidden rear wheels, most hard-core custom owners cherished certain wheel covers. Excited by the eye-catching layout of light-reflecting ridges, cruisers went ga-ga over the full-sized "flippers" found on the 1956 Olds Fiesta and late-model Dodge Lancers. During the crazy years of the fifties, some guys pushed the limits of creativity when they modified their wheel pans with faucet handles and drawer pulls! Regardless of the style, size, finish, or

This 1958 Volkswagen was co-author Kent Bash's fourth work in the mobile medium, a job that took him some 5,000 hours to paint by hand. The first year that Bash put his "art you can drive" on the street, he received 80 traffic tickets (only one conviction) for a wide variety of nonmoving violations. Sometimes, he even got tickets on the way to paying other tickets. A total of six Volkswagen Beetles were used for the mobile art series, most of which have been wrecked. Today, they are a prime example that the car was and still is a perfect canvas to express one's imagination and personality—even if it does mean getting cited for the privilege. *Kent Bash*

decoration, the lug nut covers once taken for granted became totems for creative cruise culture.

Within the tribe, full wheel covers became a requirement, led by the sombrero-style hubcaps borrowed from Cadillacs of 1949 to 1953 vintage. This bent for Caddy rim covers became the bane of ordinary car owners who happened to own a car manufactured within this span of years. Houston, Texas, bodyshop man Slim Waters was a witness to the theft, recalling problems his own father had with wheel covers. "Yessir, my pa had himself a big old Cadillac and along with it a world of hurt. He got his hubcaps stolen twice! The first time, he was travelin' when they was lifted near Eldorado, Kansas, while he was stayin' at a cheap motel. The other time, he caught the guy in the act when some kid tried to pop 'em off right in our own driveway! You never seen a body move so fast tryin' to get outta' the way of two

The Toed Inn was one of those quirky roadside restaurants of the 1920s. In those exciting days, mom-and-pop eateries with unique personalities filled up the roadsides and provided cruising havens for hot rods and custom cars. Long before fast food franchising took over the process of roadside dining, sandwich stands like this programmatic marvel were packed with cars—including some like these gleaming 1940 and 1941 Willys models. *Kent Bash*

barrels full of buckshot!" During the days of the juvenile delinquent, the "midnight auto supply" provided many cruisers with free parts.

When they weren't busy combing the streets and salvage yards for the right hubcaps, America's hot rod Picassos and custom-car Modiglianis used their extra time to develop a signature style of car painting. Unlike commercial auto manufacturers, customizers went out of their way to avoid using ordinary patterns and colors. From the suede-black primer of an unfinished hot rod to the purple radiance of a multilayer custom, the devotion to exterior shading was strong. "You can't rush it," warned

West Coast custom enthusiast Randy "Snake" Chadd. "Preparation is eight months and painting is three hours. It's just a matter of how good you want it to look. A friend wanted me to paint his car and said he didn't want it to be a real 'good' paint job, and I told him I don't know how to do any other kind! You just don't paint a car, you paint it right—that's my philosophy." It's a sentiment shared by many, as some painters believe they can transfer the personality of a car owner onto body metal with a careful application of color and pattern.

During the fifties, bodyman Joe Bailon revitalized the field of automotive painting after he devised a new paint color called Candy Apple Red. While experimenting in his Oakland, California, shop, he discovered a unique car finish by adding just a few drops of red liquid toner to clear lacquer. Bailon sprayed layer upon layer of the hybrid mixture over a gold base and discovered he had a stunning new finish. It was pure magic, since the paint looked wet even after the tinted lacquer dried! It didn't take long for the customizers to get the hots for this translucent lip-gloss look, and soon they were spraying it onto cars like nobody's business. The pearlescent variation of the candy color became a favorite. Originally, car painters blended finely ground fish scales with different shades of lacquer to create the pearlized effect (later, they substituted ingredients that were easier to obtain). After numerous applica-

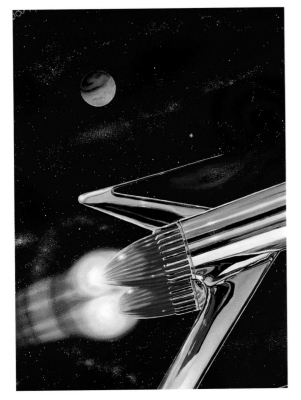

The tail fin is one of the most visible symbols of the design changes that occurred in cars during the fifties. Influenced by aircraft like the P-38, Detroit designers (such as Harley Earl) added aerodynamic visuals to their car bodies as a way of embracing the future and the promise that it might hold. Today, tail fins are potent reminders of yesterday's bold styling and flamboyant designs. *Kent Bash*

tions of paint dried, the dichroic fragments of overlapping material reflected light in the very same manner as mother-of-pearl. More daring car artists took the idea to the edge of tackiness when they used tiny shards of aluminum foil for the reflecting medium. All the rage during the sixties, customizers of present day use the metal-flake finish sparingly.

By the beginning of the 1960s, America's customizers had a tasty sampler of candies from which to choose. Improved acrylic resins gave commercial car manufacturers new choices as well. Now, there was no longer an excuse to paint a vehicle in the somber tones of yesteryear. Suddenly, a big can of Kool-Aid color, a Bink's spray gun, and an air compressor endowed the car artist with limitless creative options. As custom vehicles (and later some hot rods) began to incorporate the new look, painting an automobile changed from a boring, production line step to a bona fide expression of art.

Still, it wasn't as easy as just dipping a paintbrush into a bucket of paint (although many tried just that). To achieve the perfect, flawless finish, the craft of painting required a lot of patient practice. Even the experienced custom automobile builders

The Rocket 88 Oldsmobile—the predecessor to the radical fin jobs to be introduced in the early fifties—was a car that exhibited the sort of "jukebox" ornamentation that typified many of motoring machines of the late forties and the early fifties. In the early days, hot rodders disdained this ornamentation and stripped away all chrome and molding in the interest of speed. *Kent Bash*

While Chevrolets were available in some great color schemes during the 1950s, no commercial units were sold in this custom hot pink configuration. These days, cars frequently cross over into the category of custom—even if they don't have extensive bodywork or structural changes. All it takes to make the trip to the wild side is some crazy colors and a spray gun. ©1997 Robert Genat

The 1957 Chevrolet Bel Air remains one of the all-time favorites among cruisers who prefer their cars stock. No cruise night or trip down Main Street would be complete without seeing one of these finned beauties in action. Mike Witzel

Randy "Snake" Chadd chopping the top on a 1942 Ford Coupe. Chadd earned the unusual nickname because all of his vehicles run as low "as a snake on the grass." For a low-cost, effective security system, he often lets a few Burmese pythons loose in his car! It's a great way to keep hands off when his ride is parked at the neighborhood cruise night! Kent Bash

Contrary to macho beliefs, cruising is a pastime that's enjoyed by both sexes. Here, Gilda Hendrickson shows off her 1939 pickup, a slightly lowered ride that features a Chevy drivetrain and a custom paint treatment. *Kent Bash*

paid for their mistakes in lost time and money. Unlike the home-built hot rods assembled by trial and error, customizers sometimes used brand new automobiles as the starting point. With a major investment like that, it was best to do it right the first time.

As a result, many professional custom car shops opened their doors to offer a wide range of creative services to cruisers. One of the most successful was begun by brothers George and Sam Barris in Los Angeles, California. By the mid-fifties, the Barris Kustom Shop gained recognition with customized beauties like the *Hirohata Mercury* and *Golden Sahara*—setting new standards for the custom car builder to live up to. But that wasn't all: Barris expanded the creative parameters of the craft even further when he unveiled way-out concept cars the likes of *Miss Elegance*, *Ala Kart*, and *Fabula*. Under his direction, one-of-a-kind wheels squealed onto the silver screen and into that little box called television. Who can forget *Batman*, *The Munsters*, and *My Mother the Car*? All these shows

and many movies featured Barris creations. As a custom master, he proved the hypothesis that the car was sculpture, inspiring a new generation to create its own interpretation of mobile art.

Kenneth Howard, or "Von Dutch," as his admirers called him, was another one of customizing's great innovators. During the fifties, he became the undisputed guru of pinstriping and defined the art of decorating the car. It all started after he borrowed his father's sign-painting materials and followed his own muse on an automotive canvas. With all the skill of a great master, he proceeded to apply complex pinstriping as an addition to paint and body styling—embellishing curves and corners with abstract crests. While only he understood what the ligatures meant, the customizer's eyeballs popped out (like a crazy cartoon character) when they saw them. It was the correct response, considering that it was Von Dutch himself who created the famous "flying eyeball" that the cruisin' crowd adopted as the hobby's unofficial icon (today, it's still seen on hot rods and customs, and one can even buy shift knobs made in the form of the disembodied peeper).

Another one of Von Dutch's specialties was decorative markings known as "scallops." Applied over the base color of a car, the scallop treatment looked

This 1955 Chevrolet sports a hot 1991 Corvette 350 engine with aluminum heads. While not a vintage mill, this power-plant gives the custom the get-up-and-go that's required to hold its own among the power-hungry roadsters cruising the strip. A polished, tuned-port electronic fuel injection system is part of the configuration, as are stainless steel Corvette headers. *Mike Witzel/car courtesy Clare Patterson, Jr.*

like a planned arrangement of schizophrenic pinstriping. At their most extreme, these reverse-tip, airbrushed daggers (with carefully painted borders) ran along the entire length of a custom automobile, covering most of the hood area, body side panels, and the trunk lid. Since the heavily bordered arrangements distracted the viewer's eyeballs from slight body imperfections, the scallop technique became the saving grace for inexperienced body workers. Most of the time, scallops were an optical trick more than they were a painterly effect.

To make a car look really hot—literally—painted flames were a great substitute for scallops and flying eyeballs. A sheet of flames painted on the hood (and sometimes the body side panels) made an automobile look menacing and larger than life. Flames became a crutch for mild-mannered rods in the same way that the aggressive designs painted on

World War II fighter planes were used to intimidate the enemy. At the same time, a fiery front end made a car look like it was burning into the atmosphere, like a meteorite—a real plus if you wanted to look fast. (Today, "ghost" flames are all the rage for the understated cruiser.) Still, the burning effect was often nothing more than an illusion, a psychological trick intended to make other customizers and rodders lose faith in their cars.

Not everyone was so insecure when it came to the way their automobiles looked, however. When the cruisin' subculture known as the "lowriders" debuted on the traffic circuits of America, there was no doubting their cars, or their confidence. A product of the *Pachucos*, those flamboyant zoot-suiters of the forties, the first lowriders rolled on the streets of Los Angeles after World War II. As a form of recreation, proud Chicanos dropped the suspensions on their cars, decorated them inside and out, and cruised through the local barrios to display their handiwork. Lowriders added a new book to the American cruisin' bible. Now, the car was more than just an accessory for living, it became synonymous with cultural pride.

By the seventies, this idea of car as symbol of culture took off and suddenly, Latinos across the nation began cutting the coils on favorite cars such

Among cruisers, the fringe group known as "lowriders" finds recreation in cruising their cars extremely close to the ground. By way of chopping tops, cutting springs, and lowering the chassis, vehicles of this genre often possess a defined "rake," the rear of the car being lower than the front. In most cases, the entire car hugs the asphalt to create a low, sinister look. *Mike Witzel*

This 1959 Chevrolet is as low as it can go, creating what some cruisers would call a "weed whacker." In the background sits a classic example of the American filling station, the same sort of outfit that ruled the strip during cruising's golden age. *Kent Bash*

as the 1939 Chevrolet and the 1941 Special Deluxe. Remember the line from War's popular cruisin' ditty: "The lowrider rides a little lower"? Judging the evidence seen on the streets, it was certainly true. The lowrider community took the obsession for appearances down to road level and then beyond.

Everything the custom car had the lowrider had more of. It was lower, slower, and showed a lot more extravagance. Lowriders weren't afraid of using a liberal application of metalflake paint, either. Elaborate murals airbrushed on the trunk lid or body side panels were the rule rather than the exception. On the interior, cars often resembled a bordello on wheels, with fluffy

The showiness extended to the exterior and soon, lowriders became so low that it was difficult for cruisers to navigate the streets properly. About that time, the police started to ticket lowrider owners for illegally lowered suspensions. For many, this looked like the end of lowriding. In fact, it was just the beginning. Cruiser Ron Aguirre got an inspiration: Why not take old aircraft parts and rig up the suspension so that the driver could raise and lower it at will from *inside* the car? The idea sounded crazy, but it worked. After other lowriders saw what the setup could do, the idea of the "lifted" lowrider began to hop—literally! Overnight, lowriders transformed their rides into adjustable street machines! Without worry, they could drive to their favorite cruising venues at the same height as a normal car. When the time came to put on a show, they had the ability to drop it down for maximum effect.

In the final analysis, that's what the art of customizing a car is all about: creativity. Whether an automobile is restyled as wild, mild, low, high, raked, or radical, it's done with the same goal in mind: automotive exhibitionism. With every variation, the activity remains the same. Cruising was and always will be an American folk activity that extracts the very essence of the early coachbuilders, blends it with a need for mobility, folds in a hefty dose of good looks, tosses in a dash of exhibitionism, and shakes the resulting mixture into a delicious treat that many find very palatable.

Who were the kings of custom? You, me, Uncle Joe, your next door neighbor, the tough guy down the street, your school teacher, friends from Europe, Mexican Americans, Australians, African Americans, Asians, that little old lady from Pasadena, Eskimos, anybody qualified. When it came to showing off your personalized car in public, it didn't matter who you were, where you came from, or what color your skin was. The car became a common denominator, the great equalizer. Regardless of social position, everyone was eligible to hold title. All they needed were some wheels and the right attitude to strut their stuff on the streets.

Mouton fur for carpeting and decorative elements that would be at home in a comfortable living room. It wasn't at all unusual for a lowrider to have crushed velvet on the seat covers, pom-pons or tassels decorating the headliner, or a steering wheel made of thick, welded chain. Neon tubes lighting the undercarriage? Only the lowrider could pull it off and get away with it.

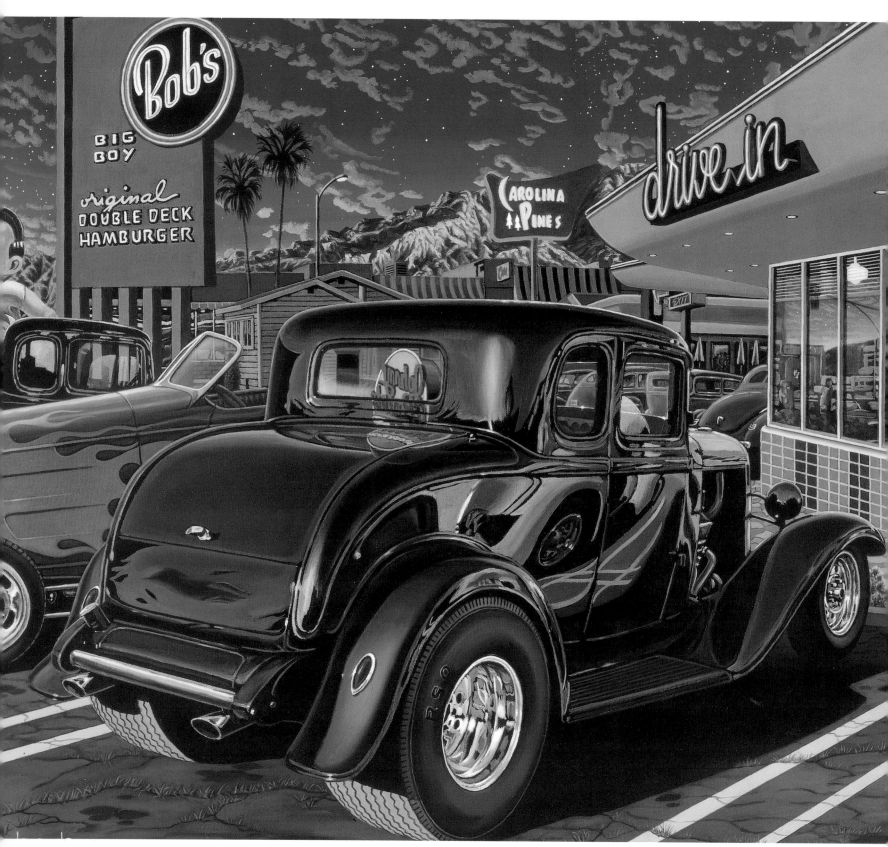

Classic Cruising Strips and Cruise Nights

Taking Back the Streets

"The thing that's attractive about cruise night and something that many people like is that it's spontaneous. Even though there's a date set and there are certain places to go, the thing that's neat about it is that unlike a car show—where people have to sign up, preregister, and pay money—a cruise night is there for you just if you feel like getting out. When the urge to cruise hits, you simply crank up the car and go! The fun of it is that you don't have any idea of who you are going to run into and exactly what's going to happen—other than once everybody's there, you will be hanging around for several hours, visiting, talking, eating, looking around, sharing car stories, and such.

In Southern California, Bob's Big Boy drive-ins were the main destinations for cruisers during the fifties, and with the resurgence of events called "cruise nights," they still are today. Parked and ready for curb service are some of the standards, including a black 1932 five-window coupe, a 1932 roadster with flames, a 1932 coupe, and a 1934 Ford truck. *Kent Bash*

Usually, the parking lot at cruise night is roped off so that only vintage cars, hot rods, muscle cars, customs, or whatever can park in the main area. Once the lot is full, the cars work like a magnet, pulling in people and lookie-lous eager to check out the vehicles and, at the same time, get a quick bite to eat. At Bob's Big Boy in Toluca Lake, comedian Jay Leno shows up every now and then—the place is just a few blocks from the studio where he does the *Tonight Show*. With excitement like this going on, most cruise night restaurants on the West Coast are inundated with customers.

Back in the old days of cruising, during the fifties and the sixties, most drive-in restaurants had car service, so you weren't really able to visit the way you can today. You had to pull your car into a space, order your food, and eat it pretty fast. Only then could you talk to the people in the cars on either side of you, if you knew them. Unlike today, getting out of your car and walking around wasn't cool. Some drive-ins had bouncers or parking people assigned to keep customers in their cars and on the move. Restaurants were in business to make money, and turning over the customers so that new ones could park was all part of it.

Today, a lot of the places that sponsor cruise nights want to give their businesses a shot in the arm. It's easy to do, as organizing a cruise night is not really a big headache unless they plan to spend the extra cash for security or a disc jockey to spin records—which a lot of the better places do. If the place that's sponsoring the event is a good one, there will always be bargains on the food menu and specials for cruisers. At Cruiser's Car Wash in Northridge, California, they have a fifties-style diner inside and serve up both fast food and contemporary dishes. For all the cruisers who don't want to leave their cars and wait inside to get their eats, they set up a barbecue pit in the parking lot and cook tri-tip sandwiches, hot dogs, hot links, and barbecued chicken."

—*Kent Bash*

Chapter Five

IF Woodward Avenue was the Indianapolis of street racing, Van Nuys Boulevard was the melting pot of cruising. It all began in 1912, when horse-drawn carriages still clip-clomped around the village of Van Nuys, California. Every Saturday night, local residents led a parade along Main Street, right through town center. As history tells it, they enjoyed the spectacle so much that they decided to turn the streetfest into a weekly tradition.

After World War II ended, many of the servicemen who shipped into Los Angeles settled down in the valley's residential tracts and continued the ritual. This time, there was a new twist to the cruising: Instead of coaches riding along the dirt, it was motor cars that rumbled down the pavement.

By the end of the fifties, the weekend celebration had grown into an automotive phenomenon. What a radical change had occurred in the San Fernando Valley! From its agricultural past, Van Nuys had grown to see criss-crossing roads replace farms, traffic lights supersede hitching posts, suburban bungalows edge out log cabins, and parking lots replace pastures. The cityscape was now defined by the automobile. The harvest parade enjoyed during olden times was replaced by car-crazed teens in a conspicuous display of personal pride. Carloads of kids converged on Van Nuys Boulevard every Wednesday, Friday, and Saturday night just to cruise up and down the street.

Cruising was such a blast that Van Nuys became the de facto Main Street cruising strip for

The Bob's Big Boy in Canoga Park was once one of the prime cruise night destinations for hot rodders and customizers residing in Los Angeles, California. Now, this former drive-in dining location is just another fond cruising memory. The Bob's Big Boy is gone, and the current owners operate the eatery as just another chain restaurant. Another cruise night bites the dust. *Kent Bash*

most of the surrounding towns. "I first heard my friends talking about the Van Nuys strip in the late fifties and all the action that was going on over there," remembered Cheryl Travers (now a full-time homemaker and mother of three). "I had a nice, white Kaiser-Frazer that my parents helped me purchase when I graduated from high school, and more times than I can recall, me and a few best girlfriends, and sometimes even guy friends, piled into it to cruise up and down the boulevard. Those outings were some of the best times of my entire life!" On Van Nuys, everyone came to see the show and take part in the pageantry, including hot rodders, customizers, mothers in their station wagons, English sports car enthusiasts, families packed in large sedans, lowriders, antique car lovers, limousine drivers, racers in muscle cars, van fans, Volkswagen aficionados, truckers, maniacs on motorcycles, street machine enthusiasts, people in pickup trucks, and many more.

As the fifties sped into the sixties, news of the exuberant street party spread up and down the coast. By the seventies, the strip had gained such notoriety that the phenomenon of cruising overshadowed most street-side business. Not that it was difficult to figure out why: Vehicles crammed with revelers streamed in from cities as far away as San Diego, Santa Barbara, and San Jose. Curiosity seekers streamed in from all over California, boosting the already-swollen crowds to well over 20,000 on the busiest nights! To obtain their vicarious thrills, area residents unfolded lawn chairs on porches and front yards and settled back with a six-pack and popcorn to watch the real-life movie passing by in the street.

Though it was heaven for cruisers, it was hell for merchants. The playful activities enjoyed by the cruisers completely jammed the main business corridor. On the busiest nights when the show was under way, cruisers took over the street and choked the economic life out of it! Crosstown travel or patronage of local businesses was impossible. Regular commuter and shopping traffic couldn't even get into the downtown area much less park anywhere along Van Nuys. To get around the congestion, the traffic department designated alternate access routes just so local residents could get home! "The traffic was pretty slow sometimes," remembered cruiser Cliff Maxwell, a regular denizen of the strip. "Sure, there was a time or two when me and my friends blocked the flow of cars, but it was all just innocent fun. One time,

we staged an elaborate 'turtle race' and lined our cars up with some other ones across one direction of the traffic lanes. Everyone in the bunch drove really slow—about five miles per hour to block traffic behind us. It was a busy night and cars were honking horns and screaming at us to move out of the way. Of course, we didn't clear out until we saw the cherry tops move in. By then, it was too late. Guys that didn't scatter got tickets!"

Out along the miles of boulevard, the huddled masses yearning to cruise free were oblivious to the problems they instigated. On the biggest cruising nights, a spectator could witness plenty of chicanery, including the ubiquitous Chinese Fire Drills (a game where car occupants burst from the doors at a traffic light and run around the vehicle

Cruising down to the local drive-in restaurant was a popular pastime of youth during the fifties and sixties. On almost any night of the week, teenagers (like the now-mature owner of this 1955 Chevrolet) would congregate in great numbers—socializing, eating hamburgers, and tinkering with their cars. It's nice to see that some things never change. *Mike Witzel/cars courtesy Clare Patterson, Jr. and Dan Daniels*

Cleaned up to eliminate all of the hood louvers, rubber on the running boards, and exterior emblems, a 1934 Chevrolet roadster like this example (on its way to a local cruise night event) would be called a "smoothie" by current fans of hot rodding. Adorned with bullet mirrors and digital gauges on the dashboard, these highly refined street rods take the best of the old school and combine it with the best of the new. *Kent Bash*

to change seats, annoying motorists waiting behind), cars bumping other cars, kids popping out of trunks, riders on the outsides of cars, flashing headlamps, musical horns, and lane blocking. "Van Nuys was a crazy scene, man. One time, we were trying to impress some chicks in another car when a friend of mine tossed a beer bottle at their car," explained an avid participant of the time

(who wished to remain anonymous). "It wouldn't have been so bad, but the bottle broke and splattered over the car, making the guy who was driving and his two friends very, very mad. They chased us all over town to beat the tar out of us and finally, we lost 'em. After that, we stored the car in a friend's garage and didn't take it out again for another year. Later, it was sold!" Whether the activities were good, bad, funny, or innocent—if it happened in a car while cruising—it was part of Van Nuys.

Sadly, though perhaps inevitably, all of the endless preening, racing, showing off, and cruising for kicks led to problems. By 1978, serious incidents of crime in Van Nuys proper were up 5 to 10 times on active cruise nights! Two years later, the

Artist Kent Bash created his own form of rolling Volkswagen art during the 1960s, long before the notion of "car art" was an accepted form. To illustrate the theme of "civilization," he finished one side of the vehicle to portray the early stirrings of organized society in the Aztec world. On the flipside, humankind's greatest accomplishments were typified by the yearning for the stars and the conquest of outer space. When it zipped around on the streets, it attracted a lot of interest from the cops and caught the imagination of cruisers up and down the West Coast. © *1997 Steph Butler*

The West Coast Kustoms car club holds cruise night events in the small town of Paso Robles, California, (near the spot where James Dean crashed his car and punched out of this world). The two-day car event has become immensely popular, with Friday night reserved for the obligatory cruise down Main Street over to a parking place at the local A & W drive-in where the parking lot is turned into a car show. *Kent Bash*

Located in Wichita, Kansas, the Kings-X Drive-In holds occasional cruise nights for local enthusiasts. Kings-X got its start in 1938, when the White Castle burger chain decided to close its restaurants west of the Mississippi. Andrew James King was employed by the square burger maker at the time, with 10 years under his belt as head of research and development. As principal "idea-man" for the company, it was his responsibility to develop new products and devise ad promotions. When Billy Ingram announced he was moving Castle's headquarters to Columbus, Ohio, King declined. He bought the three Wichita locations and tried his luck in the burger business. Later, he expanded his holdings, opening Kings-X drive-ins and coffee-shop restaurants in the city. *Mike Witzel*

patience of Van Nuys Boulevard merchants had reached its limit. With an eye toward banning cruising, merchants started bellyaching in earnest about the crowds of juvenile delinquents, the malicious vandalism, and the disgusting incidents of public urination. Ironically, cruisers weren't doing the damage—they remained on the move and inside their cars if at all possible. It was the mob of curious onlookers that was causing most of the mayhem.

Regardless of who was really to blame for all the cruising-related problems, the roadway free-for-all wasn't so amusing anymore. In the eyes of the city leaders, cruising was the root cause of too many transit problems, and with no further debate, it had to go. With that aim in mind, the town organized what it called a police "boulevard detail" in 1983. On the popular cruise nights, the cops cracked down on all drivers who had no destination in mind but were just aimlessly driving up and down the strip. To shunt the free flow of traffic that once electrified the circuit, the patrols erected sawhorse barricades at opposite ends of Van Nuys. Partying crowds who chose to drive across these circuit breakers received citations. Another strategy used warning flares to rip a hole in the night while the boys in blue made mass arrests for public drinking and loitering. Ever so quietly, the department of public works installed signs along the curbside that warned "No Stopping 9 P.M. to 12 Midnight Wednesday–Friday–Saturday." So much for life, liberty, and the pursuit of automotive happiness. . .

The loss of Van Nuys Boulevard as a cruising venue was a tragedy for southern California street enthusiasts, but it was hardly the end of the cruising craze in the United States. Most of America's small-town cruising venues weren't nearly as high-profile as Woodward and Van Nuys, and, as a result, they managed to survive. In spite of the fact that there was an ample number of traffic signs thrown up to ban the activity and plenty of news reports to denounce it, cruisers who maintained low profiles (and remained within the boundaries of the law) could still get in a few good laps on their favorite circuit.

Car enthusiasts believed they had a constitutional right to drive wherever and whenever they wanted, and they weren't going to let a few restrictions stop them. The key was to remain as inconspicuous as possible and never be seen by the black-and-white patrols more than a couple of times per night. And so, clandestine cruising continued into the eighties, and streets that had only recently gotten a reprieve from the dreaded "scourge" actually saw an increase in activity. A law-abiding, low-key, and organized, cruising renaissance had begun.

Cruisin' in the eighties exhibited some distinct differences from the fifties and sixties period—most important, the brash, cavalier attitude of the participants had mellowed. Rather than fall back into the boisterous behavior that had defined cruising during the days of carhops and curb-service, cruisers crossed over into the eighties by adapting to the situation. Automotive hobbyists forgot about fighting the law all the time and

The San Antonio location of the Texas Pig Stands has become a local landmark in the eyes of all those who love the classic steel of the fifties and sixties. With carhops providing service the same way they did 40 years ago (with roller skates), hot rod and muscle car clubs crowd the parking lanes to get a taste of the specialty, barbecued "Pig Sandwiches." ©1997 Louis Persat

decided to work with the police (it got better results when it came to the free expression of their cruising activities and kept their cars from being monitored for illegal equipment). Racing in the streets became a cruising dinosaur. Celebrating wheels for mechanical, aesthetic, and recreational values became the way of the future.

To keep the cruising hobby a vibrant pursuit and to preclude the pointless back and forth runs of yesterday, participants began to hold regularly scheduled get-togethers at nostalgic businesses (cruisers avoided franchised chain outfits). With lit-

Located in Downey, California, Friscos restaurant is one of the hundreds of favorite cruising destinations doing business in the state of California. Wherever you drive in the country, the rules of the cruising game are pretty standard: You park your car, get out, socialize, and chow down on some good old-fashioned American road food. ©1997 Robert Genat

Keller's Drive-In remains as a Dallas, Texas, landmark of car service and cruising. On any night of the week, the serving lanes beneath the canopy are packed with all kinds of customers. Families in station wagons, cowboys in trucks, commuters in sedans, businessmen in Mercedes, and road warriors in hot rods and custom cars—all are welcome at this roadside time machine. *Mike Witzel*

When vehicles visit a cruise night or other type of automotive show, their drivers often mount car service trays—complete with wax replicas of burger food and milkshakes—to get the feeling back of the way it used to be when cool cars cruised in and out of the many drive-in restaurants. It's a great way to rekindle those fond memories of days gone by and at the same time, a low-fat, low-calorie alternative to real diner fare! *Kent Bash*

tle protest, cruisers agreed that Friday night was to be the prime time for the majority of these roadside rod and custom reunions. On the weekend, surviving restaurants that featured outdoor car service and drive-in theaters that showed movies all night became top destinations to park! Car clubs added their own spin, and each developed its own protocol for taking part in the low-key automotive activities. While the race, creed, and color of the membership varied, one similarity emerged for all: These gas-saving car meets became known as "cruise nights."

The rules and regulations of the typical cruise night are straightforward: First, the members with cars drive to a predetermined spot to hang out for the evening (a place where they have advance approval to park). Often, the destination is a nearby town with businesses that welcome cars and crowds. On the way, the cruisers maintain a respectable decorum and strive to obey the posted speed limit and other related traffic regulations. The members frown upon street racing—as they do reckless driving, practical jokes, and other tomfoolery. Following these guidelines, cruisers have earned a new reputation for themselves, one that's based on public safety and civility. Consider the statement of columnist Tessa DeCarlo in the January 3, 1997, edition of the *Wall Street Journal*: It's her belief that ". . . hot rodding has aged over the last half-century into glossy respectability." With little evidence against them, the majority of modern-day cruisers would agree.

Along old Route 66 in the sleepy town of Seligman, Arizona, Juan Delgadillo and his brother, Angel, have turned their tiny drive-in eatery (and themselves) into a tourist attraction. While Angel runs a small barbershop nearby, Juan feeds the cruisers passing through with the usual roadside fare. For cruisers who make the trek from all parts of the country, stopping in for a quick bite to eat has become a prerequisite. ©1997 Jerry McClanahan

Unlike the adversarial atmosphere of 30 years ago, the modern cruise has grown into a positive win-win situation for all concerned: In exchange for providing automobilists with a gallery to display the mobile manifestations of their imagination, roadside businesses gain an increased visual profile and with it a nice business boost. Proprietors have learned that the cruise night is both an effective way to revitalize a slow operation and supercharge it with new life. Considering the curiosity factor of other car owners, it brings in a lot of extra traffic: "Every time I'm out there cruising, I get mostly positive reactions from those driving regular vehicles. Children wave at me when I pass by, old folks nod their heads at me, and young couples give me the thumbs up," explained Mel Santee, a weekend warrior who likes to check out the local drive-ins in San Francisco, California. "There's just something neat about seeing an old automobile fixed up in a group that brings a twinkle to the eye of commuters. Sometimes, people ask me where I'm going, and then they follow me there!"

And that's precisely what Americans are doing—following the cool cars to nostalgic hot spots! Today, California sets the most visible example: Out on the coast, a mild climate allows residents to enjoy 12 full months of recreational driving. On any given weekend, cruisers may choose from hundreds of venues when the urge comes to park and wolf down a trayful of burgers and fries. Robin Genat listed the most active gathering places in the August 1996 issue of *Westways* magazine. Among her favorite hangouts: Be Bop Burgers in Santa Barbara, EZ Take Out Burger in Acton, Sonic Drive-In at Bakersfield (still using carhop service, Sonic is the only surviving chain of canopy drive-ins in America), the Chicken Pie Diner in Poway, Kooky's Diner and Oscar's over in San Diego, Gigi's Grille in Tustin, Tuxies in Riverside, Hamburger Hank's in Fountain Valley, Heroes Restaurant in Fullerton, Village Grille in Claremont, Bobby's Burgers and Subs in Hemet, Red Robin Burger and Spirits in La Habra, and Frisco's Carhop Drive-In in Downey.

On Tampa Avenue in Northridge, California, Cruiser's Car Wash has become a favorite, providing a squeaky clean backdrop for motorheads eager to park and show off their armor. Washing work is done on the premises, but no respectable cruiser allows another to clean his or her hot rod or custom. The Toluca Lake Bob's Big Boy is a favorite destination. (In the old days the Glendale Bob's on Colorado Boulevard and the Van Nuy's location were infamous hangouts.) During the early nineties, the Toluca Lake location survived demolition by way of cruiser outrage.

In St. John, Missouri, the Chuck-A-Burger has been hosting cruisers since 1957. The restaurant still provides curb service, as well as a dining room and carry-out service. A future cruiser takes heed of the bold Chuck-A-Burger drive-in sign. *©1997 Shellee Graham*

The Burger Bar was a chain of hamburger diners popular in southern California during the fifties. The buildings were prefabricated units made by the Valentine Diner Company of Wichita, Kansas, and were shipped to the restaurant site in one piece. For the teenager with cars on the brain, it was burger joints like these that provided the high school jobs needed to raise the money to buy gas and custom car parts. Here, a 1955 Chevrolet two-door hardtop with chrome wheels and a 1958 Plymouth vie for space in the parking lot. While today many of the diners have passed, the cruising scene remains the same. *Kent Bash*

The Road Kings club was instrumental in saving the 43-year-old building. Later, the city designated the landmark as an official California Point of Historical Interest. Today, it's a strong pull for customs and retro fifties characters who want to relive a slice of time they were never really a part of. Management is happy for the extra business and the notoriety.

Recently, some of the small towns in the Golden State have begun to organize street fairs combined with automobile shows on the weekends. Rod and custom shows (with every other kind of car mixed in between) have popped up in locales like San Bernardino, Pismo Beach, Temecula, and Long Beach. Now, instead of banning cruising and the large gathering of cars that go with it, cities have discovered it's a good way to step up tourism and give commerce a shot in the arm. Some cities allow visitors to cruise down Main on a special night with uncorked headers (the cops turn their heads the other way)! In Paso Robles, near the site of the James Dean accident, the West Coast Kustoms hold a custom car show during Labor Day weekend every year. The town closes down regular traffic on Friday night and cruisers take over the street. Afterwards, the local A & W drive-in caters to all participants with fried foods and car service. It's literally a blast from the past.

All over America, there's a similar flurry of activity: A weekly meeting of classic cars in St. Paul, Minnesota, transforms the University Avenue strip into a jam-packed parking lot. Into the wee hours of the morning, hot rods and custom cars flash their toothy, chrome grins beneath the glowing neon of Porky's Drive-In.

While this 1940 Ford Sedan could be classified as a fifties-style rod, the tuck-and-roll upholstery inside definitely marks it as a custom job. Out-of-the-way roadside joints like Oink's are where many of today's car guys hang out—if they can find them. Fast food operations have forever changed the way mobile America eats. Many of the quaint spots of the fifties are now extinct. *Kent Bash*

Deep down in Texas, a club that calls itself the Cruzin' Cruisers reserves every third weekend in September for an automobile show and drive-in theater pilgrimage. Similarly, the Texas Pig Stand drive-in in Beaumont (the oldest remaining round drive-in diner in the United States) regularly sees its share of cruising activity—as does its sister outlet in San Antonio. Nearby in Waco, the Heart of Texas Street Machines (a mix of rods, customs, muscle cars, and other classics) makes the Healthcamp drive-in the fifties flashback of choice every third Tuesday of the month.

At the same time, the "Old Town" area of Kissimmee, Florida, erupts into what some locals describe as cruising mania: Every Saturday night, hoards of vintage vehicles converge on the tiny hamlet to vie for street space. Up and down the East Coast, it's the same story, only the names of the eateries have changed. In Churchville, Maryland, the Big M Drive-In Restaurant beckons the tuck-and-roll crowd to stoke up on fun food and films. Distilfink, one of Pennsylvania's favorite drive-ins, tempts the customers cruising in convertibles and Cadillacs to grab a bit of grub in the town of Gettysburg. Out on Long Island, muscle car maniacs (who once raced their street machines up and down Deer Park Avenue) jockey for a good space at Carmichael's. Up north in Connecticut, Mickey's provides East Hartford cruisers a visible place to park and chow down an oversized slice of cruising pie. Regardless of locality—be it a small town or large, a region in the North, East, South, or West—cruise night is a duplicated franchise.

Nationwide, cruise night participants enjoy similar activities. One of the most common rituals is to check out the automobiles in attendance for their strengths and weaknesses. To facilitate this once-

Wednesday and Saturday night have become the accepted times for the cruisers to huddle together at the drive-in restaurants of America. ©1997 Robert Genat

The Paso Robles Custom Car Show, organized by the West Coast Customs, exists as a great excuse to take out the custom beauty and cruise it on over to the local A & W drive-in. *Kent Bash*

over, it's best for cruisers to park with nose facing out, in the direction of the audience (it's a must to raise the hood and display the engine). Then, participants are free to leave their automobile and break out the California duster, a cleaning tool used to remove dust particles. Afterwards, they might mingle or strike up conversation with old friends or new. As expected, the car becomes the main point of conversation and mechanical stories the topic. There's a lot of "bench racing" too, a pastime where

racing exploits are retold for those unlucky enough not to be in attendance when they happened. Like the fishing stories about the "whopper that got away," cruisers like to stretch the truth.

But even though no one is really racing with cars these days, the aspect of competition isn't totally extinct at cruise nights. Static events are the new kick and, sometimes, loosely organized contests determine the best-looking street machine or the most radically altered custom. On some occasions,

when the organizers and venues allow it, burnout contests celebrate the cruiser who can generate the most tire smoke! Other times, cruise nights are an interesting mix of subdued sideshow events like dance contests, fifties fashion shows, and food-making festivals. (At one recent gathering, organizers tempted cruisers to enter the biggest beehive hairdo contest.) Although taking part in the fun is the primary impetus, winners usually come away with a prize.

With prizes in mind, a standby that attracts a big cruise night crowd is the raffle. Upon arrival, the ringleaders ask the cruisers (and visitors who come to drool over the vintage tin) to toss a buck into a pot and, in exchange, they hand out tickets. As the cruise night activities unfold, the crowd is free to check out the array of prizes displayed on tables for all to see. At the end of the evening's festivities, a series of drawings determines the lucky winners who will cruise home with stuff like automotive

The raised hood is perhaps the most common sight at the modern-day cruise night. With that in mind, one of the most common pastimes is talking about one's car. After that, bench racing and talking about past street (or drag) racing competitions comes in a close second. ©1997 *Robert Genat*

cleaning supplies, speed parts, and other cool accessories. When it's not an actual prize that's put up for grabs, the motor club donates the collected money to a good cause or local charity.

To the credit of the rod and custom crowd, a lot of car clubs hold cruise events for the sole purposes of raising cash, gathering canned goods, collecting Christmas gifts, and increasing public awareness.

And—as much as today's calorie-counting cruisers hate to admit it—another important element of cruise night that attracts interest is food. Is it merely a coincidence that cruisers hold car events at restaurants that specialize in junk food served up fast? It's probably by design, as the weekly reprieve

At the 1995 Route 66 Rendezvous in the city of San Bernardino, California, a total of 190,000 visitors took the "highway that's the best" and followed in the tracks of Buz and Tod. There, a 15-block stretch of the "Mother Road" became a playground for rods, customs, and other street machines. ©1997 Robert Genat

Cruising the Main Street strip is alive and well in the California town of Paso Robles. The West Coast Kustoms car club regularly takes over the central traffic corridor of town. It's all perfectly legal—the boys in blue are held in check during the event. Only normal traffic violations are prohibited. Kent Bash

There's nothing that's more appealing than getting together a bunch of friends and cruising the local strip in a convertible. The wind in your hair, the sounds on the radio, and the happy reactions of onlookers are just a few of the things that make it a worthwhile outing. ©1997 Robert Genat

Caught in mid-cruise at a busy intersection, this bold, hot yellow Chevrolet was just one of the many colorful sights and sounds seen at the Route 66 Rendezvous held in San Bernardino, California. ©1997 Robert Genat

from the suburban dinner table provides cholesterol watchers an excuse to skip the tofu-and-sprouts routine. With racing activities banned and roadway antics barred, there must be a few indulgences left that car fans may enjoy guilt-free, even if artery-glue is part of the package! Yes, the double-deck cheeseburger, the greasy french fries, the onion rings, the milkshakes mixed up with real milk, the banana splits, old-fashioned tubesteaks (slathered with chili and onions), and mugs of sweet root beer (consuming alcohol while cruising is frowned upon) are now staple cruising foods.

With the appetite satisfied, cruise nighters invariably turn their ears toward music and entertainment. In that department, a sound system or portable disc jockey arrangement become the focal point. At the best events, it's just like American Bandstand. The only differences are that 45-rpm

A parking lot full of cars would normally be a pretty mundane sight, except for when its cruise night in Tacoma, Washington. Then, the usual, mundane, everyday commuter cars are replaced with cool hot rods, muscle cars, customs, lowriders, and much more. ©1997 Robert Genat

Frank Redford's classic Wigwam motels have worked their way into the roadside culture of America and are favorite destinations for cruisers traveling Route 66, the old Mother Road. Every now and then, these motels from the past can be seen hosting visitors who arrive in cars like this 1937 Chevrolet and 1954 Buick Skylark convertible (it was Buick's 50th anniversary car). The Buick is a fine example of a car no customizer would dare change. It was perfect right off the showroom floor. *Kent Bash*

records are no longer used (it's mostly compact discs these days), and a weekend disc-jockey or local radio personality plays the part of Dick Clark. The hit parade of the good old days again holds sway, and the favorite tunes of the forties, fifties, and sixties are cruise night standards. It's appropriate that many of the radio stations that follow this same sort of nostalgia play list are also part of the cruise night concert. With little exception, they engage in cross-promotion with cruise night organizers and the venues hosting the event.

Yet, despite all of the media attention and air play, national gatherings still manage to overshadow local and regional cruises. Using the small-town cruise night as the model, major car events allow the avid cruiser an opportunity to see a lot more than the local Tastee Freeze parking lot can offer. Drawing crowds of up to 10,000, the annual Hot August Nights in Reno, Nevada, is the typical meet. Similarly, the highly publicized Americruise convenes every year, allowing cruisers to select from eight tours and to begin each one of them from starting points in various states. Highway nostalgia is now a major draw, too. At the 1995 Route 66 Rendezvous in the city of San Bernardino, California, a total of 190,000 visitors took the

The car grille: ever since the first American motor carriage rolled off the assembly line, it's exhibited some sort of human-like quality and personality. It's the metallic faces of the forties and fifties cars (like this Buick Eight), however, that are imbued with the most outrageous personalities. Perhaps that's why the modern cruise night is such a friendly, fun activity. *Mike Witzel*

Although many drive-ins welcome cruisers on planned cruise nights, there are times when idle driving is frowned upon. This Steak n Shake on Route 66 in Springfield, Missouri, welcomes nostalgia seekers, but discourages loitering in the parking lot. *©1997 Shellee Graham*

"highway that's the best" and followed in the tracks of Buz and Tod. There, a 15-block stretch of the "Mother Road" through San Bernardino became a playground for rods, customs, and other street machines. Some 1,200 vehicles joined vintage Corvettes, just like the one seen in the classic television program *Route 66*, to cruise Main.

Recently, muscle car fans enjoyed their own special cruising event: In August 1995, local cities, businesses, and car clubs in Detroit, Michigan, started up the first Woodward Avenue Dream Cruise. Three days before the event, motor homes, travel trailers, and car-haulers from all over

The "blessing of the cars" has become a tradition at many automobile shows and cruise events in southern California. This priest arrived on a skateboard then donned a flamed robe. Men of the cloth are frequently on hand to praise God and pray for the safety and good fortune of the cruisers and for good clear weather. Ironically, it's the car that has become the new religion for many Americans. The real question for theologians to ponder is this: If Jesus came back tomorrow, would he be a hot rodder, customizer, lowrider, muscle car driver—or all four? *Courtesy Fred DuPuis*

While cruising where one can be seen is the status quo, the long-distance jaunt into the country is a favorite activity among many automobile clubs and cruising fans. The call of the open highway, the lure of the unknown destination, and the journey itself are all part of the experience. A blue 1940 Chevy and a flamed 1940 Plymouth are shown here, parked but ready to roll. *Kent Bash*

America descended on the four-lane strip. Local restaurants got into the spirit and charged the same prices they had in 1966. Believe it or not, an estimated 250,000 people showed up and 10,000 to 15,000 cars turned the former muscle car strip into a parking lot. One lap around the Woodward circuit took two hours! Sock hops, car shows, movies, burnout contests, and the lure of cruising back in time packed the traffic lanes with memories. Attendees who took part in the main run got

to take a bit of memorabilia home with them: Each of the six host cities gave out a dash plaque shaped like a puzzle piece. Cruisers who made the complete run collected all of the pieces and assembled them to make one big commemorative plaque.

Along with muscle cars, every conceivable type of car slipped along Motor City's most prominent street, including funky lowriders, way-out hot rods, speedy dragsters, and customized lead sleds. But it was more than just a blast from the past: The presence

In Buellton, California, remnants of yesterday's roadside eateries provide the perfect, real-life backdrop for artist Kent Bash's T-bucket roadster. On long-distance cruise events, nostalgic scenes like this one are a resounding favorite with participants. This 1925 Ford is packed with a Buick nailhead engine (big-block 401) and features American mag wheels on a shortened and narrowed 1932 Ford frame. The beer keg gas tank is a popular fuel format for the hot rodder and used most often with the open-bodied T configuration. *Kent Bash*

Without argument, the philosophy of what a car should look like has come a long way from the day when it took four weeks to paint a Ford. With the Model T, body parts were sanded and painted five times with days of drying left between each coat. Because black pigment dried quickest, it became *the* default assembly line color. Fortunately, the drab standard was dropped—and future rod and custom builders liberated—when chemists at Dupont developed an improved lacquer that dried in two hours! General Motors was the first to use the formula on the "True Blue" Oakland Six in 1924. As the nation entered the Great Depression, cars mirrored the somber situation of the times and stylists used reserved shades of brown, blue, green, and maroon. It wasn't until after World War II that the depressing hues were lightened. Today, hot rod colors are loud, bold, and vibrant! *©1997 Robert Genat*

In California, Johnny Carson Park (within walking distance of NBC studios) is a favorite place for the car club known as the Road Kings to hold some of their major car events. Started during the late forties, the Road Kings hosts a diverse membership of rod and custom fans, and today the club continues to sponsor a number of worthwhile automotive events in the region. *Kent Bash*

of brand new motoring forms (and diverse participants) signaled that the cruising phenomenon in this country is alive and well. In fact, it's spinning off entirely new breeds. From the sort of vehicles spied in the street, it became painfully obvious that buying a replica body of formed fiberglass is

now acceptable hot rod behavior. At the same time, present-day hot rodders and customizers have the choice of fashioning their ride the way they did during the fifties, or they may return to the standards of the thirties and forties. Even lowriders looked different; suddenly, the act of lifting a chassis appeared passé. Case in point: those mini-trucks with elaborate hydraulics. Instead of controlling the suspension, the truck bed is now the object of all gyration.

Whether the hot rod and custom purists like it or not, the types of cars the next generation is choosing for cruising coaches are changing. For today's neophyte unfamiliar with the automotive arts of the golden age, it's perfectly acceptable to take a car like an Acura Integra (or other import) and transform it into a cruiser. In a trend that's alarming traditionalists, tried-and-true marques like Chevy, Ford, and Mercury are being "dissed" in favor of smaller, less imposing types of compacts including Honda Civics and CRXs, Nissan Sentras, Mitsubishi 3000 GTs, and others. The kids who don baggy shorts, backward baseball caps, and stubby goatees spend piles of cash on the sorts of automobiles that the cruising enthusiasts of old wouldn't give a second glance. Now, in addition to engine and body modifications, it's those booming, high-power audio systems that get all the attention! Overpowered stereo amplifiers and trunk-mounted subwoofers have replaced the hand-tuned flathead as the symbol of male bravado. Supposedly, the more power and higher the volume level the mobile generation X'er can sustain, the more respect he gains.

To be fair, the old-timers of cruising's golden age shouldn't be so hard on the upstarts fighting for a parking place along the mean streets of America. After all, even today's average motorist has little in common with the car owner of the early 20th century: Locked within a sound-proof cocoon of lightweight sheet metal and composites, one may recline in the comfort of four-way adjustable seats, glide down the interstate with cruise-control, monitor traffic conditions with a heads-up display, enjoy speed-sensitive steering, engage anticollision radar, groove to the sounds of compact disc music, verify

directions with a global positioning satellite and computer display, conduct conversations by cellular telephone, and even send (or receive) fax transmissions en route.

Further advancements promise to widen the technology gap even more. Aided by a digital computer and external sensors, the next generation of advanced motor vehicles will possess the ability to regulate their own speed of travel and safely guide themselves along controlled paths (engineers played with "automatic highways" as early as the fifties). Efficient motors powered by innovative energy sources will render the gasoline engine and its peripheral equipment obsolete. Compact powerplants fueled by new sources of energy are leaving the realm of science-fiction and entering the arena of practicality. With each passing decade, the gas-guzzling carriages of antiquity roll toward a future devoid of petroleum.

So, is cruising on the way out? Probably not. Even if radical environmentalists confiscate all of the automobiles and government bureaucrats outlaw all fossil fuel engines, car lovers will find entirely new ways to take a ride down the Main Street strip and show off their personalities. It doesn't matter if that new source of energy is hydrogen, solar panels, rechargeable batteries, cold fusion, nuclear fission, dilithium crystal, or flux capacitor. As long as this nation remains free, motorists will never give up their cars and the recreational outlet they provide without a fight. While walking may be good for health and flying in an airplane a safer way to travel, there's nothing quite so satisfying as strapping yourself into the bucket seat of a gorgeous convertible, cranking the ignition switch, throwing the four-on-the-floor shifter into gear, popping the clutch, pressing your foot against the accelerator pedal, slipping your arm around your date, grooving to the tunes on the radio, checking out the scene, and indulging yourself in the passion called Cruisin'.

Recommended Back-Seat Reading

Barris, George, and David Fetherston. *Barris Kustoms of the 1950s*. Osceola, Wisconsin: Motorbooks International, 1994.

Batchelor, Dean. *The American Hot Rod*. Osceola, Wisconsin: Motorbooks International, 1995.

Benjaminson, James A. *Plymouth 1946–1959*. Osceola, Wisconsin: Motorbooks International, 1994.

Boyer, William P. *Thunderbird: An Odyssey in Automotive Design*. Dallas, Texas: Taylor Publishing Company, 1986.

Boyne, Walter J. *Power Behind the Wheel: Creativity and Evolution of the Automobile*. New York: Stewart, Tabori and Chang, 1988.

Brown, Lester R., Christopher Flavin, and Colin Norman. *Running on Empty: the Future of the Automobile in an Oil Short World*. New York: W. W. Norton and Company, 1979.

Campisano, Jim. *American Muscle Cars*. New York: Metro Books, 1995.

Dauphinais, Dean, and Peter M. Gareffa. *Car Crazy: The Official Motor City High-Octane, Turbocharged, Chrome-Plated, Back Road Book of Car Culture*. Detroit, Michigan: Visible Ink Press, 1996.

Drake, Albert. *Beyond the Pavement*. Adelphi, Maryland: The White Ewe Press, 1981.

Drake, Albert. *Street Was Fun in '51*. Okemos, Michigan: Flat Out Press, 1982.

Egan, Philip S. *Design and Destiny: the Making of the Tucker Automobile*. Orange, California: On the Mark Publications, 1989.

Fetherston, David. *Heroes of Hot Rodding*. Osceola, Wisconsin: Motorbooks International, 1992.

Fetherston, David. *Hot Rod Memorabilia and Collectibles*. Osceola, Wisconsin: Motorbooks International, 1996.

Finch, Christopher. *Highways to Heaven: The Auto Biography of America*. New York: HarperCollins Publishers Inc., 1992.

Flink, James J. *The Automobile Age*. Cambridge, Massachusetts: The MIT Press, 1988.

Flink, James J. *The Car Culture*. Cambridge, Massachusetts: The MIT Press, 1975.

Ganahl, Pat. *Hot Rods and Cool Customs*. New York: Abbeville Press, 1993.

Gelderman, Carol. *Henry Ford: The Wayward Capitalist*. New York: St. Martin's Press, 1981.

Gunnel, John A., and Mary L. Sieber. *The Fabulous Fifties: The Cars, The Culture*. Iola, Wisconsin: Krause Publications, 1992.

Heat Moon, William Least. *Blue Highways: A Journey Into America*. Boston: Atlantic Monthly Press, 1982.

Hirsch, Jay. *Great American Dream Machines: Classic Cars of the 50s and 60s*. New York: Macmillan Publishing Company, 1985.

Hoffman, Robert N. *Murder on the Highway*. New York: A. S. Barnes and Company Inc., 1966.

Horsley, Fred. *Hot Rod It—and Run for Fun! How to Build and Operate a Hot Rod Safely*. Englewood Cliffs, New Jersey: Prentice-Hall Inc., 1957.

Ikuta, Yasutoshi. *Cruise O Matic: Automobile Advertising of the 1950s*. San Francisco, California: Chronicle Books, 1988.

Jewell, Derek. *Man & Motor: The 20th Century Love Affair*. New York: Walker and Company, 1966.

Keller, Ulrich. *The Highway as Habitat: A Roy Stryker Documentation, 1943–1955*. Santa Barbara, California: University Art Museum, 1986.

Kerouac, Jack. *On the Road*. New York: Viking Penguin, 1955.

Kitahara, Teruhisa. *Cars: Tin Toy Dreams*. San Francisco: Chronicle Books, 1985.

Lawlor, John. *How to Talk Car*. Chicago, Illinois: Topaz Felson Books, 1965.

Leffingwell, Randy. *American Muscle: Muscle Cars from the Otis Chandler Collection*. Osceola, Wisconsin: Motorbooks International, 1990.

Lent, Henry B. *The Automobile—U.S.A.: Its Impact on People's Lives and the National Economy*. New York: E. P. Dutton and Company Inc., 1968.

Lewis, David L., and Lawrence Goldstein. *The Automobile and American Culture*. Ann Arbor: The University of Michigan Press, 1980.

Matteson, Donald W. *The Auto Radio, A Romantic Genealogy*. Jackson, Michigan: Thornridge Publishing, 1987.

Montgomery, Don. *Hot Rods in the Forties: A Blast from the Past*. Fallbrook, California: Don Montgomery, 1987.

Don Montgomery. *Supercharged Gas Coupes*. Fallbrook, California: Don Montgomery, 1993.

Mueller, Mike. *Chevy Muscle Cars*. Osceola, Wisconsin: Motorbooks International, 1994.

Mike Mueller. *Fifties American Cars*. Osceola, Wisconsin: Motorbooks International, 1994.

Nader, Ralph. *Unsafe at Any Speed*. New York: Grossman Publishers, 1972.

Newton, Kenneth, W. Steeds, and T. K. Garrett. *The Motor Vehicle*. London, England: Butterworth-Heinemann Ltd., 1991.

O'Brien, Richard. *The Story of American Toys*. New York: Abbeville Press, 1990.

Oppel, Frank. *Motoring in America: The Early Years*. Secaucus, New Jersey: Castle Books, 1989.

Oyslager Organisation. *American Cars of the 1960s*. London, England: Frederick Warne Ltd., 1977.

Packard, Chris. *Safe Driving*. New York: J. B. Lippincott Company, 1974.

Pearce, Christopher. *Fifties Sourcebook: A Visual Guide to the Style of a Decade*. Secaucus, New Jersey: Chartwell Books, 1990.

Petersen Publishing Company. *The Best of Hot Rod*. Los Angeles, California: Petersen Publishing Company, 1986.

Post, Robert C. *High Performance: The Culture and Technology of Drag Racing 1950–1990*. Baltimore, Maryland: The John Hopkins University Press, 1994.

Roth, Ed "Big Daddy," and Tony Thacker. *Hot Rods by Ed "Big Daddy" Roth*. Osceola, Wisconsin: Motorbooks International, 1995.

Segrave, Kerry. *Drive-in Theaters, A History from Their Inception in 1933*. Jefferson, North Carolina: McFarland and Company Inc., 1992.

Seiffert, Ulrich, and Peter Walzer. *Automobile Technology of the Future*. Warrendale, Pennsylvania: The Society of Automotive Engineers, 1989.

Silk, Gerald, Angelo Anselmi, Henry Robert Jr., and Strother MacMinn. *Automobile and Culture*. New York: Harry N. Abrams Inc., 1984.

Smith, Dan. *Accessory Mascots: The Automotive Accents of Yesteryear, 1910–1940*. San Diego, California: Dan Smith Publishing, 1989.

Smith, Mark, and Naomi Black. *America on Wheels: Tales and Trivia of the Automobile*. New York: William Morrow and Company Inc., 1986

Society for Commercial Archeology. *The Automobile in Design and Culture*. Edited by Jan Jennings. Ames: Iowa State University Press, 1990.

Southard, Andy. *Custom Cars of the 1950s*. Osceola, Wisconsin: Motorbooks International, 1993.

Stambler, Irwin. *The Supercars and the Men Who Race Them*. New York: G. P. Putnam's Sons, 1975.

Steinbeck, John. *The Grapes of Wrath*. New York: The Viking Press, 1939.

Steinbeck, John. *Travels with Charley*. New York: The Viking Press, 1962.

Time-Life Books. *This Fabulous Century, 1920–1930*. New York: Time-Life Books, 1969.

Williams, William C. *Motoring Mascots of the World*. Portland, Oregon: Graphic Arts Center Publishing, 1990.

Wilson, Paul. *Chrome Dreams: Automobile Styling Since 1893*. Radnor, Pennsylvania: Chilton Book Company, 1976.

Wilson, Richard Guy, Dianne H. Pilgrim, and Dickran Tashjian. *The Machine Age in America 1918–1941*. New York: Harry N. Abrams Inc., 1986.

Witzel, Michael Karl. *The American Drive-In: History and Folklore of the Drive-In Restaurant in American Car Culture*. Osceola, Wisconsin: Motorbooks International, 1994.

Witzel, Michael Karl. *The American Gas Station: History and Folklore of the Gas Station in American Car Culture*. Osceola, Wisconsin: Motorbooks International, 1992.

Witzel, Michael Karl. *Drive-In Deluxe*. Osceola, Wisconsin: Motorbooks International, 1997.

Witzel, Michael Karl. *Gas Station Memories*. Osceola, Wisconsin: Motorbooks International, 1994.

Witzel, Michael Karl. *Route 66 Remembered*. Osceola, Wisconsin: Motorbooks International, 1996.

Young, Anthony, and Mike Mueller. *Chevrolet's Hot Ones*. Osceola, Wisconsin: Motorbooks International, 1995.

Index

ROUTE 66 *Remembered*

Michael Karl Witzel

Lowe & B. Hould
Publishers

On the frontispiece: Heading towards Miami, Oklahoma, from the Brush Creek Bridge in Riverton, Kansas, white Route 66 shields have been painted on the road surface to guide those in search of the old alignment. New asphalt has been laid as well, making easy driving for all those in search of back-road bliss. Baxter Springs, Kansas. *Author*

On the title page: The Wigwam Village in San Bernardino, California, offered the weary traveler the chance to "sleep in a teepee!" Many of Route 66's roadside establishments reflected the history and folklore of the surrounding regions. *Preziosi Postcards*

Contents

Dedication

This book is dedicated to the four-wheeled, internal combustion conveyance that became my very first motorcar: a dark azure, second-hand, two-door, 1967 model Chevrolet Malibu Coupe equipped with a 283-cubic-inch V-8 engine, an automatic transmission that jerked when you shifted into reverse, air-conditioning that blew only slightly cool air, a Delco AM radio that pulled in mostly static, vinyl split-bench seats that were cold in the winter and sweaty in the summer, and a front window seal that leaked during heavy rains. For $800 it wasn't the perfect motoring machine, but it was all mine—providing the freedom to explore the open road and discover for myself the magic and wonders that were out there, somewhere . . . beyond the distant vanishing point, over the approaching hill, or waiting . . . just around the next bend.

Acknowledgments

Without the input and assistance of Paul Taylor, editor of Route 66 Magazine, this publication would have been stuck on the side of the highway. A heartfelt thank you to all of the individuals who shared their personal "Mother Road" memories, including Ralph Bay, Allen Bell, Jay Black, Bea Bragg, Terri Cleeland, David Cole, James Cook, Glen Driskill, Ken Greenburg, Rebecca Rockwood Hill, John Houghtaling, Mildred "Skeeter" Kobzeff, Gordon Kornblith, Richard McDonald, Joe Morrow, Mildred Birdsell Pattschull, Clare Patterson, Jr., Mabel Richards Phillips, Terri Ryburn-LaMonte, Bill Stevens, and Buz Waldmire. Further appreciation is extended to all of the photographers, artists, archives, and corporations that supplied images or information, most notably: A & W Restaurants, Inc.; Airstream, Inc.; the American Automobile Manufacturer's Association; the American Petroleum Institute; John Baeder; Kent Bash; Bob Boze Bell; Bennett Pump Company; Chevron Corporation; the General Motors Media Archives; the General Stamping and Manufacturing Company; Gilbarco, Inc.; Shellee Graham; Janice Griffith of the Old Trails Museum; Diane Hamilton; Dan Harlow; the Henry Ford Museum & Greenfield Village; Joan Johnson of Circa Research and Reference; Library of Congress; Jerry McClanahan; Mid-America Designs; the National Archives; Clare Patterson, Jr.; Personality Photos, Inc.; James Reed of the Rogers County Historical Society; Jim Ross; Keith Sculle; the Security Pacific Historical Photograph Collection; Phillips Petroleum Archives; Shell Oil Company; Steak n Shake, Inc.; Texas Pig Stands, Inc.; Tokheim Corporation; University of Louisville; D. Jeanene Tiner; Robert Waldmire; June Wian; Barry Williams of the American Streetscape Society; and Gabriele Witzel. Kudos to memorabilia collectors Carl Christiansen, Hugh Clarke, John Hutinett, Jerry Keyser, Sr., Richard McLay, Don Preziosi, Chuck Sturm, Bill Thomas, and Warren Winthrop. Finally, a personal acknowledgment is reserved for my wife, Gyvel Young-Witzel—a pedestrian who has permanently hung up her Route 66 walking shoes in favor of an automotive seat (and its relative safety). Good travels to all!

Foreword

After showman and circus owner Phineas Taylor Barnum opened his side show of human oddities, folks paused at length to look upon his bizarre attraction. Barnum, aware that the delay was causing long lines of potential, but impatient, customers, placed a brightly lettered sign over a doorway at the far end of the tent; "This way to the Great Egress" it proclaimed. Curious onlookers hurried forward to examine the mysterious and wondrous Egress. What they saw when they passed through the portal was the outside of the tent, for, as Webster tells us, "egress" means way out, place of going out, or exit.

To many folks, an interstate exit sign that points the way to Route 66 is like that egress. It's the direction to just another road, they conclude. A way to nothing wondrous—an exit—just a place of going out.

In contrast, people who have discovered and rediscovered the road at the end of that exit, talk of their experiences on the old asphalt and concrete trail in terms of endearment, using words the likes of "nostalgic" and "magical."

To novelist John Steinbeck, Route 66 was The Mother Road, the road of flight, and the glory road to the land of Second Chance.

To songwriter Bobby Troup, it was "My way . . . the highway that's the best." It was the highway of kicks.

To architect Frank Lloyd Wright, it was the chute of a tilting continent, on which everything loose seemed to be sliding into Southern California.

And to travel agencies, it was the chosen thoroughfare of the discriminating American tourist.

Nobody could possibly guess how many Americans—from the Oakies, Arkies, and Texies, to the flower children—would consider Route 66 to be, first and foremost, an invitation for an extended stroll.

The nation first became aware of U.S. Highway 66 when the 1928 International Transcontinental Foot Marathon (affectionately known as the Bunion Derby) followed all of 66.

Three decades later, for a fee of $1,500, Pete McDonald walked on stilts from New York City to Los Angeles, a distance of 3,250 miles. From Chicago, the way west was Route 66. Pete was neither the first nor the last to place America's Main Street in the public eye: wild, weird, and wondrous celebrants were to follow.

Hobo Dick Zimmerman routinely walked Route 66 from California to Michigan pushing a wheelbarrow, to visit his 101-year-old mother. Dick was 78.

Another student of perambulating the old highway was "Shopping Cart" Dougherty, who, sporting a white beard and turban, traveled 9 to 16 miles a day on Route 66 with all his worldly possessions in a shopping cart.

Shopping Cart and Hobo Dick weren't the most unusual challengers and celebrants of the Mother Road. High school baton twirlers marched along Old 66 setting dubious records.

In 1972, John Ball, a 45-year-old South African, jogged from California to Chicago on Route 66, and then on to the East Coast. The journey took 54 days.

The 1920s and 1930s saw desperadoes and bootleggers the likes of John Dillinger, Al Capone, and Bugs Moran lurching down Old 66, the escape route. Occasionally, the Associated Press warned travelers of the dangers of "the criminally few who mix with the tourist throng."

National magazines called 66 "America's Worst Speed Trap," naming the tiny hamlets where cops and judges had their palms outstretched. The American Automobile Association reported towns you should avoid, or else prepare to sweeten the police treasury.

For a six-year-old child traveling with his parents in a brand new 1937 Chevy, Route 66 is memories of a canvas water bag on the front bumper, buying maple syrup at Funks Grove, Illinois, crossing the Chain of Rocks Bridge on the Mississippi River, visiting Meramec Caverns in Missouri, and listening to Dad read aloud every single Burma-Shave sign encountered along the road. I don't recall if my father used the product or not, but I do remember that his favorite verse was "Don't stick your elbow out too far/It might go home in another car." Since I always had my arm out the window, that was probably a personal message for me.

Today, with my own family, that same highway becomes more and more special with each journey. Old landmarks appear from the crest of a hill . . . a gas station or diner now closed, but still, memories flicker.

The two-laner turns, rises, and twists its way across the country. Hundreds and hundreds of drivable miles are still out there. Some of the road echoes to that familiar thump-ah, thump-ah, thump-ah rhythm as the tires bounce over separations in the WPA concrete slabs. But, in stark contrast, many miles of the old road have a surface more pleasant to drive than some parts of the interstates.

Although Route 66 is somewhat hidden in the shadows of the superhighways, progress does not necessarily conquer all. Diners and roadside attractions are still out there. Some are only gaunt images of their former selves, while others have been restored and reopened.

A glance through the pages of this book evokes memories of those businesses that once lined that scenic, narrow, two-lane, wavy old road. Author Michael Karl Witzel awakens the nostalgic era when life was less complex, when a rural economy was still dominant, when the jukebox in the back room of a mom-and-pop diner blared out "Good Night Irene," a cup of coffee cost a nickel, and there was more action in the back seat of a car at the drive-in movie than on the screen.

—Paul Taylor, publisher *Route 66 Magazine*, Laughlin, Nevada

Take a Drive Along America's Main Street

Were we really in the country? If so, where was it? The road was bordered with big hoardings, not presenting a flat surface or even painted in such a way as to create an illusion of reality, but complicated with depth and perspective; that is, made like a stage-setting with converging wings, and with figures cut out from wood in the open space in between, and at nightfall the whole thing was illuminated with rows of electrical light at top and bottom. Behind these enormous structures there may perhaps have been what passes for the country hereabouts.

–Georges Duhamel, America the Menace: Scenes From the Life of the Future, 1931

INDIAN WESTERN GIFTS RETAIL-WHOLESALE

INDIAN JEWELRY

MOCCASINS WESTERN CURIO

Tourist Traps:

Attractions

Along

the Road

Throughout the Roar-ing Twenties and straight on up to the 1960s, the roadsides along Route 66 jumped with an eclectic mix of attractions. Back then, America's Main Street was the nation's premier ride—a two-lane roller coaster of thrills that rambled through eight states and three time zones. All along the miles of the "linear midway," a diversity of car commerce combined services motorists required with the entertainment they desired.

With a full tank of fuel, a good night's snooze, and a belly filled with road food—motorized attendees of the

During the golden age of the highway, animal attractions along the road were intense by today's standards. With less concern over crowded and inhumane conditions, proprietors interested more in a fast buck than the preservation of nature established all sorts of outlandish zoos and curiosity shows. In Two Guns, Arizona, the legend of an Indian massacre where Apaches killed 40 Navajo men, women, and children provided the perfect story to promote the local tourist trade. Intrigued by the idea of an "Apache Death Cave," Route 66 travelers wheeled in to get their macabre kicks. *Courtesy Paul Taylor*

left
Amid the rabble of souvenir shops vying for attention along the old route, Joseph Joe's Big Indian Store was once an able contender. Capitalizing on the imagery of the native American (in an era when no one thought twice about exploiting stereotypes), it was a roadside curiosity shop that more than piqued the interest of the vacationer motoring down Route 66. Winslow, Arizona, circa 1983. *Jerry McClanahan ©1995*

11

roadside carnival pushed down on the accelerator to bring on the wonders. Near the highway's western limit in the city of Los Angeles, wheeling past a barbecue stand constructed like an immense pig was an everyday occurrence. Out there, short-order food shacks were shaped like giant toads and juice joints bloated up as over-sized oranges.

At the outskirts of town where traffic dwindled, automobile ownership allowed day-trippers to experience the full glory of 66. Beneath the gaping grin of a life-size dinosaur, couples could picnic without care. When a long day of explorations were concluded, it was all the rage to catch 40 winks inside an Indian wigwam, refill one's gas tank at a petrified-wood service station, or dine on a corned-beef sandwich inside the penthouse of a gigantic shoe. Route 66 held an endless array of surprises!

With turning a profit of paramount importance, the roadside businesses lining the highway employed every trick they could think of to lure motorists. They had no alternative: When automobile ownership during the teens and 1920s rose to

The Roadside Delight Called Spooklight

"Governed by seemingly magical properties, it waltzes through mesquite groves and leaps over fences, sometimes bouncing right off passing automobiles. . . ."

Since 1886, mysterious orbs of light have been bobbing up and down in the woods of northeastern Oklahoma. The Quapaw Indians caught first glimpse of these fluttering flashes, and later, residents of the town taking their name spied them as well. Local landowners nicknamed the glow "Spooklight" and began to weave tales of mystery and imagination to explain its origin. Today—the eerie phenomenon is an established Route 66 attraction, drawing throngs of curiosity-seekers to the twisting road dubbed "Devil's Promenade."

Seen mostly in July during overcast skies, the Spooklight is routinely reported as a bright, yellow-white sphere of light—one that occasionally transforms into a fiery red. Originating as a single globe of energy, it has been known to divide at will and form two bouncing blobs, each exhibiting its own directional agenda and duration. Governed by seemingly magical properties, it waltzes through mesquite groves and leaps over fences, sometimes bouncing right off passing automobiles (in one rare occurrence it entered the passenger compartment through an open window). When approached, it disappears, when chased, it eludes.

Witnesses have often described Spooklight's mimicry of a searchlight, lending credence to the skeptic's standard explanation of the anomaly. As far back as the 1920s, practical thinkers have fingered the motorcar as the most culpable suspect, describing how refracted light shone from vehicle headlamps on 66 could be the only logical source for the illumination. However, old timers vehemently dismiss the theory since many witnessed the enigmatic glow long before there were any roads or the town of Quapaw.

Some claim the puzzling lights have been around since the beginning of time. As far back as the days of the clipper ships, Mediterranean seamen were perplexed by the mercurial flames hovering about their masts. Deckhands christened the odd glow "St. Elmo's Fire"—a derivation of St. Erasmus, the patron saint of sailors. In other countries, the peculiar phenomenon has been affectionately referred to as "spunkie," "jack-o'-lantern," and "will-o'-the-wisp." In most instances, rotting tree stumps and humid marshes are the recognized haunts for this so-called *ignis fatuus* (from the Latin, meaning foolish fire).

In Oklahoma, regional folklore endeavors to demystify the conundrum with an "old" Indian tale. According to legend, a brave was prematurely relieved of his head during a domestic argument. His disgruntled spouse hid the severed head somewhere among the trees, north of Miami, Oklahoma. Spooklight simply became the earthly manifestation of his spirit—doomed to an eternal search for his misplaced head.

Nevertheless, none of these yarns formed a scientific hypothesis to explain the spectacle. So, during the 1940s, a concerted effort was initiated by the U.S. Corps of Engineers to debunk the fallacies and find the truth. As WWII raged on, they descended on northeastern Ottawa County and organized a research camp. For almost a month they explored caves, analyzed mineral deposits, sifted streams, and studied road alignments. Despite a thorough examination, the unpredictable conduct of the bizarre lights could not be reckoned with physical laws! Decades later, the "Unsolved Mysteries" television series mounted its own investigation. Once again, no concrete answers were found.

Even so, some concluded that certain geological events—combined with just the right temperature and atmospheric conditions—triggered outbreaks of these fickle flames. A spontaneous combustion of gases was given as the most logical cause. Others cited the theoretical existence of ball lightning, a specialized form of ionized gas known as "plasma" that, given the right parameters, can form at will. Like the tornado, there's no predicting when it will occur, where it will go, and how long it will last. The only absolute: The lucky few who see it will gaze with child-like wonder and amazement.

And luck has become a prerequisite, since the wily Spooklight has shifted its location over the years. Without rhyme or reason, it has steadily drifted farther and farther to the northeast, almost to the state line of Kansas. Fortunately, anticipation and a sense of adventure are more important to the two-lane travelers who come to sneak a peek at this enigmatic pixie. After all, the romantic idea of nature's mystery—something that defies our comprehension and can never be bought, sold, or bottled for sale at a souvenir stand—is what makes the quest unique. That's the real appeal of Quapaw's Spooklight. As long as there are still occasional sightings of those little white lights that "go bump in the night," it always will be.

Right off of old Route 66 in Quapaw, Oklahoma, the twisting stretch of road known as Devil's Promenade has, until recently, been the primary point for sighting the elusive Spooklight. Sightings reported during the mid-1990s have indicated that the phenomenon is now moving steadily to the northeast—right across the Kansas state line. Still, there is no way to predict when and where the next manifestation of Spooklight will occur. Quapaw, Oklahoma. *Special-Effects Recreation by Author*

become secondary only to shelter and clothing—the trading climate along America's roadsides became increasingly competitive. As a steady influx of new drivers turned a dirt artery into a transcontinental corridor, new types of industries emerged to accommodate the flow.

Before too long, services that catered to the motor vehicle were duplicated in vast numbers. With the corresponding rise in Route 66 advertisers vying for attention, the raft of billboards and snipe signs common to early motor trails became impotent. At what used to be a quiet country crossroads, Chuck's Chicken Shack now had to contend with a self-contained dining car across the street and a cafeteria on the corner. As travelers sped past with no end in sight, the friendly neighborhood filling station suddenly found itself in competition with two additional "service" stations and a lubritorium on the very same block!

The need to achieve greater visibility—and a unique hook—increased. To break through the visual cacophony, some Route 66 entrepreneurs decided to erect bigger and more brightly lit signs. Others took the craft of outdoor advertising to a new level with neon-lit creations of pressed steel and glass tubing. Born of the merchant's imagination, roadside statues made of plaster and lath were used to attract the motorist's ever-decreasing attention. A few businesses that depended directly on the car for business decided to blend both their building and billboard by utilizing the "programmatic" themes so popular on the coast. By

In June 1929, "Happy" Lou Phillips and his partner "Lucky" Jimmy Parker strapped on a pair of roller skates and rolled across America. From Washington, D.C., to San Francisco, California, they skated all the way—supporting themselves by selling their photographs, doing some vaudeville shows, and peddling newspapers in the cities they passed through. They followed Route 66 through Arizona and into California and, according to a story in the Williams (Arizona) News, explained that "[when] we travel on the roads that are not concreted, we keep the skates on and walk on them. On dirt roads, we go from 20 to 55 miles a day, but on concrete roads we make 75 miles a day." Their trip ultimately took them through 17 states and a distance of 4,563 miles! *Courtesy Hugh Clarke via Terri Cleeland*

"The Chain of Rocks Bridge," Highway 66 over Mississippi River near St. Louis, Mo.

The Chain of Rocks bridge was once the principle means for Route 66 motorists to get across the Mississippi River. About halfway across the span, a distinct curve was an integral part of the unique, steel-truss design. Today, the aging bridge has been retired and cannot be accessed from the Missouri side of the river. However, the road (right behind the chain-link fence on Riverfront Road, south of Interstate 270) can still be explored on foot. Near St. Louis, Missouri. *Courtesy Jerry Keyser*

copying the whimsical forms of animals or objects and incorporating them into their buildings, operators blended billboards with architecture. By the time construction crews were laying concrete along the final miles of Highway 66, an exciting roster of restaurants, gas stations, tourist courts, souvenir stands, and other recreational hideaways were entertaining the travelers with architectural theatrics. In Oklahoma,

a smiling blue whale splashed about in the waters near Catoosa. Just down the highway in Foyil, tourists were allowed to explore the inside of a multicolored totem pole. Meanwhile, the good folks in Texas slapped an oversized set of longhorns and a ten-gallon hat on just about everything. New Mexico traders adopted the Indian mystique, and in the stretch of road through Arizona the shapely saguaro became a predominant theme. By the time man orbited the Earth, Paul Bunyan had donned a space helmet (with hand-held missile) near Wilmington, Illinois!

As the rush to motorize changed America, the "Mother Road" became a bona fide destination in itself. Timid automobile owners who never dreamed of leaving the confines of their state took to the highway with great zeal—just to see how easy it was to travel long distances. Suddenly, the owners of roadside businesses began to realize that there was much more to making money along a busy thoroughfare than just renting out tourist cabins, pumping gas, or serving chili: When a traveler's needs were taken care of and they were ready to continue the journey, thoughts often turned to mementos of the trip. Everyone, it seemed, wanted a souvenir to show the folks back home—proof of exactly where they had been and the adventures they had experienced.

Unprepared for the rising demand, Route 66 operators learned first hand of the motorist's sentimental acquisitiveness: day in and day out, ash trays, towels, tableware, napkin holders, coffee cups, salt and pepper shakers, and anything else that could be carried off began to disappear. In an effort to discourage this depletion of operating equipment and to increase revenue, the idea of selling specialized souvenirs was seriously considered. Unsure of the territory, the trio of roadside services known as gas, food, and lodging were entering the retail world.

Big Cut on U. S. Highway 66 at Hooker, between Lebanon and Rolla, Missouri, in the Beautiful Ozarks

Between the towns of Rolla and Waynesville, Missouri, a four-lane length of Route 66 created the "deepest rock cut in the U.S." In the 1940s, the massive soil excavation was a road engineering achievement that allowed passengers inside automobiles to view a real roadside attraction without slowing down—or even leaving the comfort of their cars. *Courtesy Jerry Keyser*

The Chain of Rocks Bridge opened as a toll bridge for motor traffic in 1929. Linking the north side of St. Louis, Missouri, and the town of Mitchell on the Illinois side, it offered motorists a roadbed that was only 40 feet wide. In 1930, the St. Louis alignment of Route 66 was rerouted to avoid the bustling railroad and warehouse congestion and subsequently linked up with the Chain of Rocks. By the 1970s, the bridge was abandoned and visitors to and from St. Louis were rerouted to more modern spans. *Shellee Graham ©1995*

Of Speed Traps and Traffic Tickets

"Wide-eyed tourists out to view the wonders of America soon discovered that a revolving red light flashing in their rear view-mirror was one of the more unwelcome sights."

At the turn of the century, receiving a speeding ticket was more unlikely then being struck by lightning while fixing a flat. After all, no substantial traffic laws existed in the West until well after Ford introduced the Model T. As late as the 1930s, a dozen states had absolutely no speed limit at all! A few posted placards suggested a "safe and reasonable" rate, indirectly sanctioning motorists to put the "pedal to the metal."

Despite the lax attitudes, densely populated regions were attempting to regulate motoring's unbridled passions. In 1909, the city of Pittsburgh, Pennsylvania, set an example when they equipped their policemen with a secret weapon: the motorcycle. With a powerful V-twin engine and agility in heavy traffic, the Harley-Davidson police bike could catch up to even the speediest roadster! It didn't take long for other cities to notice. By the mid-1920s, over 2,500 towns were employing racy two-wheelers to nab traffic violators.

By the 1930s, being pulled over by a "motorcycle cop" and cited for excessive speed became a recognized risk for the car crowd. The minor trepidation sensed along the motor lanes soon grew to a panic: a few unscrupulous townships (along the well-traveled routes such as 66) calculated that the endless procession of cars cruising across their borders could be tapped as a lucrative source of revenue. Without bothering to build a motor court, restaurant, gas station, or even a tourist attraction, they proceeded to reap the road's bounty. All that was required to hook 'em was an overeager official in uniform . . . hidden behind a strategically placed billboard.

Wide-eyed tourists out to view the wonders of America soon discovered that a revolving red light flashing in their rear-view mirror was one of the more unwelcome sights. With their sirens wailing, helmets strapped tight, and ticket pads at the ready, the overzealous watchdogs of our nation's hinterlands introduced the unwary motorists to their most novel gambit: the "speed trap"! The so-called golden age of the automobile was beginning to show some tarnish.

To determine if a car was going too fast, patrolmen who were on the level usually timed a vehicle's movement between a set of marked reference points. The unfair officer casually eye-balled an approaching vehicle and determined by sight if it was exceeding the posted limits. In some cases, speed limits were left unposted at the outskirts, leaving motorists at a marked disadvantage and oblivious to the required reduction in speed. Disputing the accusations or denying to sign

off on the traffic ticket wasn't recommended—after all, these were the days when no one questioned a policeman's authority.

With kids crying in the back seat, the wife growing impatient, and egg-salad turning rancid in the picnic basket, it was easy for country cops and judges to extract inflated fines from out-of-state vacationers. Far from home and eager to continue their journeys (waiting for a trial could often take up to two weeks), most "offenders" decided to cough up the extortion dough. With their wallets lightened and their blood pressure heightened, traffic scofflaws made a quick path past the city limits—muttering obscenities under their breath and vowing that they would never, ever pass this way again.

Eventually, word of the unsavory speed scam spread around, alerting other long-distance drivers to the dangers. Sympathetic journalists also taken in by the traps began to write revealing articles about their own experiences. Over the years, stories detailing the whereabouts of "America's Worst Speed Traps" appeared in *Argosy* magazine and a host of others. The American Automobile Association maintained a national reporting bureau as well, compiling a master list of municipalities responsible for the most flagrant abuses. Believe it or not, over half the trouble spots were identified along Route 66!

To everyone's approval, the speed trap phenomenon began to diminish during the 1960s, but never died out completely. As the interstate highway planners bypassed more and more villages with endless ribbons of freeway, the traditional methods—once used for generating honest cash flow—had to be reexamined. It was no longer economically viable for one-horse towns to repel the tourist just-passing-through with a rash of superfluous traffic citations!

For some communities, the change of heart occurred too late. America's motorized river of gold was now being rerouted, guided by steel guardrails and controlled by limited access and exit ramps. Whizzing along on the elevated superslab, the next generation of would-be speeders had fallen under the jurisdiction of the state highway patrolman. The inequitable era of the small town speed trap was finally over. Or was it?

The NEW All-Solid-State MOTORCYCLE RADIO from General Electric

Before two-way radios became technologically feasible and affordable for police departments, catching speeders and other scofflaws by automobile was difficult. Unable to radio ahead and alert additional cruisers, the police were impotent when it came to rum runners in souped-up hot rods. Unfortunately, the widespread use of the vacuum tube followed by the perfection of the transistor led to the development of inexpensive and efficient transceivers. By the end of the 1950s, municipalities all over America (and up and down Route 66) were putting the squeeze on speeders. *Courtesy General Electric via Preziosi Postcards*

At the wayside cafes, cashier stations doubled as display areas for knick-knacks. Colorful matchbooks emblazoned with whimsical captions, cartoons, and other advertisements became the staple item to give away free (when one purchased a cigar or pack of cigarettes). At dining tables, some restaurants slipped imprinted place-mats under the table-settings. Featuring facts and figures pertinent to the local area along with idealized reviews of the high-way's attractions, they were inexpensive give-aways to keep on hand. Of course, nothing reminded one of eating out away from home as much as a souvenir menu. Statues were cast, coins minted, glassware etched, and guidebooks printed.

For the majority of Route 66 operators, the linen picture postcard became the most cost-effective method to advertise a road-side business and get name recognition on a national level. When it was provided gratis, enthusiastic patrons were more than willing to provide the penny postage and to mail it off—sending home what amounted to nothing more than a personalized, direct-mailer to receptive friends and family. No amount of advertising could equal the hand-written testimonials describing attractions found along the "Great Diagonal Highway."

As pictures were examined on front porches in small-town America, kids marveled at the sight of their own road vanishing into the distance—tied like a string to a world of possibilities yet undiscovered. It was a world of travel that was opening up

Along Route 66 in Groom, Texas, the Britten U.S.A. water reservoir features one leg shorter than all the others. Locals like to think of it as promotion, but those driving by just think of it as another unusual sight along the American roadscape. Panhandle 66, Groom, Texas. *D. Jeanene Tiner ©1995*

19

In towns throughout the United States, a variety of automotive repair facilities, restaurants, retail stores, and chainsaw repair shops (in this case) have employed the services of "people attractors" to lure in the motorist and his money. Giant cow heads, cheeseburgers, mosquitoes, flamingos, mushrooms, plates of ribs, guns, and ice cream cones are frequent sights up on the rooftops. This fiberglass Paul Bunyan is only one of many statues available to the modern entrepreneur not afraid of a little showmanship. North service road (Route 66) of Interstate 44, Sullivan, Missouri. *Shellee Graham ©1995*

The Launching Pad Drive-In is one eatery that Route 66 motorists find difficult to speed past. Formerly known as the Dairy Delight, this restaurant's name was changed in 1965 during the space race frenzy. A local girl came up with a memorable moniker for the parking lot giant out front, officially kicking off the advertising career of the "Gemini Giant." The larger-than-life statue (28 feet tall) was manufactured by an advertising company in California and specially modified to reflect the rocketman motif. A few years ago, local high school kids took to stealing the 10-foot-long missile cradled in his arms, and now the practice has turned into an annoying—if not expensive—ritual. Wilmington, Illinois. *Shellee Graham ©1995*

Grand Canyon Caverns is an underground cave attraction that has really nothing in common with its famous namesake. Located about 200 miles from the real Grand Canyon between Seligman and Kingman, Arizona, it's a popular roadside stop for tourists making their way across the desert on the old cut of Arizona Highway 66. A huge statue of Tyrannosaurus Rex serves as the tourist magnet and an underground tour and gift shop the entertainment. East of Peach Springs, Arizona. *Shellee Graham ©1995*

to all: In the decade following World War II, the suspension of all gasoline rationing and the production of bigger, better motorcars equated to a renewed level of mobility. Young dreamers who did without were now coming of age and taking to the highways to make their own memories. Highway volume increased so much that by the close of the 1940s, the demand for sentimental sundries spurred a handful of hopefuls in Arizona and New Mexico to jump in with full-scale retail operations.

Before tourists could hide their wallets, savvy salesmen were recruiting the local Indian crafts people and scouring trade shows for desirable products. Itching to cash in on the coast-to-coast commuter, elaborate merchandising markets—or "trad-

ing posts" as they were called—were established at various points along Highway 66. The outskirts of major population centers in the Southwest got more than their fair share, followed by adjoining states and other regions in the Ozarks. In the postwar era, taking a trip down the Will Rogers Highway meant trading with the Indians.

For the vacationing family motoring out to view the wonder of the Painted Desert, trading posts were found to exhibit even more color. The fierce competition for customers ignited an endless duel to install the most saturated neon sign, construct the

most colossal fantasy figure, or splash exteriors with the most garish paints. In most instances, all of the outside walls facing the highway became the canvas for a visual sales spiel. Three-foot-high lettering trumpeted an outfit's name as hanging sign boards (edged in jagged cuts) announced the collection of goods inside.

While the visual pulling power of the Geronimo trader had most of the nearby setups licked, one local competitor came up with a way to influence the customer hundreds of miles before they even crossed into the Grand Canyon State. James Taylor, operator of the Jackrabbit Trading Post, joined forces with Wayne Troutner (legendary owner of Winslow's Store for Men) and traveled Highway 66 on a all-out mission to advertise. Armed with a truckload of signs—bright yellow Jackrabbit signs—he plastered as much of the American roadside as possible with his namesake!

It was a hands-on approach to advertising that over the years fired up motorists' imaginations and developed an invaluable aura of mystery for his merchandising market. At the same time, it heightened the Jackrabbit's status as a Route 66 legend—fueling the interest of vacationers willing to go out and find it. One way or another, cars would eventually drive up to the Jackrabbit

During the 10-year span from 1925 through 1934, California led the way with programmatic architecture. The Mother Goose Pantry "restaurant in a shoe" was perhaps the most memorable of this design discipline, offering sit-down dining to customers inside of a replica brogue. Route 66 patrons of the late 1920s had the choice of consuming their lunch in the lower eating area of the shoe or taking the stairs to an elevated dining room. 1929 East Colorado Boulevard, Pasadena, California. *Preziosi Postcards*

Howdy Hank's was a Route 66 trading post that got its start as the Hopi Village. This whimsical character adorned the exterior wall and greeted customers in search of souvenirs. When Howdy Hank's changed ownership and was later reopened as Sitting Bull's Indian store, the future for this friendly wall painting was uncertain. By the time Sitting Bull ceased operations, the paint was already fading and beginning to peel. When a feed store took up residence and the walls were repainted, all evidence of the smiling cowpoke was hidden. Another of the unique sights along 66 had run out of time. Joseph City, Arizona, 1988. *Jerry McClanahan ©1995*

22

Trading Post. Painted in bold letters on a yellow slat billboard, a final exclamation greeted sojourners with a pithy "Here It Is." Perched atop the sign, a silhouette of an immense jackrabbit and a row of companion bunnies caught the eye of passing traffic. Of course, the three-foot-high composition jackrabbit (with yellow eyes) positioned at the front gate didn't hurt business. That was the real magnet for the kids.

In addition to memorable mascots and searing color schemes, most of the souvenir supershops borrowed extensively from Native American heritage. The connection became most obvious in their practical architecture: Influenced by the Iroquois style long house and the rectangular motifs of the Hopi pueblo, trading posts were typically long, low, flat-roofed structures constructed of cinder-block walls and finished

In Oklahoma, many closed portions of the old road may be traveled along the frontage of the new highway. While roadblocks, a lack of bridges, and removed sections of roadbed discourage any real long-distance exploring—the segments that do remain conjure up a sense of time and place unknown along the modern superhighway. Near Bristow, Oklahoma. *Author*

The Elusive Meteorite of Barringer's Crater

"Despite his inability to locate the mother of all space rocks . . . Barringer made believers out of the skeptics who ridiculed his earlier theories."

*T*he biggest Route 66 attraction is not a building, not an animal farm, not a souvenir stand, nor a restaurant. It's a natural formation, an oversized hole in the ground known as Meteor Crater, located south of the old road between Flagstaff and Winslow in Leeup, Arizona. Created more than 49,000 years ago when prehistoric man was just beginning to experiment with the possibilities of the wheel, it has been a popular "roadside" attraction ever since.

While Indians roaming the region have recognized the landmark for well over 1,500 years (some have even linked it with their tribal customs and legends), early explorers of the American West formally "discovered" the gargantuan gash around 1871. White men hastily named it "Coon Butte" and just as recklessly began to propagate unfounded theories as to its origin. At first, all logical reasoning pointed to the possibility of volcanic activity. It was said that the violent release of subterranean steam and other gases blew the colossal cavity into creation.

However, most of these uninspired explanations were dismissed when Philadelphia mining engineer Daniel Moreau Barringer took possession of the crater in 1902. In the desert territory around the site, he discovered a profusion of metallic meteorites—ranging from pea-sized bits to shards larger than a marble. Concurrently, rare minerals such as coesite and stishovite were unearthed throughout the zone of impact. Convinced that an immense object from another world was the cause of these aberrations, he filed for a mining claim to explore the site.

For the next 25 years, he embarked on a relentless campaign of scientific study to prove that the crater was formed by the impact of a meteoric mass. He began his quest by searching for what he believed to be an immense ore body—a galactic treasure buried deep beneath the desert floor. If unearthed, it would be the largest (and most valuable) meteorite ever discovered by man. Taking into account the specimen's publicity value and importance in scientific circles, conservative estimations valued the find in excess of $1 billion.

Much to Barringer's chagrin, the task of ferreting out the whereabouts of the suspect "fragment" wasn't as simple a task as he had hoped. Erroneously, he had made the assumption that the space stone had fallen from the heavens on more or less a straight course. Because of this innocent miscalculation, his excavation at the center of the crater yielded nothing more exotic than dirt. Undaunted, Barringer and team continued prospecting—confounded by the disappointing progress of the drilling.

Eventually, Barringer came to the realization that the asteroid might have entered the Earth's atmosphere at a more acute angle. But if so, would it still have created the same kind of circular cavity? A simple experiment consisting of a rifle bullet fired into a patch of mud yielded the answer: Yes, high speed objects entering the soil from a shallow trajectory do produce impact craters with round characteristics. All this time, he was prospecting for the elusive hunk of iron at the wrong coordinates!

During the twilight of the 1940s, an imposing stone structure built by Daniel Moreau Barringer stood sentinel atop a nearby hill, about 1/2 mile east of the Route 66 junction with Meteor Crater Road (north of the present-day crater exit on Interstate 40). Although the view from this lookout was less-than-ideal, the castle-like monument was touted as the "Meteor Crater Observatory." Inside, a quarter allowed access to the narrow stairs that led to the top of a viewing tower. Up above, both young and old gazed at the wonders through a telescope! In the distance, one could see Meteor Crater all right—and on a clear day, even the jagged peaks of Moon Mountain (the highest point of the crater's blasted rim) were visible. But that was only part of the fun: During twilight, the nearby Painted Desert came alive with color. As coyotes yipped in celebration, the peaks of the San Francisco mountains bid farewell to the sun while the Hopi Mesas tucked themselves in for the night. Near Meteor Crater, Arizona. *Courtesy Paul Taylor*

With this new nugget of information, puzzling measurements began to make sense. Now, there was good reason for the horizontal rock formations on the south wall to be canted upwards 100 feet higher than outcroppings on the rim. In earnest, new drilling was initiated on the southeast side. When the bit seized up at a depth of 1,376 feet, there was renewed hope. Was it jammed between hard chunks of meteor? Barringer never found out. He had already spent $600,000 on the obsession and was forced to discontinue in 1929 when funds ran out.

Despite his inability to locate the mother of all space rocks, the undertaking proved to be a success. In the end, Barringer made believers out of the skeptics who ridiculed his earlier theories. He passed away that same year, canonized as the world's first person to demonstrate that large chunks of matter occasionally intersect the Earth's orbit . . . and slam right into it. But even more important, he gained respect for his hypothesis that

in stucco. Ornamentation and decoration were kept to a bare minimum.

Ten miles west of Winslow, Arizona, Ray Meany's fabulous Hopi House set the standard for architectural aesthetics. Made of adobe set in mud mortar, it was a design that featured exposed roof timbers, an exterior staircase, and a restrained application of flamboyant advertising. With most of the tourist markets along Highway 66 designed for maximum flash, Meany's multi-level trading complex was a tasteful exception to the rule.

Despite the rare operators who showed restraint, showmanship ruled the road: At Winslow's Big Indian Trading Post, a three-story representation of an angry, tomahawk

Meteor Crater remains a bona fide tourist attraction and oddity on old Route 66. It's a natural landmark that strikes to the very heart of human vulnerability and pulls the cosmic rug right out from under those who view it. For potential visitors traveling along 66 during the heyday, the idea of an immense meteor hole was reason enough to stop their cars. From Chicago to Santa Monica--and all points in between--tourists arrived by automobile to witness the results of nature's fury (and to buy a few mementos). **Leeup, Arizona.** *Courtesy Jerry Keyser and Guy Kudlemyer*

a gigantic nickel-iron asteroid zooming in from outer space at more than 100 times the velocity of a bullet tore out half a billion tons of rock from the Arizona plain.

Years later, additional expeditions aimed at finding the physical remnants of the main mass met with similar defeat. Only when sophisticated measuring devices employing electronic sensors were brought in did evidence of the giant meteorite surface. Ironically, 10 percent of the object was located under Meteor Crater's south rim—exactly where Daniel Moreau Barringer was forced to discontinue his search.

During the early 1920s, when portions of road that were to become Route 66 were yet unpaved, motorists passing through New Mexico could routinely view native architecture. In 1923, the village of Acoma, New Mexico, existed as one of the oldest inhabited pueblos in the United States. *National Archives*

25

wielding chief (sporting a feathered head-dress and a full complement of war paint) nonchalantly rested his arm on a rooftop sign. Tepee Curios in Tucumcari, New Mexico, grafted one-half of a Plains Indian dwelling (outlined with neon tubing) onto its streetside facade. Car customers attracted by the curious sight entered through the pulled-back flap that led them to a standard-sized door opening.

In Lupton, the Tomahawk Trading Post billed itself as the last stop out of Arizona and took Indian weaponry to the extreme. In the parking lot, a massive sign depicting an idealized tomahawk loomed high above multiple lanes of gas pumps. In the "stone" portion of the giant ax, numerals were posted to alert all those zooming past of discount gasoline sold at "truckers' prices."

Inside the trading posts, the atmosphere often matched the excitement of the exterior. Everything under the desert sun was available for purchase. Jewelry was a mainstay, including handmade designs from Navajo and Zuni craftsmen. One could purchase elaborate squash-blossom necklaces, earrings, bracelets, strings of beads, belt-buckles—anything and everything that could hold a chunk of polished turquoise. The Big Arrow trading post in Houck, Arizona, even featured a line of "Squaw Dress Originals by Arlene!"

For the discriminating consumer, there were woven Indian blankets and rugs, tom-toms, belts, purses, and the ubiquitous

26

The Blue Whale used to be one of those Route 66 attractions that really packed 'em in. Hugh Davis built the whale for his wife, Zelta, and presented it to her as a wedding present in the early 1970s. Set in a spring-fed lake on their property, the whale was originally intended for the enjoyment of family members only. After local kids kept sneaking in for a dip, Davis hired some lifeguards, opened a small snack stand, and began charging a nominal fee for admission. Visitors loved to climb in and out of its grinning mouth and clamber through the portholes in its side. Inside, a ladder led to a loft. At the rear, a diving board allowed the daring to flip off from the tail. Families could pitch tents on the shore and picnic at concrete tables installed around the banks. Unfortunately, the park closed in 1988 when it became too much to handle. *Author*

genuine leather moccasins. For those restricted by budget, miniature cacti, saguaro preserves, and chunks of petrified wood provided shopping satisfaction. Even the children were accommodated with an assortment that rivaled the most modern toy store. Aisles stocked to the brim with tin toys, reproduction bow and arrow sets, cowboy clothes, six-shooter cap guns, wind-up drummers, feathered headbands, and articulated wood rattlesnakes were the reasons kids in the backseat begged their parents to stop!

Sometimes, the parents needed no prodding when it came to visiting the tourist traps—especially if they were the type that offered up real live Indian shows. In that department, the Cliff Dwellings Trading Post near Lookout Point, New Mexico, was one of the Route 66 favorites. There, a half-dozen authentic Indian dancers performed ceremonial routines inside a rustic stockade. Every half-hour, patrons scurried to the rear of the store to be dazzled by a boisterous demonstration of native culture. For the 1950s family trekking their way across the continent there was always ample time left in the itinerary to watch the ceremonial moves of indigenous Americans.

Unfortunately, the live Indian gala proved to be a little too disruptive for sales. While a great gimmick to pull in the crowds, it appeared that many visitors were only there to see the complimentary show. A more suitable equilibrium was attained by the trading posts when native silversmiths, rug makers, and basket weavers were hired to perform their work on site. As visitors watched skilled artisans creating the articles sold, it instilled a marked sense of value into the handmade merchandise. It was a great method of in-store promotion, since customers could be entertained

above
In the time before the fluorescent illumination of the highway billboard cluttered the roadscape, the painted advertisement gave color to city buildings. In the urban jungle, a canvas of brick often provided the perfect spot to hawk products and services. Today, these once common examples of commercial art exist only as ghosts—unexpectedly revealed when neighboring buildings are demolished and layers of paint peel. Galena, Kansas. *Author*

left
Many small towns along Route 66 rely on the agriculture business for their revenues. On their downtown side streets, it's not at all unusual to spy feed stores and related businesses advertising their wares. Stroud, Oklahoma. *Author*

The Jackalope is more than the name of a famous Route 66 trading post. It's a mythical animal—part Jack Rabbit and part antelope —a creature that has been firmly ensconced into the western myth. According to legend, the Jackalope will sing in a human voice under a full moon. This six-foot-tall model of chicken wire and fiberglass crafted by artist Nancy Lamb sits atop a Texas business once affiliated with an outfit by the same name in Santa Fe, New Mexico. South of Route 66 near Fort Worth, Texas. *Author*

as their sales resistance was being worn down. In the end, moving souvenirs—and truckloads of them—was the primary intention of the traders doing business along Route 66.

With that goal at the forefront, there was no limit to what the roadside tourist traps would do to boost business. In the Southwestern United States—where the nervous automobile traveler feared the desert and the creatures that lived there— this fact forged an unholy alliance between the highway retailer and the reptile world. By the mid-1950s, the combination curio shop and animal farm had evolved into a hybrid business that guaranteed visitors. Its drawing card? One of the most controversial highway hypes devised by man: the snake-pit!

For farm-raised midwesterners, travelers from the East, and folks who just plain didn't get out much, nothing back home could compare to "Reptile Gardens," the ultimate trading post and slither house located in Bluewater, New Mexico. Billed as the "largest rattlesnake trading post" along the entire length of 66, it housed under one roof all the cold-blooded creatures that anyone would ever want to view during an entire lifetime!

Leading the exotic entourage, a King Cobra 15 feet long occupied the center ring, accompanied by an immense python weighing in at a whopping 200 pounds! As sideshow filler, an amazing assortment of cobras imported from India, Malaysia, and Sumatra were put on public display. Crowds marveled

America's Heyday for Hood Ornaments

"Vehicle designers combined a variety of figurals with the car radiator, crowning unadorned reservoirs of coolant with decorative 'what-nots.'"

Around 1,200 B.C., the shipbuilders of ancient Greece tipped the long, curved bows of their seagoing ships with carved figureheads. So did the Vikings of Scandinavia, crowning the keels of their oar boats with chiseled dragon heads and other creatures. It was a practice that continued well into the 19th century, when ocean vessels were routinely adorned with curvaceous mermaids and other buxom beauties.

Unfortunately, when the era of clipper ships concluded, so ended the reign of the nautical mascot. Or so everyone thought. With the advent of the motorcar, the brazen sea statues once secured to a ship's hull were reincarnated atop the hood of an automobile! Vehicle designers combined a variety of figurals with the car radiator, crowning unadorned reservoirs of coolant with decorative "what-nots." Suddenly, the exposed radiator cap became the focal point for automotive personalization!

At first, the motoring mascots were simple. Made of cheap pot metal, the earliest examples represented brand marques and logos and were introduced by a variety of car manufacturers and supply companies. Speed became the predominant theme, with winged creatures of all sorts taking perch upon the engine cowling. Projecting an aura of strength became a favorite notion as well, accomplished by affixing animal miniatures to one's vehicle. Lions, tigers, bears, and bulls were preferred. Curiously enough, any object that could be readily converted into a hood ornament became fair game, including a pair of bronzed baby shoes!

During the Art Nouveau period of the mid-1920s, French artist René Lalique fueled the mania for mascots by mating the essence of motoring's golden era with the opulent age of elegance. His first commercial entry into the genre was a piece called "Five Chevaux" (Horses), a transparent crystal decorative crafted for French automaker Citroën in 1925. Over the next decade he fashioned over two dozen designs, choosing subjects as diverse as an eagle's head and a streaking comet! But, none compared to his streamlined "Victoire," a masterful likeness of a demigod's head representing the spirit of the wind.

Realistically, only those fortunate few who could afford a Rolls or Duesenberg had the privilege of displaying a bronze or crystal mascot. For the working Joe, humorous hood ornaments were much more appropriate—and affordable! Within this category, the selection was virtually limitless. Painted reproductions of the famous Kewpie doll, whimsical traffic cops with spinning arms, figures of Donald Duck, models of Mickey Mouse, and busts of Uncle Sam were some of the exemplars. Even Britain's bug-eyed

"Dinkie Doo" was immortalized in metal plate, along with a rogue's gallery of imps (thumbing their noses) and ghoulish skulls.

When they weren't fashioned after figures, many of the novelty ornaments were gadgets of the most inventive kind. The Wiggler Company of Buffalo introduced the "spinning rotoscope," a whirly-gig featuring four, bright red, enameled, cup-shaped discs intended to twirl in the turbulent airstream. Another unusual entry from Prossi of England depicted a scaled-down lighthouse rigged so that when the brakes were applied, a tiny searchlight was illuminated. For the early off-roaders concerned about their autos' angle of incline, the "Tel-O-Grade" indicator was invaluable. Still, none were as practical as the ingenious radiator stopper constructed to house a removable pocket watch!

Despite the preponderance of these novelty radiator finials, not all mascots were intended for simple-minded amusement. Many were designed specifically to monitor the temperature of radiator water and alert the driver to an

Motorists of the late 1920s and 1930s often adorned their motorcars with whimsical hood ornaments. This devilish imp thumbs his nose at oncoming traffic, proving that even during the 1930s automobile owners pursued their own individuality when it came to accessories. Russell Lee photo, 1939. *Library of Congress*

impending boil over. The Moto-Meter Company, Inc., of Long Island City, New York, manufactured some of the most widely purchased models during the 1920s and 1930s under its "Boyce Motometer" brand. Attached to the radiator, both the "Senior" and "Junior" versions featured a diminutive thermometer set within a circular housing. For the driver with good vision, a translucent cut-out (positioned over the "normal" range) allowed visual monitoring right from the comfort of one's front seat.

As the philosophy of streamlining began to redefine the shape of the motorcoach during the 1940s, the craze for hood ornaments subsided. The radiator itself was no longer an exterior design element. Now, it was hidden under a shroud of sheet metal beneath the hood. The celebrated radiator cap—once the primary point of attachment for the motoring mascot—was out of sight and out of mind. Decorative embellishments were no longer necessary.

Some of the first hood ornaments possessed a dual function quite important to the automobile owner: They gave one's flivver a distinctive look, while at the same time monitoring the water temperature in the radiator. The Moto-Meter Company of Long Island City, New York, supplied many of these devices to the consumer, its Boyce Motometer Universal Model one of the most common. Eagle's wings were, of course, optional. *Author*

Ray Meany's "Fabulous" Hopi House set the architectural standard for all other Route 66 trading posts. Constructed from adobe set in mud mortar, it was an eye-catching design that featured exposed roof timbers, an exterior staircase, and a restrained application of advertising. While most of the tourist markets along Route 66 were designed for gaining maximum attention through garish design, Meany's multilevel complex was a tasteful exception to the rule. Located 10 miles west of Winslow, Arizona, on Route 66, it was a complete tourist stop with coffee shop, motel, and Texaco-branded service station. *Preziosi Postcards*

below
Over the years, souvenir, curio, and gift shops located in the Southwestern states have borrowed extensively from the Native American heritage. In one form or another, the teepee and other Indian designs have found themselves incorporated into the visual front of many commercial structures. 924 East Tucumcari Boulevard, Tucumcari, New Mexico. *Preziosi Postcards*

at the sight of a Green Mamba, a hideous Gila monster, and dozens of fresh, squirming rattlesnakes! As a matter of course, most tourists checked their shopping bags for stowaways upon departure.

Unfortunately, the appeal of the snake shows wasn't enough to sustain the merchants when the Great Highway fell from prominence. With a growing addiction to shopping malls, franchised hamburger stands, thematic amusement parks, video games, and cruise control, the modern motorist began to view the quirky wayside attractions of yesterday's roadways as so

below
Since the days of dirt roads and wagon trains, Texas has promoted itself as being home to the biggest and the best. While there is some truth to the claim, souvenir postcards have always inflated that claim and taken it to the extreme. Stocked in curio shops along Texas 66, it wasn't at all unusual to see longhorn cattle depicted on the cards as elephantine giants, grasshoppers mutated to horse stature, and Jackrabbits big enough to ride. *Author*

much hokum. As vacationers' focus on destinations increased, interest in trading posts and other homespun attractions diminished. As the headlong rush to "get there" edged out simple enjoyment of the motor trip, the sights found along the way became a moot point.

At the same time, the concept of "entertainment" was being redefined by the flicker of images on a cathode-ray picture tube. Television had arrived with a vengeance, embracing the western myth with such vigor that within a few short years, the "home where the buffalo roam"

Trading posts along Route 66 often changed owners faster than you could fill up a water bag. Consider the establishment begun as Hopi Village: When the original owners sold out, the trading trap reopened as Howdy Hanks. Later, when Hank decided to get out of the trinket business, Sitting Bull's Indian Store became the new name. Evidence of multiple owners could be seen in the colorful advertising signs. The little men that were once astronauts were simply repainted to look like whimsical Indians! Sitting Bull quit the business, too, and the structure is now a feed store. Joseph City, Arizona, 1988. *Jerry McClanahan ©1995*

had been relieved of its mystique. Jaded by the endless shows, the sophisticated tourist was more concerned about whether the motel room off the next exit ramp came equipped with a television set rather than real hickory furniture.

As the high-speed interstates sucked the lifeblood from Route 66, the once bustling ribbon of road became nothing more than the molted skin of a bygone era. By the 1970s, the countrywide implementation (and completion) of the

Drive-in movies used to be a big part of getting your kicks on Route 66. Out near Barstow, California, where the old road runs along the Mojave River, remnants of the past still remain for those who take the time to look. This was the section of two-lane bypassed—and effectively put out of business—when Interstate 15 was constructed between the towns of Barstow and Victorville. Route 66, Lenwood, California. *Jim Ross ©1995*

continued on page 38

Totem Pole Park Was Nathan Galloway's Gift

"His contribution to humanity was a totem pole—a concrete-and-wire masterpiece built with an amalgam of sweat, ingenuity, and determination."

*N*athan Edward Galloway didn't discover the cure for the common cold, invent a machine to spin gold, or negotiate successfully for world peace. His contribution to humanity was a totem pole, a concrete-and-wire masterpiece built with an amalgam of sweat, ingenuity, and determination—its sole intention to make the everyday lives of people a little more enjoyable.

It was a practice that Galloway had a lot of experience with. For 22 years, he perfected his "habit of giving" as instructor of industrial arts for the Charles Page Home for Widows and Orphans in Sand Springs, Oklahoma. On a daily basis, he parceled out his precious nuggets of talent. When not guiding others, he crafted three-dimensional works for his own satisfaction, including animal sculptures, intricate pictures of wood inlay, and even violins. True to his thoughts that "the way to open doors for people is to make them something," many of these one-of-a-kind works were bestowed upon friends and acquaintances.

On days off, all of his extra time was used to develop the plot of land he owned four miles from Foyil, Oklahoma. Right alongside the unpaved cut of 28A, he continued to create—building a country home made of native stone. Six years of weekends were used laboring over the rock rambler—refining plans, fitting stones, and cutting trees. As the rustic habitat neared its completion in 1938, Galloway retired from teaching and moved with his wife to this former hobby site in rural Rogers County.

Not content to ease back in a rocking chair, his "retirement" marked the beginning of great accomplishments in the art field. Rather than continue with his usual crafts, he decided to concentrate on an idea that he had been puttering around with over the last 12 months: an immense, multistory totem pole—positioned right near the road! Motorists would be able to view it from their cars at any hour of the day, seven days a week, without charge.

It was an ambitious project to say the least. Surplus wire rescued from the railway in Sand Springs was combined with other reinforcing to form a working skeleton. In all, over six tons of steel were used to make the internal superstructure. On this bracing, Galloway hand-plastered a mortar mix that required 28 tons of cement. From a nearby creek, over 100 tons of sand and rock were hauled with a five gallon bucket!

Because specialized tools for his unique method of carving were not available, he employed some old-fashioned ingenuity to devise his own instruments from scrap metal and wood. While preliminary sculpting of the foundation's "turtle" was done with ease, carving complex reliefs near the pinnacle required more bravado. As the design stretched ever skyward, reaching the 90-foot mark with building materials proved a problem. As always, Galloway met the challenge and constructed a handy system of scaffolding and pulleys to hoist himself up!

In spite of his homemade fixtures and sometimes eccentric construction methods, the towering monolith emerged as Galloway's ultimate creation. On the exterior, 200 detailed carvings paid homage to a hodgepodge of famous Indian chiefs, mythical raptors, familiar flowers, fanciful fish, and other symbols. A bright rainbow of paint provided the finishing touch. Inside the tapered spire, murals depicting memorable events through history adorned the walls.

After eleven years, the nine-story, five-level totem pole was completed! Next, a twelve-sided edifice resembling an Indian hogan was built—providing "museum" space to house some 300 fiddles Galloway had already carved (each from a different type of wood). For lunching tourists, a whimsical road-

Edward Nathan Galloway began the construction of his giant totem pole in 1938 and finished it 11 years later. As more and more motorists took to the roads in search of recreation and adventure, it became a much-visited and admired roadside attraction and remains today as a tribute to what imagination, hard work, and purpose can achieve. Foyil, Oklahoma. *Author*

side table was crafted. To keep the totem company, a larger-than-life arrowhead (topped with weathervane) joined the menagerie of creatures in the concrete garden. Additional sculptures were planned but never built. Galloway had too many ideas left and simply not enough time to see them through.

In 1962, the artist who throughout his life petitioned others to "work on your imaginations" passed away at the age of eighty-two. On his deathbed, he summed up his attitude toward his fellow man when he wrote the words that could have well served as epitaph: "All my life I did the best I knew. I built these things by the side of the road to be a friend to you."

As a motoring Mecca for the millions of pilgrims seeking the real meaning of Highway 66, the "world's largest totem pole" has become that gift. Today, it remains an outstretched hand of friendship—put there by Edward Nathan Galloway, a folk art genius who gave himself away both in his life and in his work.

On the exterior of Ed Galloway's main totem pole, 200 detailed carvings pay homage to a hodgepodge of famous Indian chiefs, mythical raptors, familiar flowers, fanciful fish, and other symbols. A bright rainbow of paint provides the finishing touch. Inside the tapered spire, murals depicting memorable events through history adorn the walls. The totem poles are currently being restored and may still be visited. Located off of Old Route 66 on Highway 28A. Foyil, Oklahoma. *Author*

During the early 1960s, television producer Sterling Siliphant created the popular "on-the-road" program "Route 66." Featuring George Maharis and Martin Milner as two high-energy youths screaming around the countryside in an equally energetic Corvette, it epitomized the fantasy of automotive escape. From the comfort of their easy chairs, viewers across America could ride along and experience the adventures of the open road. *Personality Photos*

continued from page 35

freeways instigated by the Interstate Highway Act of 1956 brought an end to the merchandising mania of the old road. In small towns, Wal-Mart discounters usurped the obligations of the curio shops. Along the impersonal miles of the interstate, sprawling truck stops and feeding facilities assumed the responsibility of trading trinkets. Real leather products were now "crafted" in China from genuine imitation vinyl, turquoise stone became colored plastic, and the only reptiles were either flattened on the freeway or made of rubber.

A Southern Pacific railroad advertising billboard strikes an ironic contrast with a pair of migrant workers making their way along the Mother Road toward the city of Los Angeles. Down on their luck and unable to afford an automobile, many out-of-work men had no other choice but to walk during the height of the Great Depression. Dorothea Lange photo, 1937. *Library of Congress*

The Querino Canyon Trading Post is one of the ghosts of the old road decaying in Northern Arizona. Located on a stretch of road where the pavement has been removed, it's not a convenient place to stop anymore for a bottle of pop or souvenirs. The stretch of Route 66 that once ran by it has now returned to dirt. This former Chevron refueling stop was abandoned and finally burned down during the early 1990s. Querino Canyon, Arizona, 1991. *Jerry McClanahan ©1995*

Today, only a few of the tourist traps remain along the road-less-traveled. Most of the extravagant operations have long since gone out of business, their original owners retired, deceased, or disinterested. Other outfits have evolved with the times, but remain mere shadows of what they used to be. While some of the trading post structures have found new uses, the majority have been abandoned. For the adventurous motorist who steers clear of the superhighway in deference to the free road, only crumbling walls, faded murals, and fragments of neon remain as evidence of the way Americans used to get their kicks . . . on Route 66.

Miles Mahan was a retired carney and roadside character who decided to set up a little roadside "museum" along Route 66 during the 1950s. Located near Victorville, California, he called the place Hulaville and touted his big "Hula Girl" as the main attraction. Featuring an odd assortment of things he had found or visitors had left him, Mahan's unusual curiosity display was a pleasure for motorists to visit. A miniature golf course made with junk was one of the highlights, as was poet-laureate Mahan himself. Sadly, Mahan's Hulaville has become a casualty of time. Because of Mahan's advancing age and illness, the site was dismantled in 1995. Currently, the city of Victorville has most of the items packed away for safekeeping and future display. *Dan Harlow ©1995*

left
Just east of Alanreed, Texas, on the former four-lane stretch of 66 (built during the late 1940s), expansive signs once advertised all sorts of rattlesnake attractions. During the height of roadside reptile shows, the Regal Reptile Ranch was one of the most recognized. Today, the giant cobra statue that used to pull in the business holds a place of prominence in the Devil's Rope Museum of McLean, Texas. The Regal Reptile Ranch closed during the 1980s. Alanreed, Texas, 1983. *Jerry McClanahan ©1995*

During the 1950s and 1960s, the Rio Pecos Ranch Truck Terminal was one of the classic truck stops along Route 66. Out front, a gigantic neon sign featured a cartoon semi truck with an attached trailer. Up on the sign, the truck cab itself was outlined with neon tubing as were the wheels. Inside the cab sat an engaging little character that looked a lot like Howdy Doody. Santa Rosa, New Mexico, 1993. *Jerry McClanahan ©1995*

below
During the golden years of the Highway 66 trek, the Tomahawk Trading Post billed itself as "the most complete comfort stop along Highway 66." It was a claim substantiated: on the premises, a full-service filling station featured gasoline at trucker's rates and, of course, clean rest rooms. All at one stop, tourists traveling by car could eat in a restaurant, shop at a small grocery store, down beers in a cocktail lounge, and shop for curios in a well-stocked trading post. Twenty-one miles west of Gallup, New Mexico, in Lupton, it really was the first and last stop out of Arizona. *Preziosi Postcards*

Linen postcards manufactured by the Curt Teich postcard company have emerged as desirable mementos of the old road. Throughout the decades of motor travel, countless tourists purchased these colorful remembrances from curio shops, five-and-dime stores, and other roadside attractions to mail off to friends and relatives back home. With many of the original sights along the highway lost, they exist as two-dimensional time-capsules of the way things used to be along our blue highways. *Preziosi Postcards*

And Then There Were Traffic Signals

"Designed for overhead suspension on a single span of wire, the classic traffic light featured heavy-duty wiring and a cast-aluminum housing."

The world's first traffic signal flickered to life on a bustling street corner in Westminster, England, in 1868. As the story goes, horse-drawn surreys, pushcarts, pedestrians, and other vehicles were clogging the square outside the Houses of Parliament. To alleviate the crossing hazard for elected officials, signaling engineer and idea-man J.P. Knight was contracted to design and construct a device to regulate the flow.

The contraption was simple enough, appearing very much like the typical railway signal of the era. Two moveable "semaphore arms" and a small lamp compartment were mounted atop a tall pipe. A policeman was required to operate the device manually, moving the location of the alert flags by means of a mechanical linkage as well as switching the rotating, colored lenses.

During daylight, the position of the metal flags indicated whether to proceed with caution or to stop. When these flared appendages were fixed downward, persons "in charge of vehicles and horses" were to continue with care—keeping constant watch for foot passengers. Extended flags indicated the "all-stop," alerting traffic to halt and pedestrians to cross. At night, the green and red lamps took over these functions, green representing the caution and red the stop.

Members of Parliament adored the device and marveled at its seemingly flawless operation for almost a year. Then—just when it seemed the traffic problem had been licked—disaster struck. A discrepancy with the gas-illumination system caused the traffic gadget to explode, blowing both the signal device and the assigned duty officer to smithereens! After news of the tragedy spread, a lack of volunteers to operate a new signal marked the end of England's experimentation with street signals.

More than four decades later, the signal saga continued in the United States. According to one account, the first red and green traffic lights were installed in Salt Lake City by policeman Lester Wire in 1912. Even so, The American Traffic Signal Company claims that in 1914, it installed Cleveland's first electric unit (with buzzer). However, most historians give credit to inventor Garrett Morgan as Cleveland's original signal sage with his four-way creation of 1923. Regardless, the electric light replaced gas lamps in all accounts, increasing both brightness and safety.

One of America's first traffic signals appeared in the city of Detroit, Michigan, in 1914. While it was an improvement in the field of traffic control (it was really nothing more than a hand-operated "stop" light), officials still found it prudent to post a policeman with the new gadget. *Reprinted with permission of the American Automobile Mfg. Assoc.*

With the practicality of the traffic signal proven, municipalities across the nation began installing their own units. Along Fifth Avenue in New York city, gilded columns adorned with ornamental statuettes supported a trio of lights. Along the congested streets of Los Angeles, showmanship prevailed. Out there, automated traffic control went totally Hollywood and featured animated semaphore arms and clanging bells!

Despite the showy example set by America's larger cities, most towns chose to install "four-way" traffic signals. Designed for overhead suspension on a single span of wire, the classic unit featured heavy-duty wiring and a cast-aluminum housing. A quad arrangement of red, amber, and green lights (with eight-inch lenses optically engineered to inhibit reflections) allowed complete car control in all directions. From the 1930s until the 1950s, the demand from traffic departments kept manufacturers such as the Darley Company of Chicago and Eagle Signal of Moline, Illinois, busy with orders.

By the dawn of the 1960s, the increased volume of traffic on America's streets threatened the future of the four-way signal. As traffic engineers widened corridors and added turning lanes at intersections, the Federal Highway Administration revised the traffic codes. New laws called for additional signal units to be posted at all major crossings. The installation of these "dual indications" would preclude burned out bulbs or mechanical failure in a single unit.

A handful of cities circumvented the updated rules by hanging additional four-way clusters, while others dumped their "antiquated" flashers in order to collect monies offered by the Highway Trust Fund. Without concern for historic preservation or aesthetics, a majority of American municipalities went for the green and opted for the installation of updated lights. By the time motorists were stuck in long gas lines during the 1970s, most intersections were festooned with multiple constellations of lamps.

The distinctive yellow, multicolor four-way traffic light had blinked its way into obscurity, an unfortunate casualty of progress. It was now a novelty—a nostalgic relic destined for use along abandoned main streets and in towns time forgot. Quiet stretches of roadway (like old 66) became its final domain, where, swaying gently to and fro in the breeze, it continued to wink in memory of the way motoring used to be.

During the early 1910s and on into the 1920s, corduroy roads were a familiar sight for automobile owners endeavoring to cross the desert by automobile. To form a driveable surface, planks of wood were arranged in an assembled structure that sat on top of the earth. When two cars met on narrow portions of the roadbed coming in opposite directions, it was prudent to keep one set of wheels on the wood to prevent one's car from being stuck in the sand. Near Yuma, Arizona, circa 1925. *Library of Congress*

Migratory cotton pickers travel the old road to connect with Highway 99 between Tulare and Fresno, California. This driver and his family have motored the Mother Road all the way from Independence, Kansas, and have been in California for six months looking for work. When this photo was taken in 1939, the family was off to find employment chopping cotton. Merced, California, Dorothea Lange photo, 1946. *Library of Congress*

"The Route 66 Travel Game" features the smiling faces of Martin Milner and George Maharis streaking over the blacktop in a cherry Corvette convertible. Originally intended for players between the ages of 8 and 12, it was marketed by the prominent game manufacturer Transogram and was sold in toy stores when the "Route 66" television series was at the height of its popularity in the early 1960s. Inside, car-shaped game pieces and colorful play money complement a playing field that takes travelers from a garage in Los Angeles all the way to Las Vegas. In the process, towns along the length of 66 are visited, bringing monetary penalties and rewards. *Courtesy Warren Winthrop*

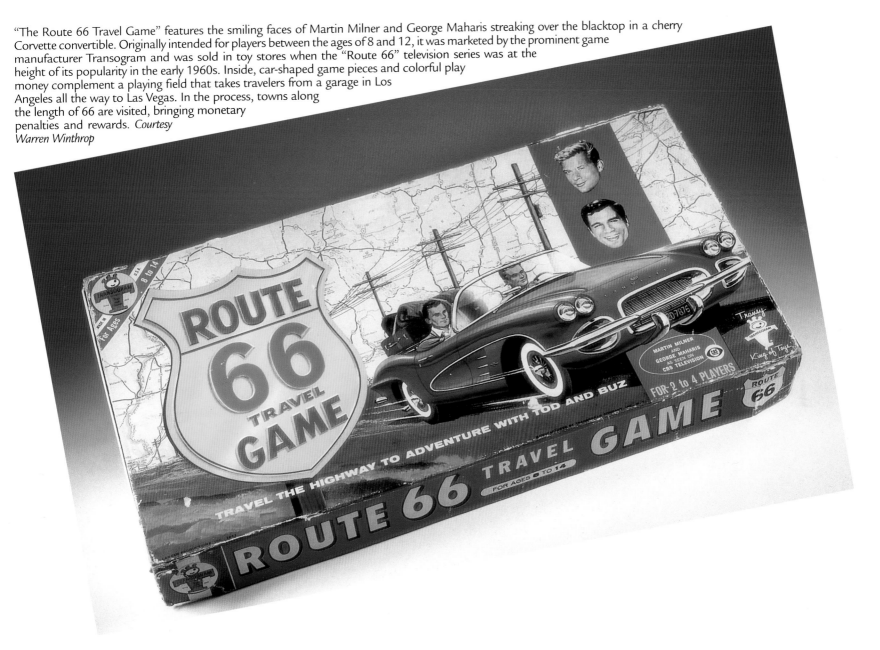

Virtually, this is how Chicago grew: around a trading-post. May it not be that new villages and towns and, ultimately, cities will grow up around some of the best located of our roadside filling stations? It is conceivable that they will, for they are generally on highways that are served by modern bus transportation, swift and flexible. And near many of them flat fields are available for airports. A center need no longer be located on a railroad in order to develop into an important spot on the map. Watch the roadside filling stations of America . . . many of them may even now be cities in embryo."

—The Literary Digest, "Filling Stations as Embryo Cities," 1930

Filling Stations:
Highway Pump and Circumstance

In 1904, Missouri motorists who sought adventure out along the "Old Wire Road" faced considerable adversity. That year, the U.S. Office of Road Inquiry reported that out of the 2,151,570 miles of roads nationwide, 93 percent were comprised entirely of dirt. The passage winding its way south from St. Louis to Joplin was no exception. Nothing more than a cleared course with soil at its base, it was a path frequented by horse-drawn carriage, delivery wagon, or other conveyance pulled by animal power.

A clean windshield has always been a primary concern for the motorist traveling by automobile over Highway 66. During the 1940s, service stations still had an emphasis on "service." A large part of that service was washing, drying, and buffing the window glass to a sparkling sheen. Cairo, Illinois, Arthur Rothstein photo, 1940. *Library of Congress*

left
During the early years of the horseless carriage, the country store was one of the businesses where motorists could purchase gasoline. Along with soap powder, grain, biscuits, and thread, the owners of a motorcar could stop in front of a tall, visible-register gasoline pump and have their tank refilled. Because fledgling oil companies didn't want to spend the huge amounts of capital required to obtain real-estate, existing retail operations were solicited to sell motor fuel and associated products. It was a system that worked—until competition necessitated the move to an arrangement that catered strictly to the automobile. Soon, specialized structures like this modern Phillips station of the 1950s housed power lifts, mechanics, and car accessories all under one roof. Route 66, 36th and Shartel, Oklahoma City, Oklahoma. *Courtesy Phillips Petroleum Company*

47

For the automotive enthusiast, driving this future alignment of Highway 66 was arduous. Jagged rocks and other road hazards wreaked havoc on fragile balloon tires. When the rains came, wheels tilled the unprotected roadbed into a treacherous bog of mud. In the frenzy to keep rolling, axles snapped, radiators bubbled over, and engines blew up. At the turn of the century, transportation corridors were ill-suited for the horseless carriage.

To make matters worse, service amenities were scarce. Carriage works had headquarters in larger cities, as did the livery stables and bicycle shops that often carried car accessories sought by the motoring crowd. Because there were no specialized car repair garages to speak of, vehicle owners were required to be mechanical experts. Fixing an automobile between towns was a frequent occurrence. Still, the ingenuity of the motorcar operator could only go so far. A motor might very well be repaired en route if it failed—but when the fuel supply in one's gasoline tank dipped below a safe level, nothing more could be done. Since the average motor coach of the age could only travel about 70 miles on a full tank of gas, an additional canister filled with an emergency supply of fuel was always carried along. A second tin of lubricating oil was usually stored under

Vintage gasoline dispensers are becoming an extremely rare commodity along our modern roadscape. Suddenly, yesterday's machinery has become tomorrow's treasure—a fact of life dictating the hasty removal of anything and everything deemed valuable from the narrow shoulders lining this nation's asphalt. This dispenser pumped fuel (for station use only) at the Wagon Train Automotive shop near Cajon Pass, California. *Jerry McClanahan ©1995*

the seat. Once these reserves were consumed, luck—or clever timing—played a large part in completing the journey.

To enable automobile owners to experiment with their "horseless car-

Pie Town, New Mexico, is a small community south of the old road that was settled by about 200 migrant Texas and Oklahoma farmers who filed homestead claims. During the 1940s, the automotive stage run by Santa Fe Trail Stages, Inc., was a vital transportation link to the outlying towns along Route 66. Here, the post office served as place to refuel, catch a ride, and mail a letter. Russell Lee photo, 1940. *Library of Congress*

riages," small quantities of gasoline were sold in pre-filled containers at drugstores, general merchandise suppliers, blacksmith shops, and other vendors in major cities like Missouri's Stanton, Waynesville, and Carthage. But unlike the modern service station markets of today, retailers that stocked motor fuel were in business mainly to sell other products—gasoline was an insignificant sideline. Motoring

49

was still considered a pastime for those with money to burn.

In most instances, the enthusiastic car lover turned to an operation known as the "bulk depot." In a commercial setting, the major oil refiners sold a variety of processed petroleum products—including kerosene, axle grease, motor oil, and gasoline. Usually situated in the sparsely populated area of town near the railroad tracks or on the outskirts, they were more sympathetic to the awkward task of refilling an automobile's fuel tank. No one raised a concern over a gasoline-stained driving coat or boots splattered with oil. Since most of the business was conducted on an outdoor lot in the open air, appearances didn't matter.

At the bulk depot, motor spirits were stored in a large cylindrical storage vessel perched atop a wooden support structure. To refill a car's gas tank, a depot operator—who wasn't afraid to soil his trousers—drained gas into a portable can of five gallons or less provided by the car owner. Gingerly, this canister was carried to the parked vehicle. Next, one

above
In a scene straight out of *The Grapes of Wrath*, a migrant farm worker from Chickasaw, Oklahoma, is stalled in the Southern California desert with no money, no extra gasoline, and no prospect for work. He and his 10 children are facing an unknown future in the fields of California. Dorothea Lange photo, 1937.
Library of Congress

Although the introduction of the visible register gas pump was an improvement over "blind" pumps, they were still subject to cheating. Disreputable stations doing business in tourist trap towns could readily place a brick or other object in the tank, inflating gallon readings to the operator's advantage. More sinister schemes included the misalignment of the measuring rack or improper numbering. Still, customers had certain advantages as well: During the heat of the day, warm motor fuel would register higher in the tank. As a result, it was advantageous to fill up in the cool of the morning and get the most volume for one's money.
Courtesy Tokheim Corporation

The Rest Haven Motor Court is a typical example of the tourist court and gas station combination so prevalent during the 1940s and 1950s. No doubt, the gleaming box-style Phillips station was the first structure built, followed by rows of overnight cabins. With five gasoline pumps and an interior gift shop taking the place of the usual auto accessories, it was obviously an outfit designed for maximum revenue and product turnover. Springfield, Missouri. *Preziosi Postcards*

The Hi-Line Modern Motor Court was located where U.S. 66 meets U.S. 89 in Ashfork, Arizona. This advertising postcard touted "New, strictly modern cottages with and without equipped kitchenettes." Of course, tiled showers and closed, attached garages made staying overnight a joy. Twin Wayne 60 gasoline pumps and a matching Art-Deco sign pulled in customers low on gasoline. *Courtesy Chuck Sturm*

assistant steadied a large funnel on the filler tube and helped to guide the liquid into the tank. To trap sediment and other debris, a second helper thrust a piece of chamois or other makeshift filter over the funnel. A third person tipped the storage can and with great care, began pouring the precious gasoline into the automobile.

Because there was no accurate method devised to alert the pourer as to when he should stop, fuel spilled over hands and clothing and often onto the automobile itself. Wooden measuring sticks marked with indications gauged to a handful of popular tank sizes helped, while at the same time creating more peripheral equipment prone to accidental ignition. Patrons

Pay Less for Gas at Hedges

GAS
25½ 28½ 30½

HEDGES OIL CO.

WE HONOR ALL OIL COMPANY CREDIT CARDS

FISHING TACKLE LICENSE

FISHING SUPPLIES LICENSES

REG. 28½

GAS 25

The Hedges Oil Company chain of gas stations had a small network of 16 gasoline stations in major New Mexico cities. With heavily discounted prices and clean rest room lounges for the ladies, they did a thriving business during the postwar surge of vacations taken by automobile owners. Albuquerque, New Mexico. *Preziosi Postcards*

careless with an open flame caused horrific fires, greatly limiting the appeal of motoring to a brave minority.

Thankfully, progress was being made to replace this crude refueling method of "drum and measure." The changes began almost one year after the Office of Road Inquiry's report when entrepreneurs Clem Laessig and Harry Grenner debuted a radically new type of fuel depot in 1905. They called their operation the Automobile

Gasoline Company and began recruiting customers motoring in and out of the bustling trading hub of St. Louis.

Their location would prove to be a good one: the meandering telegraph route that was to be designated as part of the Ozark Trails (and later Highway 66) was nearby. It was a perfect location to get the attention of the growing legions of car owners taking to the roads. As the popular bromide of the time boasted:

The American roadways have always been rich with signs and billboards attempting to capture the motorist's attention. When these painted message boards fail to shock or amuse, one of the last methods they employ is an appeal to the pocketbook—a direct hit for many travelers motoring long-distances on a budget. Attention-grabbing slogans such as "Never Undersold" or "Our Prices Can't Be Beat" play on the price-conscious driver, already low on cash from the gouging experienced at the overpriced greasy spoons and motels along the route. For the harried traveler, it's often hard to compare prices when far from home. When the fuel gauge drops below the empty mark and the kids in the backseat are crying for a rest room, the world of choices found along the road shrinks to what's accessible within the next two miles. Santa Fe, Dorothea Lange photo, 1938. *Library of Congress*

Al Bell's Fantastic "Flying A" Filling Station

"Beneath the glow, the promised land of petroleum awaited new arrivals—complete with four service islands, twelve fuel pumps, and five drive-through lanes."

*F*or travelers cruising into Kingman on a hot summer's eve, Al Bell's "Flying A" Service Station appeared to be a roadside apparition—one that belonged more on the Las Vegas strip than the quiet community of Hilltop, Arizona. The reason? A double-sided, 209-bulb, show-stopping sign featuring a swooping arrow lit with sequential flashers. Below, blazing tubes of neon announced the promise of refreshment to desert drivers. "Jugs Iced Free" really hooked them in!

From Memorial Day until the last week of September, the elevated sparkler illuminated the Arizona nights. Luckily, Bell worked out a deal with his oil supplier to cover the cost of the staggering electric bill. It proved a beneficial arrangement, since the three story signpost pulled over $150 worth of raw current in just one month! A more power-hungry (or memorable) marquee could not be found along the entire expanse of the Will Rogers Highway.

During the dog days of summer, hundreds of vehicles in need of service were drawn by the sight—many coasting in on fumes and a prayer. Beneath the glow, the promised land of petroleum awaited new arrivals—complete with four service islands, twelve fuel pumps, and five drive-through lanes. Four attendants decked out with bow ties and white overalls (names embroidered on the breast pocket) serviced the cars simultaneously. While the first pump jockey inquired whether he could "fill it with 100-plus octane," a second lad proceeded to wipe the windows crystal clear. Meanwhile, a third checked the tire pressure as the fourth topped off the crankcase.

As the ultimate in American gas station service was being perfected, Bell's young son Bob sprinted out to the driver's side window and poked in his head. "Got any jugs you want iced?" A heavy-duty York ice machine cranked out the precious cubes at the steady rate of 450 pounds per day—providing a summer job for the enthusiastic Little Leaguer. In exchange for tips, he began toting the frozen crystals to the cars when he was only nine years old and worked every season until high school graduation.

Bob Boze Bell recalls those days with fondness: "What was amazing about working at the station was that everybody during the 1950s was bound for California. Many thought it was the promised land out there. You could see it in their eyes. During July, it was around 103 degrees in Kingman and they would all get out of their cars wilted from the heat and ask, 'How far to California?' I'd say, 'About 60 miles.' Almost every time, they would smile and blurt out, 'Oh . . . thank God!' Well, I didn't have the heart to tell them that 60 miles away was California all right—the inferno town known as Needles, California, one of the hottest locations on the planet other than Death Valley!"

But everybody asked those questions. What really stood out about the Flying A station was the sheer adventure of just working there. One afternoon, Bob was filling up a tank when he heard sirens. With filler nozzle in hand, he

The year was 1947 when Al Bell got hooked up with a Whiting Brothers station down in McConnico along the old road. It pumped out a fair amount of gallonage, but not enough for Bell. At the end of nine months, he mastered the refueling basics and decided to move on to a more lucrative position. A Mobil station on the Walapai Indian Reservation in Peach Springs, Arizona, became his new responsibility, this time in a leasing arrangement. A couple of tourist cabins out back provided extra income, and later—trouble. Young Bob Bell was playing where he wasn't supposed to and got his hand caught in the maid's washing machine wringer! They rushed him to the nearest doctor in Kingman and fortunately, his arm was saved. *Courtesy Allen P. Bell*

observed Floyd Cisney (local highway patrolman, Little League coach, and part-time driver in the demolition derby) pull up alongside a speeding car, pass it, and turn—forcing both vehicles off the road. "That part of 66 was a bottleneck for hot cars," remembers Bell. "Cisney held the record for nabbing stolen vehicles with over 5,000 arrests to his credit!"

For Bob's dad, the station was a rewarding adventure of another kind. In 1959, he attained his goal of bringing in $100 a day. When Tidewater Oil analyzed his receipts, they bluntly told him that he was "makin' too much money!" When their demands for new lease terms elevated into a fight, Bell walked—taking his service station savvy along with him. Another operator took control of the circuit breakers and as Bob Bell so aptly describes, "the Flying A went successfully downhill." Al Bell proved that there was much more to running a gas station than simply flicking on a flashy sign.

Eventually, Phillips Petroleum purchased the Associated Flying A stations in the West and the winged trademark glided into obscurity. But that wasn't important. The 1960s were half over, the country was undergoing radical changes, and Al Bell was retiring from the business of refueling. He was having problems with his legs and his doctor advised him to hit the bleachers.

Still, it didn't really matter that the highway was losing one of its heroes. When the implementation of freeways rerouted traffic around Kingman, the classic pumping venues were already relieved of their status as highway havens. After the great river of cars flowing along 66 reduced to a trickle, there weren't enough customers to keep the refuelers profitable. By then, classic gasoline oases typified by Al Bell's fantastic Flying A filling station were relegated to memories. The age of self-service had begun.

Working for tips, Al Bell's son, Bob, spent most of his childhood toting ice at the Flying A. Curiously enough, the pocket change paled in comparison to the goodies picked up by other means: Every other day, another customer would ask if they could trade gas for merchandise. "We're out of money and we gotta' make it to California," they all said. Bob's dad was sympathetic to their plight and always found something he could use in exchange for a tankful. The great highway brought in more stuff than could ever be imagined, including a set of WWII binoculars, cameras, a Bowie knife, drums, fishing poles . . . everything boys dream of. Kingman, Arizona. *Courtesy Allen P. Bell*

Clines Corners on Highway 66, New Mexico

"The world passes through St. Louis!" While much of that traffic was powered by beasts of burden, it would soon be dominated by the internal combustion engine. Gasoline—and large quantities of it—would be required to feed the coming onslaught of automobiles.

With experience in the business as bulk fuel distributors, Laessig and Grenner witnessed for themselves the growing demand for the "waste product" gasoline. As more and more piston-powered carriages appeared streetside, they acknowledged the limitless potential of the motorcar and endeavored to change the onerous refueling procedure.

Clines Corners is one of the oldest establishments along Highway 66. During the 1940s, it was equipped for "super service to the motoring public" and included one of the most modern cafes and curio shops. Roy Cline founded the New Mexico tourist stop back in the late 1920s. Today, it still exists as a souvenir shop and refueling oasis along 66 and features nothing more than a couple of gas stations and a sprawling gift shop. The "town" of Clines Corners is merely a place for those traveling by motorcar to stop and spend. Clines Corners, New Mexico. *Courtesy Chuck Sturm*

To achieve this goal, they devised a process that took the art of refueling to the next level: First, an upright storage vessel about the size of a small hot water heater was used to store the gasoline—fed from a larger tank nearby. This upright container was fitted with a hand-operated valve at its

base, connected to what looked very much like an ordinary "garden" hose. When a car drove in to be refueled, an employee placed the end of this hose into the customer's gas tank. Then, he opened the spigot and let gravity push fuel directly into the stomach of the famished flivver.

At long last, motorists could steer into a roadside business and have their tanks refilled without the bother associated with visiting the bulk depot. Because cars could pull up right next to the small holding tank,

Up and down the pathway of old 66, the service station attendant appeared in a variety of forms. Many donned the one-piece overall and cloth cap, while others were adorned in fancy uniforms and elaborate hats. Fifty years ago, they all had one thing in common: Take care of the customers and make sure they return. Along old 66 in Oklahoma. *Author*

metal cans once used to pour fuel remained strapped to the sideboard. The cumbersome funnel was history, along with the chamois screen that "filtered" out contaminants. Now, an integral filter system ensured that the gasoline served was pure. Missouri—and the highway that would rise to glory as America's Main Street—finally had its first real "filling station."

By the time Route 66 was officially commissioned in 1926, the filling station had evolved into a self-contained business format *continued on page 60*

Imagine pulling into a gasoline station and having your car serviced by multiple attendants! For today's jaded motorist, it's the stuff of which dreams are made. However, during the 1950s, it was no dream: Phillips stations like this classic full-server in the company territories along Route 66 sold products with an unparalleled style and grace. Wiping the windows, checking the oil, airing up the tires, and topping off the fluid in the radiator was all part of the deal. Will Rogers Airport, Oklahoma City. *Courtesy Phillips Petroleum Company*

Chronicle of the American Roadmap

"By the time the roadmap entered its heyday in the 1930s, virtually every refueling stop along Route 66 offered colorful gatefolds to its patrons."

*E*mperor Augustus of Rome knew a great road map when he saw one. Mounted on his private bedroom wall was what most historians agree constituted the most elaborate highway diagram ever created. Artfully engraved upon a sheet of hammered gold, glistening lines described the empire's entire network of transport. Principle towns were highlighted with rubies. Secondary settlements were marked with emeralds.

Though not as ostentatious, the simple road map manufactured of ink and paper was just as precious to the intrepid motorist attempting to navigate America's early trails. No self-respecting automobilist would leave civilization without one, unless he knew exactly where he was going and what facilities he could count on for gas, food, and lodging. During the early teens, crude roads or "blazed trails" were the only paths overland. Routes were poorly marked—if at all. Becoming lost out on the fringes was the rule.

Progress was made, however, when pioneering motorists with similar interests banded together. With an eye toward improving roadways and the maps that defined them, organizations such as the Automobile Association of America introduced road guides in an effort to assist members. In 1910, AAA debuted its "Official Automobile Blue Book" featuring multiple maps. These state and regional charts were well received by horseless carriage enthusiasts, despite the often arcane instructions used to guide adventurers.

With the lack of any real system to classify and designate corridors of travel, well-traveled routes were routinely navigated by means of "landmarks." Guidebooks described directions in relation to natural formations such as cliffs, boulders, and streams. These geographical features provided reliable reference points, along with man-made structures of substantial design such as buildings, bridges, or windmills.

Still, it was tough going for the motorist. Typical guide entries could alternate between clear or cryptic depending on the reference features. A typical entry might have read: "drive 6-1/2 miles, turn right at the school house, proceed 10 miles, then turn left at the stone wall." When visual aids such as directional arrows and photographs were added, the guides improved—marginally. Swelling to more than 1,000 pages with the extraneous information, impracticality soon outweighed any usefulness.

Around the same time, automobile manufacturers, tire companies, and even some motels, began passing out complimentary maps to regular customers. While less detailed than the complicated guidebooks, they were nonetheless welcomed by the motorist. After all, they were free! It didn't take long for the promotional frenzy to command the attention of petroleum refiners: In 1914, Gulf Oil joined corporate trendsetters such as White Motor and Pierce-Arrow in the practice of distributing gratuitous road diagrams.

It all started when Pittsburgh advertising guru William B. Akin advised Gulf Oil to distribute free maps to prospective customers. Executives liked the idea, and as fast as they could print a double-sided, tri-fold mailer it was delivered to 10,000 registered motorists residing in Pennsylvania's Allegheny County. Business at Gulf's drive-in service station (it was its first) boomed!

With Akin's idea proven, additional roadmaps were quickly drawn up for Pennsylvania, New York, New Jersey, and New England. A total of 300,000 were handed out to customers by Gulf's friendly service station attendants or delivered by mail.

By the time the roadmap entered its heyday in the 1930s, virtually every refueling stop along Route 66 offered colorful gatefolds to its patrons. Romanticized renderings of classic pumpers graced the covers along with exaggerated visions of powerful motorcars cresting hills and swooping through racy curves. Motorists inebriated with the thrill of driving (and purchasing gas) were depicted in their convertibles—smiling, waving, scarves flying—enjoying life to the fullest. The image of the square-jawed pump jockey was quickly becoming an American icon.

Regrettably, the colorful heyday was doomed to extinction. The famed oil embargo of the 1970s dealt the first blow with long gas lines delivering the knock-out punch. For the oil conglomerates, free maps had suddenly become an unnecessary expense, liability, even an embarrassment. Policies embracing the promotion of motoring and the massive consumption of motor fuel were suddenly no longer commercially viable. Refined gasoline was to be conserved, saved, and revered. The cartographic canvas of the free, service station roadmap was an advertising medium that had outlived its usefulness.

Automobile aficionados who found themselves traveling just south of the La Bajada Lava Cliffs during the year 1911 did not have the luxury of reaching into the glove compartment and pulling out a service station road map. During the 1910s, guidebooks detailing motoring roads were rare and many routes in remote areas were as yet, undocumented. Back then, a good sense of direction and a compass were two of the best things a vehicle owner could possess. New Mexico, A.L. Westgard photo. *National Archives*

When the roadside service station in America was in the midst of its teenage years, road maps were colorful tools intended to aid motorists with their driving pleasure. Every imaginable theme was used for artwork, including young women in beachwear. Of course, the designs never strayed from one of the most important parts of the journey: the ever-present automobile was always pictured somewhere in the foreground. **1933 Missouri Road Map.** *Courtesy Phillips Petroleum Company*

Back in the "good old days," tourists traveling the old road for pleasure relied on the service station road map to find their way. Today, the maps remain as unique artifacts of **Route 66.** *Author*

The life of Two Guns, Arizona, was directly linked with Route 66 and the amount of traffic that passed. During the zenith of highway touring in America, it was a must-see tourist attraction for vacationers, traveling salesmen, and truck drivers speeding across the country. Caged lions, bobcats, and other wild desert animals were the settlement's main drawing cards, backed up by the obligatory restaurant and filling station. After the freeways decimated the flow of cars along old 66, business dropped and eventually ended. Another highway tourist trap bit the dust. Two Guns, Arizona. *Shellee Graham ©1995*

Two Guns got its name from a man named Two-Gun Miller who claimed to be an Apache Indian. During an argument with a neighbor, he killed the man and was later acquitted of all charges. On the grave marker, friends of the dead man wrote "Killed by Indian Miller." Miller found out, got mad, and decided to put his own epitaph on the marker. Much to his chagrin, he was subsequently thrown in jail for defacing a grave. Folklore has it that he lived for years in a cave along the banks of the Canyon Diablo. Two Guns, Arizona. *Courtesy Paul Taylor*

continued from page 56

along the road. In the interim, the gasoline dispenser had progressed far from its humble beginnings. Now with a chassis made of forged steel, brass fittings, and a silhouette of

curves, it exuded a living presence! All along America's highways, the era of the "visible register" gasoline pump was beginning.

Originating from the "blind pumps" developed by inventors in the early part of the century, the visible register gasoline pump addressed many of the motorist's concerns: Customers wanted to see the gasoline that was pouring into their tank— and rightly so. For years, unscrupulous operators were rigging indicator dials to give false gallon readings and watering down motor fuel with other liquids.

With the visible register, consumer confidence blossomed. Perched high atop a

heavy base formed of cast iron, a cylindrical crucible of glass served as a transparent holding tank for gasoline. Within this elevated bowl, graduated markings "registered" (in gallon intervals) the amount of distilled liquid pumped from an underground storage tank. Motorists could actually see the product, inspect its quality, and measure its volume with their own eyes!

When the desired amount for sale was reached, the pump operator turned a lever to release the fuel. Through a flexible rubber hose, the precious fluid gurgled into the car's gas tank. For the few who remember what it was like, there was nothing like

seeing your gasoline before it was pumped into your motorcar!

With the physical and technical aspects of refueling an automobile streamlined, it was easy for anyone to get into the sales business. Free from excessive regulations

These days, classic station scenes from our roadside past are becoming more and more infrequent. Vintage Pepsi-Cola and Dr. Pepper signs like these are now treasured collectibles—along with the visible register unit still intact within this frame. Taken by photographer Harold Corsini in 1946 for Standard Oil of New Jersey, this Mannford, Oklahoma, refueling stop has seen its share of customers bound for glory on the Mother Road. *Courtesy Standard Oil (New Jersey) Co. Collection, Photographic Archives, University of Louisville.*

and licensing procedures, a prospective gasoline seller could make a deal with an oil refiner on Monday, have a trio of gasoline pumps delivered on Wednesday, and begin selling gas on Friday. As a result, proprietors made deals with multiple refiners. At certain points along Route 66, so-called "gasoline alleys" appeared overnight—distinguished by rows of gas pumps each dis-

playing a different brand of fuel. Route 66 was suddenly awash with gasoline.

Despite the mad rush to secure marketing arrangements, many gas stations decided to channel their energies into other directions. Rather than concentrate solely on the sale of gasoline (and hand over the bulk of revenues to the oil refiners), family operations found it profitable to offer food to the motorist. With customers frequently inquiring as to where one could get a good meal, many station owners began making sandwiches in back room kitchens and stocking soda pop.

Point-of-purchase items such as cigarettes and candy were added and before too long, the business that began as a filling station had evolved into a full-service cafe. By the time an expanded dining room, full-time cook, waitress, and jukebox were added to the equation, the trio of gasoline pumps that stood beneath the neon "Eats" sign were forgotten.

Some gasoline stops took notice of the lack of private roadside accommodations and decided to get into the business of lodging. Proprietors realized that there was much more to serving the vehicle owner than just offering a full tank of gasoline, quart of oil, or new fan belt. A good night's rest was an important part of completing the journey.

During the 1940s, when roadside services were not yet perfected, finding a rest room along the highway was difficult. Tourist camps were some of the first to erect public toilets for their customers—a precursor to the era when gasoline service stations would take care of the motorist's personal needs. Near the Old Road, Missouri, John Vachon photo, 1942. *Library of Congress*

The Fastest Filling Station in the West

"Capable of handling virtually any service station assignment, the rolling refueler turned every parking space into a potential garage."

*B*y the mid-1960s, the majority of refueling stops hustling gas along Route 66 shared a common denominator: They were "stations," that is fixed businesses at unchanging roadside positions. In order to get service, vehicles had to leave the road, drive across an air hose, and park near a fuel dispenser. No accommodations were made for the occasional automobile stranded miles down the road.

Enter inventor and service station proprietor Raymond Dietz of Borger, Texas. It was his position that if the customers couldn't make the trip to him, he would drive his entire station out to them! The key to this radical new strategy was a late-model, open-bed Ford Econoline van. Fitted with the latest equipment required to refuel, repair, and maintain a modern motorcar, the "Service Station on Wheels" rumbled out on its maiden voyage in early 1964. Selling gas would never be the same.

At first, the motorists moving south on state Highway 117 (on their way to Route 66) didn't know what to think of it. While the curious rescue rig appeared to be a truck, it featured an arrangement never before seen. On both body side-panels, a bold Phillips 66 insignia lent the vehicle an official air. At the same time, dual racing stripes of white and orange hinted at speed. Overhead, a small triangular canopy copied the architectural stylings of the refiner's turnpike superstations. Filling station apparatus—and plenty of it—filled the small rectangular bed space behind the driver's seat.

Bolted onto the truck bed, a full-sized gasoline pump of the Bowser brand poked up as its most prominent feature. Identical to the units installed at stationary applications, it sported a flexible hose, electric motor, and digital calculator. For extended roadside sales, two specialized storage containers held a considerable supply of gasoline. The main tank contained 110 gallons of Phillips 66 and a smaller receptacle the premium Flite-Fuel. To allow an operator to switch quickly between the different grades, a selection valve was installed.

Besides convenience, operating safety was a prime consideration of the patented gas station truck. To inhibit accidental ignition of fuel reserves, the power feed for the pump motor was located away from vapors inside the truck cab. Likewise, the external electrical terminals used for boosting batteries were controlled by a starter-relay switch designed to retard sparks.

For occasional engine or suspension work, a conglomeration of tools and other fixtures were kept on board. As a result, most malfunctions encountered along the road were easily remedied—including broken fan belts, burned-out alternators, and fouled spark plugs. For structural damage, an acetylene welding torch proved invaluable. Removing tires for the repair of punctures was assisted by a Coats Iron Tireman (attached securely to the rear tailgate). A miniature air compressor with an upright tank ensured refilling to the proper pressure.

Capable of handling virtually any service station assignment, the rolling refueler turned every parking space into a potential garage. At the same time, it became a showcase for the latest automotive products: Specialized racks fastened to port and starboard held more than 40 cans of motor oil in the one-quart size. From its well-stocked "parts department," streetside patrons could select from an eclectic mix of paraphernalia, including household cleaning fluids, furniture wax, tow chains, inner tubes, windshield wiper blades, light bulbs, and even antifreeze.

Despite this marketing bonanza, the wheeled wonder remained true to its primary directive. In the process, a priceless amount of good will and free publicity spelled the promise of new customers. It didn't take a rocket scientist to figure out that if a stranded traveler were rescued on just one occasion,

About 20 years ago, oil cans were regarded as throwaway items. Those that did survive the final cut either ended up on the workbench holding screws or as a handy canister to clean dirty paint-brushes. As time progressed, a few forward-thinking individuals realized that many of these tin containers featured pleasing graphics and corporate designs. Ever so slowly, a few eccentrics saved all the cans they could get their hands on and were soon scouring garbage dumps and other locations for new ones. As they worked their new "hobby" in secret, the interest in filling stations increased. Suddenly, collecting oil cans was no longer a fringe activity. Desirability grew as values increased. For anyone interested in American road culture, the collection of oil containers became serious business. The Red Horse Museum, Kansas. *Author*

the word of mouth spread along the motorway could be a boon for business. On the return leg of the trip through town these saved customers could show their appreciation by patronizing the main Dietz & Sons Phillips 66 service station—the one permanently anchored to the roadside at 1000 South Main Street in Borger, Texas.

As traffic trickled south on the great web of feeder roads to join with the mother motorway of the mid-1960s, countless car customers were introduced to the real meaning of gasoline service. After all, Raymond Dietz was out there—somewhere—cruising the backroads and byways in search of an empty fuel tank. With one hand laid firmly on the steering wheel and another gripped tight around a pump nozzle, he and his amazing Service Station on Wheels raced to legendary status—the fastest filling station in the West!

During the mid-1950s, Raymond Dietz operated the Service Station on Wheels and literally brought the filling station to the customer. For motorists stranded along Route 66, it was a practice that brought new meaning to the term "full service"! Borger, Texas. *Courtesy Phillips Petroleum Company*

Often using whatever materials they could find (such as native worm rock, scrap lumber, or logs), jack-of-all-trade types nailed together one or two tiny cabins out behind their station house. In short order, the duties of the gas station operator expanded well beyond the task of pump jockey to part-time bellboy. With gas tanks topped off, crankcase filled with oil, and tires inflated, tired travelers rented rooms for the night. As business from tourists increased, many of these moonlighters

developed into full-fledged motor courts—relegating the sale of refined gasoline to secondary importance.

By 1931, it was clear how much gasoline had affected the development of highway commerce: In the United States, government statistics revealed that there were a total of 110,000 roadside-stand owners in operation. Out of this number, almost all were expanded from filling stations. Gasoline was transforming the face of the American road. To some, it seemed like the

The Iceberg Cafe and Gas Station was built during the mid-1930s in Albuquerque, New Mexico, on the site currently occupied by the old Lobo Movie Theater. Just east of the University of New Mexico on East Central Avenue, it was a popular hangout for college students fond of ice cream. In the late 1930s, it was moved farther up Central to the 5300 block to make way for a new development. In 1953, it was moved again to a spot just north of Albuquerque on old Highway 85, somewhere near Bernalillo. After its final relocation, the former Route 66 landmark sat neglected for many years and was finally demolished in 1972. Albuquerque, New Mexico, Russell Lee photo, 1940. *Library of Congress*

When the "gas crisis" of the 1970s ended, many of the roadside gasoline businesses that once flourished had to close their doors permanently. Now—more than 20 years later—many of these bankrupt operations can still be found along the roadways, mere shells of their former selves. Like the ruins from a lost civilization, only crumbling brick, stone, and faded paint remain to remind us of just how quickly highway commerce can change. Moriarty, New Mexico, 1983. *Jerry McClanahan ©1995*

right
For the family off to see America on the open road, saving money on gasoline was one way to make the trip last longer. Stations such as this classic three pumper (a former motel office) were once numerous along the original alignment of the Mother Road, enticing business with nothing more than honest-to-goodness low prices. How did they do it? Volume, volume, volume! Santa Rosa, New Mexico, 1983. *Jerry McClanahan ©1995*

Midas touch of motor fuel held no boundaries for the enterprising operator.

It was a false assumption. The dominance of the individually owned, diversified gas station was destined to end. Large petroleum refiners—aided by the income derived from the outlets flooding Route 66 with gasoline—were accumulating the capital needed to buy more of their own land and build additional company-owned stations. By gaining control over the majority of their outlets, marketing strategies could be standardized on a national level.

This idea was nothing new. As early as 1914, Standard Oil of California had opened a chain of 34 stations on the West Coast. In the process, they learned that factors such as station appearance, architecture,

STANDARD OIL COMPANY OF CALIFORNIA

Standard Oil of California began its gas station operations on the West Coast in 1907. Following the lead of the Automobile Gasoline Company in St. Louis, they spread up and down the coast with small, similar-looking station huts. While basic in their design and layout, Standard Oil was the first company to make the move toward the unification of station architecture throughout a wide territory. *Courtesy Chevron Corporation*

and extra amenities related directly to brand loyalty. By combining full service with knowledgeable attendants, a refueling stop could pull in more patronage and influence its existing clientele to come back. For the small-time operator with nothing more than a shack as an office and two aging gravity pumps, standardization meant the

beginning of the end.

However, the improvements implemented by the major oil refiners were not limited to attitude and aesthetics. Public rest rooms that could be used on demand became a major sales tool for the post-Depression service station. While the concrete privies erected nationwide by the Works

Progress Administration were an improvement over the home-made outhouse, they were hardly the class of bathroom refined tourists desired. Frightened by the scourge of crippling microbes, society was growing increasingly aware of the unseen germ.

In 1938, the Texaco Company addressed those fears when they debuted the "registered rest room" to the motorist. As part of a nationwide promotional blitz, each of the company's gas station bathrooms were officially registered and individually numbered. Touting the toilets as a "Texaco Dealer Service," curb placards were placed along the shoulder to attract the interest of passing vehicles. For stations in the Texaco sales territories along Highway 66, it was a sales-boosting move.

Behind doors posted with green and white rest room signs signifying "Men" and "Ladies," there existed public powder rooms without peer. Inside the sanitary compartments, tiled interiors sparkled with an unprecedented cleanliness. Modern commodes of porcelain accompanied gleaming sinks. Fully equipped with fresh soap and fluffy

When toll roads such as the Turner Turnpike took over many of Route 66's duties, a new type of highway rest stop emerged. Phillips Petroleum introduced its Vendorama stations in the early 1960s to meet the expected demand. Like the world-famous Horn and Hardart automat in New York City, the Vendoramas allowed visitors to select products from machines and serve themselves. Oklahoma City, Oklahoma. *Courtesy Phillips Petroleum Company*

When Highway 66 was in its glory, the service station attendant was a dedicated roadside servant. With a courteous smile and a friendly attitude, America's pump jockeys were expected to carry out the basic rituals required to ensure the utmost in motoring pleasure. Checking the oil level and tire pressure was required, as was checking mechanical components for signs of failure. Ensuring that the windshield was free from grease, grime, and insects was high on the list of station priorities, too. When a car pulled up to the pumps during the 1930s and 1940s, an attendant was always there to greet it. Without hesitation, the eager-to-please serviceman pleasantly inquired as to the amount of gasoline desired and set upon the task of operating the dispenser. *Courtesy Chevron Corporation*

Rock-Wool Insulated against Heat and Cold

PUEBLO COURT

OFFICIAL AAA MOTOR COURT

STANDARD DEALER

WINTER AIR CONDITIONED CENTRAL HEAT

STANDARD OIL

PUEBLO COURT OFFICE J. WILKIE TALBERT

RPM

ON U. S. 66 and 60 at EAST CITY LIMITS, AMARILLO, TEXAS
— *Authorized Standard Oil Lubrication* —

J. Wilkie Talbert was the owner and manager of the Pueblo Court. Featuring ultramodern accommodations with the charm of "early American Pueblo Indian architecture and furniture," it doubled as an authorized center for Standard Oil Lubrication. An adjoining restaurant served food approved by none other than Duncan Hines himself. Amarillo, Texas. *Preziosi Postcards*

towels, the Texaco registered units delivered a new level of personal comfort.

To make sure that the pristine washrooms lived up to the ads, Texaco maintained a fleet of "White Patrol" Chevrolets. All 48 states fell under the white-glove scrutiny of these water closet watchers. Undaunted by rain, sleet, and snow—they rode the highways and byways of America so that the gas station customer would remain safe in the assurance that

their appointed rest room was free from dirt or germ.

As our nation prepared to enter World War II, Phillips Petroleum introduced its own campaign for polishing up the public privy. Its team of registered nurses ensured that all "Certified" facilities throughout the Phillips sales region were immaculate. Six of these "Highway Hostesses" took to the Will Rogers route to validate conditions at random. If they

The Fact and Fable of Phillips Motor Fuel

"An excess of amusing yarns and unbelievable anecdotes have persisted as explanations for the double-digit, road-related, brand-name choice."

Among the endless catalogue of gasoline trademarks once spotted along America's Main Street, no refined motor fuel has been obfuscated with as much controversy as the Phillips gasoline brand. Ever since its first gallon of go-juice gurgled up through a visible-register fuel pump, an excess of amusing yarns and unbelievable anecdotes have persisted as explanations for the double-digit, road-related, brand-name choice.

The most common tale explaining the choice of the "66" designation is based solely on a numerical myth. This fable relates details of the first Phillips station built in Wichita, Kansas. According to the legend, the flagship refueling depot sold exactly 6,600 gallons of gas by the end of the first day's business. Supposedly, the station manager turned to a company representative standing nearby and dubbed the new fuel with the comment: "Boy, 66 is our lucky number!" Unfortunately, the report is historically inaccurate. That heartland haven for cars dispensed over 12,000 gallons on grand-opening day!

Another fictional fallacy that endeavors to explain the origin of the brand is that Frank and L.E. Phillips, prior to founding the company, had only $66 left when their first successful oil well struck black gold. Because of the timing of their lucky strike, they decided that if they ever marketed gasoline to motorists, it would be christened "Phillips 66." Sounds believable, but it's untrue too. While it's known that the Phillips brothers stretched finances to the limit with their oil explorations, no evidence shows the dollar amount of capital remaining when their Anna Anderson oil well blackened the sky as an Oklahoma gusher.

One exceedingly bizarre tale boasts of high stakes gamblers and luck: According to legend, a Phillips official won the company's first Texas panhandle petroleum refinery in a game of dice! The owner of the facility rolled "double-sixes" in an unlucky toss . . . and lost it all! Back in Bartlesville, company directors liked those unlucky boxcars so much that they named the refinery's product "Phillips 66." A colorful episode, but false. Most likely, this story originates from the oil distillery's infamous neighbor, the 6666 Ranch. Reportedly, the cow corral was won in a poker game with a hand of four sixes!

A few scientifically oriented scenarios have been perpetuated to explain the name too, including the unfounded report that Phillips gasoline was 66 octane and that its much touted "controlled volatility" feature was perfected after 66 lab tests. The truth is, no one knows for sure how many experiments were performed, not even the company. Furthermore, methods for determining gasoline octane wouldn't be adopted until five years after the selection of the original trademark!

The true story of Phillips 66 gasoline begins when the first gallon was offered to motorists in Wichita, Kansas in 1927. Preparations made prior to opening kept corporate employees busy for months. Only a decade old, the company was previously involved only in the production of crude oil. Now, it was venturing into the consumer market for the first time. In the frenzy to perfect its product, selecting an appropriate title to represent their innovative new motor fuel was delayed until the last possible moment!

Still, there was ample time to proclaim one important desire: the name for Phillips' new liquid had to have a hook. A catchy brand identifier stood more chance of garnering the motorists' attention at the pumps. In an effort to meet this criterion, researchers recommended using the benchmark for implying quality in that era, namely "high gravity." Because the new fuel was in the range of 66, it was suggested the numerals be used as a moniker. But, as the choice was logically analyzed, scientists surmised that a colophon linked to one specific gravity wouldn't mesh with Phillips' concept of varying gravity and controlling volatility to fit a range of seasons and locales.

Finally, a special committee was organized for the sole purpose of determining a new trademark. On the night of the meeting, a Phillips official was returning

During the 1930s, oil companies advertised their goods and services in a variety of formats. Phillips distributed colorful movie slides to motion picture palaces across the country to inform theater patrons of their great gasoline. *Courtesy Phillips Petroleum Company*

to the Bartlesville headquarters in a company car—a vehicle being used to road test its new motor fuel. "This car goes like 60 on our new gas!" announced the official. "Sixty nothing," retorted the driver (eye-balling the speedometer), "we're doing 66!" The next day, somebody asked where this dialogue occurred. The answer came back: "Near Tulsa, on Highway 66." Electrified by excitement, the executives took a vote—and finally reached a unanimous decision: Phillips Petroleum would kick off the sale of its powerful new gasoline under the distinctive brand, "Phillips 66"!

Originally introduced to kick off the sale of its first gallon of new gasoline at its inaugural Wichita station, the Phillips 66 trademark is viewed as one of the most widely recognized in America. Many amusing stories and explanations have sprung up over the years attempting to explain the origin of this distinct logo, readily perpetuated by imaginative consumers and those taken to craft romanticized road yarns. While many of these stories are based on fact, others remain mired in myth. Some come across as quite believable, while a handful are crafted in the same vein as fantastic works of fiction. For Frank Phillips, founder of Phillips Petroleum, "66" proved to be an appropriate choice for personalized license plates. Bartlesville, Oklahoma. *Courtesy Phillips Petroleum Company*

Route 66 Motors and General Store is one of today's thriving gift shops doing business along the old alignment of Route 66 (right off I-44 at exit 189, located 1.3 miles east of North Outer Road). Owned and operated by Wayne E. Bales and his wife Patricia, it's stocked with virtually every type of Route 66 memento—including T-shirts, mugs, books, repro signs, auto memorabilia, country accents, and much more. With an adjoining car lot, this dual-function business is a great place to peruse special interest autos and see a variety of vintage advertising signs. It's a must-see stop along the old road. Rolla, Missouri. *Author*

opposite
Migrants who relocated from Oklahoma to New Mexico in the great exodus of the 1930s decided to open up a gas station for their brethren. For all those making their way to the promised land of California, the Oklahoma Service Station was a roadside stop that offered up a little bit of reassurance—and part of the home they had left behind. Oklahoma newspapers, as well as other Oklahoma products, were among the items offered for sale. Questa, New Mexico, Russell Lee photo, 1939. *Library of Congress*

met up with a rest room they didn't like, it was promptly reported to company headquarters back in Bartlesville, Oklahoma.

As news of the Texaco and Phillips units spread along the miles of Route 66, other oil companies began to scrub up their own version of the service station bathroom. For a brief moment in the history of the highway, the cross-country adven-

turer who desired a carefree comfort stop could count on the impeccable surroundings of the roadside rest rooms. The American gas station had reached its zenith.

By the end of the war, the ability to once again purchase gasoline without restrictions edged out all concern over bathrooms. Once again, Route 66 was flooded with gal-

left
From the Top of the Ozarks to Conway, Missouri, Route 66 had a reputation as being a bloody killer. With more than its share of automobile accidents occurring along that infamous stretch of concrete, the piece of road passing through the town of Devil's Elbow was regarded by many as the "death corner of the world." The Cedar Lodge and Gasoline station was one of Devil's Elbow's more popular places to stop and get refueled. Hooker, Missouri. *Courtesy Chuck Sturm*

In the small towns along Route 66, evidence of yesterday's gas stations is slowly being erased. In the mid-1980s, this downtown gas station in Galena, Kansas, still sported three gasoline pumps and a price signboard. As collectors began to view old pumping equipment and signage with a different eye, scenes such as this became a rarity. Anything and everything that wasn't nailed down was removed, looting the roadsides of much of its legacy and simple treasures. *Jerry McClanahan ©1995*

lons of "go juice" and Americans were getting into their cars in record numbers. In 1949, more than five million passenger cars were manufactured—sold as fast as they could be made to a public eager for postwar luxury. The entire country was off to see the U.S.A. in their Chevrolets.

Commerce adapted to field the new influx of car customers. Now, instead of driving up to a business, parking, and then walking inside—merchants began catering to the growing obsessions of car culture. Restaurants offered carhops that served cus-

when he opened the nation's first self-service gasoline stations in Los Angeles. These "Gas-A-Terias" consisted of 18 to 21 gasoline pumps set on islands lined up at right angles to the street. In the interest of reducing expenses, station attendants once on duty to check the oil and wipe windows were sacked.

Six girls in tight sweaters raced around the lot in roller skates—much like their satin-clad counterparts at the corner drive-in. Gliding from island to island, they collected money amidst a mad frenzy of vehi-

Selling food and gasoline from one business outlet was the perfect choice for many entrepreneurs setting up shop along Highway 66. With one structure, two demands of travelers could be met with a minimum amount of investment. Near Springfield, Illinois. *Courtesy Jerry Keyser*

tomers in cars and drive-in theaters allowed vehicle owners to watch movies from the front seat. But at the local gasoline station, the effects were quite different: Instead of serving arrivees in their automobiles, customers were urged to pump their own gas!

George Urich started the trend in 1947

cles and whirring pumps. The snazzy pump man with bow tie and cap was waiting on the unemployment line. It was a harbinger of things to come.

While the industry tried to dismiss the phenomenon as a dangerous fad, the format held on. By the late 1960s, it was firmly estab-

When cars were less reliable and the population density was lower, the "last chance gas" station poised at the edge of the desert struck fear and loathing into the hearts and minds of the Route 66 adventurer. To prepare themselves for the crossing, customers were warned to fill up their tank with gas, top off the water bag, and buy plenty of provisions. Somewhere in the desert, California. *Shellee Graham ©1995*

lished in the gas station culture of the road and a recognized way of doing business along Route 66. Crazy thing was, hurried customers were getting used to pumping their own gas and really enjoyed the discount prices. The service station attendant's days were numbered.

In the meantime, the Environmental Protection Agency deemed glass containers to be unsafe for gas storage. With great haste, their use

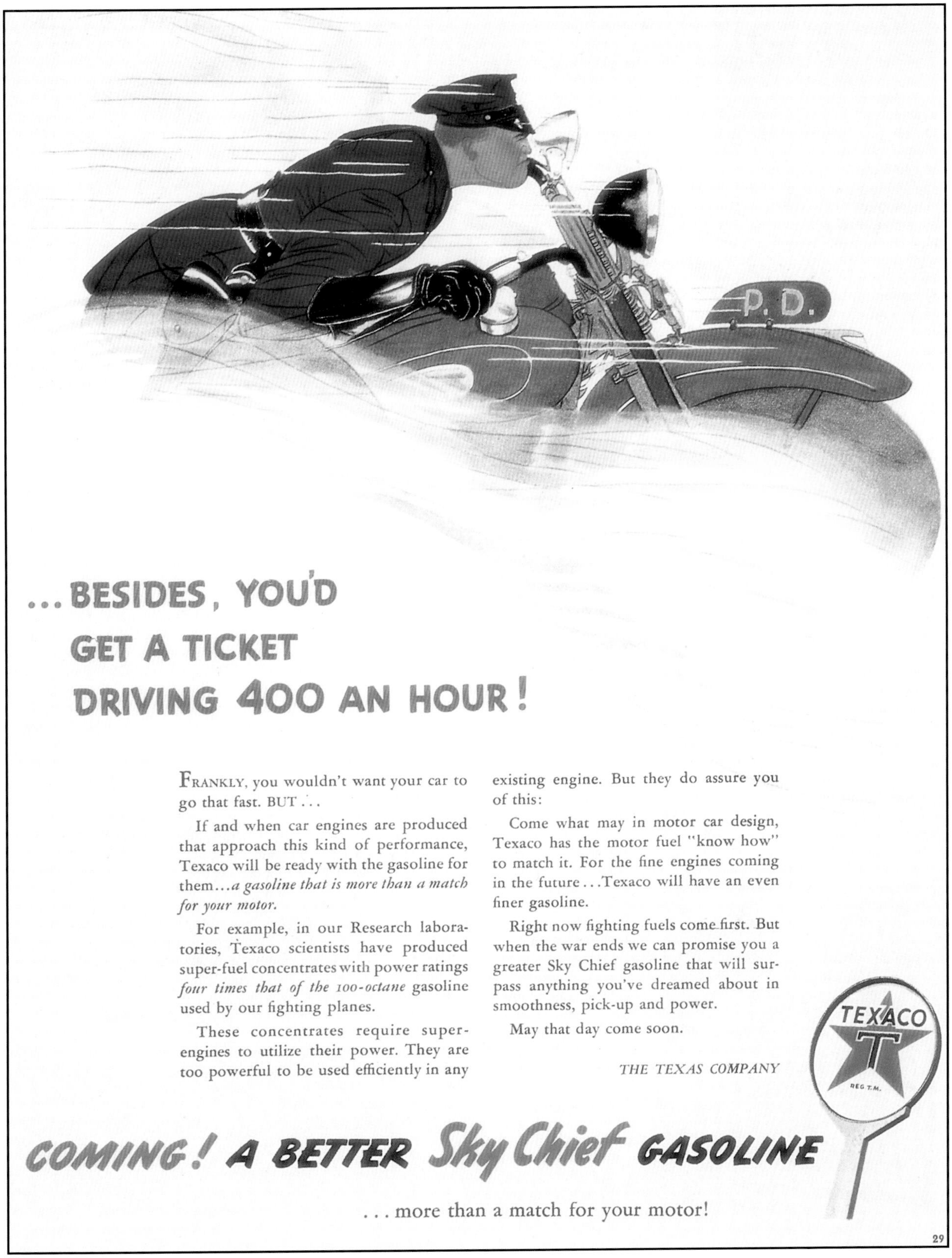

P.D.
...BESIDES, YOU'D GET A TICKET DRIVING 400 AN HOUR!
FRANKLY, you wouldn't want your car to go that fast. BUT ...
If and when car engines are produced that approach this kind of performance, Texaco will be ready with the gasoline for them...*a gasoline that is more than a match for your motor.*
For example, in our Research laboratories, Texaco scientists have produced super-fuel concentrates with power ratings *four times that of the 100-octane* gasoline used by our fighting planes.
These concentrates require super-engines to utilize their power. They are too powerful to be used efficiently in any existing engine. But they do assure you of this:
Come what may in motor car design, Texaco has the motor fuel "know how" to match it. For the fine engines coming in the future...Texaco will have an even finer gasoline.
Right now fighting fuels come first. But when the war ends we can promise you a greater Sky Chief gasoline that will surpass anything you've dreamed about in smoothness, pick-up and power.
May that day come soon.
THE TEXAS COMPANY
TEXACO
T
REG. T.M.
COMING! A BETTER Sky Chief GASOLINE
... more than a match for your motor!
29

opposite below

As commercial architecture, the "house" became a surrogate home for millions of motorized patrons in search of that safe feeling along America's highways. After Pure Oil architect C.A. Petersen found success with his "English-Cottage" design of the mid-1920s, other refiners picked up on the motif. By the close of that decade, residential sites and corner lots were being purchased by many of the large oil concerns in the hopes of constructing new domestic stations. Phillips Petroleum invested heavily in the style with many of their Oklahoma stations on Route 66 embracing the homespun look. Eleventh and Lewis, Tulsa, Oklahoma. *Courtesy Phillips Petroleum Company*

left

By the 1960s, petroleum refiners developed new gasolines on a continual basis, many touting secret chemical additives or revolutionary refining processes. All claimed superior performance and quality, making it difficult for the motorist unschooled in chemistry to discern exactly what was flowing into their car's tank. Texaco introduced the Sky-Chief brand and reinforced its climate-controlled qualities with a series of print ads in national magazines. Specially blended to deliver top performance in each of the 25 weather areas in the country, this "Volatane Control" motor fuel was just the ticket "for quick starts, fast warm-ups, smooth getaways, and power-a-plenty on the highways and up the hills." *Courtesy Texaco Inc.*

The Silent Sentinels of Route 66

"Soon, the silent sentinels of 66 will vanish forever—leaving only faded photographs to validate the hasty evolution of the internal combustion refueling stop."

They stand as lone obelisks along the unused stretches of America's "Mother Road." They sit empty now . . . silent, waiting. The rust and corrosion of the years slowly engulf their exteriors. Like faded billboards, their message has vanished. They are following the hamburger stand and the drive-in theater to extinction. Only a few decaying gas pumps remain. The new wave of superstations has arrived. The era of "wipe the windows and check the oil" has ended.

Today, mini-markets stationed along the interstate have filled the void, offering everything from cheap sunglasses to frozen yogurt. Technology has made it easier for 20th-century motorists to fill their tank, stuff their face, and empty their pocketbooks. The free car wash has become a roadside obsession, and the colors of redesigned petroleum trademarks cast their impersonal glow over the motorways. Like so many other American icons, the filling station has mutated into something unrecognizable.

These days, travelers can look forward to a major consumer project when buying motor fuel along the superslab. First, a search of the general area in and around the parking lot is in order. Where is the pump unit and exactly how does it work? The eager-to-please station attendant canonized during the golden age of motoring is now a legend—and nowhere to be found!

Money-changing pump jockeys now occupy bullet-proof cubicles, isolated from the public. Currency is exchanged through a stainless steel drawer with prepayment after dark. A sophisticated intercom system broadcasts the operator's thanks—a burst of garbled noise abruptly completing the sterile transaction. Afterwards, attempting to use the rest room to wash up is impossible—the door is locked. Toilet paper theft forces the harried customer back to the pay kiosk for the key—attached to a bowling-ball-sized object to prevent its theft!

Remember the days along old Highway 66 when tires where greeted by the familiar "ding-ding" of the driveway air-hose? Those were the days when attendants checked under the hood and attitudes were friendlier. Station employees still had personality then, refining companies a reputation. "A Tiger in Every Tank," the "Flying Red Horse," or "Man with the Star" stirred our imaginations. These were the honeymoon years of America's automotive love affair. Cheap gas with full service! Hubcaps

adorned walls and Greenstamps filled glove compartments. With a friendly ring, gas pumps sounded-off at one-gallon intervals. A visit to the super service station was still a favorite ritual.

Now, only remnants of these classic stations populate the back roads. Many have been converted into used car lots, others just demolished. Usually, a stripped-down pump is all that remains, its removable parts and brand placards cannibalized by overzealous "petroliana" collectors. With only their shells remaining, they echo values from another era, another way of life.

Worn out by a society faithfully served, the aesthetic preferences of former generations permeate every molecule of their structure. With an ethereal character all their own, they decay in glory. Transformed, they measure the advance of time as roadside barometers. The wind, rain, and sun have interacted with their external surfaces causing a transformation. Whether altered by the elements, a well-intentioned station owner with spray paint, or a hammer-wielding vandal, they are windows to another time.

Sometimes, along the forgotten miles of old road—where weeds have grown high and the memories of yesteryear move along the whispering wind—one can almost hear the sounds of old attendants gassing cars. Unfortunately, the recollections grow quieter with every passing year. The surviving relics are slowly

During the 1930s, Ed Edgerton established an outpost along Route 66 at a place in the Black Mountains called Sitgreave's Pass. It started out as a gas station and a cafe, but when the interstate pulled the traffic south, it was transformed into a repository for "stuff." Edgerton worked most of his life as a miner and at one time built a gold-processing mill. In his later years, he gained notoriety when he cured himself of cancer through the use of high temperature and radioactive pads. Rusting visible register pumps are all that remain to remind travelers of the man who discovered "Edgertonite." West of Kingman, Arizona. *Jerry McClanahan ©1995*

being eliminated from America's roadside, replaced by mega-malls, parking garages, and improved freeways. Soon, the silent sentinels of 66 will vanish forever—leaving only faded photographs to validate the hasty evolution of the internal combustion refueling stop.

So look now for the last of the refueling classics that remain. Take a break from the frenzy of the interstate and explore the wonders of the two-lane. The landscape encountered across this mobile America is your museum, the pavement your viewing point. The vehicle you pilot to arrive there is your point of common connection—the transitional link to the consciousness of the road and the generations who constructed it, traveled it, and were born on it.

The major oil refiners didn't miss a trick capitalizing on the success of the visible register pump design. By the end of the 1920s, many began to offer different grades of gasoline dyed with a variety of hues. Texaco sold green gasoline, Esso red, and Sunoco blue. Gilmore promoted their Blue-Green brand of gasoline. Reasoning had it that if normal, uncolored gas sold well, colored mixtures could sell even more. At the same time, a certain sense of mystique could be added to an otherwise mundane commodity. Pie Town, New Mexico, Russell Lee photo, 1940. *Library of Congress*

at filling stations was outlawed. Coincidentally, the majority of mom-and-pop independents unable to afford the latest dispensing equipment relied on the visible register pump (with its glass tank) for their livelihood. Now, restricted by government bureaucracy, the graceful machines that stood as silent sentinels along Highway 66 were just so much scrap metal.

When the so-called oil crisis of the 1970s reduced the flow of gasoline to a trickle, many of the family-run establish-ments that pumped gasoline along Route 66 dropped from the scene. As fuel supplies were limited by a de facto rationing plan, 5 percent of the 218,000 gas stations in business at the start of 1973 ceased operations. Within this depressed business climate, the major oil refiners wrested the refueling business away from the operators that got it started in the first place.

In the end, only memories of what motor fuel made possible remained: For the farmer fleeing days of dust, it ful-

The Tower Station was opened in Shamrock, Texas, back in April 1936, at the busy intersection of Route 66 and Highway 83 (the Canada-to-Mexico Highway). John Nunn had scratched the design for the building in the dust with a nail. Shamrock businessman J.M. Tindall had a local architect draw up the Art-Deco plans and the station was built. Upon opening, John Nunn and his wife Bebe sponsored a contest to find a catchy name for the new restaurant. A local eight-year-old boy won with the name "U-Drop Inn" and took home a week's worth of waitress pay. T.W. Kines photo, 1948. *National Archives*

If the roadbed is considered to be the soul of Highway 66, it could be argued that the gasoline station is its very heart. From the days of dust bowl flight to modern-day travelers seeking adventure on the open road, the filling station continues to be an important part of the journey. A man can go for six days without water and more than a month without food—but once a gasoline tank is empty, a few feet of forward momentum are all that remain in a powerless automobile. Feeder Road, north of Route 66, Oklahoma. *Author*

filled the promise of the West. For the long-haul trucker, it provided a paycheck at the end of a run. For the traveling salesman off to make a pitch, it was a tool of the trade. Even for the family on vacation, it provided the means to experience a wondrous end. Though some may curse it and others dismiss it, gasoline was the elixir that provided the power to make the motor trip along Highway 66 possible. It was, and always will be, the key to America's Mother Road.

Today's race to get from one part of the country to another in record speed has taken the magic out of travel. Multilane interstates and freeways confine the motorist. Off-ramps and pre-determined exits dictate when and where motorists may eat, sleep, and refuel their gas tanks. Fortunately, alternative corridors such as Route 66 are still thriving. For those that relish the journey and the unexpected sights and sounds a two-lane fandango might bring, America's back roads await. Has the old-time gasoline station faded into obscurity? Not really—life in the fast lane has just foreshortened our view through the windshield, making it difficult to see the few survivors that remain. Chandler, Oklahoma. *Author*

MOTOR INN COURTS
On U. S. 66 - Elk City, Okla.

RECOMMENDED (AAA) MOTOR COURTS

Recommended by the AAA, the Motor Inn Courts featured a full-service Texaco gasoline station in combination with 11 beautifully furnished cabins. Inside, the finest Beauty-Rest mattresses soothed tired backs. They were cool in summer, heated in winter, and even featured hot and cold running water! Their motto? "Where Tired Tourists Meet Good Eats and Good Beds." West Edge of Elk City, Oklahoma. *Courtesy Chuck Sturm*

left
At the road's end in the city of Los Angeles, the gas stations frequented while on Highway 66 were suddenly transformed into colorful visions of neon. Big-city operators spared no expense in their efforts to attract business. Hollywood, California, Russell Lee photo, 1942. *Library of Congress*

Doubling as ambassadors for the company, the Phillips highway hostesses "helped to sell Phillips 66 by their courteous manner, pleasant personalities, and willingness to aid anyone in distress." Cheerfully, they directed tourists to suitable restaurants, hotels, and scenic attractions, as well as took the time to discuss infant hygiene with traveling mothers. Dressed in light blue uniforms and military-style caps, they reminded one of Women's Air Corps recruits. Their white shoes, stockings, and vest pocket handkerchiefs also conjured up images of the local waitress who poured coffee at the neighborhood pancake house. *Courtesy Phillips Petroleum Company*

Certified CLEAN REST ROOMS

In the Route 66 towns of the Arizona desert, gas station owners often fixed prices 2 cents higher than the stations out of town. During the 1950s, the common question was "what have you got in this gas—gold?" At the time, ethyl fuel was almost 42 cents per gallon! The Whiting Brothers chain of stations decided to capitalize on this price gouging by offering gas at a discount. Immense billboards alerting those traveling Highway 66 about upcoming stations were once a common sight along the old road. Continental Divide, New Mexico, 1988. *Jerry McClanahan ©1995*

left
Methods for road building in 1922 relied primarily on manpower and the brute force of animals. This section of the Santa Fe Trail in San Miguel, New Mexico, (from Glorieta to Panchuela) is being surfaced with a layer of crushed rock. When Route 66 was formally commissioned, many sections of roadbed shared a similar design. Until gasoline-powered tractors, graders, and other heavy machinery came into general use, it was slow going for roads in America.
National Archives

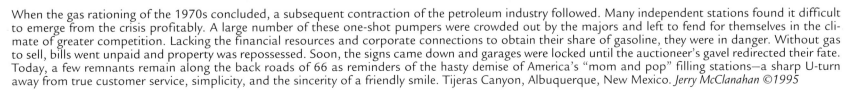

When the gas rationing of the 1970s concluded, a subsequent contraction of the petroleum industry followed. Many independent stations found it difficult to emerge from the crisis profitably. A large number of these one-shot pumpers were crowded out by the majors and left to fend for themselves in the climate of greater competition. Lacking the financial resources and corporate connections to obtain their share of gasoline, they were in danger. Without gas to sell, bills went unpaid and property was repossessed. Soon, the signs came down and garages were locked until the auctioneer's gavel redirected their fate. Today, a few remnants remain along the back roads of 66 as reminders of the hasty demise of America's "mom and pop" filling stations—a sharp U-turn away from true customer service, simplicity, and the sincerity of a friendly smile. Tijeras Canyon, Albuquerque, New Mexico. *Jerry McClanahan ©1995*

The Flying C Cafe and Gas Station was a Route 66 operation begun by Roy Cline, an Arkie who came to New Mexico during the mid-1920s after he was driven off an Arkansas farm. Cline tried farming, then ran a post office at Ruthern. Later, he bought another spread near the town of Moriarty that was eventually traded for a small hotel in town. He founded the well-known tourist trap known as Clines Corners and through a combination of stubbornness and self-promotion, got the name for his town put on service station road maps. The Flying C was another of his many projects along the old alignment of Route 66. East of Albuquerque, New Mexico. *Courtesy Chuck Sturm*

While many former gas station structures have found new uses in urban areas, those in the outlying regions have had a hard go of it. For the most part, they were abandoned were they stood—making way for the raft of freeway super-stations and self-service discount markets assuming dominance over the automobile. Texola, Oklahoma. *D. Jeanene Tiner ©1995*

Grady Jones ran the DX Gasoline station in the town of Arcadia, Oklahoma, for quite a number of years. When he closed down the operation, an impromptu memorial and roadside display of curiosities ensured that his legacy would be remembered. Today, it's one of many service station attractions that draws visitors to the Will Rogers Highway outside of Tulsa. *Author*

In 1905, the Automobile Gasoline Company in St. Louis opened its first "drive-in" filling station featuring a gravity tank and garden hose. Starting primarily in the business as bulk fuel distributors with huge above-ground storage tanks, Harry Grenner and Clem Laessig calculated that their overall volume (and income) could increase by offering gasoline for sale to motorists in a quick, efficient, and practical manner. With the total elimination of the exceedingly impractical method of drum-and-measure refueling, their experiment proved a success. Motorists liked the idea of filling a gasoline tank with a flexible garden hose, and soon the enterprising pair operated about 40 outlets in Missouri, plus a depot. *Courtesy American Petroleum Institute*

87

At the last roadside hot-dog stand you patronized how clean or otherwise were the dishes, the knives, the forks, the spoons, the glasses? How clean do you surmise, were the utensils in which the food had been cooked? Was there an opalescent skin of soap or grease on top of the water in your glass? Did you have an urge to give your coffee spoon a going-over with your sleeve, handkerchief or napkin while the lady or gentleman behind the counter wasn't looking? Did you by chance pick up a stomach-ache or a case of trench mouth at the place?

—"Ptomaine Joe's Place," Collier's, October 1, 1938

Roadside Food:
Dining Out
and
Dining In

Rod's
**STEAK
HOUSE**
WILLIAMS, ARIZONA
"GATEWAY TO GRAND CANYON"

During the salad days of the 1950s, Route 66 was a great smorgasbord of regional fare. All along the miles simmered a boundless brunch, an exciting variety of food and beverage that could be sampled at greasy spoons, roadside diners, frantic truck stops, trading-post lunch counters, drive-in dinettes, ramshackle hot dog stands, and elaborate sit-down restaurants.

In Illinois, it was perfectly "normal" to chomp on delicious Steakburgers and gulp Tru-flavor milkshakes. Over in Missouri, Ted Drewes' old-fashioned custard cones put the

Rod's Steak House was started in Williams, Arizona, by Rod Graves and his wife in 1945. At one time, Graves had a Hereford ranch east of Williams. His cattle were branded with his Bar Mary Jane brand, the restaurant's trademark. The eatery itself is located in a long, rather nondescript building that takes up the whole block between Williams and Railroad Avenues. Today, Stella and Lawrence Sanchez own and operate this Route 66 standard and continue to satiate the appetites of all those motorists in search of a real American steak. Williams, Arizona. *Courtesy Chuck Sturm*

left
Along Route 66, Juan Delgadillo and his brother, Angel, have become living legends. While Angel runs a small barbershop in Seligman, Arizona, Juan entertains (and feeds) customers at the Snow Cap Drive-In. Quite the practical joker, he has prepared a number of surprises for unsuspecting patrons. Fortunately, the food is no surprise: It's a classic mix of simple road food served up with speed and style. *Jerry McClanahan ©1995*

Jim's was just one of many eateries along the old road that tried to capitalize on friendly familiarity. Whether it was Bob's Grill, Alice's Restaurant, Joe's Bar and Grill, Rosie's Diner, or Kathy's Cafe, most roadside dining spots had one attribute in common: great customer service. In the days before the impersonal attitudes found at today's fast-food restaurants were accepted as the norm, friendly waitresses, talkative fry cooks, and helpful busboys made dining along the highway a real treat. Vinita, Oklahoma. *Preziosi Postcards*

chill into summer. Meanwhile, the Kansas heartland set the standard for baked breads. Cruising the "Lone Star" state, drivers dined on Texas T-bones as jalepeños tickled taste buds. Across the border, the meals of New Mexico and Arizona set mouths ablaze with savory spices. For dessert, Southern California served up a delight of squeezed citrus—providing a "flavorful" ending to the motor trip.

Inundated with this cornucopia of the highway, it was difficult for the motorist to imagine that just 30 years prior the road was limited in its ability to feed. Back then,

ignored. As the automobile rose to dominance, the petroleum peddlers of the 1920s began to view "edible" fuel as just another aspect of car commerce. With underfed travelers already parked at the pumps, it was only good business to provide them with the victuals they desired.

As a consequence, the sale of "road food" became inextricably linked with the sale of gasoline. The diversification required no great sacrifice, since the bulk of refuelers operating in the rural territories of 66 were often owned by families that lived on site. In these instances, a backroom kitchen and well-stocked larder were the only prerequisites. All one had to do was add a Coca-Cola cooler, make a deal with the iceman, and wait for the hungry to drive in.

It was a marketing plan that worked well for George Morrow, a one-time farmer and retail merchant hailing from Iberia, Missouri. The year was 1932—the very height of the Great Depression—when he decided to start his own refueling business along the nation's most traveled route. With an investment of $1,500, he purchased 3-1/2 acres of frontage on the West Kearney "bypass" and began building his personal vision of a roadside oasis.

Constructed with a veneer of fossilized "worm rock," Morrow's station was planned to serve as both an auto facility and as permanent shelter for his family. The dual-purpose "housestore" was a natural choice for the rural operator planning to prospect the highway for gold: It was inexpensive to build,

car owners had to rely on themselves when it came to refilling the human tank. Between the towns along Highway 66, it was easier to find a gallon of gas than it was to rustle up a square meal.

Even so, the symbolic relationship between food and gas was not one to be

Ed Waldmire Builds a Better Hot Dog

"Although the secret formula for Waldmire's batter casing was patented, clever cooks across the country began developing their own version of the vertical hot dog."

*N*estled between two halves of a fluffy bun and topped with a dollop of mustard, the common frankfurter has been quite content for more than 100 years. The public had universally accepted this format as the norm—that is, until Edward Waldmire came along and decided to turn the wiener world on end—literally—and reinvent the beloved, hand-held comestible most Americans know and love as the hot dog.

This incredible rethinking of a culinary icon began during the early 1940s, when Waldmire was visiting his brother in Muskogee, Oklahoma. There, a hash-slinger working a local greasy spoon flaunted a homemade specialty featuring three wieners cooked in batter! To solidify the eccentric entree, it took 15 minutes of baking in a strange contraption resembling a waffle iron. While lacking points in aesthetics and presentation, the brothers agreed the dish was a flavor combination to remember.

Still, it wasn't until Waldmire was drafted into the military that the possibilities of building a better hot dog were seriously pondered. Stationed in Amarillo, Texas, with the Army Air Corps, his assignment mustering out returning servicemen left him with ample time to think. When an idea popped into his head for a radically new way to prepare tubesteak, he phoned one of his old college buddies, Don Strand (his father ran a bakery in Galesburg, Illinois) and inquired about a special batter concoction with just one important property: The edible formula had to remain stuck to an Oscar Mayer wiener while submerged in the deep fry!

Waldmire received an experimental batch of mix from Strand and proceeded to tinker with various formulations at the base PX. His efforts paid off in 1945 when he emerged triumphant from the kitchen—his vision of a self-contained, great-tasting finger food a practical reality. It didn't take long for the unusual hot-dog-on-a-stick to gain a following with fellow enlisted men bored with the military's unexciting bill-of-fare. Surreptitiously named the "G.I. Hot Dog" by appreciative airmen, it was officially dubbed the "Crusty Cur" by Waldmire.

Upon return to Springfield, Illinois, his wife, Virginia, suggested that he consider a less salacious sobriquet for the fried frankfurter. While Crusty Cur may have scored a direct hit with his Army pals, she felt it was an inappropriate trade name for civilians. After careful deliberation, they agreed on the more appetizing "Cozy Dog." Virginia sketched some preliminary designs for the trademark and refined them into a logo featuring an amorous hot dog duo. They were ready to take the wiener world by storm.

Waldmire organized Cozy Dog Incorporated and in 1946 introduced America's first dipped-dogs to revelers attending the Illinois State Fair. The response was overwhelming and word of the delicious specialty spread countywide.

Encouraged by his popular success at the exposition, Waldmire opened the Cozy Dog House between Fifth and Sixth Streets in Springfield. A year later, he introduced a second eatery across town. By the dawn of the 1950s, car customers were gobbling up so many of the skewered hot dogs that he was inspired to build a third eatery along the Main Street of America. Grand-opening ceremonies for the new Cozy Drive-In commenced on September 10, 1950, with batter-dipped dogs selling for just 15 cents and burgers for 20!

Although the secret formula for Waldmire's batter casing was patented, clever cooks across the country began developing their own version of the vertical hot dog. Whether it be concession operator, theater snack bar, drive-in, or diner—all began to spread news of the savory sausage. The "corn dog" had gone nationwide.

For the next 40 years, Ed Waldmire and his corn-coated creation grew to become a highway

Springfield, Illinois', Cozy Dog Drive-In as it appeared during the 1960s, still featuring the amorous hot dog couple and the great-tasting fast-food dishes developed by founder and Route 66 personality Ed Waldmire. *Courtesy Buz Waldmire*

legend. For motorists passing through Illinois on their way across the great continent, his walk-up drive-in—with its simple menu of home-cooked food and friendly service—became synonymous with good taste. In 1991, his unwavering dedication to food service was recognized with the restaurant's induction into the Illinois Route 66 Hall of Fame. It was a fitting memorial for the inventive Waldmire who took the highway's heavenly off-ramp in 1993.

These days, the Cozy Drive-In and its namesake endures among the fast food franchises doing battle along Springfield's old road. Son Buz and his wife, Sue, perpetuate the legacy by offering the same batter-dipped-dog Ed Waldmire pioneered over one-half century ago. With its future secure, the Cozy Dog remains proof that if you build a better hot dog, the world will truly beat a path—or even a highway—to your door.

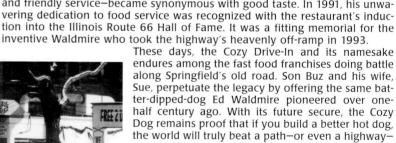

Ed Waldmire opened his first Cozy Dog House between Fifth and Sixth Streets in Springfield, Illinois (pictured here). A year later, he introduced another batter-dipped hot dog eatery across town. By the close of the 1940s, customers arriving by car were wolfing down so many of the skewered wieners that he was inspired to build a third drive-in along Highway 66. While today the Cozy Drive-In still serves the same great grub as it did on its grand-opening (1950), the batter-dipped dogs don't sell for 15 cents anymore. Springfield, Missouri. *Courtesy Buz Waldmire*

economical to operate, and allowed for 24 service.

From the road, Morrow's operation looked like almost every other filling depot of the day. Three visible-register fuel dispensers attracted customers with regular, ethyl, and white grades of petrol. But if one looked closer, the domestic clues were everywhere: Between the pumps and the road, a decorative flower box suggested a woman's touch. Behind the store, the family's Guernsey milk cow grazed the pasture.

Inside the structure, two bedrooms, a living room, and a dining area were reserved for the family. In the kitchen, a gasoline stove allowed Morrow's wife, Ethel, to work her craft, mostly preparing simple sandwiches and other short order meals (her culinary skills later earned her a job at the Grove, a restaurant in Springfield). Her home-baked pies enticed motorists to pull up a stool and eat lunch.

And that they did, consuming dinners at the serving table set up near the front window. From this vantage point, customers perused an assortment of goods—including breads, milk (supplied by the bovine out back), and the usual traveling supplies one might need for the open road. Kids drooled at the sight of Baby Ruth and Hershey bars, and their parents opened their wallets to quell the crying.

For its time, the combined grub and gas stop pioneered by the Morrow family was an appropriate way to provide roadside amenities to the Route 66 traveler. But despite its obvious utility, the housestore

Route 66 was the home for countless drive-in restaurants during the 1940s and the 1950s. Unlike the occasional mom-and-pop motels of the same era that occasionally survived the invasion of franchising, the majority of the curb servers were forced out of business. The introduction of the fast-food hamburger and the assembly-line techniques used to make and serve them literally fried the competition. Carhops and window trays were no match for the fast, impersonal, food service of the future. Peach Springs, Arizona. *D. Jeanene Tiner ©1995*

QUMACHO INN. PEACH SPRINGS. ARIZONA
RESTAURANT AND MODERN MOTEL. INDIAN CURIOS. GIFTS

From the earliest days of the internal-combustion engine, truckers, travelers, and other denizens of the highway have relied upon the humble cup of coffee to keep them awake while in transit. Over the years, a variety of restaurants, cafes, diners, and greasy spoons have made a livelihood out of serving up a basic brew. At Formica serving counters across America, "espresso" is a foreign term reserved for shopping centers and strip malls. Albuquerque, New Mexico. *Dan Harlow ©1995*

The Qumacho Inn was one restaurant (with motel out back) that didn't try to disguise itself as something it wasn't. It was simply a cafe—a quick, inexpensive place to get a cup of coffee and a blue-plate special. Even so, it was a Route 66 business that still wanted to stay current with the latest architecture. The circular window installed in the front facade was an obvious attempt to keep up with the craze for streamlining begun during the 1930s. *Courtesy Chuck Sturm*

CHICKEN "66" - ON U.S. 66 AND 75 - TULSA, OKLA.

Of all the restaurant styles begun along the Route 66 Highway, no other kind of eatery was as easy to set up as the chicken stand. During the 1930s, the virtual absence of government regulation and red tape made it easy for grandma to exploit her culinary talents. Unfortunately, the success of the automobile and the commerce created by it spelled the end of the individual operator. The franchised, homogenized chicken shops were destined to take over, relegating homespun outfits like "Chicken 66" to obscurity. Tulsa, Oklahoma. *Courtesy Chuck Sturm*

did not rise to dominate the highway restaurant trade. By the close of the Roaring Twenties, the art of feeding the motorist had already evolved far beyond this limited format. One of the most visible mutations was dubbed the "truck stop."

In 1928, J.P. Walters and his son-in-law John W. Geske stumbled into the truck stop game when they decided to try their hand at the oil business. Their idea was a jobbership to sell refined product to commercial and retail customers. They leased a Route 66 location in McLean, Illinois, and to capitalize on the idea that southern states had the best hospitality, they christened their new building the "Dixie."

After a short while, they realized that the evening hours brought in a whole new set of customers. Unlike the motorist, commercial truck drivers hugged the road all night long—hauling their freight under rigid time restraints. To make the trip, they required gas, oil, and a strong cup of coffee. In order to maximize turnover (and to ensure their success), Geske and company decided to stay open all night.

Before too long, the big rigs became the primary focus. To aid the night time drivers, the Dixie started selling the truckers coffee and sandwiches. As news of the highway

When McDonald's announced in 1967 that is was going to increase the price of its burgers to 18 cents, shock waves rocked the industry (the average price of a burger had remained at 15 cents for years). Blamed on rising beef costs and spiraling expenses, the hike was an ominous precursor to the great burger battles to come. Labeled by the press as "Black Wednesday," the stage was set for the elimination of many smaller chains. After a period of unprecedented growth, the proliferation of the McDonald's hamburger clones was over. The casualties lined Route 66 like so many fallen soldiers. Bridgeton, Missouri. *Shellee Graham ©1995*

hospitality spread, more and more drivers making the run between Chi-town and St. Lou wheeled in for a bite. When the demand for food exceeded the demand for fuel, the menu stretched to include plate lunches. By the time dinner and dessert were added, a wall in the dining room had to be knocked out to accommodate the crowds!

As the 1930s came to a close, business at the Dixie boomed. On an ordinary Saturday night, more than 1,000 visitors jammed the parking lot to fill up fuel tanks and sample the broasted chicken. By then, the specialized truck stop was an established resource of Highway 66 and a dependable place for any traveler to dine.

At the same time America's truck stops and house stores were honing their services, other eateries were emerging in the shadow of the gas pump. By clustering near established businesses geared to the tourist, operators hoped to recruit excess customers. There were more than enough customers for the cafes, diners, and coffee shops to come: by 1949, more than 43 million motor vehicles were whizzing down the nation's highways.

For Harry Tindle, it was the perfect time to get into the roadside restaurant business. His location was Kingman, Arizona—a major stop for motorists crossing the desert into California. Right there on the dusty ribbon of Route 66, he opened a small dining spot in the space adjoining Allen P. Bell's "Flying A" Service Station. It was called the Tideway Cafe.

By the 1960s, the Steak n Shake chain of drive-in restaurants was well-known throughout the Midwest—especially along Route 66. Gus Belt's original formula for serving up a complete meal consisting of Steakburger and a hand-dipped milkshake became the roadside standard. "It's a Meal" was the company's popular slogan. Because the customer could see the order being prepared, "In Sight It Must Be Right" became another car-dining catch-phrase. Webster Grove, Missouri. *Shellee Graham ©1995*

The Rocket Drive-In exists as a hamburger-stand flashback doing business along one of the most nostalgic stretches of the old road. While the juicy, dripping-with-fat hamburgers depicted on their sign are no longer sold for 10 cents, the Rocket's nostalgic atmosphere transports visitors back to a time when carhops zipped around on roller skates and clipped trays full of comfort food on the windows of parked cars. Main Street 66, Afton, Oklahoma. *Author*

Before the McDonald brothers enlisted the services of Ray Kroc to franchise their hamburger stands, they attempted to tackle the task themselves. Of those early burger outlets, this Azusa, California, location was constructed in 1954 and is one of the last extant examples to be found along old Route 66. Architect Stanley Meston and assistant Charles Fish designed the candy-striped structure, but it was Richard McDonald himself who actually came up with the idea of the golden arches. This unit was closed in February 1984. *Jerry McClanahan ©1995*

Like many of the competing restaurants in Kingman, the Tideway was a no-frills diner without tables—customers were provided with nothing more than 14 stools around a small counter. Along with the beverages and carry-out snacks expected by the postwar traveler, the standard road food fare was served.

Bell recalls the complementary arrangement with great fondness: "We worked together . . . somebody would come in and ask where they could get a good sandwich and I would tell them 'right next door.' Somebody would ask Harry where they could get a tire fixed and he would tell them 'right next door!' Yeah, we ran a real good business there, we helped each other out." But it was more than just hype. The Tideway Cafe served up some great food.

"I'll never forget the breakfast" brags Bell. "Boy . . . he had a grill right in front where you could sit and watch him cook—he was sharp! Bacon, eggs, hash browns, toast, coffee—all for one buck!" With all the motels in the area, the traffic was brisk enough to afford Tindle a pink Cadillac and a matching power boat! Both were parked nearby, evidence

Robert C. Wian was the brains behind the counter of a 10-stool hamburger stand purchased from two little old ladies in 1936. To raise the money needed to buy this Glendale, California, eatery, he sold his prized 1933 DeSoto. Unfortunately, the sale only netted $300—the women were asking $350! Still, he scraped up the balance and renamed the joint "Bob's Pantry." Then, when local bass player Stewie Strange asked for "something different" one night in 1937, Wian created a new sandwich and made history. The double-deck cheeseburger was an immediate sensation and was later dubbed the "Big Boy," a name inspired by local lad Richard Woodruff. A cartoonist regular sketched the portly kid on a napkin and later, statues of the burger-toting boy became a familiar sight along portions of the old road. 900 Colorado Boulevard, Glendale, California. *Courtesy Richard McLay*

of an American dream come true—one built with an ocean of coffee, eggs-over-easy, and a side of hash browns.

Meanwhile, similar dreams materialized along Highway 66. By the early 1950s, a drive-in style that catered to people in their cars rose to become one of the most popular modes for dining. It was a concept that gained notoriety in 1921 when Dallas

mercantile magnate Jessie Kirby convinced physician Reuben Jackson to invest in his idea for a drive-in sandwich stand. His sales pitch: "People with cars are so lazy they don't want to get out of them to eat!"

Their first Texas Pig Stand was built along the busy Dallas-Fort Worth Highway and served up a basic repertoire of barbecue and beverage. Unschooled in the practice of four-wheel dining, commuters passing by eased up on the gas to satisfy their curiosity and to do what the porcine sign board suggested: "Eat a Pig Sandwich!" They weren't disappointed.

Although the food wasn't anything out of the ordinary, nothing could prepare the staid motorist for the Pig Stand's service: When a car drove up to the curb, a young lad jumped up onto the running board before the driver could even come to a complete stop! Clinging to the side, boys clambered on and off to gather their orders. After someone referred to the waiters as "carhops," the craze for curb service was on.

News of just how fun it was to eat in the front seat traveled. As fast as four wheels could carry it, details of the unique drive-in filtered out along the connecting roadways. Within the span of two decades, carhops were serving food throughout most of the Route 66 territories.

For those who revere the golden years of touring food, drive-ins make up the most vivid memories. After all, face-to-face service was the rule of the day. Carhops clad in satin majorette uniforms skated among the cars. Serving trays clipped onto the steering wheel or window and were stacked high with sizzling burgers, golden French fries, and ice cream milkshakes.

In the city of Los Angeles, visitors arriving by way of Route 66 were thrilled by the neon visions lining the boulevards. Out there, most of the drive-ins employed circular architecture to maximize parking and minimize labor. To circumvent local laws barring oversized signs, resourceful restaurateurs mounted elaborate advertising pylons on their rooftops to get attention.

Showman Harry Carpenter erected one of the most ostentatious stands at the intersection of Sunset and Vine in the early 1930s, causing quite a stir for locals. As reported in a 1946 issue of *The Diner*, Carpenter "dressed up this basic idea [drive-in service] with typical Hollywood glitter. He paved his lot, put up a building that looked like a cross between the Taj Mahal and Mary Pickford's swimming pool bath house and found a batch of would-be stars starving to death while waiting for the big chance."

However, the architecture reminiscent of a giant, skewered hamburger was not limited to California. The quest for road food razzle dazzle influenced many of the drive-ins along Route 66. In Tulsa, Bishop's "driv-in" emulated the West Coast motif with a multi-layered octagon. Illuminated by spotlights, it appeared as a jewel in the western night. Garland's Oklahoma City eatery had a similar effect: with a massive tower shooting up from its forward bow, neon tubes bathed the parking lot with a warm glow.

continued on page 104

In 1940, the McDonald brothers sliced their "Airdrome" orange juice stand located in Arcadia, California, in two pieces and transported it to a new site at Fourteenth and E Streets in San Bernardino, California. It was remodeled, reorganized, and outfitted with a bevy of 20 carhops in satin uniforms. On weekend nights, 125 cars jockeyed for position in the parking lot! *Courtesy Richard McDonald*

101

Spencer Groff Unearthed a Roadside Diamond

"Groff realized that if he could figure out what these pleasure-bound excursionists needed,
he could eke out a living—right in his own front yard."

At the turn of the century, Spencer Groff left the family farm in Villa Ridge, Missouri, to pursue his dream of becoming an attorney. His studies were cut short, however, when speculation on the St. Louis Mercantile Exchange led to financial ruin. Using the old homestead as collateral, he returned home broke— determined to somehow pay back the accumulated debt.

Fortunately, the two dirt paths that ran alongside his acreage on Altamont Hill brought the promise of new fortune. Sputtering motorcars now speeded past on roads previously occupied by covered wagon, stagecoach, and buggy. Groff realized that if he could figure out what these pleasure-bound excursionists needed, he could eke out a living—right in his own front yard. Plums from the orchard became his first product, an item that sold out on a busy Labor Day weekend. He was in business!

Bolstered by the success of his first retail endeavor, he decided to turn over the profits and buy a supply of soda pop. An old washtub with ice held the bottles beneath a tattered umbrella planted near the shoulder. As the hot summer temperatures created thirst, he and his helper, Mack, exchanged colas for coins and established their presence along the road-

Known as "The Old Reliable Eating Place," The Diamonds was one of the most visited restaurants along Highway 66. Located at the junction of U.S. Highways 50, 66, and Missouri 100, it had a location that would be the envy of any restauranteur. Former busboy Louis B. Eckelkamp (he started there in 1933) took over the operation from founder Spencer Groff and turned it into a roadside travel center of renown. In the early 1960s, he rebuilt the old Diamonds destroyed by fire (shown) at the cost of $350,000 and reopened it as a combination restaurant, cafeteria, coffee shop, curio shop, bus ticket office, travel bureau, popcorn stand, and filling station. Villa Ridge, Missouri. *Preziosi Postcards*

soon the aroma of homemade pies filled the air. The year was 1923 when the little store at the crossroads became a recognized fixture.

Still, Groff's neighbors were skeptical of the eclectic stand. They perceived it as a whim, unaware that it represented his sole income and relief from debt. It had a similar effect on customers: One day, a highway official stopping in for a drink commented that the ramshackle gazebo reminded him of nothing more than "Adam's Banana Stand!" Amused more than insulted, Groff pondered the significance and decided to capitalize on the curious observation.

So, without any formal blueprints or specifications—there in the dust to which he had bowed in defeat—he measured off a diamond of undreamed value. Using a pick ax, he scratched out the rough outline of a what was to become a new building, aligning it with the fork in the road, with two sides paralleling the highways. Before the first nail was struck, an appropriate exterior was already in mind: White clapboard— painted with big bunches of bananas!

Even this new structure was eventually outgrown. As the talk of highways became a serious fact in the state capitol at Jefferson City, traffic at the junction grew. Within months, the new Banana Stand was surrounded by concrete rib-

way. When the weather turned frigid, sales dropped dramatically and plans were formulated for a much grander stand that could operate year around.

When spring arrived, Groff was ready: He planted four posts into the ground and topped them with a dilapidated roof from an old grain silo. Boards were nailed to the sides to form an enclosure and a small stove brought inside to provide heat during winter. A small railing was installed around the perimeter of the hut to keep customers at bay. Inside, tobacco, gloves, overshoes, overalls, gingham shirts, and socks lined the shelves. Outside, a fuel dispenser was installed so that the depleted tanks of automobiles could be refilled with gasoline.

By that time, the farm was once again producing edibles, so it seemed only natural to offer food to customers. The main course became none other than Frankfurter sandwiches, supplemented by fresh, chilled buttermilk at five cents a glass. Vegetables from the garden were harvested for sale and fruits used for delectable pastries. Groff's sister, Ursula, joined the endeavor and

bons. Motorists visited in numbers like never before, and of course, Groff was ready. He was dreaming of his greatest gem of all—a full-service restaurant dedicated to delicious dinners and service. On "road opening day," July 3, 1927, he greeted the world with his finest jewel. It was called "The Diamonds."

News of "The Old Reliable Place" spread by word of mouth and soon it became a favorite stop for bus companies, soldiers on their way to Fort Leonard Wood, and an endless procession of hungry sight-seers. Celebrities often popped in. On Sundays and holidays, the walls seemed to bulge with customers who came to taste the famous food. With every blue-plate special served, Groff's tremendous debt dwindled away.

In the end, it could be stated that Spencer Groff stumbled upon his life's work right outside his front door. Through a combination of faith, luck, and patience, he turned an ordinary fruit stand into one of the most memorable landmarks along the Mother Road. For him, all it took was a little time—and effort—to uncover the most valuable diamond of them all.

After opening his roadside refreshment stand, neighbors began to wonder about the strange course Spencer Groff had taken. They looked upon the stand as a whim, not knowing it represented his sole income and path out of debt. He ignored their comments and hoped that one day his stand and the surrounding knoll would be called Altamont Park (after his old school). He had visions of Sunday afternoons with cars parked four deep for service and even erected a sign on the old building nearby with the title "Altamont Park." One day, fate stepped in when a highway official stopped for a drink and commented that the place reminded him of nothing more than "Adam's Banana Stand." Finally, Spencer Groff's Route 66 stand had a name. Villa Ridge, Missouri. *Author*

The Diamonds is a Route 66 landmark to this day. However, it's not the original structure built by Spencer Groff and rebuilt (it was destroyed in a 1949 fire) by Lewis Eckelkamp. During the 1960s, Highway 66 was moved when I-44 came through. Eager to remain near the traffic, the Eckelkamp management decided to abandon the Diamonds and construct a new structure at the end of the freeway's access ramp (two miles away). At the same time, the path of the highway shifted from the Franklin County ridgetop, it

The motto at the Diamonds was "Service is First, Courtesy Always." The ultramodern (for the 1960s), California-streamlined building was designed by architect Frank Hayden and constructed by Oliver L. Taetz, general contractor. The fire-proof structure covers a half acre and features a concrete foundation and a brick exterior. Villa Ridge, Missouri. *Courtesy Chuck Sturm*

encroached on the Tri-County Truck Stop in Sullivan, Missouri. Owners Arla and Roscoe Reed were forced to shut down and began looking for a new business home. After they rediscovered the Diamonds, it was refurbished, cleaned, and polished. In 1971, they moved in and the old yellow brick Diamonds building was reborn as the Tri-County Truck Stop. (Behind little girl: Spencer Groff, right; Lewis Eckelkamp, left). Villa Ridge, Missouri. *Courtesy Ralph Bay*

Along the old road, local hangouts and other undiscovered eateries remain an untapped resource for automotive explorers. Routinely, present-day Route 66 adventurers pass them by. While the standard dining venues have received more than their fare share of press, the mom-and-pop cafes, neighborhood beer joints, honky-tonks, and other rustic bar and grills seem content just to be themselves. On the Kansas/Missouri Border. *Author*

continued from page 102

Unfortunately, the average restaurant owner who managed to weather the Depression had little capital left for upgrading architecture. As a result, the focus of many eateries became the food. Some cafes made a deal to sell the ever-popular "Chicken in the Rough," while others concentrated on improving the hot dog. To the delight of highway travelers, specialized dishes and original entrees ruled the day.

Along Illinois 66 in Normal, A.H. "Gus" Belt took over the old Shell Inn after the Depression and converted it to a neighborhood tavern. He sold chicken dinners and experimented in the kitchen, testing a greaseless grill for cooking up ground steak. When the town enacted a "no liquor" law, he made plans to convert the cafe into a burger bar and dropped beer in favor of hand-dipped shakes. By 1934, he perfected the "Steakburger," a ground beef sandwich fortified with cuts of T-bone, strip, and sirloin.

Armed with a sure road food winner, Belt introduced "Steak n Shake" restaurants to the Illinois motorist. Car customers responded enthusiastically to the four-way service known as "Takhomasak" (take home a sack) and came to trust the gleaming, white drive-ins as reliable rest stops. With food orders made where patrons could see them, "In Sight, It Must Be Right" became the creed for other greasy spoons to copy.

Nearly 1,700 miles west—at the opposite end of Highway 66—Richard and

Maurice "Mac" McDonald were preparing to conduct some food experimentation of their own. While struggling to make a movie theater called the Beacon profitable, they noticed that a local hot dog vendor was attracting a remarkable amount of business. Realizing that they might be in the wrong line of work, they decided to open their own stand. It was 1937, and money was tight.

As luck would have it, they learned that a local Sunkist packer was selling bruised fruit at a bargain. So, they made a sweet deal to buy twenty-dozen oranges for a quarter, borrowed money from a local bank, and went to work. Using borrowed lumber, they erected a gazebo along Arcadia's Huntington Drive (Route 66). On top, they crowned it with a large replica of an orange juice drink. Since Monrovia's airport was nearby, they called it the "Airdrome."

When the McDonalds learned how much demand there was for fresh-squeezed juice, they opened a second stand right across the street! To impress the thirsty travelers driving in from Needles and the Arizona desert, they

crafted the edifice to look like a piece of fruit. During the summer months, motorists by the hundreds stopped off to down an icy chalice of juice and to take snapshots of the orange-shaped hut.

Bolstered by the resounding success of their refreshment stands, the McDonalds decided to enter into the drive-in

The Big Texan Steak Ranch is one of those stops along Route 66 to be made on an empty stomach. Why? If you can finish their famous 72-ounce steak (along with all the side dishes and trimmings that come with it), it's free! Hopefuls may not leave the table once they have begun and may leave the fat behind (to be judged by the management). The restaurant was originally located on Amarillo Boulevard but was relocated by the owners when the interstate cut off business in 1968. Presently, it occupies a site along Interstate 40. Amarillo, Texas. *Dan Harlow ©1995*

Featuring an octagonal layout and massive advertising pylon jutting from its rooftop, Bishop's Driv-Inn was once a roadside gem. Located on Highways 66 and 44 in Tulsa, Oklahoma, it was a classic example of the circular carhop eateries popularized in Southern California during the 1930s and 1940s. *Courtesy Chuck Sturm*

below
The Boots drive-in featured the classic styling of Streamline Moderne architecture complete with wraparound windows and side-mounted portholes. Twin canvas canopies provided protection from the elements and multiple Coca-Cola buttons the perfect complement for colorful paint. Positioned at the busy junction of U.S. Highways 66 and 71, its souvenir shop was always ready with inexpensive trinkets. Carthage, Missouri. *Courtesy Chuck Sturm*

opposite
Many drive-in restaurants located on the busy cross streets of Los Angeles were considered "taxpayers." Never intended to become permanent landmarks, they typically operated for a short life span of 10 years or less. As real estate values of these prominent plots rose, the buildings that occupied the space could no longer support the value of the land. During the 1950s, restauranteur Stanley Burke bought out all of the remaining Simon's units and converted them to Stan's drive-ins. Eventually, none of the operations survived. Classics like Simon's were memories when high-rise towers and shopping malls took over the streetside territory. *Security Pacific National Bank Photograph Collection/Los Angeles Public Library*

business with full force. In 1940, they sold the oversized orange stand and sliced the Airdrome in two. It was moved to a new location at Fourteenth and E Street in nearby San Bernardino where workers enlarged, remodeled, then carefully reassembled it.

Richard McDonald introduced "Speedy" as their mascot and installed a neon sign featuring the blinking chef roadside. Inside, a

Located on the busy stretch of Central Avenue in Albuquerque, New Mexico, the El Sombrero Drive-In was the quintessential blend of object and architecture along Route 66. For a drive-in restaurant of circular design, a sombrero provided the perfect format for the display of rooftop neon, brim-side advertising, and protection from the rays of the sun. Could there have been any question from those driving past as to what kind of food was served here? *Preziosi Postcards*

grill cook made up hamburgers, hot dogs, and barbecue plates. Out on the parking lot, twenty carhops donning satin uniforms handled the crowds of customers: during weekend nights, 125 vehicles caused a curb service traffic jam! By 1948, their revenues topped the $200,000 mark.

Despite the overwhelming success, the McDonald brothers grew restless. After

World War II they could sense that customers were growing impatient with carhop service. On a hunch, they decided to fire all the hops, pare down the menu, dump the dishes, and store the silver. Three months later, they reopened with a limited menu and a new style of service: At tiny walk-up windows, customers were required to make and carry off their own food orders!

I'll Gladly Be Fried for Chicken in the Rough

"In 1937, their unique grill was patented and the soon-to-be famous rooster trademark registered—signifying the arrival of America's first franchised food."

For more than 60 years, a specialty platter known as "Chicken in The Rough" has satiated appetites at table-service restaurants, carhop drive-ins, motel dining rooms, and nightclubs along Route 66. Consisting of half a golden brown chicken served with a side of shoestring potatoes, hot buttered biscuits, and jug 'o honey, it was the ultimate—and tastiest—entree to emerge from the kitchens of the old road.

It all began in 1921 with fledgling restaurateurs Beverly and Rubye Osborne. As legend has it, they borrowed 15 dollars from their milkman, hocked Rubye's engagement ring, and sold the family car—just to scrape up the down payment on a modest, six-stool dinette in Oklahoma City. They packed the tiny eatery on 209 West Grand by offering 19-cent meals and perfecting their secret recipe for pancakes! As profits piled up, the enterprising duo purchased another outfit—a little drive-in on 2429 North Lincoln, right along the original alignment of the Will Rogers Highway.

By 1936, they were both ready for a vacation and began motoring out to the Golden State. Along the way Beverly hit a pothole, causing Rubye to dump a lunchbox full of chicken to the floorboards. As battered breasts and drumsticks were picked up, she remarked, "This is really chicken in the rough!" The spontaneous comment clicked with Beverly and set his imagination to sizzle. By the time they returned home, plans were made to create a radically new dish based on Rubye's observation.

At first, the Osbornes fried up the unjointed birds "pan style" since they believed it was the only method of cooking that would bring out the true flavor. Unfortunately, it was slow and tedious. As popular demand for the new poultry platter swelled to over 1,500 orders per day, it became apparent that a faster and more efficient preparation method was required. So, Beverly collaborated with a local machine shop owner and proceeded to devise a shallow-pit griddle designed to cook with minimal grease.

The resulting brazier was a specialized unit featuring "built-in" burners for even heat distribution. A shallow slope allowed the fryers to be submerged only half way—regardless of their thickness. Simultaneously, the clever cookplate both pan fried and steamed the pullets to perfection. With a capacity for preparing 30 orders (150 pieces) at one time, it afforded the production-line cooking method necessary to turn a profit—without sacrificing the "home-style" flavor the Osbornes had so beautifully perfected with their single stovetop fry pan.

In 1937, their unique grill was patented and the soon-to-be famous rooster trademark registered—signifying the arrival of America's first franchised food. A marketing plan was hatched, spreading the culinary delights of Chicken in The Rough to numerous venues along 66. Among the earliest eateries to pluck the opportunity were Abbot's Cafe in Berwyn, Daniel's Duck Inn at Joplin, Elliott's Court Cafe of Albuquerque, and Kingman's Lockwood Cafe. Oklahoma grew to seven outlets, the original expanding from four booths and nine stools to a behemoth with 1,100 seats. After Shamrock's U-Drop-Inn and Galena's Tivoli signed up, "I'll Gladly be Fried for Chicken in The Rough!" became one of the most remembered slogans for car customers along the historic highway.

By 1958, the Osborne's hands-on approach to chicken had spread all the way to the road's end. In California, the drive-in craze was reaching its zenith and shrewd operators were trying everything to make a buck. Los Angeles landmarks like Henrys, Carpenter's, and McDonnell's added the unjointed entree to infuse their burger-based menus with variety. The car crowd responded with salivating mouths and open wallets and it wasn't long before the Osbornes were overseeing 156 locations—some as far away as Hawaii and South Africa!

During the 1920s and 1930s, etiquette expert Emily Post proclaimed that every fried chicken dish should be consumed with a knife and a fork. Fortunately, Beverly and Rubye Osborne disagreed with this restrained opinion and served up their hand-eaten poultry entree without restraint. Known in the trade as "Chicken in the Rough," the couple's culinary creation became a franchised delight up and down 66. People loved the homey platter consisting of half a fried chicken with side of shoestring potatoes, rolls, and "pot o' honey." **Oklahoma City, Oklahoma.** *Courtesy Chuck Sturm*

Eventually, the franchising of America and the rise of the fast-food industry overtook the Osborne's famous recipe. In 1974, rights to the process were sold to Randy Shaw, an early partner. He subsequently purchased the remaining restaurants in Oklahoma City and continues to manage day-to-day operations at Beverly's Pancake Corner—one of the original locations still extant along the Northwest Expressway.

Today, Route 66 "roadies" may still enjoy the original Chicken in the Rough their parents (and grandparents) smacked their lips for during the early days. It's still eaten the very same way—with a hearty appetite, no silverware, and plenty of napkins. Sometimes, the tastes of the past do survive the present—and for that—we may all cluck quietly with delight.

For motorists on a budget, dining along Highway 66 often meant an impromptu running-board picnic. Anything and everything that could be taken along in an automobile was consumed, including fried chicken brought from home. When finances allowed, a visit to a Chicken in the Rough franchise was the next best thing to mama's frying pan. **Russell Lee photo, circa 1930s.** *Library of Congress*

above and opposite
From 1941 to 1959, Elmer and Rosa Lea Elliott owned The Court Cafe and served great dishes from its kitchens. They offered a wide variety of food there, including entrees as exotic as oysters and others as basic as the "blue-plate special." As a Chicken in the Rough franchise, The Court Cafe was a popular spot for tourists eager to get a taste of the unjointed bird perfected by Beverly and Rubye Osborne. Albuquerque, New Mexico. *Courtesy Chuck Sturm*

Accustomed to drive-in dining, the local teenagers didn't take kindly to the new "speedy service system." On Friday nights, the lot was conspicuously absent of hot rods. The carhops cruised by to heckle, informing Dick and Mac that they had their uniforms ready. Worried that they might have made a big mistake, the McDonalds almost switched back the format.

Three months later, their patience was rewarded. Suddenly, the travelers traipsing in from Highway 66 began making regular stops—along with taxi cab drivers, sales clerks, construction workers, and door-to-door salesmen. A diverse clientele discovered that assembly-line cooking translated into fast service and 15 cent hamburgers. As an added bonus, there were no carhops to tip!

"Sometimes we'd have over 100 people in line," remembers McDonald. "But—if we waited until they got up to the window to find out if they wanted a milkshake—the line would have snaked to Los Angeles!" To satisfy the demand, shakes were mixed in advance and stored in a freezer. Two single-shaft, Hamilton Beach mixers were in constant use, occasionally burning out from the stress.

When Ray Kroc, ever-eager representative for the Prince Castle Sales division received an order for ten heavy-duty "Multimixers," he was dumbfounded. Why would one hamburger stand need so many five-spindle mixing units? Filled with curiosity, he got into his car, pulled out onto Highway 66, and pointed his hood toward San Bernardino, California.

CHEESE - After Dinner Portions (Toasted Crackers)

Roquefort ......25c   Camembert ......25c   Imported Swiss ...25c
American ......15c   Cream Cheese ....15c   Pimento Cheese ...15c
Cottage Cheese ...15c   Philadelphia Cream 25c   Limburger 20c

SANDWICHES
We Use Our Large Sandwich Bread — Making a Large Sandwich

Cold Pork Sandwich 15c	Bacon and Tomato 20c	Toasted Cheese 15c
Cold Beef Sandwich 15c	Oyster Sandwich 25c	Melted Cheese 30c
American Cheese 15c	Tuna Fish, Mayonnaise ...20c	Roquefort Cheese 20c
Sausage Sandwich 15c	Baked Ham 20c	Jelly Sandwich 10c
Cold Ham 15c	Fried Ham 15c	Fish Sandwich 25c
Tongue Sandwich 15c	Olive Nut 20c	Ham and Egg 25c
Pimento Cheese 15c	Chicken Salad 20c	Liverwurst 15c
Lettuce Mayonnaise 10c	Bread and Butter 10c	Deviled Ham 20c
Lettuce Tomato 15c	Cold Chicken 25c	Pineapple Cheese 20c
Hamburger 15c	Sardine Sandwich 15c	Cold Turkey & Mayonnaise 30c
Salisbury Sandwich 15c	Bacon and Egg 20c	Relish Spread 15c
Gooseliver Sandwich 15c	Imported Swiss Cheese ...25c	Deviled Egg 15c
Fried Egg 15c	Stuffed Olive 25c	Philadelphia Cream
Peanut Butter 10c	Caviar, Chopped Onion ...50c	Cheese 20c
Hard Boiled Egg 15c	Denver on Toast 30c	Imported Salami 15c

HOT SANDWICHES With Potatoes and Gravy - Open Face

Hot Beef or Pork 25c	Hot Roast Veal 25c	Hot Turkey 35c
Hot Roast Lamb 25c	Hot Chicken 30c	Hot Ham 25c

Any Sandwich you do not see we will prepare it on request.

FOUNTAIN SPECIALS

ICE CREAM
Vanilla or Chocolate
  Plain 10c
Sherbet 10c
Sundaes all Flavors 15c
All Sundaes with Nuts ...20c
Bittersweet 15c
Banana Split 25c
Parfaits, all flavors 25c

Hot Fudge Sundae 15c
Ice Cream Sodas
  All Flavors 15c
Malted Milk all flavors ...15c
Double Thick Malted
  Milks 20c
Malted Milk with Egg ...20c
Chocolate Milk 05c
  with Float 10c

BEVERAGES
Coca Cola 05c
Root Beer 05c
Fresh Orangeade 10c
Fresh Limeade 10c
Fresh Lemonade 10c
Lime Rickey 10c
Ginger Ale per glass ...10c
Bottle Sodas, all flavors ...10c

Whipped Cream Used in all our Fountain Service.   *Our Fountain Service is Complete*
We will be glad to make any Fountain Special for the Asking.

DESSERTS, Pies Cakes and Pastry Made on Premises

Home Baked Pies, per cut 10c	Doughnuts, two for 05c
Layer Cake per slice 10c	Sweet Rolls, 2 for 05c
Danish or French Pastry "Home Baked" ...10c	Cheese on Pie, Extra 10c
Fruit Cake 15c	Fruit Jello, plain 10c
Cookies, two for 05c	with Whipped Cream 15c

Pie or Cake Topped with Ice Cream 5c Extra; with Whipped Cream 10c

HOT AND COLD BEVERAGES

Coffee is richest and best when made immediately after the freshly roasted bean is broken. Court Cafe Coffee is therefore ground only as used — just before it goes into the big urn. You get all the flavor and goodness of good coffee in every cup. Blenders of Our Own Coffee.

Coffee per Cup 05c	Sweet Milk Individual Bottle 05c
Buttermilk, Individual Bottle ...05c	Instant Postum per cup 05c
Ovaltine, Hot or Cold 15c	Iced Coffee or Iced Tea 05c
Cocoa ......10c with Whipped Cream 15c	
Hot Chocolate ......10c with Whipped Cream 15c	
Green or Black Tea per Pot 10c	

Our Own Soft Water Well Furnishes The Softest Water in the City.
It is Pure Take Home All You Like.

GRAND CANYON

MISSION CHURCH

NAVAJO CHURCH

THE MONUMENTS CANYON DE CHELLEY

KID CARSON'S CAVE

INDIAN WARRIOR

INDIAN MEDICINE MAN

Court Cafe
ALBUQUERQUE, NEW MEXICO
A La Carte Menu

Be Sure to See

The extra day you spend in Albuquerque will reward you with never-to-be forgotten experiences. Example, the breath-taking "Rim Drive", which takes you through interesting, primitive Tijeras Canyon to the crest of the steep Sandias east of the city. There, 11,000 feet above sea level, and 6,000 feet above the valey, your eyes sweep a hundred-mile view, with Albuquerque lying in the center, like a tiny, flattened ant hill.

West of the city, an easy drive, you find a group of extinct volcanoes. Over beyond, in the Rio Puerco valley, plenty of agate and other unusual rocks.

South thirteen miles you visit the Indian village of Isleta, which was there when Coronado came in 1540, and carries on its communal life today very much as it did then.

Stay another day in Albuquerque—take home life-long memories.

Our Curio and Gift Shop

Don't fail to visit this finely stocked department of the Court Cafe. In order to provide you with all that is unique and worth while in Southwestern curios, Indian jewelry, Indian pottery and basket work, imported Mexican novelties, wares and handicrafts. The space is small but the choice is extensive, as you will see when you look through its glass cases and open displays.

We are careful to keep the prices down to popular levels. Many local people find it an ideal place to purchase bridge prizes and other small personal gifts to send away. Before you go out, be sure to see what there is of interest for you in our curio and gift department.

Blue Room

This is our cocktail lounge, bar and dispensary. Try its comfortable chairs, its quick, accurate service. Drop in after the theatre, dance or party.

SOUVENIR MENUS

Our Menus make an interesting souvenir of your trip through Albuquerque. We have provided Mailing envelopes to send them home in. PLEASE ask Cashier for one if you wish, but DO NOT take this one.

WINDOW ROCK

GOVERNOR'S HOUSE INDIAN PUEBLO

TAOS INDIAN PUEBLO

Upon arrival, Kroc couldn't believe what he saw: at each of the order windows, lines of people were waiting to purchase food. In all his miles of travel, he had never witnessed anything like it. Then and there, he made up his mind that he would become part of the operation. As it turned out, he got his wish: The McDonalds hired him as their franchise agent and within ten years, he spread the

left
In the fall of 1948, the McDonald brothers closed down their San Bernardino, California, drive-in and fired all of their carhops! After a brief shutdown, they reopened with a new food serving plan based on what they called the "Speedy Service System." Its main features were self-service, minimal choice, and fast turnover. The 15 cent hamburger stand—and the American fast food industry—were born! *Courtesy Richard McDonald*

In 1949, Nash promoted its latest automotive model to the American family with images of recreation and comfort. With twin convertible beds and a more-than-roomy interior, Nash's latest offering appeared to be the perfect vehicle for the family eager to take to the roadways and venture into the great out-doors. With the latest Nash, motoring down Route 66 was a highway dream. *Reprinted with permission of the American Automobile Mfg. Assoc.*

fast-food gospel of the burger, fries, and Coca-Cola nationwide.

By the mid-1960s, people traveling down Route 66 couldn't drive very far without seeing those golden arches. Competitors cloned the concept and soon, sprawling cities and their suburbs were brimming with franchised food.

As more and more sections of two-lane 66 were bypassed by new routes, hamburger bars with styrofoamed foodstuffs and plastic utensils vied for position at the freeway exits and access. For those devoted to life in the slow lane, it appeared that the variety of eateries that made up the two-lane were in danger of extinction. The future of road food—or so it was thought—would be devoid of home-style food.

Meanwhile, a great number of restaurants settled in for the duration. With time on their side—they watched as freeways, turnpikes, and interstate highways soaked up customers. Many could not endure the onslaught and died out.

Then, something wonderful bloomed: Route 66 evolved into a certifiable artifact—an oddity, an aberration, a destination in itself. Modern automobilists began to rediscover the dining spots spoken so highly of

Roadside businesses along Route 66 have to change at a moment's notice. They may start out as a dining cafe and when economic conditions change, transform into an automotive repair shop. Passing motorists seldom notice the change until years later when advertising signs begin their slow fade. It's not at all unusual too see the various iterations a business has gone through once the layers of peeling paint reveal the truth: Mom's Cafe or Tire Repair? Riverton, Kansas. *Author*

Hoyt's Highway 66 restaurant featured famous foods that garnered the approval of Duncan Hines. For early restaurateurs, earning the Duncan Hines seal of approval equated to guaranteed success. Hines started out in the restaurant review business by a fortunate stroke of fate. A well-traveled salesman, he had compiled a list of favorite eateries for his friends and family. The public's interest prompted Hines to expand the list and publish it as a book, entitled *Adventures in Good Eating*. By 1939, it was selling at a steady clip of 100,000 per year! Albuquerque, New Mexico. *Courtesy Chuck Sturm*

113

Route 66 road rumors have it that the Club Cafe made famous by Ron Chavez might reopen. Currently closed and out of business, the restaurant was at one time billed as an "original Route 66 Restaurant since 1935." For years, the smiling mascot known affectionately as the "Fatman" caught the eyes of hungry travelers driving down Route 66. Sadly, after Ladybird Johnson implemented her plans for "Highway beautification," (the grinning Fatman and the billboards he brought to life became few and far between. Santa Rosa, New Mexico, 1983. *Jerry McClanahan ©1995*

by their parents! Hidden for so many years in the eddies and whorls of the forgotten road, classic restaurants were once again in great demand.

Today, the eateries found along America's Main Street have become classics. For all those traveling the old road, standards like the Snow Cap, the Club Cafe, the Cozy Drive-In, Rod's Steakhouse, Pop Hicks, the Dell Rhea Chicken Basket, Barney's Beanery, and the U Drop Inn have come to signify the old road's flavor. They are the pit stops that make up a tasty motor trip. Because—no matter how you bake, boil, fry, or microwave it—Route 66 motorists still travel on their stomachs.

Those Dreaded Days of Desert Water Bags

"When draped outside of a window, slung over the hood ornament, or hung on the side-mounted spare, air rushing over their exterior created an effect likened to 'wind chill.'"

For the traveler trekking across America during the 1920s and 1930s, transportation by car was rife with problems. Tires went flat regularly, if they didn't blow out! Engines threw rods, transmissions seized, and crankcases cracked. But, nothing inspired more dread than a plume of steam billowing from a screaming-hot radiator.

There was good reason: Radiators of the era were often delicate and frequently underrated for their applications. They were quick to overheat in traffic, during hot weather, and on steep inclines. The most inefficient designs even exhibited thermal problems under marginal circumstances, especially if a wad of leaves or splash of mud restricted their air flow. Certain automobiles of the age like the Wasp phaeton (with Continental T-6 engine) added inherent design flaws to the equation: Its lack of side ventilation louvers on the engine cowl worsened the overheating problems.

In urban areas where water and other amenities were plentiful, these technical matters rarely aroused concern. However, when long-distance travel dictated the navigation of unpopulated regions of the Southwest—especially over the Sitgreaves Pass in Arizona—thoughts were quickly dominated by desolate desert stereotypes. So-called "last chance" gas stations didn't waste time capitalizing on the worries: posted warnings implored motorists to fill up with fuel and water. Billboards adorned with skull and crossbones reinforced the message, conjuring images of stranded travelers perishing of thirst.

To ease their panic, motorists relied on portable "water bags" to carry along extra liquid. Originally intended to transport drink-

The canvas water bag was at one time a familiar sight along the distant miles of Highway 66. To complete the desert crossings in Arizona, motorists relied on the portable container to hold their drinking (and sometimes radiator) water. Slung over the hood of a speeding car or hung outside a window, evaporation cooled the contents of the bag making it more palatable to drink. *Author*

ing water for human consumption, these soft containers were universally adopted by cross-country drivers as insurance policies for radiator boil-over. During the heyday of America's maternal two-lane, the practice of topping off one's bag before a journey heightened to near religious fervor. It was a ritual repeated along the entire length of the 2,400 mile strip, rivaled only by gas tanks being filled with motor fuel!

While design of the bags varied, the standard models were specially woven from Scotch Flax or "genuine imported linen." For less than a one-dollar bill, the conscientious vehicle owner could purchase a sack from well-stocked service stations, auto supply houses, and general stores. Rectangular in configuration, the typical canvas container featured heavy border stitching and a removable cap—secured from loss by string or chain. Some sported a flat, wooden carrying handle with hand-hold. To facilitate easy hanging on the exterior of the vehicle, most came with a heavy-duty rope looped through eyelets.

On the exterior, bold graphics distinguished the competitors: the well-known "Safari" brand featured a roaring lion, "Hirsch Weis" a vaulting buck, and "Water Boy" a feathered Indian. W.A. Plummer's classic pick and shovel design flaunted the worrisome bromide, "Desert Water Bag." Even the Pep Boys got in on the action! Speeding across the desert in a convertible, the grinning caricatures of Manny, Moe, and Jack appeared fearless as they hurtled across the no-man's land of sagebrush and saguaro.

It was an appropriate image, since forward motion is what actually made the bags work. After filling with water, they began to perspire with moisture as liquid leached through the special strands of cloth. When draped outside of a window, slung

The Elmer Thomas family of migrants stopped in the Oklahoma town of Muskogee for some water in 1939. To refill the reservoir, the combination hood ornament and radiator cap was removed (note the elaborate crest he is holding) and the water poured in. Specialized antifreeze was the least of Mr. Thomas's worries. Russell Lee photo, 1939. *Library of Congress*

over the hood ornament, or hung on the side-mounted spare, air rushing over their exterior created an effect likened to "wind chill." The intense evaporation caused contents inside the pouch to cool. So, instead of heating up to the outside ambient air temperature, water remained "cool and palatable."

Despite the clever principles involved, the chilling novelty of the desert water bag eventually faded. For the thirsty, the insulated ice-chest and vacuum flask Thermos became standard equipment for mobile dining. Automotive technologies advanced as well, resulting in the introduction of improved formulations for artificial coolant. Chemically protected in conditions hot or cold, engines evolved into efficient and powerful machines—virtually free from the specter of thermal breakdown.

By the 1950s, the requirement to tote a dripping udder of extra water east and west along Route 66 was all but eliminated. The venerable water purse was tossed into the trunk, discarded, and gladly forgotten. It was—and always would be—a reminder of the days when motoring across America required a pioneering spirit, a full gas tank, and a bulging desert water bag.

Wichita, Kansas, was the home for Valentine Diners, a post-WWII manufacturer that made prefabricated dining units for the roadside trade. A variety of aluminum models were offered, all numbered and leased to operators eager to make a fast buck. While most diners are typically located in New England, the Valentine units are found all across the country, and of course, various spots on Route 66. The Birthplace Diner was located on the site of Winslow's first dwelling and at one time had a miniature stork planted on top of it (to honor its historic location). Thelma Holloway was the first to manage this minuscule lunch counter. Most recently, it changed to Leon Dodd's One Spot Grill. *Jerry McClanahan ©1995*

AT THE CROSSROADS
OF U. S. HIGHWAYS
66 AND 77

GARLAND'S
DRIVE-IN
RESTAURANT

OKLAHOMA'S
FINEST

22nd and Broadway

OKLAHOMA CITY

Phone 5-8811

SEA FOOD   BARBECUE   CURB SERVICE

U. S. HIGHWAY 77   22ND STREET

At the crossroads of Highways 66 and 77 in Oklahoma City, Oklahoma, Garland's Drive-In took its rooftop sign to the limit. Originally incorporated into building architecture to circumvent local sign regulations, the idea of a tall, central spire bedecked with neon lettering was a concept embraced by curb servers all across the country. *Preziosi Postcards*

During the 1930s, California Route 66 was thick with orange juice stands. Everybody it seemed was getting into the orange juice business, eager to sell their crop of squeezed citrus to the carloads of arrivees coming in on the great diagonal highway. Many larger restaurants and dining chains got their start in this manner, including a small refreshment stand run by Richard and Maurice McDonald, founders of the now ubiquitous McDonald's chain of hamburger eateries. Route 66, Rialto, California. *Author*

The ribbons of Route 66 roadway like the one found near Fenner, California, are the lengths of vintage highway that often stimulate the appetite. During miles and miles of long-distance driving, evidence of civilization is often sparse—driving the motorist's imagination to visions of full-service gasoline stations offering ice water, drive-in restaurants delivering cold drinks, and wayside cafes serving up freshly grilled cheeseburgers. *D. Jeanene Tiner ©1995*

chapter four

ROUND-UP

MOTEL

VACANCY

AIR CONDITIONED

FREE TV

To a man or woman fond of the bignesses and the mysteries of the open, it is the nights on the trail that form the greater part of the joy of transcontinental motoring. You can spread your blanket beside the Santé Fe Trail or the Overland Trail or the Lincoln Highway, and if God has given you any imagination whatsoever, you can forget that there are six-cylinders and an electric starter within forty feet of you, and can imagine yourself going with Fremont out toward the unknown, or laboring westward to find a foothold in a great new land.
Edward Hungerford, "America Awheel," Everybody's Magazine, 1917

Motor Hotels:
America's Home on the Road

Regarding convenience and comfort, the slow-moving tortoise has an obvious advantage over the speeding motorist! When a day's travel comes to a close, he has no worries over where he might sleep. He simply picks out a serene spot, withdraws his appendages, retracts his head, and remains still until rested. Inside his shell he is safe, warm, and protected. When circumstances call for relocation to a new environment, his self-contained, portable accommodations move right along with him. It's an idea that has been admired by the automobile owner since the debut of the gas-powered engine and a concept that has been experimented with since the dirt road days of Route 66.

Of all the collectibles pertaining to Route 66, the common matchbook remains one of the easiest artifacts to acquire. In the days before smoking was considered a nuisance, hotels, motels, and other roadside businesses distributed these hand-held gems to advertise their accommodations. *Courtesy Chuck Sturm*

left
Along the shoulder of the old road, Western themes have always dominated motel sign graphics. In Oklahoma, Texas, New Mexico, and Arizona, the predominant subjects were, and continue to be, rough-riding cowboys, colorful Indians, Longhorn cattle, and the ubiquitous Saguaro cactus. It's all part of the illusion designed to make travelers feel as if they have reached the destination imagined in their mind's eye. Claremore, Oklahoma. *Author*

121

The Boots Motel is prime example of the architectural stylings popularized during the 1930s and 1940s. With its rounded corners, distinctive "speed lines," and pastel accents, it's one of the roadside resources of Route 66 that should not be missed. Carthage, Missouri. *Shellee Graham © 1995*

Unfortunately, the pioneering motor vehicle operator of the early 1900s didn't have such an easy go of it. Back then, a long-distance journey across the expanse of America was described best by the etymology of the word "travel." Originally, this innocuous expression was derived from the French *travail*, meaning work and trouble. Further iteration cites the Latin *trepalium*, a three-staked instrument of torture! It's an apt description, since the pitfalls and problems encountered by the automotive enthusiast at the turn of the century were numerous. Spending the nights along the trail meant a reliance upon one's own resources.

In that regard, automobilists so inclined to risk life and limb simply to prove that they could drive a motor coach all the way across America and "dip their wheels in the Pacific" found it prudent to stock up on equipment germane to the explorer. Tents, kerosene lanterns, portable cooking equipment, bedrolls, hunting gear—and a myriad of other camping paraphernalia—became required baggage for would-be adventurers hooked on four-wheeled overland transportation.

On occasion, car travelers could take advantage of the hotel facilities offered in some of the larger cities. But for numerous reasons, these were avoided by intrepid explorers addicted to the smell of gasoline and burning motor oil. With money reserved for more important incidentals such as tire patches, extraction from mud holes, or mechanical repair, paying for the

122

Although closed and abandoned, the Rest Haven Motel still boasts a fetching roadside sign. While much of the neon is broken and the electricity disconnected, it continues to attract the gaze of all those in search of the past. Afton, Oklahoma. *Author*

privilege to recline on a lumpy mattress and have a tip-hungry bellman carry one's baggage was the last thing any self-respecting adventurer wanted to do.

At the same time, there were obvious issues of appearance to consider. Entering an establishment with grease-splattered driving goggles, soiled gauntlets, and a duster thick with road dirt was often viewed with great trepidation by both the desk clerks and hotel management. At the boarding houses that catered to a less affluent class, the reverse was true: Those arriving in the motorcars were the ones uncomfortable with the surroundings and social strata of the clientele.

As a result, the open spaces that bordered the public highways and byways became attractive venues for travelers to set up temporary sleeping accommodations. When tired eyes called for rest, one simply decelerated, turned the steering wheel right or left, and coasted into the nearest clearing. Outdoors, natural amenities provided roving travelers with free facilities, unencumbered by monetary and social constraints often imposed by the urban hotel.

In the "great outdoors," wood for campfires was readily accessible, water could be carried from streams, and personal facilities were abundant. When answering the call of nature, one sought refuge behind a substantial tree and took care of business. In the natural environment of the undeveloped roadside, there were no monitors, no rules. Best of all, there was always plenty of free parking!

At first, landowners who found themselves host to visitors tolerated the infrequent forays onto their property and sometimes even offered the hand of hospitality. The friendliness proved short-lived, however, and even turned to loathing as more and more motorists ventured past city limits in search of scenery and solitude. When Henry Ford introduced the affordable Model T in 1908, the days of

unbridled activities along the roadside were destined to end. Within two short years, there were 468,500 registered motor vehicles plying the roadways with a substantial number placing undue demands on rural real estate.

To quell the unsupervised actions of overnight freeloaders, farmers and landowners with property bisected by highways began to adopt a stricter attitude

continued on page 128

In the beginning, America's auto camps offered little luxury. In most cases, visitors arriving by automobile had to fend for themselves when it came to water and toilet facilities. Fortunately, the situation began to improve by the 1940s with the advent of "sanitary facilities." Slowly but surely, the American outhouse was fading into oblivion. Southern California, Russell Lee photo, 1940. *Library of Congress*

125

Frank Redford's Wigwam Village Motels

"Occasionally, customers got more than their money's worth when Native American dancers imported from Oklahoma demonstrated the lost art of rainmaking."

During the 1950s, "cowboys and Indians" was a favorite game for children. Back then, the airwaves were populated by characters like Buffalo Bob Smith, Hopalong Cassidy, The Lone Ranger and Tonto. A craze for the West permeated American popular culture and businesses along 66 did all they could to fuel the frenzy. Motel showman Frank Redford led the pack.

It all started in the early 1930s with a cone-shaped ice cream stand in Long Beach, California. Inspired by the design, Redford built a filling station and cafe in Horse Cave, Kentucky. When it opened in 1933, the tourists visiting nearby Mammoth Cave could hardly believe their eyes: Indian teepees were sprouting along Highway 31E! The "main office" was a 60-foot tall construction of wood and stucco, enhanced by a matching pair of "wigwam" rest rooms.

After repeated requests from customers for overnight cabins, Redford added six "sleeping rooms" in 1935. A year later, he patented the exterior design of the teepees and proceeded to field inquiries from entrepreneurs eager to open their own roadside camp. Over the next 15 years, the Wigwam Villages grew into a modest motel chain with seven sites in six states. Two of the most celebrated reservations made their home along the Will Rogers Highway.

Appropriately, Wigwam Village number six occupied a lot on Hopi Drive in Holbrook, Arizona. As Route 66 rose in prominence, it became a premier tourist attraction for motorists traveling through "the heart of Indian country." When number seven was completed in 1947, the Foothill Boulevard section through San Bernardino, California, gained new status on the road maps. Curious carloads came to take snapshots, stay overnight, or just plain look. Both locations became recognized landmarks—part and parcel of getting one's kicks along Route 66.

For the unjaded motorist on holiday, the Indian motif had unquestionable allure. And why not? Near the road, a teepee-shaped sign provided a modern version of the smoke signal in neon, imploring all those who passed to "Eat and Sleep in a Wigwam!" Auto excursionists were enchanted by the idea and eagerly checked-in to experience the wonders. Upon their departure, teepee-shaped menus and plaster replicas were purchased as treasured souvenirs.

Redford was more than willing to feed the fantasies, at one point hiring a trio of young Indian lads as helpers. Occasionally, customers got more than their money's worth when Native American dancers imported from Oklahoma demonstrated the lost art of rainmaking.

Fortunately, the teepees were impervious to the elements and well insulated for the "peace and quiet" of overnight patrons. The internal framework consisted of wood timbers arranged to form a multi-sided cone then covered in tar paper. Stucco was plastered on to fashion the faux "cowhide" skin, artfully sculpted at each entryway to give the appearance of a rolled back flap. Similarly, the four lodgepoles that projected up through the tip were for visual effect only.

Outside, the exterior paint scheme was decidedly subdued, enhancing the roadside illusion. The majority of the teepee surface was finished with a coat of bright white paint. At the vertex of each hut, a contrasting splash of red was edged with a sublime border of zigzag. A similar course of colorful rickrack encircled the middle circumference of each cabin, leading the eye to an ornamental line surrounding the unit's diamond-shaped window.

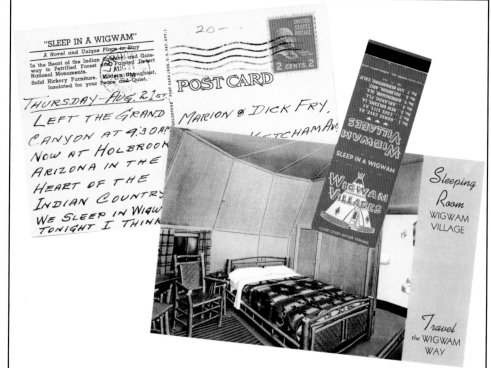

One of the most memorable attributes of the Wigwam Villages were their interiors. Proprietor Frank Redford furnished the cabins with authentic Navajo and Apache rugs and blankets. A suite of real hickory furniture—with the bark still in place—completed the rustic atmosphere. Holbrook, Arizona. *Courtesy Chuck Sturm*

Inside, all of the modern conveniences were available. Full bathroom facilities with a shower, sink, and toilet pleased even the most discerning tribe. While a fire would have been stoked in a real wigwam, heating was provided by a thermostatically controlled steam radiator. Electrical outlets delivered power for Mom's portable iron and Dad's Zenith Trans-Oceanic radio.

In the decor department, the teepee interiors were carefully orchestrated to indulge the notions of what a "real" western lodge should look like. A suite of rustic furniture included a bed, night stand, and chair—all fashioned from natural hickory wood with the bark still in place. Redford supplied the rooms with authentic Apache Indian blankets, Navajo rugs, teepee-shaped table lamps, and wigwam ashtrays. Of course, the wall-to-wall paneling was knotty-pine!

With that accomplished, Redford's Wigwam Villages satisfied two of the traveler's most important needs: lodging and adventure. For a single fare, the typical family was allowed to stay in a comfy motel room and experience the delights of an authentic roadside attraction. Along the marvelous miles of old Route 66, no amount of wampum could buy a better deal.

Partners Frank Redford and his wife, Vetra, operated Kentucky's Wigwam Village Motel with the help of Redford's mother, Sally Ann. Through a combination of unusual architecture, teamwork, and high moral standards, they made the Wigwam Villages into the most-recognized icons of Highway 66. *Keith A. Sculle Collection*

When compared to common building methods, construction of the teepee sleeping units was unconventional. At first, they were made with a steel framework covered by lath and plaster. After a number of chronic problems surfaced with that design, the method was modified to make the buildings more like boat hulls. Applied to each steel cabin frame was a layer of wood, a layer of felt, and a covering of canvas. Finally, a generous amount of linseed oil was applied to shrink the structures until they were finally covered with stucco and painted. Wigwam Village No. 5, Birmingham, Alabama, 1940s. *Keith A. Sculle Collection*

The Wigwam Village (located on Hopi Drive in Holbrook, Arizona) is one of the last pristine examples of the teepee motel chain begun by Frank Redford after World War II. Today, all those in search of the old road—and the landmarks that made it what it was—may still spend the night there. Although the modern motel chains are nice, there's still nothing that can beat the fun of "sleeping in a wigwam." *Shellee Graham ©1995*

ENJOY REAL WESTERN HOSPITALITY

SILVER SPUR MOTEL

EAST AMARILLO, TEXAS — ON U. S. HIGHWAYS 60 & 66

IC-H656

Americans vacationing by car have always been enamored with the concept of the West, and Route 66 motels fueled the fantasy with a variety of cowboy themes. But whether it was the Silver Spur, the Longhorn, Golden Saddle, Wagon Wheel, or the Branding Iron, it really didn't matter. All served up a heaping helping of the "real western hospitality" so craved by the public. East Amarillo, Texas. *Preziosi Postcards*

right
While Bailey's Motel was basically a simple, contiguous structure under one roof, it really painted a romantic image for itself with its lasso-roping postcard. In the real world, the rooms featured pretty much the same type of furniture and bathroom fixtures found at a majority of the motels in town, although "Panelray Heat" was touted as one of the unique amenities. What was it? Simply a vertical gas burner set into the wall and individually controlled by the room's occupant. It was the next best thing to a real campfire on the open range. Amarillo, Texas. *Preziosi Postcards*

continued from page 125

toward the ever-increasing swarms of motorized locusts descending on their land. And who could blame them? The thoughtless crowds arriving by car were making a mess of the countryside, helping themselves to shrubs, trampling fields, and picking orchards clean. Cows were milked dry without permission and crops harvested for a quick roadside snack. In one dramatic incident, a crowd of car campers accidentally set fire to a landowner's woods while another bunch tore off entire branches from the trees.

By 1925, the unbridled activities had reached the breaking point, and a number of national magazines published scathing articles critical of the

AILEY'S MOTEL

TH AVE.   PHONE 2-0423   AMARILLO, TEXAS

The rustic log cabin was a popular structure for independent motel operators in the Missouri Ozarks. They were a common sight along Route 66 during the 1940s and 1950s. John's "Modern" Cabins have stood the test of time, and although completely abandoned, they have become a much-admired and visited landmark along the old road south of Rolla, Missouri. Bypassed by new asphalt, the decaying shells may still be visited along a dead end stretch of Route 66 frontage. *Dan Harlow ©1995*

phenomenon. One fed-up farmer summed up the problem when he explained how motorists "would turn into the meadow without saying so much as by your leave; pitch their tent, collect firewood, cook supper, and then start hell-raising as if the whole place had been made over to them by deed!" A change was coming.

Part of the new relationship with automobile owners was to prohibit their entry onto private property. Barbed wire was strung along the shoulder, joined by fencing and other barriers to keep the so-called "hurrah boys" from spoiling areas adjacent to the public corridors. "No Trespassing" and "Keep Out" signs became a part of the scenery. To emphasize their position, a few farmers kept watch with their shotguns close at hand. To deter would-be visitors from setting up overnight encampments, a vicious-looking dog secured by what appeared to be a weak chain proved to be one of the most effective strategies. Like it or not, the uninhibited lifestyle of the motoring camper was drawing to a close.

At the same time, businessmen in towns along Highway 66 and other routes realized that this unorganized rabble of "game, fish, and flower hogs" could be readily tapped as a substantial source of income. The consensus was that if the throngs of sputtering

Some trailer courts and auto camps furnished laundry facilities to their boarders. Because there was an additional charge levied to use electric washing machines, an area was reserved for the manual agitation and rinsing of clothes. Of course, there were certain rules and protocol to follow to ensure that the equipment was clean and in good order for the next customer. Southern California, Russell Lee photo, 1940. *Library of Congress*

automobiles could be influenced to set up their camps in organized parks near the city limits, all the businesses lining Main Street and other urban areas would be patronized for groceries, clothing goods, automotive supplies, and other services.

To test the theory, many towns erected municipal camps that offered free space where motorists could

left
The 66 Motel is one of Tulsa's surviving motor courts. Found at the outskirts of town on a part of the old road alignment that cuts through an industrial area, it continues to house travelers exploring the back roads. Noma Undernehr is the current owner of this forgotten treasure on the edge. *Author*

131

Highway 66 remains home to many small motor courts and overnight facilities that are individually owned and operated. Giant lodging chains such as Holiday Inn, Best Western, and La Quinta now choose to concentrate their business efforts at the freeway off-ramps—leaving the slow-lane trade to the survivors. Still, there's competition to worry about, evidenced by the variety of amenities and extras some of the independents offer their customers. Vinita, Oklahoma. *Author*

pitch a tent, roll out a bedroll, or slumber in their rumble seat. Along with complimentary campsites, the municipal operations featured all the basic conveniences so sorely lacking along the nation's highways. Public privies were installed for personal hygiene and there was even running water available for washing clothes and cooking. At some of the better camps, one could find playgrounds for the children, bathing facilities,

and electrical hookups. At long last, America's hoards of auto-campers had a cheap, easy-to-access oasis at their disposal. Along Highway 66 and other roads like it, the municipal camps surged in popularity.

Like the cities, the manufacturers of travel gadgets saw a great potential for sales and soon introduced a host of products geared to the car club. One of the most popular contrivances was the "auto-

Massage of the Magic Fingers Mattress

"Sampling the subtle waves of relaxation emanating from his reconfigured recliner, he coined the phrase 'Magic Fingers' and set upon the task of marketing it to the masses."

During the twilight of the 1950s, the Englander Company manufactured a commercial mattress with a mechanical vibrator at its core. One of its top salesmen, John Houghtaling (pronounced hotel-ing), peddled the unit to customers in the lodging industry. When a number of clients complained that the massagers were burning out, he took it upon himself to find out why.

For almost two years, he conducted a relentless campaign of under-bed research. Mattresses were dissected, bedsprings analyzed, and motors monitored. After disassembling the mysterious motion transducer and studying its intricate workings, he discovered that "there wasn't much to it." Inside, what was initially perceived as a mechanized marvel consisted of nothing more than a simple electric motor with a small counterweight attached to its driveshaft.

Houghtaling began to tinker on his own and soon devised a much more reliable version. It was small, powerful, and a snap to replace. Best of all, his visionary design had a specific advantage over the existing competition: it could easily be mated with any mattress. Now, anyone handy with a screwdriver could install one of these new massagers—right to the inside of a bed's box spring! A quad arrangement of special, grooved mounting posts made easy work of attaching the vibromodule between the cushioning coils. The inventive Houghtaling wisely patented his unique design approach.

Sampling the subtle waves of relaxation emanating from his reconfigured recliner, he coined the phrase "Magic Fingers" and set upon the task of marketing it to the masses. Sales representatives from across the country were recruited in a loose franchise arrangement. For an investment of $2,500, would-be dealers received 80 of the vibrator units, three days of training, and audio-visual materials. After that, it was the dealer's responsibility to locate potential customers, handle installation, facilitate repairs, and finally, collect the sacks of coins accumulated at the end of each month.

A compact control head (attached by wire) held the loot and activated the magical oscillations. Bolted down securely (in later years) to the night stand, it served as both a pay receptacle and housing for the timer. When sleepy overnighters dropped one quarter into the coin meter, it tripped a mechanism—allowing 15 minutes of operation. The setup worked without a hitch for a number of years until basic honesty went the way of the dodo. Suddenly, anyone and everyone (including some motel employees) began breaking into the coin meters to help themselves to the proceeds!

For the hapless distributor, the resulting losses could be quite substantial. During the heyday of Magic Fingers mania, over 250,000 units were buzzing along at both the independent and major chain accommodations nationwide. With an average of eight quarters brought in by each unit during the time span of one month, an entrepreneur maintaining a few hundred vibrators could pull in a considerable chunk of change. Since Houghtaling didn't demand royalties, top salesmen could make a good living.

By the 1970s, an aggressive attempt was made to thwart the pilferage by employing magnetic stripe technology.

Room renters received a card from the desk clerk during check-in that could be credited with incremental amounts of time. Back in the privacy of their rooms, a modified control head read the debit card and activated the Magic Fingers. Unfortunately, costs to continually upgrade the system to reflect the latest technology were prohibitive. Card readers that were initially "high-tech" were quickly rendered obsolete by the fast pace of progress.

Eventually, coin theft became such a problem that Houghtaling couldn't sell distributorships with a clear conscience. Somebody would set up business and effectively go broke in just a few months.

During the halcyon days of roadside lodging, the progressive proprietors of hotels, motels, and tourist courts like the Blue Swallow learned of the Magic Fingers unit in industry publications like *Tourist Court Journal*. Along with the coin-operated radio and the soda machine, it was perceived by some as a cost-effective way to maximize profits from overnight patrons. With its ease of installation and affordability, Magic Fingers quickly joined "refrigerated air" and "a television in every room" as yet another popular amenity. Tucumcari, New Mexico. *Jerry McClanahan ©1995*

But the Magic Fingers wasn't licked yet: In the early 1980s, the General Stamping and Manufacturing Company of Hialeah, Florida, acquired rights to the gizmo and began marketing it to residential customers. While demand from the motel industry waned, seniors remembered the therapeutic gadgets from their cross-country journeys on Route 66 and eagerly purchased them for home use—albeit, without the coin meters.

Today, fully functional models of the venerable Magic Fingers mattress can still be discovered—and enjoyed—at a smattering of tourist courts, cabins, and no-tell motels along the retired recesses of Highway 66. Along with "refrigerated air" and "a television in every room," Houghtaling's shimmying shaker has found a place of permanence in the pop culture of the American road. Anybody got change for a buck?

During the days before extensive thought was put into auto interiors, motoring vast distances along Route 66 could be quite grueling. After all, spartan bench seats offered little support for the lower lumbar region. Without cruise-control, the accelerator foot tired quickly. The absence of power steering brought on tired shoulders and wrist cramps. Lacking today's ergonomics, cars could be rolling torture chambers. Fortunately, America's burgeoning motel industry came to the rescue by equipping rentals with therapeutic aids. During the 1960s, travelers obsessed with arriving in "Tucumcari Tonight" were rewarded with a massage therapist in every room! How could they do it? Simple: Every bed was equipped with a shimmying shaker. For only 25 cents, a bed vibrator soothed spines, relaxed muscles, and calmed travelers to a restful slumber. *Courtesy General Stamping & Mfg. Co.*

During the 1940s, the Hotel Franciscan was one of the highlights of staying overnight in Albuquerque, New Mexico. An initial glance suggests another incarnation of the adobe Pueblo, but further examination reveals distinct Art-Deco overtones as well as hints of the International style. As part of the concept, roof timbers have become idealized drainpipes and windows stylized portals. Note the unique sign on the gun store to the left of the building. John Collier photo, 1943. *Library of Congress*

Along the Santa Fe Trail in Missouri, travelers of the early teens had only two choices when it came to lodging: sleep in established hotels in the cities along the way, or make a camp out in the open wilderness. Horseless carriage owners were sometimes frowned upon because of their disheveled appearance, hence the wide open spaces were often chosen to avoid scrutiny. Missouri, A.L. Westgard photo, circa 1912. *National Archives*

tent," a collapsible camping device that mounted right onto the running board of an automobile. When time came to set up camp, it was unfolded by the enthusiast into a full-sized shelter—complete with a cot for sleeping, support springs, and a built-in headrest (the running board). For the growing ranks of car owners anxious to experience the adventures of auto-camping, it was the perfect vacation accessory for the open road.

Warner's Autotrailer "Prairie Schooner" took the tent idea to the next level with a collapsible sleeping unit that attached to

134

DEDICATED TO WILL ROGERS, THE WORLD'S GREATEST HUMORIST. CLAREMORE, OKLA., U.S.A.

HOTEL WILL ROGERS

WILL ROGERS HOTEL

the rear bumper. A distant cousin to the "pop-up" trailers that would appear decades later, it sported two wheels attached to a compact trailer compartment. Inside the box, a rather complex arrangement of poles and canvas were stored until it was time to set up camp. Once assembled, the Auto-trailer was the envy of all the auto-

campers—that is—until time came to put it all back in the box again. For those who experienced difficulty in folding a service station roadmap, breaking down this unit and fitting it back in the rolling compart-ment was a daunting task. Onlookers gained a new admiration for the simplicity of a pup tent.

The Hotel Will Rogers was dedicated on February 7, 1930. After the ceremony, Rogers himself said, "I was more proud to see my name in electric lights in my old home town on an institution built for service to the public, than I ever was on the biggest theater on Broadway." Since the hotel made a commitment to offering "That Eastern Atmosphere, Western Welcome, and Southern Hospitality," Rogers' statement was more than mere hyperbole. Claremore, Oklahoma. *Courtesy Chuck Sturm*

The Nelson Dream Village was an annex to the famous Nelson Tavern. On the grounds, visitors could thrill to the Musical Fountain and drive right up to rooms that featured a free garage. The individual "Guest Houses" were built to resemble storybook cottages and allowed renters to lose themselves in a distinct roadside "world." While such an establishment might be considered hokey if judged by today's standards, it was an appropriate format for an age that lacked Disneyworld, Six Flags, and the Universal Studios Tour. Lebanon, Missouri. *Preziosi Postcards*

Still, the availability of new camping equipment wasn't the only force that contributed to the municipal camp's success. The profusion of new vehicles taking to the highways was a more likely cause. Statistics released in 1924 by the Automobile Association of America revealed that well over 16 million motor vehicles were in operation nationwide. It was estimated that each motorcar was driven an average of 5,000 miles every year with 10 percent of the travel time

devoted to what the pundits referred to as the "gypsy pilgrimage."

As patronage of the municipal camps swelled, a whole new set of problems developed. First and foremost were concerns about the ability to overnight at a camp for free. While the complimentary arrangement was a desirable incentive for the typical traveler, it attracted a fair number of "undesirables." Unemployed drifters, con-artists, ex-convicts, door-to-door salesmen, and other shifty characters arranged semi-

Reed's Cabins were some of the coziest on the Missouri side of the Mississippi. Sure, they weren't anything fancy, but at least they provided a cheap place to stay for a family heading west. Today, simple overnight courts like Reed's are getting harder to come by. A sparse few remain as forgotten footnotes to the golden age of Highway 66. Carthage, Missouri. *Courtesy Chuck Sturm*

During the mid-1920s to late 1930s, the average conveniences along Route 66 were quite modest. Motel accommodations were simple, unadorned, and utilitarian in nature. After all, people traveling away from home by automobile were happy enough just to get a roof over their heads. It seems curious that in those days, society got along just fine without all the swimming pools, fitness centers, and fax machines so cherished by today's highway adventurers. Vinita, Oklahoma. *Courtesy Chuck Sturm*

permanent housing simply by driving up with an old clunker and setting up housekeeping on the running boards. Their freeloading was causing both a monetary and social strain.

As the problem worsened, legitimate customers who had funds to buy fuel from the camp-run gas station or foodstuffs from the adjoining grocery store grew concerned over the declining ambiance. As news of the conditions spread throughout the regions of Route 66, the idea of a "free" motor camp took on a decidedly negative connotation.

In an effort to rehabilitate the public's perception of their facilities, many camp outfits decided that it would be best to charge a nominal fee to motoring campers. That way, the increasing mob of out-of-gas malingerers and motor-hobos would be

½ Mi. South of Vinita, Oklahoma on U.S. 66 - 69 - 60

137

Signs—especially brightly lit neon signs with loud colors—are what once attracted customers to the highway motor courts. Out on the road, these glaring messages mounted high atop a pole were often the first thing seen amid the cacophony of billboards and roadside advertising. During the 1950s, a neon clock mounted above the front entryway was standard. Tulsa, Oklahoma. *Author*

forced to relocate when their money was depleted. The concept worked, allowing the proprietors of the municipal camps to effectively relocate the shiftless overnighter.

Unfortunately, the implementation of this pay-as-you-stay policy came too late. The damage was already done and it seemed that no amount of public relations could polish the tarnished image of the organized roadside camp. For all intents and purposes,

The Pueblo Bonito Motel was one of Albuquerque's finest accommodations. Located on Highway 66 (2424 West Central Avenue), it featured the adobe Pueblo style of architecture so admired in the Southwest. Large, three- and two-bedroom apartments with kitchenettes were available, each room featuring air-conditioning, an automatic floor furnace, tile bath, custom-built Franciscan furniture, and an enclosed heated garage. During WWII, defense workers used the facilities as temporary housing. Albuquerque, New Mexico, John Collier photo, 1943. *Library of Congress*

Sign Language Neon of the Motel Marquee

"Ever eager to please, the proprietors of hotels and motels incorporated a variety of regional stereotypes into their signage."

Forty years ago, nothing could compare to the razzle dazzle of lights witnessed along roadside 66. As twilight descended upon the two-lane, the illuminated signs of motor courts, motels, and tourist cabins assumed dominance over the night. In a kaleidoscope of color, miles of neon flickered to life with a new language—an iconic code intended solely for automotive occupants.

Leading the dialogue in this lexicon of light was the unpretentious indicator of availability: the "vacancy" sign. If accommodations were booked solid, the dimmed portion of this signal was illuminated. From the highway, one could tell at a glance whether or not a motel had empty rooms. For the motorist, it was the one key element of an advertising billboard that determined whether or not to read on.

At the next level, tourist court terminology required a bit more scrutiny. While the ice blue characters of "air conditioning" teased the senses with frosty twists of neon, a degree of caution was called for before one actually signed a guest register. In the formative years preceding the perfection of personal indoor comfort, this deceptive catch-phrase routinely referred to an ordinary heating system or centralized fan!

Likewise, the words "air-cooled" couldn't be relied upon to provide substantial heat relief. The reality of this slogan was more suggestion than actual fact. In layman's terms, it described the possibilities of a process known as evaporative cooling—a crude arrangement that relied on a water-breathing leviathan, known affectionately (to traveling salesmen and residents of Arizona) as the "swamp cooler." The only sign language that guaranteed a chilled breeze was "air-cooled by refrigeration."

With matters of comfort addressed, the motoring crowd looked to the motel sign for entertainment clues. For some, the ability to catch the latest episode of "I Love Lucy" was just as important as indoor climate. But simply qualifying a sign for the word "television" wasn't always enough. By the time the would-be watcher realized the screen was coin-operated, it was too late. "Free T.V." was the correct combo to look for if one desired unlimited tube time.

For vacationers unconcerned with the pratfalls of the Ricardo family or the humidity of their cabin, a sign that stirred the imagination was often reason enough to pull over. Ever eager to please, the proprietors of hotels and motels incorporated a variety of regional stereotypes into their signage. Recurring themes included past presidents, animals, the westward movement, Indians, and of course, cowboys.

Not surprisingly, the western mystique was the most popular theme along Route 66, even in the Midwest. Consider the rustic Wagon Wheel Motel in the village of Cuba, Missouri: with an uncluttered arrangement of bow-legged letters and a wooden-spoke wheel, it rustled up childhood fantasies filled with prairie schooners and cattle drives. Once upon a time along the Will Rogers Highway, just the idea of the "West" was enough to sell motel rooms.

As the real gateway to the West was breached in Oklahoma and then Texas, the down-home dialect of the motel signs turned to twang. Suddenly, idealized depictions of cowboys riding the range on horseback whooped it up in blazing

A view looking west down old Route 66 in Holbrook, Arizona. As in many of the tourist towns found along the great diagonal highway, Holbrook's motel row is a neon dream of the urban boulevard. *Jerry McClanahan ©1995*

color. Wild stallions reared, snorted, and galloped in curves of animated neon. The lasso—primary tool for the cowpoke—became an integral part of a sign's message. In most cases, it twirled out from the roper's hand to spell out a variety of catchy come-ons in golden strokes of yellow light. It was one wild ride!

Of course, Native Americans received an equal amount of sign coverage, minus the buckaroos. The proud profile of a generic Chief wearing a feathered headdress became the most common design, a tomahawk-toting brave running close second. Some court-tels tried to model their signposts after totem poles or Hopi Kachinas, but most remained true to the fanciful perceptions born of the tourist's vivid imagination. For the drowsy driver exploring 66, the visual vocabulary of the American motel marquee made up one convincing sales pitch. *They* were the reason we chose to exit the road—because when it came right down to it, rented bed and bathrooms were almost identical. The real differences were burning brightly up on those amazing billboards of light, electrified representations of what ideal overnight accommodations could be, should be and not what they really were.

The Cotton Boll motel probably saw more travelers heading to western vacations than it did cotton pickers. Consisting of a small L-shaped motel without garages, it remains as a prime example of the simple motel structure with connected sleeping units. As of the mid-1990s, the "vacancy" sign was still lit. East of Elk City in Canute, Oklahoma, 1983. *Jerry McClanahan ©1995*

the idea of parking bumper-to-bumper with perfect strangers in a roadside auto-camp had lost most of its appeal. The motorized vacationer was growing more sophisticated.

With the premise of paying for a place to spend the night established, the way was cleared for a new type of accommodation that would solve many of the privacy issues of the public camps: the rented cabin. As municipal concerns were scrambling to refine their services, a handful of trendsetters along America's Main Street anticipated the trend toward fully enclosed sleeping quarters and began constructing modest bungalows on property adjoining the highway.

While the pioneering units were Spartan affairs that offered no more than four walls and a floor, they ushered in an era of

The snorting Palomino Motel sign is convincing evidence that the American cowboy and his trusty steed were (and in some cases still are) staple images of Highway 66 advertising. Throughout the western states along the route, neon tubing has routinely assumed the shape of cattlemen, Longhorn steer, cowboy boots, and a variety of related archetypes. Unlike today's unattractive signboards with their internal lighting and vacuum-formed plastic, the illuminated salesmen of yesterday's road possessed a charm all their own. Tucumcari, New Mexico. *Jerry McClanahan ©1995*

66 Courts in Groom, Texas, was the typical small town motel with a house converted to an office flanked by a row of stucco sleeping units for overnighters. Although the house is now history, the stucco units are still standing, along with the roadside sign. Beneath, a rusted, derelict Edsel riddled with bullet holes provides an engaging photo-opportunity for all those passing through. *Jim Ross ©1995*

privacy previously unknown by auto-campers. After a long day's drive , both pilot and passenger could relax in their skivvies without worry. There were no limitations to the freedoms that might be enjoyed behind closed cabin doors.

The advantages were numerous. By renting a cabin, tourists could travel lighter. No longer was there any need to carry all the equipment required of a safari when embarking on a motor journey. Since cabins provided a watertight roof, insulation from the cold, and a heating stove, conveniences like the auto-tent became outmoded. The need to lug along utensils for meal preparation was now moot: cabins were frequently outfitted with miniature kitchens and equipped with all the pots and pans one would ever need for a day, week, or month of lodging.

At the outskirts of towns, near the major crossroads, and at strategic points along 66, entrepreneurs jumped into action. Farmers handy with a hammer and saw chopped down a grove of trees, threw up a half-dozen rustic cabins, and they were in business. Filling station operators slapped together a couple of native rock buildings out back and began renting them to the occasional customer stranded by mechanical problems. It seemed that everyone was trying to get in on a good thing—including the restaurants and cafes that already had an established clientele.

Within a few years, little white cabins that featured clapboard siding, exposed eaves, white picket fences, and flowering window boxes had changed the face of the Route 66 streetscape. Escape to the roadways now included personal privacy. The era of municipal camps was unofficially over—auto-camping was dead.

Suddenly, the rush to build sleeping units was on. In the years between 1929 and 1933, "more than 400,000 shacks for autoists" were erected nationwide. Because these units typically displayed a semi-circular or "U-shaped" arrangement with central office structure, common lawn area, and access to the bungalows by way of a dedicated driveway, they came to be known in the trade as "courts." Depending on the preference of the operators, a variety of adjectives were paired with the identifier

Signs of defunct motor courts abound along the Route 66 roadsides. Even after buildings and other structures have been stripped of their valuables, its the signs that often remain high above—isolated and protected from the vandals' hand. Near St. Clair, Missouri. *D. Jeanene Tiner ©1995*

143

-for REST and COMFORT TOWER COURT MODERN IN EVERY DETAIL

Stop

West on Hiway 66 Albuquerque, N. Mex

144

resulting in signs that read "tourist court," "motor court," "cottage court," and a variety of similar combinations. Appropriately, the individuals that operated this style of lodging were called "courters."

Some of the courters doing business along the old highway took the Native American angle and extrapolated the possibilities to the limit. After World War II, Frank Redford surfaced as the undeniable king of the wigwam sleeper, erecting a pair of "Wigwam Villages" in the Route 66 towns of San Bernardino, California, and Holbrook, Arizona. In later years, a few imitators like the Motel Conway in El Reno, Oklahoma, tried to copy the eye-catching formula but never attained the same level of style.

Despite their appeal, fantasy structures did not rise to dominate the architectural philosophy of the motor court. By the late 1930s, industry publications continued on page 148

left
Mr. and Mrs. J.D. Meredith owned and operated the Tower Court in Albuquerque, New Mexico, and entreated guests to stop "For Rest and Comfort" with their promotional postcards. Rooms in this Art Deco dream were completely modern and air-cooled: During the cold winter months, frigid air seeped through the windows and during the summer, evaporative "swamp coolers" pumped in a moist breeze. The technology required to create "refrigerated air" was still many years in the offing. *Author*

Regional styles of motel construction are typical along Route 66. In the southwestern states, facsimiles loosely based on the adobe brick architecture of the Pueblo Indians were once widespread. Back in the 1940s and 1950s, New Mexico became a bastion of the Pueblo cabin, with Albuquerque its capital. All along the commercial strip leading to and from the city center, tidy groups of squat, flat-roofed haciendas greeted the Route 66 motorist. *Preziosi Postcards*

Wally Byam's Amazing Airstream Clipper

"Speeding through a desert landscape full of sand and Joshua trees, it appeared to be an apparition streaking right out of a Buck Rogers serial!"

It was Wally Byam's dream to "place the great wide world at your doorstep, for you to yearn to travel with all the comforts of home." He knew there was a more satisfying way for motorists to travel with complete independence, wherever the road might lead. It was an ideal he realized by the creation of one of America's most gleaming icons: the venerable Airstream trailer.

The story of the silver legend began back in the late 1920s when Byam was making a living in the advertising field. He crossed over into the world of publishing and introduced several newsstand magazines, one concentrating on the do-it-yourself craze sweeping the nation. When he published an acquired article on the construction of a travel trailer, readers wrote in with complaints! The plans were unsound and impractical to build, leading Byam to initiate some backyard experimentation of his own.

After developing a workable design, he penned his own article outlining the assembly of an inexpensive, $100 trailer. When he offered booklets detailing the clever plans by mail, he was overwhelmed. Eventually, he improved his original concept and was doing a brisk business supplying pre-built units. With the success of a tear-drop-shaped, 13-foot, canvas and Masonite marvel dubbed the "Torpedo," he promptly dropped other career plans to manufacture trailers. With the belief that his unique models slipped along the byways "like a stream of air," he adopted the name "Airstream" in 1934.

Around the same time, aeronautical genius William Hawley Bowlus was busy developing a radically new trailer concept in the San Fernando Valley. As head of Ryan Aircraft's shop in 1927, he gained valuable expertise on the famed *Spirit of St. Louis* project. By the 1930s, he was riveting together a streamlined, monocoque fuselage—skillfully applying proven principles of aircraft design to the art of trailer construction. He called it the Bowlus Road Chief.

The important strength-to-weight ratio was optimized with an internal labyrinth of tubular steel frames providing a skeleton for structural panels of aluminum alloy. While most trailer configurations incorporated a bulky superstructure, the Bowlus model relied primarily on exterior skin panels for the distribution of stress loads. This skyworthy assembly technique improved overall resistance to flex and vibration, improving both mileage and towability.

In 1936, the January issue of *Trailer Travel* magazine featured a full-color illustration of the "Road Chief" on its cover. Speeding through a desert landscape full of sand and Joshua trees, it appeared to be an apparition streaking right out of a Buck Rogers serial! With its streamlined rooster-tail, Moderne windows, and polished aluminum, it was an aerodynamic embodiment of the future. Still, there was one design feature that didn't receive many accolades: the entry door. It was positioned at the front of the rig, right above the towing attachment!

Whether it was the door or the lack of marketing panache exhibited by Bowlus, the model failed to sell very well. Enter Wally Byam, part showman, part promoter—with his stockpile of advertising ideas and the pizzazz to make them work. After taking over the bulk of the Bowlus inventory, he relocated the entry and reintroduced the trendsetting trailer as the Airstream "Clipper." With the 1936 debut of the Bowlus cum Byam amalgamated streamliner, the machine age of transportation had arrived in style.

But, there was much more to the flashy trailers than mere aesthetics. Inside, the sleeper was built to accommodate four. Even seats converted into beds. A dinette of tubular frame was employed for dining and a diminutive galley to prepare food. An advanced heating and ventilation system (augmented by insulation) increased comfort—along with electrical lights, storage cabinets, and eight, fully opening side windows. Top-of-the-line models even included an experimental, dry-ice air-conditioning gizmo!

During the 1920s, trailer visionary Wally Byam found success with a tear-drop shaped, 13-foot, canvas-and-Masonite marvel dubbed the "Torpedo." Almost seven decades have passed, and today the travel trailer has evolved far from its humble beginnings. Motorhomes are now the perfect union between the automobile and the home, some featuring 118 gauges and instruments, the ability to store 400 gallons of fuel on board, microwave ovens, electrical beds, radar, satellite navigational systems, electronic maps, and even automatic leveling devices. *Courtesy of Airstream, Inc.*

When the war came, parts became difficult to obtain and aluminum was a critical war material. Consequently, Byam suspended Airstream operations and began work for a Los Angeles aircraft contractor. After the war, Airstream was taken out of mothballs and re-emerged stronger than ever to build the gleaming classics that made it an American original.

Today, the original Clipper, "old granddad" as it is now called, occupies a place of prominence in history—and the hearts of Airstreamers—at the company's headquarters in Jackson Center, Ohio. The graceful Airstream is a true survivor, one of only a handful of trailers made in America with the same standards of quality begun over 60 years ago. Wally Byam's vision and trailering dream is still rolling on!

The earliest RV'ers in America were a group of people who got together in 1919 in Sarasota, Florida. Known as the "Tin Can Tourists," they started with 22 families and within 10 years had grown to well over 100,000 members. They organized into camps, and suddenly southern towns found themselves in competition to host them. Much to the approval of businessmen, trailer people were interested in local events and boosted economies by purchasing food and supplies. As trailering gained in popularity, the appearance of overnight facilities featuring running water, bathrooms, and electricity made the lifestyle more appealing to the average family of the 1950s. In the postwar era, Americans rediscovered the joys of the open road. Many took to Highway 66 with their homes in tow and went off in search of the great American West. *Courtesy of Airstream, Inc.*

continued from page 145

The Old Hotel Beale was Kingman, Arizona's, hub during the Roaring Twenties. Beneath the sleeping rooms were most of the services required by the lodger or guest just passing through. For buying ready-to-wear clothing goods, having one's hair cut, and even stocking up on cigars, it was one-stop shopping at its finest. The appearances of many small towns along Route 66, haven't changed all that much. Lieutenant Edward Fitzgerald Beale was a naval officer and explorer who surveyed a route from Fort Defiance (180 miles southwest of Santa Fe) to the Colorado River and California (with the assistance of camels) during the late 1850s. *Library of Congress*

extolled a radical rethinking of the cabin and began outlining their ideas in print. Always eager to modernize, leading architects canonized the concepts of streamlining within the pages of *Tourist Court Journal*. The campaign worked.

Following the lead of service stations and Los Angeles drive-ins, courters accepted the ideas and began implementing an architectural facelift. Route 66 became a hotbed of style. In Carthage, Missouri, the Boots Motel emerged as a trendsetter by incorpo-

rating the rounded corners and speed lines favored by gas station architect Walter Dorwin Teague. But nothing could compare to the Coral Court in St. Louis: dominated by a minimalist rationale of ceramic tile and glass block, it was the quintessential incarnation of Streamline Moderne.

While the tourist cabins raced to upgrade, a new method for housing motorists began its slow encroachment on the business of lodging. Rumblings of the changes to come began as early as 1925

more contiguous structures. Arranged in a row parallel or perpendicular to the highway, rooms shared common walls—interrupted only by integral garage bays. Now, lodgers could back up to the front of a cubicle, pop the trunk, and unload baggage directly into the room. For the customer, the advantages of easy access were welcomed.

Even so, it was the roadside proprietor who came away with the best deal. With an

when architect Arthur Heineman designed an overnight establishment called the "Milestone Motels" in San Luis Obispo, California. The combination of the words "motor" and "hotel" spread quickly along the highway, providing a catchword to promote sleepers that looked like nothing more than elongated stables for cars.

By the mid-1950s, the villages of separate cabins that once decorated Highway 66 were replaced by

The Casa Linda was one of many motor courts influenced by the Indian Pueblo. Individual garage units were available for every room, but the lack of air-conditioning made visits during the hot months of summer a trial. When this photo was taken, Route 66 was still a dirt path through New Mexico. Gallup, New Mexico, G.B. Gordon photo. *National Archives*

The Coral Courts were a complex of 30 buildings (expanded to 77) that set a precedence for Moderne styling along Route 66. Built in 1941, they were designed by architect Adolph L. Struebig for the late Johnnie H. Carr, a colorful personality who was widely admired by the local community of Marlborough but held in dubious regard by the local police. Over the years, the Courts were the center of shady circumstances on a number of occasions. In October 1953, Carl Austin Hall stayed there the night before his arrest for the kidnapping and murder of Bobby Greanlease, the six-year-old son of a Kansas City auto dealer. The $300,000 ransom money that was paid him was never found—leading many to wonder if the hollow walls at the Coral Court may hold more than air. St. Louis, Missouri. *Shellee Graham ©1995*

150

WAL-A-PAI COURT HEATED
KINGMAN, ARIZONA

Air Cooled

Right in Town, on U. S. 66

With its close proximity to the Wal-A-Pai Indian Reservation, Kingman, Arizona's, Wal-A-Pai Court took full advantage of the Native American association. From the perspective of the present, it seems a bit ironic how poorly our nation has treated these indigenous people—yet freely exploited their words, images, and customs for use in commercial advertising and promotion. *Courtesy Chuck Sturm*

Vintage postcards depicting the Pueblo Bonito Court and the Koronado Kourts illustrate the contrasting styles of architecture employed by courters in various states along Route 66. In Joplin, Missouri, the overnight cottages are reminiscent of vacation bungalows whereas in Albuquerque the long strips of sleeping quarters evoke the visual and structural properties of the Native Pueblo longhouse. *Courtesy Chuck Sturm*

all-inclusive structure, motels provided a dramatic reduction in the amount of real-estate needed, as well as lower material and construction costs. Maintenance was cheaper, too. One maid could service a row of rooms in less time than it took to clean a sprawling layout of bungalows.

In the broad overview, it appeared that the simplified motel was the ideal solution for the traveling salesman, tourist, trucker, and highway adventurer of the modern motoring age. In reality, the motel was merely a

PUEBLO BONITO COURT
ALBUQUERQUE, NEW MEXICO

KORONADO KOURTS
ON HIGHWAY 66
WEST OF MAIN STREET
JOPLIN, MISSOURI

151

distant cousin of the early camps. Instead of the privacy afforded by one's own cabin, motels crowded patrons together in one building that had more in common with an impersonal military barracks than a resort. Surroundings were designed for efficiency—not relaxation.

Across the eight states connected by 66, the idea of a home-on-the-road had returned to one of communal togetherness. The blare

Approved AAA Courts   **CAFE GOLF**   *Lakeview Courts*   Member United Motor Courts   **BOAT RIDES**   **Selected By Duncan Hines**

COOL IN SUMMER - FACING ONE OF OKLAHOMA'S LARGEST LAKES

8 MILES WEST OF OKLAHOMA CITY LIMITS   3 MILES WEST OF BETHANY   4 MILES EAST OF YUKON ON 66

Phone Bethany 612 and 322   TELEGRAPH   Mail Address R. 3, Box 23-A, Yukon

Lakeview Courts had it all: They were approved by the American Automobile Association, featured a cafe, had golfing facilities, boat rides, and were selected by restaurant reviewer Duncan Hines. Inside the rooms, things just got better with Simmon's Beds, Ace mattresses, electric refrigeration, and Magic Chef stoves! For the 1940s, these were roadside accommodations to write home about. Near Bethany, Oklahoma. *Courtesy Jerry Keyser*

from a television speaker and snore of a neighbor became modern replacements for the coyote's call. Lodging was now quick, convenient, and hassle free. Without any desire to linger, packing up the station wagon and speeding back onto Highway 66 became more important. In the rush to complete the journey, the special magic that was once associated with camping out along the American roadside was lost.

CORAL COURT
Ultra-Modern
One of the finest
in the Mid-West
on U. S. Highway 66
City Route, one mile
west of City Limits,
three miles east of
intersection of By Pass,
Highways #61, 66, 67
and 77

70 rooms, tile cottages
with private tile bath
in each room.
Hot and cold water
porter and maid service
—Beauty Rest Spring
and mattresses—
Hot Water Radiant
Heat—24 Hour Service
7755 Watson Road
(Highway 66)
St. Louis 19, Mo.

WOODLAND 2-5786

Desirous of a commercial structure that would require little maintenance, visionary John H. Carr chose hollow ceramic blocks manufactured by Architex Ceramics, Inc., of Brazil, Indiana, for the exterior of the now-demolished Coral Court Motel cabins. When applied as a veneer over standard concrete block, they made the outside walls of his Art Deco compartments one foot thick. St. Louis, Missouri. *Courtesy Chuck Sturm*

153

Hotel *el Rancho*
TURNER TOURIST HOTELS, Inc.

E. W. TURNER, Pres.
Managing Director

GALLUP, NEW MEXICO -- ON U. S. HIGHWAY [U.S. 66]

The Hotel El Rancho was once known as "The World's Largest Ranch House." Accommodations for 250 guests made it one of the biggest operations catering to the tourist trade in the New Mexico area. Some of the more unusual features available there were cowboy bunks for the children and "sleeping porches" for the adults. Gallup, New Mexico. *Courtesy Chuck Sturm*

right
A street scene along the Atchison, Topeka, and Santa Fe railroad between Seligman, Arizona, and Needles, California. Note the commerce thriving along this urban strip: Lockwood's Cafe (with Chicken in the Rough sign), a Chevrolet car dealership, a Conoco gasoline outlet, the Hotel Beale, various bars, and other sundry stores. Kingman, Arizona, Jack Delano photo, 1943. *Library of Congress*

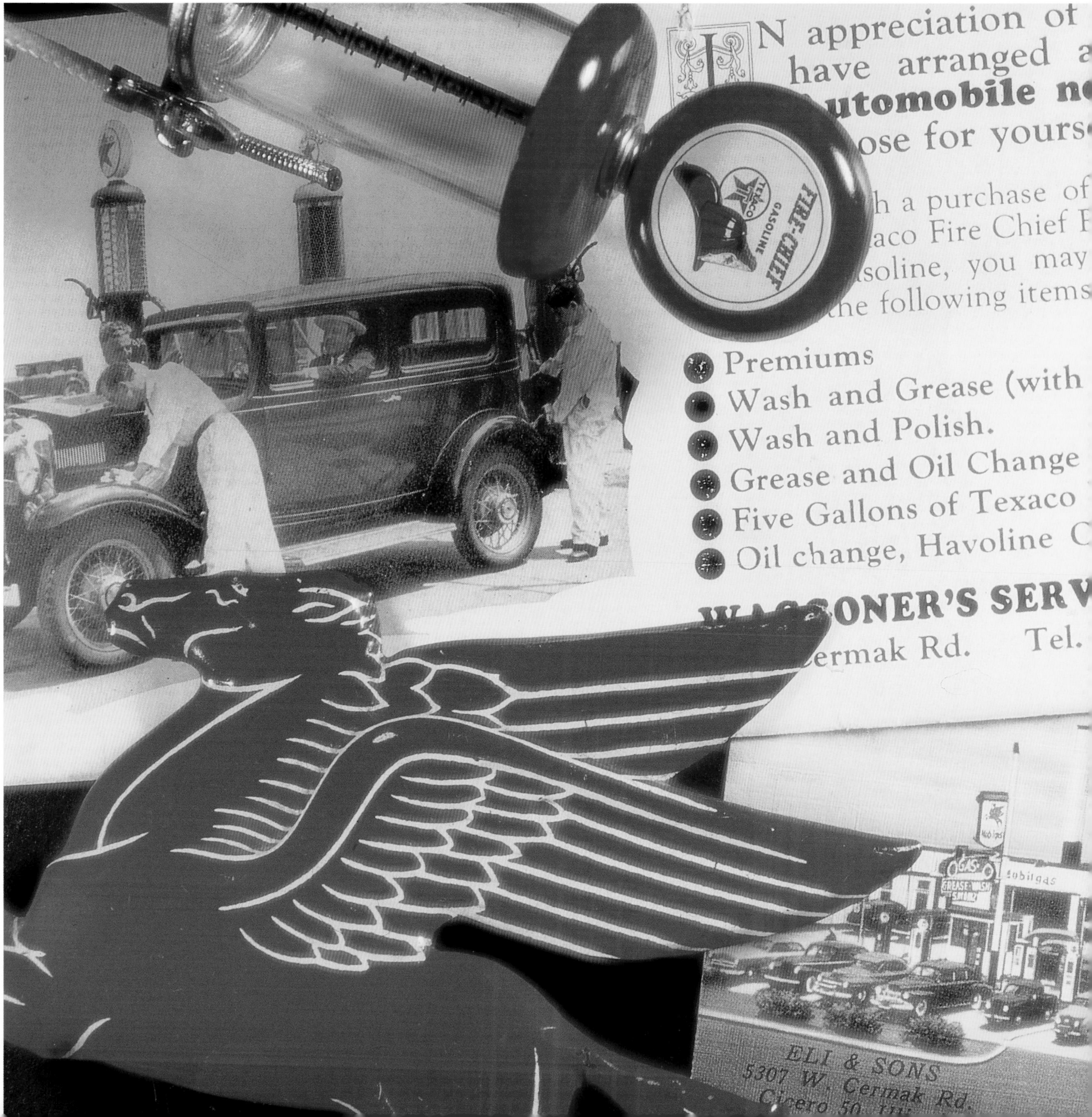

chapter five

IN appreciation of
have arranged a
utomobile no
ose for yours

h a purchase of
aco Fire Chief
asoline, you may
the following items

- Premiums
- Wash and Grease (with
- Wash and Polish.
- Grease and Oil Change
- Five Gallons of Texaco
- Oil change, Havoline C

WAGGONER'S SERV

ermak Rd.   Tel.

ELI & SONS
5307 W. Cermak Rd.
Cicero 50 Ill

Mother Road Memories:
Life on the Road

U.S. Route 66 is a highway made up of memories. It always has been. From the very early days of the blazed trails until the roadway's official birth during the 1920s and right on through the years leading up to its rediscovery during the 1990s, it has functioned as both an inspiration and a facilitator for an expansive realm of human experience. While intended to function as a purely utilitarian conduit for the purpose of car travel, the highway and its businesses have doubled as a base for memories.

While the various experiences of the millions of motoring Americans (and countless others from around the globe) who drove Highway 66 might be unique, a common thread of

Crossing the state line from Arizona to New Mexico along Highway 66 was a dramatic experience in 1940. Crowned with a Highway 66 shield, a massive portal welcoming newcomers to the state created an impressive sight for all those in the front seat. Of course, gasoline and curios (note small stand on lower left) awaited all those making a run for the border. Arthur Rothstein photo, 1940. *Library of Congress*

left
During the 1930s, Elias Kornblith ran Waggoner's Greasing Palace Number 33 in the Route 66 town of Cicero, Illinois. In addition to selling Crosley cars, they served a short order fare from a tiny lunch room on the parking lot. Up on their flashy sign, a young lady in a car was outlined in neon lights. To attract attention, her scarf flew up and down as the wheels on her vehicle turned. *Postcard and blotter courtesy Gordon Kornblith*

157

Jim Bragg reclines in the grass while preparing a peanut butter sandwich for a quick roadside lunch. While most of the couple's meals consumed while driving Route 66 were made with potted ham, fresh fish was an occasional treat. Bea caught her first fish in a river somewhere near old Route 66. *Photo courtesy Bea Bragg*

happenstance and incident bonds all of those who traverse its path. The incidents that take place upon this inanimate aggregate of concrete are universal. The problems encountered are endemic. The solutions found along the way are obvious. With little exception, the destinations reached, the locales visited, and the attractions viewed are all similar.

In most cases, the reasons for travel are related in both cause and purpose.

When viewed from a larger perspective, the resolution of each individual "trip" is less unique than actually perceived by its participants. Whether it be the migrant farm worker or displaced laborer seeking a new chance out west, the truck driver hauling products to market, vacation-goers packed into a station wagon, or a carload of insurance salesmen heading to a convention in Las Vegas, traveling along

Highway 66 eventually dictates a similar fate for all those who roll over its path.

Is there any dispute that all automobiles break down, radiators overheat, tires go flat, gas tanks run dry, and engines cease to spin? For the driver and his passengers, the schedule of events encountered during the journey is predictable: appetites must be quelled with food and occasional breaks be made for the rest room. Additional stops must be made for sleeping and also sights viewed. Money is spent, money is found, money is lost. Meanwhile, a tragic accident claims yet another victim. Inside the car compartment, people either get along famously or they spend their entire trip in pointless argument.

Nevertheless, this reality of the road's physical realm is quickly forgotten. More important in the long term are the lasting memories that are made along the way. Although the myriad of road-users who have driven this route represent diverse philosophies and lifestyles, the two lane slab of 66 has been—and continues to be—a point of intersection for a collective automotive experience. An American road experience. Within this continuum, new friendships are forged and old acquaintances revisited. Lost loves are found and old flames are rekindled. Thoughts are inspired and minds expanded. As motorists speed off to reach that distant vanishing point, new discoveries, adventures, disappointments, awakenings, and heartbreaks await. In the end, these are the elemental properties that real Mother Road Memories are made of.

We Found Our Road

You can't always find the right road on a map, but in 1939, two years after we were married, Jim and I found it: Route 66 from Oklahoma City to Los Angeles. It was more than just a road from here to there. On this road came joy and sadness. Our children were born nearby, and more than 50 years after our first anniversary, Jim died in Albuquerque near the old road.

War clouds were very dark that year. Rumors were strong that Hitler would invade Poland. More important to us newlyweds was that the Great Depression still lingered.

We lived in a $35 a month apartment in Oklahoma City with a living room so small our knees touched when we sat across from each other. We didn't mind that. Jim took $80 a month from his real estate business, and I earned 10 cents a page typing. We saved $125, ample for a three-week trip West to glamorous California or even east to wicked St. Louis or Chicago. The year before we had gone on family business to St. Louis, a well-known Route 66 stopover, but we went by train. We were still to experience the magic of Route 66.

At last, we would drive west toward the sunsets we watched from 39th Street, Route 66's path through the city. This would be our real honeymoon! Not like the weekend "honeymoon" after our wedding in 1937 which was—well, I can't tell you about that.

Our budget included gas at 12 cents a gallon for the 2,000-mile round trip. Our 1930 Chevy, which coughed above 40 (but was in good condition), got about 15 miles per gallon. Estimated expenses for the trip looked like this: gas, $16.00; motels (growing more plentiful westward), $1.50 to $3.00 per night; and food (for both of us), $1.00 a day. Anticipated total: $79.00. This left us with at least $45.00 for unforeseen expenses and perhaps one evening at a nightclub in Los Angeles! Wealth!

We packed 21 cans of potted ham, seven cans of tomatoes, and a can opener. Through dust storms in Amarillo, a cold spell in Gallup, and searing heat at Needles, we were sustained—mostly by excitement.

In Los Angeles we saw the museums and dipped our toes in the Pacific, but nothing could compare with the huge Hollywood nightclub. I must tell you, we were shocked! Sixty scantily-clad dancing girls had their bare backs painted with noses, mouths, and eyes. They faced the rear of the stage as they danced. That wasn't what shocked us. It was the one girl who was facing the audience, painted just like the others. Those who saw her—and of course, Jim did—roared with laughter. Everyone else was bewildered, for not all could see the dancing girl with wobbly eyes.

The International Golden State Exposition that year took us to San Francisco's Treasure Island. How could we have resisted? We were beginning to like potted ham! My biggest thrill? I got to type on a new product: an electric typewriter!

This momentous event rivaled a side trip on the way back home to Oklahoma City. Route 66 passed near Grand Canyon National Park. We had to go. With not much money and only two cans of potted ham left, we couldn't take expensive burro trips down into the canyon. We WALKED in, and WALKED out by sundown! The distance, 8-8/10 miles, seemed like 88 back!

Eagles soared and chipmunks chattered, but three people we met on that hike were the most curious of all. Jim, an avid camera fan, was curious about the famous Leica camera carried by the young man in front of us. A Leica! Almost in a class with the electric typewriter! Jim sprinted up to him. Their conversation was over in seconds. The youth stopped, turned to face Jim, raised his hand in a Nazi salute, and barked "Heil, Hitler!"

Jim stood stock-still, his jaw slacked in surprise, but our curiosity led us to persuade him to talk in his broken English. We learned that he was a Nazi student among hundreds traveling through the civilized world. All he would talk about was the "maliciously lying newspapers" in America.

At the bottom of the canyon, the student handed Jim his camera and indicated he wanted his picture taken. As Jim focused, the student clicked his heels, straightened his shoulders, and raised his hand in a Nazi salute. "Danke," he said, bowed, took his camera, and disappeared up the path.

Halfway out, we struggled for breath under a nut-pine tree. Two fellow hikers stopped to chat, asking questions about the Nazi. We got goose bumps when we learned they were FBI agents.

By 1940, we had a little better car and celebrated by driving Route 66 to Chicago where we saw Vivien Leigh, the controversial choice for Scarlett in *Gone With the Wind*, and Laurence Olivier in *Romeo and Juliet* on stage.

Jim and I traveled more widely in the years following, he to the South Pacific during World War II and, years later, both of us to Europe, Africa, Mexico, and Central America.

In 1991, we moved to Albuquerque, Route 66 country, where Jim died. Since his death, I have moved to an apartment where I can overlook Interstate 40, the highway that replaced Route 66. It leads to where Jim—and yes, I also, saw the girl with the wobbly eyes. The road where I touched the electric typewriter, where we saw George M. Cohan, Laurence Olivier, and Vivien Leigh, all gone now, and where the Nazi student and the FBI agents almost met.

Occasionally, as I watch the traffic, I think I hear our old Chevy coughing down Route 66.

—Bea Bragg

Marked for Life

Is it possible to "mark" a child, as old wives are fond of saying? My mother says my father "marked" me by threatening to move the whole family from Illinois to California while she was pregnant with me. She cried all day, every day, which she insists ensured that the child she carried would have the wanderlust my dad was never able to shake. As a result of Dad's need to travel, we moved often. I attended seven grade schools (including three third grades) and two high schools.

One trip I especially remember, however, took the family along Route 66. It was 1953, and I was five years old. Dad finally made good his threat and uprooted us from our home to move near his elderly mother in California.

Using his carpenter skills, Dad worked busily in the driveway, building what I believe to be the first camper—ever. On our old pickup truck, he constructed a frame of two-by-fours and covered it with chicken wire. Meanwhile, Mom did her part by giving away everything that wouldn't fit in the "camper." She hurriedly stuffed our clothing and other belongings into gunny sacks, which were placed in the bed of the truck and covered by a mattress. Other gunny sacks were attached to the sagging chicken wire overhead and, finally, canvas was draped over this lumpy, and obviously homemade, contraption.

Raymond Ryburn, Sr., with Theressa "Terri" Victor, David, and Raymond, Jr., pose for a snapshot in front of the camper that would become the Ryburn home during their 1953 Route 66 journey. To the left, Victor; Raymond, Jr.; David; Terri; and four-legged friends Spic and Span are pictured relaxing on the running board of an automobile—totally unaware of the traveling adventure the future holds. *Photos courtesy Terri Ryburn-LaMonte*

What didn't fit in the truck, Dad burned in a huge bonfire. Having not one sentimental bone in his body, he decided that toys took up too much room and promised that he would buy replacements when we arrived in California. Tearfully, I sacrificed my favorite and best loved "Linda" doll to the flaming funeral fire of practicality. My brothers were brave. They described our destination as a magical place where the sun shone every day, you never had to wear a coat, and you could pick oranges from the trees in your yard!

In preparation for our odyssey, Dad tied firewood to the running boards of the truck, and strapped two canvas water bags to the front for that long, hot trek across the desert. We were off for California on Route 66—a 2,000-mile adventure! We must have looked like the Joad family from *The Grapes of Wrath*. I was, of course, far too young to be embarrassed by our appearance, but I can now imagine what we looked like to others as we set off—canvas and children flapping in the wind!

Besides my dad, and Mom (who was pregnant and suffering from morning sickness), there were my three older brothers, Junior (who was car sick), David, Victor, myself (also car sick), my baby brother, Roger (who was in diapers), and our two dogs—Spic and Span. Dad spent more time waiting, sometimes patiently and other times not so patiently, at rest rooms, rest stops, and alongside the road than he did driving. The trip must have seemed an eternity for my dad—especially since the truck, at full ramming speed, couldn't have exceeded 35 to 40 miles per hour.

Route 66 was two lanes, bumpy, and very narrow. Rest stops were few and far between. A deluxe rest stop was an especially wide place in the road, a carved-up and falling-apart picnic table, and a 55-gallon drum for trash disposal. It was necessary, then, for obvious reasons, to stop at gas stations, and my brothers and I soon became rest room experts. Only Phillips 66 rest rooms met our exacting standards of cleanliness. At one gas station, however, we found a surprise. Victor and I each jerked open a door and found ourselves looking at each other across the toilet in the small room. Depending on which door you used, this particular rest room was either a boys' or girls'. The trick was to lock both doors once inside. We used up valuable time arguing about who was there first, but mom finally arrived to settle the issue, and ordered the boys out back.

Mom, the cleanest person in the world, spent all of her time fussing over us. She carried a washcloth in a bread wrapper and every time we stopped, she tried to clean us up, which was nearly a full-time job. As she washed faces and hands with cold water— the only faucet that ever worked—she would say, "We may be traveling, but there's no excuse for being dirty." We squirmed as she scrubbed our necks and then ran off to air dry while she turned to the next victim. I vowed that if I ever had children I would let them be as dirty as they wanted—I would never wash them!

Meals had a comforting sameness along the road. Dad stopped at a grocery store each morning for a package of cinnamon rolls or donuts and a half-gallon of milk. Of course, at every stop, he bought a paper cup of coffee to keep himself going. Lunch was a picnic: a hunk of bologna and bread to make sandwiches, milk, and if we were really good and Dad felt especially solvent, there might be cookies.

Some nights Dad kept driving; other nights he needed to sleep. One night, he found a quiet place near water to set up camp. He pulled the truck to the water's edge and unstrapped the firewood and pots and pans so that Mom could cook a hot meal. After dinner, my brothers spread a canvas under the truck where they slept. "Get to sleep you kids," was Mom's lullaby from the lumpy mattress she shared with Roger and me. Dad stretched out on the front seat of the truck and tried to sleep. I listened to the unaccustomed sounds of the night and thought I heard a mountain lion. I fell asleep hoping that Dad, the intrepid builder-of-campers and long-suffering trailblazer—or Spic and Span—would be able to save my poor, defenseless brothers. In the morning, my brothers were alive but covered with mosquito bites. I laughed at their splotchy appearance. After that, Dad was careful to choose camping places away from water!

In the back of the truck, we tried to entertain ourselves. We sang "California, Here I Come," over and over and over, that being the only line that we knew! We sang it with great gusto, however! Sometimes my brothers, who were older and more worldly, sang "Get Your Kicks on Route 66," imitating the sophisticated vocal stylings of Nat King Cole. They too were limited—having learned only the title verse to the song!

My brothers also entertained themselves by fighting. Once, when they jockeyed for position at the tailgate, Junior and David began to scuffle. Soon they were both hanging over the pavement. I just knew they would fall from the truck and be killed. I had never seen brains, and I had never seen them bashed out on the highway either. Victor shouted "Stop!" and I began to cry and pound on the cab of the truck. "Raymond, pull over," Mom barked. "We'll never get there at this rate, Hazel," grumbled Dad as he rolled to yet another unscheduled stop. Mom and Dad had mistaken my desperate pounding for "the call of nature." I blubbered the truth and my brothers denied it. "I don't know where you get these stories," scolded Mom. I vowed then and there that I would never try to save the lives of my lying, but very much alive, brothers again.

We pulled into San Bernardino at night and while the truck was being filled with gas by a friendly man in a uniform and bow tie, Dad got permission to stay overnight on their lot. I felt safer there; it was well lighted, but the sleeping arrangements were rather cramped. David, Victor, and I stretched out, almost full length, in the bed of the truck; Junior slept lengthwise against the tailgate. Mom and Dad couldn't have gotten much rest, sleeping upright in the front seat with Roger between them. Spic and Span took their places in the truck.

Although I was stiff and sore in the morning, I was grateful to be near the rest rooms—this was the most convenient place we had stayed. We stretched, yawned, and ate our customary road breakfast. Dad rolled up the canvas sides of the camper and tied them securely. "Kids, let's go," Mom shouted, counting aloud as we got into the back of the truck. "Five . . . okay, Raymond, we're all in." The truck began to roll toward the ocean. A slightly modified version of our favorite song wafted from the back—"California, Here I Am!"

I stuck my head out the side of the truck and let the air buffet my face. It was different than any air I had ever felt—warmer and moister, with a smell I would later identify as the ocean, although I had no idea what that might look like. But, I soon found out.

Dad stopped the truck at the beach; we had reached the end of Route 66. My brothers and I clambered over the tailgate and ran toward the water. I moved slowly as my bare feet sank into the sand. The waves made me gasp as they washed over my feet and the wet sand ran quickly from under my feet and back into the ocean. It was colder than I expected, and loud. I turned and looked back at the truck. Mom was holding Roger and shouting, "Get back from there! What are you boys doing?" My brothers had already found a beached jellyfish to torture. Dad walked toward me and I ran to hug him. In that moment, I didn't care if he ever replaced

my "Linda" doll. He had given me the road and the ocean! I was "marked" for life.

—Terri Ryburn-LaMonte

We Called Ourselves the Joy Boys

Looking back, it seems like we packed a lot of living into that golden summer of 1954. Of course, a year lasted longer then. In fact, some hours were interminable. We'd sit in class at Flagstaff High School and listen to the Santa Fe trains rumble through town. There were still mournful steam whistles mixed among the diesel air horns, and they all made us want to be anywhere but Flagstaff.

Not that Flagstaff was a bad place to grow up. But we were restless teenagers at the crossroads of Northern Arizona, where Route 66 and U.S. 89 intersected. We'd sit in a booth at the Round Up Cafe watching the world pass, daydreaming aloud of the time when we would join that passing crowd. Like many people in those postwar years, we Route 66 kids dreamed of California.

The Round Up was at the corner of Leroux Street and Santa Fe Avenue in downtown Flagstaff. Santa Fe, the Main Street in Flagstaff, was also U.S. 66, the Main Street of America.

In summer, cars were bumper-to-bumper on the narrow street: lots of older cars, of course, but also the boxy post-1949 Fords, bullet-nosed Studebakers, Buicks with portholes, Cadillacs with fins. You didn't see many foreign cars then. Sometimes the cafe was so crowded with travelers that the management didn't appreciate teenagers hanging out, nursing coffee or Cokes, and ogling the tourist girls.

But in winter, the cars were few and far between. Flagstaff sits at nearly 7,000 feet elevation, and sometimes 66 was icy, or slushy. Our resident highway patrolman had a sneaky patrol car, a white-over-maroon Ford hardtop with the white star stenciled on the off side, away from traffic. When things were slow, the cop tied down his buggy-whip antenna and baited out-of-state motorists into dragging Main Street. Then he'd nail them with the flashing lights installed in his grille.

We called ourselves the Joy Boys: Mark, Kirt, and I. Mark worked in gas stations and garages, of which Flagstaff had plenty, so he always had some sort of car. We'd pool money for gas and explore 66 as far as Holbrook, 90 miles to the east, or Ash Fork, 45 miles to the west.

With morbid fascination, we inspected mangled wrecks towed in from "bloody 66." Someone used to put a white cross at the scene of each traffic fatality; the shoulders of some dangerous intersections, like Cottonwood Wash east of Winslow, looked like veterans' cemeteries!

After we graduated from high school in 1953, my three buddies moved to the Los Angeles area and got jobs. My parents set a lot of store in my getting an education, so I entered tiny Arizona State College at Flagstaff, now Northern Arizona University. But at the end of my freshman year, I couldn't stand it any longer. I had to see what lay beyond Ash Fork.

I soon found out that the first thing that lay beyond Ash Fork was one long, long day. I caught a ride with a college buddy who was going home to Los Angeles for the summer. He had a 1936 Ford coupe with a cracked head. We stuffed our belongings into the little car, along with a Jeep-can of water and a few cans of oil.

That day, I was introduced to Seligman, Peach Springs, Truxton Canyon, Valentine, Hackberry, then the long, straight drive across the plains to Kingman. A couple of years earlier, the "Grapes of Wrath" road had been pulled out of Goldroad and Oatman. The newer, straighter Route 66 went south from Kingman around the end of the Black Mountains, then bent west toward Topock, following the Sacramento Wash.

Today, it is fashionable, or at least politically correct, to admire deserts. But crossing the Mojave that first time, I concluded that

Jim Cook (pictured third from the left), Bob Atkinson, Mark McGrew, and Kirt Hart called themselves the Joy Boys. They discovered Route 66 and headed out to Los Angeles, California, in 1953 to get jobs. When they weren't on the beach, they spent a lot of time in a variety of automobiles (some with major mechanical problems) hanging out on Colorado Boulevard and cruising the Main. *Photos courtesy James Cook*

the supply of desert exceeded the demand (the last time I drove that area, traveling Interstate 40 in an air-conditioned Buick in the summer of 1992, I had the same feeling).

West of Needles, Route 66 veered south of today's Interstate 40 to touch Essex and Amboy, tiny oases on that long, bleak road. Amboy was one of the several places we stopped to put more water in the Ford and add a little oil. We pressed on through Daggett and Barstow. It was night when we got to Victorville, and near midnight when we cruised along Colorado Boulevard into Pasadena, where my buddies were living.

I moved in with Mark and Bob and they got me a job at the factory where they worked; Kirt lived alone in Glendale and worked in a bakery. I was in Pasadena two days before the smog cleared enough to show me the San Gabriel Mountains towering over the metropolis. At the factory, I worked days, spending the summer polishing the heads of tiny screws that went into drafting machines. But, the nights and weekends were ours to roam the wonders of the big, sprawling Los Angeles complex.

Being young and full of vinegar, we adapted quickly to the frenetic L.A. lifestyle, driving long distances on boulevards and freeways to find a beach or a concert. The Joy Boys spent a lot of time hanging out at one of the three original Bob's Big Boy drive-ins on Colorado Boulevard (these hip teenage hangouts eventually evolved into today's J. B.

The Horn Brothers Gas Station was a Route 66 landmark at 5418 East Central Avenue in Albuquerque, New Mexico. In 1946, Otho Driskill (near the pump) and station worker Manuel sold a White grade of gasoline at 15-1/2 cents and a Bronze grade at 17-1/2 cents per gallon. Six gasoline pumps widely spaced on a narrow gravel driveway allowed for high sales volume. *Photos courtesy Glen Driskill*

restaurants). Mark had a picturesque 1941 Plymouth sedan, painted primer gray. Its single exhaust pipe had a glass-pack muffler that gave it a throaty roar; most of the time, we couldn't get it into low or reverse gear, which resulted in some creative driving.

On weekends, we went to the beaches and baked ourselves in the sun. We danced to Les Brown's Band of Renown at the Hollywood Palladium and bought records in the round Capitol Records store on Hollywood Boulevard. Lynn, Mark's girlfriend, sat on my 78-rpm recording of Ray Anthony playing "As Time Goes By," and I've been trying to replace it ever since. We listened to "Sh-Boom," the original rock 'n' roll song that came out that summer. That first version, by The Chords, and the quick cover by The Crew Cuts, was all over L.A. radio. It was a novelty, and we never figured it to last.

I met a petite girl named Anne, whose brown hair was bleached by the California sun. We spent some pleasant, innocent times together. We held hands, necked at drive-in movies, and stumbled around a dance floor or two. We not only didn't get to first base, but weren't sure where the ballpark was.

Looking back from long perspective, I think I made two good decisions that summer. The first was going to Los Angeles; I might not have made the trip that gave new depth to my life. The second good decision was going back to Flagstaff and college.

Mark needed to tie up loose ends in Flagstaff so he could go into the Air Force. We left Pasadena at midnight to avoid some of the August heat across the desert. Mark drove hard to Needles, where we had breakfast at dawn. Unfortunately, when I started the Plymouth after breakfast, we heard an unmistakable knock. "Oh boy," Mark said, or words to that effect, "she's about to throw a rod!" I nursed the Plymouth along Route 66 at 35 miles per hour, hoping the piston connecting rod didn't let go. It didn't, but that was a long trip from Needles to Flagstaff.

We never heard from Bob again after that summer. Mark and Kirt have lived in Southern California for a long time. Mark and I keep in touch, and we hear from Kirt once in a blue moon. My wife died in 1991 and Kirt's in 1993. Anne visited Flagstaff one weekend in 1955 and later enrolled at ASC. She married a guy named Bob Cook, and they're still happily married. Bob's not related to me, but Anne says if she hadn't met me, she wouldn't have met him. So, the summer of 1954 was a watershed in her life too.

A couple of years ago, Anne asked me to autograph a book I had written "to the dumbest California girl I ever knew!" I changed that to "the most innocent California girl . . ."

—James E. Cook

Horn Brothers Gasoline

In the summer of 1945, I sat on an old wooden bench with my dad and Manuel, one of his gas station employees, drinking an R.C. Cola. We watched as the traffic moved through Albuquerque along U.S. Highway 66. The highway ran straight from Tijeras Canyon to the east, through town, and then up Nine Mile Hill to the west. People were on the move during the last year of World War II.

My dad's Horn Brothers station at 5418 East Central was typical of the independent stations of the 1940s. It had six pumps widely spaced along a narrow gravel driveway. A large sign above the driveway proclaimed "HORN BROS." and underneath, "never undersold!" Smaller signs attached to the single large light pole which lit the driveway at night advertised gas prices to back up the claim: "White" at 15-1/2 cents, "Bronze" at 17-1/2 cents.

As we relaxed in front of the station, a 1928 Pontiac, moving slowly west, made a left turn into our driveway, the car's wooden spoke wheels creaking under the heavy load. The engine side access doors were folded under the top part of the hood to help cool the hot motor. Mattresses and bed springs were tied to the top and all kinds of luggage and household items were strapped to the back over the rear bumper. A spare tire with an nasty looking bulge in the sidewall rode atop the luggage. The driver, a haggard looking man, shared the front seat with a tired, stringy-haired woman nursing a baby. Four kids with unkempt white hair hung out the rear windows. The car stopped at a pump marked "Bronze."

"What'll it be, mister?" my dad asked as he approached the car

"What's this here Bronze gas?" the man asked.

"It's white gas with lead added. It's cheaper than Regular and the lead keeps the engine from knocking."

"I'll take a gallon of it. And I'll need this here can filled up with kerosene."

Dad put in a gallon of gas and Manuel took the five-gallon can to the back and filled it with kerosene. "That'll be 18 cents for the gas, 50 cents for the kerosene and a gallon ration coupon," Dad said as he returned to the car.

Reaching deep into the back pocket of his tattered overalls, the man pulled out a small leather coin purse and counted out 68 cents, then dug a tattered government issue Rationing Book from another pocket. His large weathered hand fumbled nervously as he tore out a coupon, leaving only six.

"Where you headin'?" my dad asked.

"We're trying to get to California. We've gone broke farming in Oklahoma. We heard there's jobs in the war plants out in Los Angeles. We sold everything 'cept what we're carrying."

As he pulled out onto Highway 66, my dad said, "Watch what he does now!" Dad had seen it many times before. The man drove a hundred yards down the road, pulled over and poured the five gallons of kerosene in the gas tank of the car. He then drove to the Iceberg Cafe and Gas Station to repeat the process. He had to fill his tank with kerosene in Albuquerque so he could make it to Gallup. He did not have enough ration stamps to buy gas all the way to California and it was illegal for gas station operators to sell kerosene for cars. The old cars with low compression engines would run on kerosene if they were started on gasoline and kept warm.

"I'd like to help that feller out, but I ain't got nothin' either," Dad lamented as he returned to the bench.

A steady stream of cars passed the station during the day. Many of the cars carried poor farm people heading west along Highway 66. They were the tail end of the "Great Migration" which had peaked during the Dust Bowl years of the 1930s as described by John Steinbeck in *The Grapes of Wrath*. Everyone going either east or west, except the few who took the northern route, passed along the narrow two-lane paved road known as U.S. Highway 66. Most of the towns in the West were built along Highway 66 which for much of the way, was also the route of the railroads. Everyone traveling the highway had to plow laboriously through the traffic and slow speed zones in each town on the way. Many of the towns' economies were based on tourism which blossomed after World War II. Albuquerque set the pattern for the towns. The highway through town was a 20-mile stretch from the Sandia Mountains in the east to the steep climb up the West Mesa. Small motels, curio stores, bars, and greasy spoon restaurants lined the road.

During World War II, the government attempted to restrict travel by rationing gasoline and tires in order to conserve oil and rubber resources for the war effort. It didn't stop the migration of starving people from the farms of Oklahoma and other states still feeling the effects of the Great Depression. The ones left out of the war effort as soldiers because of physical or family situations had to move where the jobs were—the flourishing West Coast war industries.

Many of the people who came through Dad's station were hungry, tired, and broke.

They were risking everything to get to California. They couldn't afford to buy tires and didn't have ration stamps to buy them anyway. Dad sold "boots" to be installed between the inner tube and the tire to cover the holes in the tire. Tubes were patched and repatched until they looked like checkerboards. People carried canvas drinking-water bags which were cooled through evaporation.

We sold bulk oil from barrels because it was cheaper, and we drained the empty bulk oil bottles and cans into a waste can so we could sell the drippings cheaper still. Desperate people would try to barter anything they had to get what they needed to complete their trip. Dad had a soft heart and managed to secret away a few ration stamps that "fell through the cracks." He used them to help a few of the most desperate people.

Native New Mexicans from the other side of the mountains, east of the Sandias and Manzanos, were also feeling the pinch of dried-up farmland. Some were moving to Albuquerque for work, but many were sticking it out—waiting for the return of seasons of even sparse rain; adequate for the western technique of dry farming beans and potatoes. Dad provided them with credit for gas and oil. Much of the money was not repaid,

The U-Drop Inn has evolved to become one of the most popular standards along Highway 66 in West Texas. John and Bebe Nunn were the original operators of the restaurant, which they sold in the 1940s, then repurchased in 1950. They renamed the landmark Nunn's Cafe and set upon the task of feeding the throngs of back road adventurers in search of the past. Today, it is a "must see" and "must eat" stop along the Texas track of Highway 66. Shamrock, Texas. *Dan Harlow ©1995*

Joe Morrow (posed by the truck with his wife, Leta) relied on the business of trucking for a livelihood. In 1950, he bought his own rig and operated as a "wildcatter." Hauling freight and produce all over the United States, Route 66 was always a part of his trips. For him, the highway was an economic "lifeline." His brother, Jewell, (now deceased) and wife, Brownie, (posed with a Tydol Gasoline sign) ran the family gas station after their father, George Morrow, passed away. *Photos courtesy Joe Morrow*

which contributed to my dad's parting with the Horn Brothers.

For many years, the only other structure near the station was the Iceberg Cafe and Gas Station, located across the highway and a few hundred yards west (now the corner of Central and San Mateo). The Iceberg Cafe was fabricated from wood and metal lath and plastered to look like a large iceberg rising from the stark desert. The cafe and a smaller iceberg used for the station office were landmarks for many years. The two were later moved and unceremoniously dumped out near Bernalillo, where they sat for many years before being destroyed. The Tewa Motor Lodge was built across the highway from the station in 1946. Dad's station was torn down in 1955 to make way for the Trade Winds Motel. A Chinese restaurant now occupies the site.

Thinking of that station on Highway 66 reminds me that the "good old days" were not so good for some people, but their move West made it better for their children.

—Glen W. Driskill

My Route 66 Lifeline

When I was a small boy my dad bought three acres of land on Route 66, west of Springfield, Missouri. He built a service station complete with living quarters alongside the highway.

The place was built out of beautiful, native worm fossil rock. Inside was a large room with shelves and a counter with stools where travelers' supplies, such as bread, milk, and candy were sold. He had planned to build six or eight cabins for tourists (that was before the word "motel" was in the dictionary). He completed two cabins before ill health stopped his project. The doctors referred him to the Mayo Clinic in Rochester, Minnesota. He died there in 1935. After Dad passed away, my oldest brother took over the operation of the station and the cabins.

During my childhood I was fascinated by the big trucks that went by our home and our station. To me they were huge, though they were only single-axle tractors and single-axle trailers, nothing like the giant rigs of today.

I found an old pair of steel roller skates that someone had discarded and took the front rollers off of one skate and hooked it on the other skate. Hey, I had myself a trailer truck! I cherished that homemade toy for a long, long time and never did get over my fascination for the big trucks.

I enlisted in the Navy on my 17th birthday, near the end of World War II, and was discharged in 1948. I got a job driving a truck for a creamery company that had a government contract to supply milk to Fort Leonard Wood. Seven days a week, Springfield to Fort Leonard Wood, all on Route 66.

In 1950, I bought my own tractor-trailer rig and operated as what we used to call a "wildcatter." I hauled freight and produce all over the United States, but almost everywhere I went, Route 66 was a part of the trip, because Springfield was my home. Many times I loaded in Chicago for a haul to California and vice versa, heading along old Route 66 all the way. There were other routes I could have taken—the northern or southern routes—but for me it was always 66. I could stop at home, get rested, grab some clean clothes, or a home-cooked meal before hitting the road again.

In 1956, I went out of business. I always considered myself to be a good driver and figured if I had an accident it would be the other guy's fault. So when I paid off the rig, I dropped my collision insurance because it was very expensive. Well it didn't turn out as I had planned. Yes, I had an accident. Yes, it was my fault. I ran into the back of another truck. And, yes, it was on Route 66, just outside of Hamel, Illinois.

I got a job driving for Powell Brothers Truck Line. Most of the runs were from Springfield to St. Louis—good old 66 again. Then I drove for Voss Truck Lines, whose home office was in Oklahoma City. They moved freight between Chicago and Oklahoma City—yep, Route 66! In 1960, Voss sold out to Western-Gillette, which had its home office in Los Angeles, and in 1977, Western-Gillette sold out to Roadway Express. I retired in 1985.

I have no way of calculating how many miles, hours, days, or even years of my life have been spent on Route 66. I know the old highway contributed a great deal to my source of income and livelihood. I believe I can truly say, "Route 66 was my Lifeline."

—Joe Morrow

Waggoner's Greasing Palace

My father, Elias Kornblith, had the idea that anything a friend of his could do, he could do just as well. So, he jumped headfirst into the business of selling refined petroleum—just like his friend Phil Sloan, a man who started in the gas station business from scratch in the pre-Depression late 1920s. Sloan teamed up with his brother and managed to amass a large number of gasoline outlets and in the process inspired my dad to take action.

Eager to get started, my father asked his brother to be his partner, and after soliciting a loan from my uncle's father-in-law, they constructed a sprawling gasoline station that featured five grease pits, a car wash large enough to handle four cars at the same time, and a brake shop with three service stalls. Out front, they put in a big parking lot so there would be enough space for a large number of cars.

To the locals—and all the other customers filling their tanks before venturing out onto Route 66—the business was known as Waggoner's Greasing Palace Number 33. Don E. Waggoner was the regional sales manager for the refueling operation, and consequently, all of the gasoline stations used his name for many years after that.

Well, although Dad and his brother didn't amass a large number of stations like Sloan and company did, they managed to pump more gasoline than anyone else in the entire area. During the 1930s, the increased competition from gas wars and labor strikes didn't hurt them a bit. They simply set their gas prices ridiculously low and concentrated their efforts on top-quality service. As fast as the delivery tankers could off-load the fuel into their station storage tanks, it was sold.

Clever marketing was part of the great sales success: Open 24 hours a day, Waggoner's Greasing Palace gave out a premium of four quarts of motor oil with every eight gallons of gasoline purchased. The public response to the gimmick was so good that not only were enthusiastic customers filling their auto tanks with fuel—they were taking some extra liquid home in a variety of portable containers!

After the first week, the Cicero, Illinois, fire chief begged my father to stop the promotion and to take heed of the fact that people were going home and draining their car tanks into 55-gallon barrels. As he figured it, all across the suburbs of Chicago, motorists were hoarding hundreds of gallons of gasoline in their garages. "One spark and the whole town would burn for a week!" was his worried warning.

Originally, Dad opened the gas station as a Texaco. After buying his brother and the other partners out, he switched to the colorful brand of the Flying Red Horse. Of course, the company that would one day become Mobil was still known as Socony-Vacuum back then, the result of the giant Standard Oil conglomerate merging with the much smaller Vacuum Oil Company. For business, it was a wise switch. Through the experience of servicing all the Western Electric Company service trucks, we found out that the quality of Socony-Vacuum oil products were very consistent. Not surprisingly, we later realized that Mobil Oil products were always on a higher plane than most of the other brands.

Fortunately, the Mobil name not only proved to be a mark of quality, but one perfect for all types of promotion. With that in mind, Dad asked a man by the name of Zed Gerwe (Illinois head of the Mobil Oil Company) to install something more attention-getting in place of the porcelain enamel shield sign that represented Socony-Vacuum. The following week, Dad got his wish. Gerwe delivered an immense, blazing Red Pegasus outlined in bright neon! It was exactly what Dad had in mind: an attention-getting billboard that plainly illustrated the ideas of speed, flight, and horsepower.

Unfortunately, even the powerful red horse could not stop the march of time and progress. Those unforgettable days of wiping the windows and checking the oil were bound to end sometime. And end they did!

My brother and I sold the Greasing Palace property in 1979, and the gallant red steed that once greeted car customers was taken down and retired.

Even so, the memories remain strong. To this day I still have many friends who remember the good old days. Back then, I could actually call all of the customers by their first names and watch as their children grew up to drive (and follow) in their footsteps. Although the town of Cicero, Illinois, and the many events that made history there are slowly slipping into obscurity, the sign of the Flying Red Horse remains as a vibrant reminder of the golden age when gas stations were called greasing palaces and station attendants pumped the gasoline.

—Gordon Kornblith

We Almost Made It

In 1950, the Korean War was escalating. As a 19-year-old facing possible military draft, all I really wanted to do was experience the ultimate driving/sightseeing adventure—Chicago to Los Angeles on Route 66. There were still some rough, narrow, desolate roads to challenge the traveler, and no car air-conditioning, superhighways, motel and fast food chains, credit cards or jet airliners to pamper him. Often, there were lengthy stretches along which no radio stations could be picked up.

On the plus side, gas was 20 cents a gallon, Cokes and candy bars were a nickel, and motels could be found for $5 a night. Best of all, the posted speed limit was often 70 miles per hour, and in some places there were no signs, which meant any speed that was "reasonable and proper."

My father died that summer and as the only licensed driver in the family, I got his 175,000-mile 1941 Buick Century to use as my own. With its dual compound carburetors it easily hit 30 in first gear and 60 in second. And boy, was I anxious to discover the top speed. When driven reasonably, it would deliver 18 miles per gallon on the highway.

My friend Harvey Mayer and I scraped together a total of $125, packed three dozen cookies my sister baked for us, and jumped on Route 66 where it began, at Michigan and Jackson in Chicago. Due to youthful impatience, we wanted to see Los Angeles as soon as possible, so we drove over 1,000 miles straight through to Amarillo, Texas. We stopped only for gas, washrooms, milk for the cookies, and unfortunately, tires.

Our persistent car trouble began in St. Louis when I noticed that what had been perfectly good front tires when we left were now very badly worn on the edges to the point where the rubber was gone and the interior cords were exposed. They were unsafe and

Ken Greenburg poses with the familiar "Arizona Welcomes You" sign at the border of New Mexico. With friend Harvey Mayer, Greenburg crossed the continent in the year 1950 driving a 1941 Buick Century fraught with tire problems. Although the team ultimately had to turn back before getting to California, they both realized that the journey is often more important than the destination. *Photo courtesy Ken Greenburg*

useless, so we bought two pair of used tires for three dollars each. At the same time, a mechanic examined the front end and pointed out all the worn parts that made it impossible to align the car. It needed a major repair with new parts at a cost we could in no way afford. Relying on our youthful wisdom again, we decided to keep heading west and to watch the tire wear very carefully and buy more used tires as needed.

We looked around in Springfield, Missouri, and took some pictures, with my oddball Whittaker Micro 16 miniature camera. We then sped on to Tulsa where we had to buy two more tires. The oil wells pumping all over the place were fascinating. It was either in Missouri or Oklahoma where we saw our first red dirt, which became red mud in the rain and really stuck like glue to the car. So far, the drive had been mostly boring. We wanted to see mountains, desert, and mostly, jump into the Pacific Ocean. The flatlands did not capture our imagination.

I did most of the driving, and because it was an old car, I usually kept the speed under 75. However, much to my unhappy concern, when Harvey drove and I dozed, he kept the needle at 85 or 90. We argued about this a lot, and I let him drive less and less. I was driving somewhere in Oklahoma, when a front tire disintegrated, causing us to leave the road, crash through a thin wire fence and finally bounce to a stop several hundred feet into a field! We were lucky the car didn't flip over.

Still shaking from the near miss and driving a little slower, we got to Amarillo very tired. There we bought three more tires, had another mechanic look at the front end, and he gave us the same dire diagnosis. This was our first night in a motel or as they were called then, a motor court. After a good night's sleep, we looked around the city, and all I can remember was that a lot of people were wearing cowboy boots and hats. It was obvious we were tourists.

As we drove to Albuquerque, the scenery was definitely getting more interesting. We could see the great Rocky Mountains way off in the distance. Now the adrenaline was beginning to flow. In Albuquerque, we bought two more tires and some kind of canvas-covered water bag to hang on the front bumper like everyone else was doing, I guess in anticipation of crossing the desert. The hills began getting steeper and taller and from the top of each one, all we could see was an endless ribbon of concrete seemingly vanishing into infinity.

As the road grades got increasingly steeper, I nervously watched the temperature gauge climb dangerously close to the overheat point, but with much relief, I watched it recede to normal on the way down. We began seeing signs telling drivers to shift to a lower gear when going downhill.

At last, we arrived in Gallup, which was not very much at that time. We slept in our second motel there. The drive from Gallup to Flagstaff was uneventful, but the scenery was improving all the time. I don't remember anything about Flagstaff except that the ride from there to Kingman was brutally hot—115 degrees was not uncommon and at 75 miles per hour the air felt like it was exiting a blast furnace. It was oppressive and very uncomfortable. I knew it was best to travel at night when it's that hot, but we just couldn't wait to see California. I clearly remember in a remote area seeing signs advertising water for 25 cents a gallon. The heat made us cranky and at this point we began getting on each other's nerves.

When we got to Needles, we took stock, looked at our expense record, and realized that food, gas, motels, and tires had used up more than half our money. We could in no way make it to Los Angeles and back home on less than $50! With great sadness, we had to start back home without even seeing the Pacific Ocean.

There are several postscripts to this story: When we got home, Harvey discovered his Army Reserve unit had been activated the day we left. Within a month, he was shipped to Korea. I finished college and one week after I graduated, I was drafted into the Army. A major disappointment was that all the many pictures I took were either lost or more likely intentionally destroyed, because I had unwittingly mailed cash along with the film to be developed! That film could only be developed by the company in Los Angeles that had manufactured the camera. It was heartbreaking. I don't know what happened to all the pictures Harvey took with his camera. The photo of me by the Arizona sign is the only one I have from our trip.

On a brighter note, in 1955, on my honeymoon, I finally drove Route 66 all the way to the Santa Monica Pier, this time in a 1946 Buick Roadmaster. Things were beginning to change along the old road, but it was still a wonderfully romantic drive, and people along the way were still universally friendly and helpful to tourists. A few years after that, my wife and I made the drive one more time in a new station wagon with our two young kids who complained, whined, and fought most of the way. But, that's another story.

—Ken Greenburg

The Fearless Foursome

They were not Tod and Buz in a Corvette nor the Joad family in a truck escaping the Oklahoma dust bowl. Nor were they Thelma and Louise in a Thunderbird headed for disaster. They were just Mildred, Emily, Lucille, and Hazel, four young women who left Clear Lake, Iowa, in 1932 aboard a Model T Ford

Mildred Pattschull (above right) hitched up with three friends and drove a 1925 Model T Ford across the country in 1932. Although the rickety bucket-of-bolts cost her only $75, the car (middle frame) made it to California in just 10 days! Mildred is pictured behind the steering wheel with her friends Emily, Hazel, and Lucille looking on. *Photos courtesy Mildred Pattschull*

175

Chicago, Illinois, was the point of origin for Highway 66 and holds the distinction of supplying the eastern portion of the road with plenty of automobiles. It still does. John Vachon photo, 1941. *Library of Congress*

with a madcap idea to take a road trip on Route 66 to California.

"At first I really didn't have a strong desire to go," said Mildred Pattschull, now 82. "California seemed like a million miles away at the time. But my three friends were just dying to go, so I finally agreed to drive my car until it quit running. Then we would scrap it and come home."

As luck, or fate would have it, the 1925 Model T Touring car, purchased two years earlier for $75, was up to the task. It took them from Mason City, Iowa, to Los Angeles and back with few problems, a total of 3,900 miles!

Not many people made such trips in 1932, especially young single girls. Most women didn't even drive at that time, let alone take off on their own. And, to spend hard-earned cash during the Depression on a zany motor trip

would have been considered a foolish idea by many.

But not to Mildred. She was a spunky forerunner of independence and freedom before feminism was a movement. Mildred was simply too busy being Mildred, a person on her own road of discovery.

"My mother was convinced she'd never see me again," said Pattschull. "Both my parents openly cried in the front yard of our home the day we drove away. They just didn't understand."

She was just 20 years old. Today's equivalent might be the shock a parent would experience if a daughter announced her intent to canoe across the Atlantic Ocean. After all, most roads in America then were rutted dirt lanes with few services. And the Wild West was still considered, well, wild. But, Mildred and her friends were out to "get their kicks on 66," which in 1932 was still more a gravel path than paved highway.

Mildred's Model T Ford—a cramped, narrow, rickety-bucket-of-bolts had no windows, side curtains, or reliable tires—let alone air-conditioning, stereo, or cellular phone. She had driven the car for two years and named it "Ben Hur." It didn't have a top, but she found one just before they left.

"In the winter, I just piled on more clothes," explained Pattschull. "And I'd turn the seat upside down to keep the snow off while it was parked outside." Pattschull grew up in Iowa where winters are notoriously cold and windy.

The four young women—ages 19 to 22—drove south on Iowa Highway 65 through

Missouri and Kansas and hooked up with Route 66 at Oklahoma City. "We each had $100 cash," related Pattschull. "It was an enormous sum with the Great Depression descending hard on everybody. I don't even remember how we were able to accumulate that amount, but we did!"

Back then, however, meals in restaurants cost around 25 cents. Mildred's diary of the trip lists every dime she spent. One entry is for a bowl of chili at 15 cents and another is for a roast beef dinner for 35 cents. Gasoline was about 20 cents per gallon.

The group stayed in tourist cabins along the way—the forerunner of motels—for $1 per night! Each unit was only a small single room with a bed. Showers were in a separate building and the toilets were outhouses. All four young women slept in one double-bed—two at the head and two at the bottom with their legs intertwining at the middle. It was cheaper to rent one cabin and they felt safer being together.

Even though the song "Get Your Kicks on Route 66" (made famous by Nat King Cole) had not yet been written by Bobby Troup, Mildred and her friends "motored West and took the highway that's the best." They went through Oklahoma City ("looking mighty pretty"), Amarillo, Gallup, New Mexico, Flagstaff, Arizona, ("don't forget") Winona, Kingman, Barstow, and San Bernardino. They left Mason City May 28, 1932, and arrived in Los Angeles on June 7— 11 long days of driving. They had little human contact on vast stretches of empty road between towns and road conditions

kept "Ben Hur" chugging along faithfully, mile after hot dusty mile, at about 20 miles per hour. Arizona had only been a state for 20 years when they drove through it, and the population was numbered less than Iowa's— fewer than 500,000 people.

"There was nothing—not one living thing—except sagebrush and sand along much of our trip," exclaimed Pattschull. "It was a real no-man's land, and it took about three hours to drive between any signs of civilization—if you could call some of these tiny towns along the way civilization."

The burning sun and the hot winds of the southwestern desert forced two of the women to wear men's long sleeved work overalls and drape a bath towel over their heads to protect their skin. Their only real brush with trouble came in Las Vegas, New Mexico, when they took a wrong turn and ended up in an unfamiliar neighborhood.

"All the signs were in Spanish, which we couldn't read, and we ended up on a one-way, dead-end street," Mildred recalled. "We apparently made an illegal U-turn and got arrested by a Spanish-speaking policeman and hauled off before some magistrate and a young teenage interpreter!" Ordered to appear the next morning in court, they got up at 4:00 a.m. and made a quick getaway out of town in the dark.

They all marveled at the lush green valleys and bright blue skies around San Bernardino after driving so long in the desert. They were especially impressed with the thousands of orange groves in that area and the limitless clear blue skies. The term smog had yet to be coined!

"It just seemed there were millions of orange trees everywhere," said Pattschull. "People had them in their front and back-yards and there were roadside stands selling oranges and juice." In a picture postcard sent to her parents during the trip, Pattschull said, "I would love to live on the beach in California or in some parts of Arizona. We all like it in New Mexico."

One of their foursome is now deceased, but the other three continue to be close and frequently write and telephone one another. Hazel Mitchell died in 1984. Emily Abbott lives in Glendale, California, and Lucille Lackore lives in Winona, Minnesota. "We never lost touch with each other," said Mildred, "but we didn't all get back together for a reunion until five years ago. We relived the entire trip, of course, and laughed and howled over our memories.

"I'd love to do that trip all over again today," said Pattschull as she sat behind the wheel of a 1921 Model T Touring car owned by Tom Wick of Clear Lake, Iowa. She hadn't gripped a steering wheel like this one since the day she sold Ben Hur in 1933—the year she got married. "That trip was a highlight of my life," exclaimed Pattschull, beam-ing a wide smile through the wind-shield. "I can feel the memories roll over me. Even though we were only gone a month, I felt as if I'd been transformed into adulthood when we got back."

—Jay Black

Patterson's Route 66 Milk Run

When I was nine years old, my family was preparing for a two-week automobile trip to see my father's relatives in California. It was going to be the first (and last) major vacation the entire family—my mom, dad, and three brothers—would take from our dairy farm in Augusta, Kansas. In prepara-tion for the trip, mom got us all excited by showing us literature, maps, and other things about where we were going and what we could see along the way. I was pretty excited and so were my brothers Dalton, seven, and Allen, three.

But before we could leave, my mom and dad (Clare and Jessie Patterson) had to get someone to take care of the dairy farm and make sure that our registered Hol-steins were kept in good shape. After some searching for qualified caretakers, Dad hired local boys Bill and Peewee Duncan. For about a month prior to the trip, they were shown how to milk the cows, take care of the livestock, do the bottling, and make the deliveries to the people in town. Once Dad was satisfied that everything wouldn't fall apart in his absence, we were ready to hit the highway.

It was July 1948 when we loaded Dad's brand new, maroon Ford woody (he bought it only four months before we left) and pulled out of Augusta—heading due south. Route 66, the great highway that connected the Midwest to the West Coast waited for us at the southern tip of the state. We were all excited at the prospect of driving across the country.

For the first portion of the journey, my mother had packed sandwiches, home-baked cookies, and other foods to eat as we wound through the backroads. After we joined up with Highway 66, roadside stands and restaurants were so plentiful that we soon switched to other foods. When the family got hungry, we just stopped in the little towns along the way and bought meals. For Mom, this was a real vacation from the kitchen!

As far as I can remember, Dad always ordered the chicken fried steak. The boys had more variety, including chili and, one of my favorites, hot roast beef sandwiches. In the mornings, it was the standard breakfast: eggs with biscuits and gravy on the side. Other times, my brothers and I filled up on soda pop and candy. Grapette was our favorite Route 66 flavor!

When we weren't stopping to eat or visit the bathroom, my mom dreamed up games for us to play. As we came upon Burma-Shave signs, the first to see them would get the privilege of reading them out loud! Other times, we enjoyed identifying the cars we saw, calling out the colors, and counting how many Indians we encountered. Mom would always have some sort of reward for the "winner" of these motoring pastimes. Usually, it was a dime we could use to buy goodies at the next filling station. For such a long trip, Mom did a tremendous job of keeping us all busy.

My favorite car game was counting horses. We all knew that when we got to California we were going to get to see Roy Rogers and Trigger. For us, it was a big thing because

we watched their exploits nearly every Saturday night at our local movie theater.

To sleep, we stopped at little auto courts—the kind where one could pull the car right in beside the room. We always got two beds: Mom and Dad slept in one, the three boys in the other. Before continuing the next day, we got some time to play around outside and let off a little steam before we climbed into the crowded car and drove back onto 66.

When we reached Arizona, Dad took a little side trip up to the Boulder Dam. When we got there, it was so big that Dad refused to go down into the dam! We were eager to see it, however, and without hesitation went down on the elevator. We were impressed by the massive turbines and the rushing water. It really got our attention, and we've been talking about it ever since. On the way back

In 1948, Clare Patterson, Sr., drove the entire Patterson clan in his brand new Ford Woody to see the sights at the Boulder Dam. Taking a vacation from their Augusta, Kansas, dairy farm, they headed to Van Nuys, California, by way of Route 66. Although his dad decided not to accompany the family down into the dam to see the sights, Clare, Jr., remembers the road trip as one of the best vacations of his life. *Photos courtesy Clare Patterson*

to Kingman and the highway, we stopped at a filling station where Dad gave us some nickels to play the slot machines!

From what I can remember, we went through the desert early in the morning, and it didn't seem that hot to us. We just opened up the windows—I guess we didn't know any better.

What really stands out above the heat was the fun we had in the car: On parts of the highway in the Southwest, the roadbed sometimes followed the contour of the land. As we went over the tiny dips and hills, my dad started to inch down the gas pedal and soon we were flying up and down. We kept yelling "faster, faster" as my Mom warned "you better slow down, you better slow down!" It was one of the best thrills we had along the trip!

When we finally arrived in California, we headed to the city of Van Nuys which at that time, was in the outskirts of Los Angeles. For fun, Mom and Dad took us to Pacific Ocean Park. It was the first time that any of us were around seafood so we decided to sample some of the fare. Unfortunately, my dad and I had a bad reaction to lobster and we both became ill. But that wasn't the most exciting part. We got to ride a real roller-coaster (that went out over the ocean) which made our fun and games along the highway pale in comparison. I had such a great time that I had to do it again, marking the high point of one of my family's greatest adventures. Without a doubt, that summer trip in 1948 was, and always will be, my most memorable trip along Route 66.

—Clare Patterson, Jr.

Crossroads of America

In the 1920s and 1930s, we called my home town of Sapulpa, Oklahoma, "The Crossroads of America." Highway 66 went right down our Main Street and the main north-south route, Highway 75, intersected 66 in the center of town. Highway 75 went from South Texas all the way into Canada.

In 1927, I traveled with my parents and two brothers along Highway 66 from Sapulpa to Los Angeles, California. We had a Hudson touring car and all our camping equipment. It was quite an experience for a five-year-old girl.

One of the more troublesome things on that trip was that the highway was not marked going through towns and cities. One had to keep stopping and asking how to find 66 on the other side of town.

We had a lot of rain on that trip. I remember this because the Hudson's windshield wiper was not electric, thus the person sitting next to the driver had to operate the wiper manually. Also, there were no windows as such, and each time a rain started, there was a mad scramble to get the side curtains out and installed. Much of the highway was not paved, and in June 1927, some of it was underwater. Fortunately, someone had placed poles along each side of the road so that you could see where the roadway was. Cars stuck in deep mud had to be pulled out by mules or tractors.

Whenever we stopped to camp, if we saw another car with Oklahoma license plates, it was like old-home week. We quickly learned that if we left our campsite to visit nearby points of interest, such as the Petrified Forest, Meteor Crater, or the Grand Canyon, wild creatures up to and including bears were quite likely to vandalize the camping area in search of our "grub box."

We had many flat tires and several broken fan belts. My father and brothers had quite a time changing and patching all those tires. When we needed a fan belt, one of my brothers would hitchhike to the nearest town to get one and then catch a ride back.

Mountain roads at that time were one lane only. If we were unlucky enough to meet another car, either they or we would

Rebecca Rockwood Hill (at age five) camping with her father and two brothers near Flagstaff, Arizona. Though not evident in this photograph, her mother is most likely off somewhere performing duties related to the preparation of food. The Hudson touring car parked to the right of the tent is loaded down with spare tires. *Photos courtesy Rebecca Rockwood Hill*

have to back up to the nearest turnout to let the other car pass. On one occasion, we met a woman who refused to back up. Many angry words were exchanged. It was only a short distance for her to backup to a turnout, but my father finally had to backup quite a long distance so that we could let her pass.

When we finally reached the Pacific coast, we treated ourselves to a nice motel on the beach—such a luxury after all that camping and cooking under difficult circumstances.

—Rebecca Rockwood Hill

California Bound in Ford's Flivver

My parents, Harry and Grace Richards, departed the town of Summersville, Missouri, in the spring of 1919 for a road trip across America. At the time, I was 18 years old and my sister, Carol, only eight. It was no leisure trip: we were moving to the West and driving all the way. San Dimas, California, was our final destination, one we would reach by motorcar in an age long before there were any hard-surfaced roads, multilane freeways, or even a Route 66.

The arduous journey that lay ahead promised to be an adventure of a lifetime and on that account, it did not fail to disappoint. Seventy-seven years have passed since that eventful trek, but the memories still replay in my mind as vividly as if they had happened yesterday.

My mom and dad didn't have a fancy phaeton or any type of trailer, but they did own a simple Model T Ford Touring Car that featured "isinglass" side curtains. Its running boards were used to store things, and a utility trunk strapped on the back housed all of our food and supplies. Inside, Dad toted a round, coal oil (kerosene) stove, which we used for extra heat at night. Space was limited on board, so each of us were allowed to bring only one suitcase—four in total, the youngest member of our clan bringing along a "keyster"(suitcase made of straw)!

In those early days of motor travel, things taken for granted today didn't even exist. The going was really rough out there between the large towns. Between towns, there were no filling stations or amenities of any kind to be found—no fast-food service, no campsites with electricity, and definitely no motels in this final year of the teens. This made for some very exciting times and dictated that three very special tanks had to be kept full at all times. One was a gasoline canister, another an oil container, and the third a large canvas bag filled to the brim with water (it hung from the radiator and had to be refilled without fail daily). These reserve supplies were our own special form of trip insurance!

For food, we usually ate meals at truckers' stops or other places in towns. This was only once in a while, so most of our "dinners" consisted of cold lunches and other foods we could easily carry with us. My parents purchased fruit and other snacks that were eaten along the way, and I remember that I ate enough cheese and crackers to last a lifetime! Of course, Dad always started the day by filling his Thermos full of coffee, something the

When she was 18 years old, Mabel Richards Phillips (second from the left) made the trip across America long before there were any hard-surfaced roads, multilane freeways, or even a Route 66 to speak of. Her mother, Grace (left), sister, Carol, and father, Harry, accompanied her on the trip from Summersville, Missouri to San Dimas, California. *Photos courtesy Mabel Richards Phillips*

rest of the family members did not drink. I guess he needed the extra energy considering all the responsibilities of the journey.

When we reached Oklahoma by means of the Old Wire Road—the rough pathway that later became the Ozark Trail and even later part of Route 66—we met a couple of young men by the names of Vance and Henry who were also venturing by automobile out to the West Coast. We struck up a conversation, and it didn't take long for the pair to ask us if they could follow us. After all, we were all going the same way and in those days, everyone helped each other while crossing the country by car. Vehicles often formed a kind of caravan, much like the old wagon trains of the pioneer days. That way, everyone

wasn't so alone in the remote wilderness and we could count on one another for obtaining help during times of trouble or mechanical breakdown. Besides, it also created a certain camaraderie that buoyed our spirits throughout the treacherous journey into the unknown territories of the West.

We routinely spent the nights under the open skies, since hotels in towns were usually extravagant affairs that were too expensive with rooms too fancy for a dust-covered family on a tight travel budget. Nevertheless, we always found a place to stay along the trails, often bunking down in deserted houses, quiet school yards, or any other place along the roadside that looked like it had a large enough clearing to set up our

A circa-1911 truck crosses the Colorado River by ferry between Arizona and California at Ehrenburg Scow, pushed by a power boat ferry. Fortunately, modern bridges made this precarious crossing considerably easier once Highway 66 was paved from end to end. A.L. Westgard photo, 1911. *National Archives*

tent. When possible, we even gathered up tumbleweeds and newspapers so that we could insulate our cots at night to stave off the high winds and low temperatures. Of course, public bathroom facilities were non-existent in those days, and we had to make do with what nature provided.

Because of the open design of our modest family flivver, the weather often posed considerable problems for us on the journey. In the prairies of Kansas, we experienced such strong winds that seeing the highway through the blowing dust and dirt was almost impossible. When it rained, driving was difficult at best—windshield wipers were not a feature of the simple Ford. After a long deluge, the dirt roads that we traveled became nothing more than

muddy ruts. As a result, my parents' biggest fear was bogging down in the mud with no way to get out. Near larger towns, teams of horses were often used to haul stuck vehicles out of mud traps. In remote regions, however, there was often no assistance available. One had to rely on their wits and ingenuity, of which I learned my parents had a considerable amount.

At one point during this great overland journey, things were feeling pretty crowded in the small compartment of our Model T, so the two young men we met offered to take little Carol in their car for a while. It sounded like a great idea to everyone, except that she ended up crying for her mother so much that the boys wondered if they had done the right thing. Mother Grace was so concerned about not seeing Carol that she carried on as well. It only took one day of that to reunite our small family in a common vehicle!

Not surprisingly, these personal problems were the least of my father's worries. As pilot, mechanic, and navigator, the trip was rife with all sorts of difficulties and concerns for him. It was slow going, with little mileage accumulated. Flat tires had to be dealt with on a continual basis, and my father always had the same thought in the back of his mind, "just where are we going to get our next tank of gasoline?" Oil and water were an important commodity as well—but of secondary ranking when the fuel tank appeared to be down to its last drop. Antifreeze was unheard of, so in the mountainous regions along the way, my father had to actually drain the entire radiator of its fluid so that during the frigid nights the cooling system would not freeze up and crack the engine block.

In New Mexico, we were looking for a place to sleep when father got a tip from some people to drive up an old dirt road and look for an abandoned miner's cabin. The "road" was very difficult to cross and led us high into the hills. Around that time, the worst possible thing that could happen did: the old Ford started acting up and making really strange noises. The radiator needed water and we were all out, so my dad drove across a very bumpy field where he spied a small herd of cattle huddled around a windmill. Unfortunately, the water in the small stock tank we came upon was frozen solid. Undaunted, Dad retrieved a hand-held hatchet from the tool box and started to

chop up the ice layer. Using the trusty old canvas water bag, he scooped up a bagful of frigid water and refilled the radiator. We were back on our way.

When we finally reached the border of Arizona, the dirt trace dubbed the National Old Trails Road came right up to the great Colorado River and stopped! It wasn't until then that we learned there were no bridges to be crossed. The only way to get our automobile to the other side was to drive onto a rickety old ferry that didn't look like it could support its own weight much less the heft of our fully loaded rig. Still, there were no other practical means to ford the water, so we had to swallow our fears and brave the rushing waters. Amazingly, we managed to get across without incident.

Looking back from today's perspective and 95 years of living, it seems amazing that we made it safe and sound across the country to California without any major mishap. It was a big accomplishment, since the roads we traveled on were nothing more than blazed trails—youngsters who would later grow to become the smooth concrete roads with official-sounding names such as Highway 66. In 1919, we endured hardships and made sacrifices that today's traveler would never dream of. Still, my parents' old Model T was a hardy machine; it got us all the way to a new life in California, put a little adventure into all our lives, and kicked up quite a bit of dust along the way. And that my friends, is what traveling across country is all about.

—Mabel Richards Phillips

Hicksatomic is one of the smaller Illinois gasoline marketers that faded into obscurity. Today, reminders of the diverse selection of gas brands existing just 20 years ago are all that are left along Highway 66. Wilmington, Illinois. *D. Jeanene Tiner ©1995*

Epilogue

Route 66: Memories of a Forgotten Highway

A Tribute to Jack Kerouac

What does one remember of Route 66? Is it the sound of the tires as they hum along the pavement? The whine of an engine straining to top a hill? Is it the pictures of street signs flashing past like so many frames in a nickelodeon?

Perhaps it's the conversation of the road or the songs heard on the radio—the sounds broadcast from unfamiliar towns and mysterious disc jockeys howling in the western night. Could it be the look of excitement in a child's eyes or that feeling of joy experienced when crossing a state line or making one's mileage goal before dusk? It could very well be all of these.

For some, it's the service stations and the gasoline they provide, the smell of evaporating motor fuel, the fragrance of burning oil, and the ammonia of windshield cleaning spray as the attendant wipes the windows. It's the cold soda pop pulled from an icy machine and the simple pleasure of popping the top on a machine-mounted bottle opener while a gas pump rings and the hood slams down. It's visions of fan belts, car parts, and gadgets seen through the plate glass window of the station office, the idle curiosity about what these people do when they close down at night. Where do all these people go after a day of dedication to the road and the stream of travelers that anonymously patronize their businesses?

Route 66 is also the meals eaten along the way, and the amazing variety offered the palate. It's the candy bar gobbled in the front seat, or even a chunk of Spam wrenched right from the can with an old pocket knife, after driving for endless hours with no food in your stomach. It's the taste of a simple sandwich lovingly slathered with deviled ham by your wife, mom, or grandma—wrapped in wax paper and stacked like bricks in your cooler—and washed down with chilled water chugged from a collapsible drinking cup. It's the thick diesel-and-bacon smell of a truck stop.

It's the indelible impression made by a cheap hamburger and French fry combination—the homemade kind—complete with all the grease and trimmings that

Far from the hurried climate of the interstate highways, the "free road" routinely offers up the unexpected. Along the quiet miles of cracked asphalt, travelers may experience the wonders often missed. Life in the "slow lane" has its advantages over an addiction to cruise control. Between Miami and Afton, Oklahoma. *Shellee Graham ©1995*

always drip down your chin and get the seats all messy no matter how careful you are and how many napkins you have handy. It's the friendly service of a gum-smacking, drawling waitress with a little apron and cat's-eye glasses—the "ya'll come back now" as you head out the door with a stomach full of grits and gravy.

It's the tasty memories of home-fried chicken just like mama used to make, the barbecue, the pan-fried river trout, the broiled rabbit, and the handmade tortillas formed and fried right before your eyes as an old woman

Courtesy Chuck Sturm

all-you-can-eat frenzy of the dinnertime traveler's buffet.

When the stomach is full and the food forgotten, Route 66 is the amazing sights encountered along the roadside and all the wonder of our weird, wild America. It's gigantic dinosaurs, drive-in restaurants adorned with swooping neon, unexplained phenomenon, and sad and crazy shrines to human individuality—like giant balls of twine or the world's largest bundle of barbed wire—displayed with the sole intention of causing the tourist to stand back and utter "wow!"

It's the vivid images of a snake handler as he thrusts his pole into a cage and pulls out a gigantic rattler ready to strike. It's the wriggling wonder of an alligator paraded in front of the public like some freak of nature, and the homemade "museum" featuring a two-headed goat preserved in formaldehyde displayed right next to a stuffed javelina with glass eyes and horrible teeth scaring little children and providing your subconscious with nightmare fodder for years to come.

It's the rubber Indian hatchet or cheap, imitation moccasins—made in Japan—that were purchased in the adjoining trading post that was open 24 hours for customer convenience. It's watching the throngs of tourists, dressed in loud, patterned bowling shirts and print tunics with polyester pants and bolo ties, drinking in the sights and sounds

in the back hand-grinds corn meal just like her ancestors have for the past 500 years.

It's how cool and tasty the water was and "wasn't that just about the best tasting iced-tea we ever drank?" It's the sizzle that remains in the mind long after the steak is digested and the memories of what the town even looked like disintegrate into thin air.

It's the lobster bibs that you have to wear just to eat some seafood in a joint that tries real hard to be classy despite the glittery vinyl upholstery and the cheap table candles with fishnet coverings to set the mood. It's even the cockroach that waltzes boldly across your table that no one notices or cares about as much as the plates piled high with vittles from the

they can't see at home—all the while their pocket Instamatic cameras clicking and whirring.

For all motorists, Route 66 is driving all day and then finding a tourist court that looks cozy and inviting, its "vacancy" sign drawing the motorist to its hearth—a genuinely friendly and homey place that really does invite the road weary to "just stop and rest a while." It's an Indian wigwam one can actually sleep in when the time comes to turn out the light and wait for the moon to make its arc across the night sky.

It's the secure feeling of knowing your car is parked right outside your room and that the desk clerk really does care "if you need anything." Its the friendly attitude of the maid who lives in her own cabin right out back. It's all part of the experience, including the television that only receives two fuzzy channels, the threadbare pillowcases, and the bedspread that hasn't been laundered since Roosevelt held office.

It's the telephone with the rotary dialer and the inability to access long-distance without the operator listening in on your calls. It's the shower curtain that sticks to your body as you try to take a bath and the few postage-stamp-sized towels available to dry yourself off.

In the final analysis, what's really remembered of Route 66 are those small towns and bustling main streets, the filling stations, the tourist courts and ramshackle roadside cabins, strange attractions, the endless parade of curio shops, the restaurants, the greasy spoons, the diners, the ice cream stands, the drive-in theaters, and a myriad of other wonders that make it worthwhile to hop in a car in downtown Chicago and roll over the great groaning continent to meet the sun-drenched shores of the Pacific. The beginning of a journey and the point of arrival are often just that: the beginning and end. Real memories—and life itself—are made up of all the sights, smells, sounds, and tastes along the way. Events that can only be experienced . . . on the road.

—Michael Karl Witzel, the Texas Hill Country, 1996

Lester Dill acquired ownership of Meramec Caverns in the early 1930s and turned the cave into a well-known Route 66 landmark. Newspapers in St. Louis described Dill as a "self-styled caveologist, promoter of the P.T. Barnum school and a quiet benefactor of both causes and persons in need." Through an unabashed campaign of promotion and highway publicity (he once touted the caves as Jesse James' hideout), he developed a natural wonder and made it into a much-loved tourist destination now remembered as a Mother Road favorite. His numerous barn paintings that advertised the caverns ("See Meramec Caverns, Route 66 Mo.") rose to become almost as famous as the signs of Burma Shave. Today, the caves are still a vital part of the Route 66 legacy. Near the Meramec River, Stanton, Missouri. *Courtesy Jerry Keyser*

Recommended Two-Lane Reading

Anderson, Warren H. *Vanishing Roadside America*. Tucson: The University of Arizona Press, 1981.

Andrews, J.J.C. *The Well-Built Elephant and Other Roadside Attractions: A Tribute to American Eccentricity*. New York: Congdon & Weed, Inc., 1984.

Baeder, John. *Gas, Food, and Lodging: A Postcard Odyssey Through the Great American Roadside*. New York: Abbeville Press, 1982.

Belasco, Warren James. *Americans on the Road: From Autocamp to Motel, 1910–1945*. Cambridge, Massachusetts: M.I.T. Press, 1979.

Blake, Peter. *God's Own Junkyard: The Planned Deterioration of America's Landscape*. New York: Holt, Rinehart and Winston, 1964.

Boyne, Walter J. *Power Behind the Wheel: Creativity and Evolution of the Automobile*. New York: Stewart, Tabori & Chang, 1988.

Buckley, Patricia. *Route 66: Remnants*. Arizona: Historic Route 66 Association of Arizona, 1989.

Butler, John L. *First Highways of America*. Iola, Wisconsin: Krause Publications, 1994.

Clark, Marian. *The Route 66 Cook Book*. Tulsa, Oklahoma: Council Oaks Books, 1993.

Crump, Spencer. *Route 66: America's First Main Street*. Corona Del Mar, California: Zeta Publishers, 1994.

Curtis, C.H. *The Missouri U.S. 66 Tour Book*. St. Louis, Missouri: Curtis Enterprises, 1994.

Davies, Vivian, and Darin Kuna. *Guide to Historic Route 66 in California*. LaVerne, California: California Route 66 Association, 1993.

Finch, Christopher. *Highways to Heaven: The Auto Biography of America*. New York: HarperCollins Publishers, Inc., 1992.

Flink, James J. *The Automobile Age*. Cambridge, Massachusetts: M.I.T. Press, 1988.

Hart, Virginia. *The Story of American Roads*. New York: William Sloan Association, 1950.

Heat Moon, William Least. *Blue Highways: A Journey Into America*. Boston: Atlantic Monthly Press, 1982.

Heimann, Jim, and Rip Georges. *California Crazy: Roadside Vernacular Architecture*. San Francisco: Chronicle Books, 1980.

Hess, Alan. *Googie: 1950s Coffee Shop Architecture*. San Francisco: Chronicle Books, 1985.

Hilleson, K. *Route 66 Revisited: A Wanderer's Guide to New Mexico—Volume 2: Albuquerque to the Arizona Border*. Albuquerque, New Mexico: Nakii Enterprises, 1988.

Keller, Ulrich. *The Highway as Habitat: A Roy Stryker Documentation, 1943–1955*. Santa Barbara, California: University Art Museum, 1986.

Kerouac, Jack. *On the Road*. New York: Viking Penguin, 1955.

Kurtz, Stephen A. *Wasteland: Building the American Dream*. New York: Praeger Publishers, 1973.

Langdon, Philip. *Orange Roofs, Golden Arches: The Architecture of American Chain Restaurants*. New York: Alfred A. Knopf, 1986.

Leavitt, Helen. *Superhighways Superhoax*. New York: Doubleday, 1970.

Leverton, Bill. *On the Arizona Road*. Phoenix, Arizona: Golden West Publishers, 1986.

Lewis, David L., and Lawrence Goldstein. *The Automobile and American Culture*. Ann Arbor: The University of Michigan Press, 1980.

Liebs, Chester. *Main Street to Miracle Mile: American Roadside Architecture.* Boston: Little, Brown & Co., 1985.

Marling, Karal Ann. *The Colossus of Roads: Myth and Symbol Along the American Highway.* Minneapolis: University of Minnesota Press, 1984.

Moore, Bob, and Patrick Grauwels. *A Guidebook to the Mother Road.* Del Mar, California: USDC, Inc., 1994.

Noe, Sally. *66 Sights on Route 66.* Gallup, New Mexico: Gallup Downtown Development Group, 1992.

Patton, Phil. *Open Road: A Celebration of the American Highway.* New York: Simon & Schuster, 1986.

Phillips Petroleum Co. *Phillips: The First 66 Years.* Edited by William C. Wertz. A public affairs publication of Phillips Petroleum Co., 1983.

Rittenhouse, Jack D. *A Guide Book to Highway 66.* Albuquerque, New Mexico: University of New Mexico Press, 1989. (Reprint of 1946 issue).

Rose, Albert C. *Historic American Roads: From Frontier Trails to Superhighways.* New York: Crown Publishers, 1976.

Ross, Jim. *Oklahoma Route 66: The Cruiser's Companion.* Bethany, Oklahoma: Ghost Town Press, 1992.

Ross, Jim, with art by Jerry McClanahan. *Route 66: The Map Series.* Bethany, Oklahoma: Ghost Town Press, 1994.

Rowsome, Frank, Jr. *The Verse by the Side of the Road.* New York: The Stephen Greene Press/Pelham Books, 1990.

Schneider, Jill. *Route 66 Across New Mexico: A Wanderer's Guide.* Albuquerque, New Mexico: University of New Mexico Press, 1991.

Scott, Quinta, and Susan Croce Kelly. *Route 66: The Highway and its People.* Norman, Oklahoma: University of Oklahoma Press, 1988.

Silk, Gerald, Angelo Anselmi, Henry Robert, Jr., and Strother MacMinn. *Automobile and Culture.* New York: Harry N. Abrams, Inc., 1984.

Snyder, Tom. *The Route 66 Traveler's Companion.* New York: St. Martin's Press, 1990.

Society for Commercial Archeology. *The Automobile in Design and Culture.* Edited by Jan Jennings. Ames: Iowa State University Press, 1990.

Steinbeck, John. *The Grapes of Wrath.* New York: Viking Press, 1939.

Steinbeck, John. *Travels with Charley.* New York: Viking Press, 1962.

Stern, Jane, and Michael Stern. *RoadFood.* New York: Harper-Collins Publishers, Inc., 1992.

Teague, Thomas. *Searching for 66.* Springfield, Illinois: Samizdat House, 1991.

Wallis, Michael. *Route 66: The Mother Road.* New York: St. Martin's Press, 1990.

Wallis, Michael, and Suzanne Fitzgerald Wallis. *Route 66 Postcards.* New York: St. Martin's Press, 1993.

Wilkins, Mike, Ken Smith, and Doug Kirby. *The New Roadside America.* New York: Simon & Schuster, 1992.

Witzel, Michael. *The American Gas Station: History and Folklore of the Gas Station in American Car Culture.* Osceola, Wisconsin: Motorbooks International, 1992.

Witzel, Michael. *The American Drive-In: History and Folklore of the Drive-In Restaurant in American Car Culture.* Osceola, Wisconsin: Motorbooks International, 1994.

Witzel, Michael. *Gas Station Memories.* Osceola, Wisconsin: Motorbooks International, 1994.

Index

THE AMERICAN DRIVE-IN

STEAKS CHOPS CLUB BREAKFAST FRIED CHICKEN SODA FOUNTAIN

Michael Karl Witzel

Lowe & B. Hould
Publishers

Dedication

For Dad, my original roadfood mentor, who transported me in the "green slime" to the Wanaque Drive-In for hot dogs, the Milk Barn for chocolate almond ice cream, the Chuck Hut for Bacon-Lettuce-and-Tomato sandwiches, and down Route 23 to Lami's for sausage and pepper sandwiches. Those were some of the tastiest road trips I remember . . . and will never forget.

On the frontispiece: The famous Porky's Drive-In in St. Paul, Minnesota. *Michael Dregni.* The well-stacked hamburger meal served with a plate of French fries and extra large Coca-Cola. *Michael Karl Witzel.* Pig Stand carhop Ruth Forke. *Dallas Public Library*

On the title page: Katson's Drive-In circa 1940, located in Alburquerque, New Mexico. *Courtesy Chuck Sturm*

On the verso and contents pages: Walt's Bar Restaurant Grill on US Highway 46 in Essex County, New Jersey, in July 1947. Is there any doubt that this stand was built by an ex-wartime aviator? *Standard Oil (New Jersey) Co. Collection, Photographic Archives, University of Louisville*

CONTENTS

ACKNOWLEDGMENTS

A triple decker thanks to the individuals who donated time, knowledge, remembrances, photographs, advertisements, contacts, and suggestions. Most notably, Will Anderson, Nancy Baker, Joan Baxter, Joseph R. Blackstock, Brian Butko, Martin Cable, Pat Chappell, David Clements, Dan Daniels, Mike Dapper, Michael Dregni, Albert Doumar, Tom Duffey, Bill Dushatko, Amy Eliezer, Wanda Faist, Ruth Forke, Ralph Grossman, John Hanks, Frank Haywood, Edith Hoover, Charles K. Hyde, Harvey Kaplan, Jerry Keyser, Eric H. Killorin, Bruce Kraig, Arthur Krim, Mildred "Skeeter" Kobzeff, Pat Krohlow, Philip Langdon, Teresa Linscott, Robert Linscott, Ramona Longpré, Richard Longstreth, Lorraine Magowan, Wayne McAllister, Richard McDonald, Richard McLay, Boe Messett, Tom Morrison, Biff Naylor, Greg Naylor, Victor Newlove, Chris Nichols, Clare Patterson, Jr., Dale Poore, Bill Roberts, Kyle Roberts, Ted Roen, Keith A. Sculle, Louise Sivils, Troy N. Smith, Melba Stapleton, Ronald N. Schneider, Chuck Sturm, Jeffrey Tennyson, Buna "Johnnie" Van Hekken, Buzz Waldmire, Marc Wanamaker, J. Frank Webster, and June Wian.

A generous slice of appreciation is reserved for the stock photo agencies, historical archives, photographers, and artists that supplied images, including Warren Anderson, the Atlanta Historical Society, Inc., Arizona Historical Society, Kent Bash, The Texas Collection at Baylor University, Annabelle Breakey, Burbank Historical Society, the Cambridge Historical Commission, Chicago Historical Society, Culver Pictures, Inc., Craig Curtin, the Dallas Historical Society, Georgia Historical Society, Henry Ford Museum & Greenfield Village, Historical Society of Seattle and King County, Kansas State Historical Society, Karl Korzeniewski, Steven Lewis, The Museum of Modern Art, National Archives, the National Museum of American History, The New York Historical Society, Oregon Historical Society, Los Angeles Public Library Photo Collection, Louis Persat, Personality Photos, Inc., Photosource International, Preziosi Postcards, Quincy Historical Society, Renton Historical Society, the Sacramento Archives & Museum Collection Center, Saline County Historical Society, Security Pacific Historical Photograph Collection, Andy Southard, Jr., Standard Oil of New Jersey Collection, Unicorn Stock Photos, Randy Welborn, and of course, Gabriele Witzel.

An extra-large order of fries should go to the libraries, librarians, and researchers who assisted, namely Kim M. Miller and the Antique Automobile Club of America Library and Research Center, Joan Johnson of Circa Research and Reference, Detroit Public Library,

Courtesy Metro ImageBase

Carol Roark and the Dallas Public Library, Howard University Libraries, Brita Mach and Jenny Watts of the Huntington Library, The Library of Congress, Caroline Kozo-Cole and Jane Nowak of the Los Angeles Public Library, Michigan State University Library, Spokane Public Library, Laura Barnard and Christine Firth of the Seattle Public Library, Bill Carner and the University of Louisville Ekstrom Library, Dace Taube of the University of Southern California Library, Washington State University Library, and Wichita Public Library.

Without the assistance of certain organizations and associations, this project would have stuck to the grill. "Order up" goes to Christopher Raab of A&W Restaurants, Inc., Karen Johnston of Beatrice/Hunt-Wesson, Elizabeth Eller, Georgia Grove, Lori A. McManes, and Linda Williams of the Coca-Cola Company, Mildred Walker of the Dr Pepper Museum, Michael Dunlavey and Yvonne Guerra of The Dunlavey Studios, Inc., Kathy Lendech of Hanna-Barbera Entertainment Company, the Hot Dog Hall of Fame, Elizabeth Snyder and the Ice Screamers, the Kansas City Museum, Wayne King of Kings-X Inc. and Jimmie's Diner, Katherine Hamilton-Smith and Debra Gust of the Lake County Museum, George Lucas and Lynne Hale of Lucasfilm, Ltd., Joan Costigan and Doris Morris of Marriott Corporation, Jennifer K. Sebree of MCA/Universal Pictures, Steven Weiss and Mels Drive-Ins, Metro Imagebase, Larry Wagerle and the National Association of Soda Jerks, Phillips Petroleum Company, Schiffer Publishing, Ltd., Seaver Center for Western History Research of the Natural History Museum of Los Angeles County, the Society for Commercial Archeology, Nancy Robertson and Sonic Industries, Inc., Janet P. Boston and Steak n Shake, Inc., Rus Riddell and Swensen's Ice Cream, Dwayne Jones of the Texas Historical Commission, Richard Hailey of the Texas Pig Stands, Inc., Linda Tibbetts Buckley of Universal Studios Florida, Susan H. Gordy and Gordon Muir of The Varsity, Inc.

Finally, a special topping of thank yous to my wife, Gyvel Z. Young-Witzel for her tireless editorial assistance, fact-verification, research, accounting services, moral support, and otherwise unsung duties relating to the completion of this project.

Courtesy Gabriele Witzel

FOREWORD

by Philip Langdon

From their beginnings in the 1920s until their astonishingly sudden fall from grace during the 1960s, drive-in restaurants were some of the most spontaneously enjoyable diversions ever produced by American road commerce.

Without giving up the semi-private world of their automobile interior, motorists could summon service simply by flashing their headlights or depressing the switch on a speaker-box. In a flash an eager carhop would arrive—perhaps dressed in a colorful majorette uniform—or in some instances, sporting roller skates. Gliding across the asphalt with a tray full of hamburgers, French fries, and milkshakes, the curb-girl was an unforgettable sight.

The drive-in itself was a youthful vision of paradise. Youth liked its food tasty, moderately priced, and quick—just the way the drive-in served it. Equally important, teens liked their restaurants to have a stimulating atmosphere, and successful operations rarely disappointed on that score. The continual comings and goings of an eclectic caravan of customers made the dining-room-on-a-parking-lot the ideal spot for people-watching, making new friends, confronting rivals, and sparking romance.

Families were beckoned by the magic of the drive-in, too. This was one kind of restaurant where parents could enjoy taking their children—

without all the worry about behavior or kids making a mess. Here, personal freedom reigned. Customers of all ages were liberated from the expectations and inhibitions that governed the confining conventions of indoor dining.

The uniquely American experience of the drive-in restaurant reflects the twentieth century's ascent of unprecedented mobility and informal living styles. Whether, in the end, the drive-in exerted a desirable or a disruptive influence on the character of America's highways and cities is debatable. However, there can be no doubt that it mirrored a nation's movement toward mobility, changing the roadways…forever.

Today, the imagery of drive-in dining and all its trappings evoke fond memories. Those were the days of so many pleasurable memories—times of relaxation, times of excitement, times when owning a jalopy was a big thrill, and chomping a burger at one's favorite carhop restaurant was a pleasure.

While many of the classic operations have disappeared, they will not be forgotten. And, for all those nostalgic diners with a yearning for the way things used to be, Michael Karl Witzel's book provides the vehicle to revisit the past—a unique opportunity to experience the taste, sound, and atmosphere of some of America's best drive-in restaurants.

INTRODUCTION

As a small fry growing up in the 'burbs of New Jersey, my palate was yet untouched by fast food and its frozen, prefabricated wares. My eager young tastebuds had only experienced the culinary feasts of Mom and Pop eateries that thrived along the Jersey roadside.

Unique food specialties were still the norm back then—staple entrees influenced by a diverse range of ethnic tastes. From the tall oaks of Ringwood to the beaches of Wildwood, every type of family-operated hamburger, hot dog, pizza, sandwich, or ice cream "joint" could be frequented along the commercial corridors. When it came to the simple preparation of roadfood and serving it up to motorists with a practiced style and braggadocio, New England was thicker than the ketchup made famous by Heinz.

Saturday was the special day my Dad and I reserved to explore those flavorful roadways. Pulling out of the driveway from our suburban outpost we embarked on a mission to indulge in the simple pleasures of the motorcar, spend time together, and secretly sample the best junk food that ever tickled our tastebuds.

Although Mom could cook up a superb sauer braten dish, the addictive lure of roadfood and the magic that it promised to add to our vehicular adventures were an addiction we couldn't resist. Hooked, we pledged our culinary allegiance to the offbeat eateries serving the roadside genre.

Through small townships and boroughs we rolled, a piston-powered juggernaut headed far from the suburban sensibilities of my Mother's home kitchen. Within the confines of

Courtesy Metro ImageBase

Suskana Saran Seat Covers
Automotive seat cover manufacturers demonstrated the stain-resistant properties of their fabrics during the fifties and sixties. For a society in love with their automobiles, it was welcome news. Now, dining in the car—whether that meant greasy hamburgers or drippy ice cream—could be worry-free. Oh, the joys of in-car dining!

the family automobile, we talked, consuming the visual wonders of the roadway rushing towards us through a curved panorama of glass. Roadfood mecca was waiting for us...just around the bend.

While we scanned the horizon for just the right dining spot, I played many of the games youngsters play within a moving vehicle: pushing radio buttons to rock'n'roll stations my Dad didn't like, imitating race car sounds, and sprinting alongside the car—in my imagination. Not one obstacle on the sidewalk proved a match for my high-speed fantasy jumps.

Sometimes, my flattened palm became airborne. Like a jet plane, it streaked through the air, diving and climbing in the thick airstream flowing by my open window. Intoxicated with the speed of the internal-combustion engine, telephone poles and street signs rushed past in a myopic blur. I fell in love with the road!

The Wanaque Drive-In was always first in line, located just over the town line. A simple structure situated at an angle to the roadway, it beckoned passing customers with three oversized garage doors opened wide. Visible from the roadway, its long serving counter and menu signboard became a backdrop for the silhouettes of happy diners, wolfing grilled delights. Inside, a dozen tiny tables were outfitted with standard-issue salt and pepper shakers. Wooden chairs of every variety set the informal atmosphere with condiment squeeze bottles containing mustard and ketchup providing a decorative splash of color. Without fail, the house specialty was always a classic hot dog, prepared with mounds of fresh kraut and piles of tangy relish. Greedily, my father and I grabbed our orders and headed for the four-wheel dining compartment, content to observe the pageantry of cars and customers as we filled our tummies with tubesteak.

On the rare occasions when we had room left over for dessert, the craving for home-made ice cream set the course for our next stop. Without exception, that meant driving just a few miles down the avenue to our favorite outlet for frozen treats: the Milk Barn.

A one-of-a-kind establishment dedicated to ice cream, it was covered in weathered cedar shingles and featured an oversized parking lot. Inside, the cavernous interior held dozens of roomy booths and oversized picnic tables. Riddled with knot holes and other imperfections, all were constructed of thick wood. Every visible surface was deeply engraved with thousands of messages carved by an uncountable procession of patrons. Heavy layers of shellac made possible all variety of graffiti, from generic, friendly greeting to undying pledge of love.

While sitting at one of the tables licking a double-scoop cone of chocolate almond or devouring a banana split deluxe, it was easy to let imaginations drift. Whatever became of the people who left behind hand-scrawled triptychs such as "Johnny Loves Suzy," "Greetings from Fort Lee," or "The Andersons were here January 14, 1967"?

At the Milk Barn, the inborn desire to leave proof behind of one's visit and make a mark on the physical realm created a unique dining atmosphere. More important, it gave what would have normally been just a great roadside ice creamery real soul.

Sometimes, we would forego the hot dog and ice cream routine and save our appetites for pizza. Larry's had its share of character, too—but there, the food commanded our complete attention. With no regard for indigestion or abdominal distress, we eagerly coated twenty-five-cent wedges of cheese with copious amounts of red pepper sprinkles and hot yellow seed! A large Pepsi washed down the saucy snack as we gazed in awe at the Old World pizza master pounding, flipping, massaging, and pulling raw dough into the edible product we revered.

Silently, the flabby disc twirled in the air, assumed a perfect shape, then landed, a light breath of flour exhaling from its final contact with the marble. It was magic! With a graceful flourish, Larry—or one of his sons, or brothers, or cousins, or uncles—ladled a healthy dollop of tomato sauce upon the flattened bread. In an ever-widening spiral, he carefully coated the pie in preparation for the generous shower of mozzarella that followed. As we devoured our triangles, we watched it all with reverent silence, hypnotized by the culinary miracle of new pies being born.

Eventually, I outgrew those weekend journeys with my Dad and assumed my rightful place behind the steering wheel among the machines on the highway. The trials of growing up and the demands of everyday living edged out the leisure time once used to watch a pizza man work. Still, I look back fondly on those wonderful times and feel fortunate that the formative years of my streetside schooling included the distinctive restaurant operations we discovered together.

I learned well from them all, memorizing the boomerang patterns of their tabletop Formica, consuming the whimsy of their homemade billboards, etching the twisted traces of their colorful neon into memory. To this day, the swirling imagery of ice cream cones, Coca-Cola buttons, polished diners, fruit stands, advertising mascots, drive-in theaters, carhop restaurants, lunch counters, freeway exits, intersections, and the occasional glimpse of an abandoned automobile take me way, way back to those flavorful days of my youth.

Michael Karl Witzel
Wichita, Kansas
August 1993

AMERICA'S NEW MOTOR LUNCH

Once upon a time in the far, distant past over one hundred years ago—long before there were any plans devised for McDonald's, Wendy's, Burger King, Little Caesars, Carl's Junior, Kentucky Fried Chicken, Whataburger, Jack in the Box, Hardee's, Roy Rogers, or even Taco Bell—the acts of traveling and dining were still considered separate events.

For the most part, the horse-drawn covered wagon proved to be an impractical vehicle for dining on the go. Early carriage designs made no accommodation for beverage holders, and there was no safe place to clip a serving tray. Similarly, four-hoofed transport atop a saddle provided little convenience or comfort when it came to breaking sourdough. While horses were well suited to graze freely of grasses along the route, hungry drovers fared best to ignore hunger pangs until dismount.

When all the frontiers were finally conquered and the population began to fill in the space between each coast, trains, carriages, and horse-drawn travel were overtaken by an economical motorcar for everyone. Once Henry Ford eliminated the kinks from his assembly line operation in 1913 and set the course to replace the iron horse, mobile dining conditions promised to improve. Now, instead of relying on a train line's "butcher boy," the proud owners of a Model T could strap their picnic baskets onto the running board, throw Junior into the backseat, and motor as far and wide as a tank full of gasoline would take them.

Despite the newfound mobility promised by the automobile and its undeveloped potential for dining, there were still limited choices to consider when thoughts of passenger and pilot turned to food. Of course, there was the occasional wayside inn or resort hotel with dining facilities, but with roads still undeveloped, conveniences "out in the sticks" were largely unheard of. Once the limited buffer zone of civilization surrounding a town was breached, automobilists were on their own until they reached the next settlement or nearest grove of fruit trees. In the days when gasoline was purchased from depots on the outskirts of town, refined dining establishments were often as scarce as a fuel pump.

Not surprisingly, planning ahead also became the watch words for those anticipating any sort of meal along secluded routes. A small wicker basket filled to the brim with dishes, silverware, and the foods normally reserved for the sit-down supper became part of many journeys. Containing an overflow of home-cooked goodies such as fried chicken, pork chops, and a loaf of bread, the picnic basket was the portable larder to feed the family on the go. To that end, it wasn't always necessary to stop: sandwiches could be eaten and drinks chugged from a bottle in the front seat—even while the pistons popped!

Realistically, Sunday sightseers and cross-country vacationers made up only a small percentage of the growing rabble of motorists taking to the roadways. Despite Ford's reduction in auto prices, the majority of motorized Americans were working hard just to keep up

continued on page 18

In the far, distant past over one hundred years ago, the acts of traveling and dining were still considered separate events. Despite the newfound mobility promised by the automobile, there were still limited choices when thoughts of passenger and pilot turned to food.

Roadside Picnic Table Scene
Former Farm Security Administration photographer John Vachon froze the family picnic for future study while visiting High Point State Park in Sussex County, New Jersey, in June 1947. Although drive-in eateries were common during that era, the family picnic on the side of the road was just as enjoyable. There was less car exhaust, and a lot less noise. Standard Oil (New Jersey) Co. Collection, Photographic Archives, University of Louisville

SPLENDOR OF THE SODA FOUNTAINS

When the temperature movement forced many states to prohibit the sale of liquor during the 1870s, America's parched populace began turning to the corner drugstore for relief. Eager for liquid refreshment, it was only natural that their search would lead them to the friendly pharmacist: after all, he was once the leading dispenser of alcohol.

Soda Fountain
Walgreen Drugs was one of the Midwest's largest drugstores chains during the late twenties. Not only did they feature fountain service, many had lunch counters that could serve well over a hundred people per hour. In 1929, Ray Kroc, salesman for the newly merged Lily and Tulip Cup Company, approached Walgreen Drugs with a revolutionary new concept—carryout food! By replacing their current glassware with disposable cups, folks could order "to go" shakes and drinks. Walgreen's business doubled and ten years later they were convinced (once more) to try a new concept—this time it was the rapid-action Multimixer. Hedrich-Blessing photograph. Courtesy the Chicago Historical Society

Pharmacy owners lost no time in acclimating to the new situation. By heavily promoting carbonated beverages, an all-out campaign was launched to regain revenues lost from alcohol sales. Obsolete liquor advertising signs were tossed regretfully into the storage room. Oversized display racks were hastily removed, too, clearing way for tables and chairs.

To entice new patronage, the creation of cozy conversation areas became an integral part of the revamped marketing plan. Now, folks could linger—all while sipping the effervescent liquids produced by the Lippincott and Puffer fountains.

Eventually, the competition that followed spurred many drugstore operators to construct elaborate fountain areas. Gleaming counters of marble and alabaster replaced homely wood. Ornate mirrors and lamps added an air of elegance. Crafted in the form of goddesses, gargoyles, and sphinxes, intricate spigots yielded sparkling fluid with a turn of the wrist. This union of polished stone and mirrored back bar soon became an integral part of the modern drugstore.

To America's alcohol-deprived, the effect of fountain drinks and sundaes was one of deep satisfaction. Who could resist carbonated waters blended with ice cream, syrups, marshmallows, and nuts? At long last, the public's parboiled palates were quenched! Fantasy mixtures like the "Catawba Flip," "Panama Cooler," and "Black-Eyed Susan" became popular tonics of the era.

Commanding the spigots was a new youthful wonder: the soda jerk. With his skillful manipulations, generous supplies of whipped cream and syrup joined with the bubbling waters. Highly coveted, his position was the product of many months, and sometimes years, of menial tasks performed around the store. As consummate showman, innovator, and freelance linguist of the drugstore stage, America's soda jerk became the pop culture star of the Gilded Age.

As fountain popularity swelled, many drugstores lacked the interior space to accommodate the onslaught. To handle the rush, young curb servers soon joined the soda jerks. Visionary operators determined that the lads could deliver soda fountain creations outside to the waiting buggies. Since they were paid by customers' tips, the monetary risk was minimal. Without moving or remodeling, the drugstore operator could increase sales volume and convenience.

Within a short time, curbs were lined with carriages. Energetic curb servers relayed requests for a "barked pie" (with upper crust), one "in the hay" (strawberry shake), and Java to the inside soda jerk—all prepared to "go for a walk."

Unfortunately, this leisurely style of ice cream parlour service eventually gave way to the bustling frenzy of drive-ins and walk-up fast-food stands. Flamboyant soda jerks were replaced by grill men and fry cooks. Assembly-line burgers became the new art form. Soon, curb boys sporting cow-licks were dumped for carhops in form-fitting fashions.

As the exodus to the suburbs sounded the final death knell during the fifties, the cultural phenomenon of the American soda jerk and fountain had all but expired. Only fond memories of sweet sodas and smooth milkshakes—and the legacy of the greatest of all American creations, the soft drink—were left behind. ■

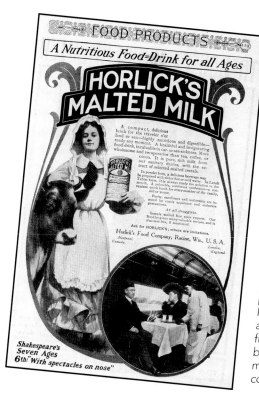

Horlick's Malted Milk

In 1886, Wisconsin dairyman William Horlick developed a new food made from whole milk, extract of wheat, and malted barley. Touted as a healthy and invigorating drink, its popularity grew rapidly. A few tablespoons mixed briskly with water turned an ordinary glass into a liquid lunch, packed with instant nutrition. Innovative soda jerks gradually added milk, ice cream, and flavored syrups to the beverage, transforming the malted milk into a new fountain concoction.

Chocolate Milkshake

"Shake, rattle, and roll"—the words of this popular song certainly describe the methods used by early milkshake pioneers as they attempted to create that perfect shake without the aid of electric mixers. In 1920, a single-spindled blender manufactured by Hamilton Beach entered the arsenal of soda fountain tools. Now, the true nature of the shake could be experienced. As tiny blades whizzed and whirled—gently aerating the mixture—a new blend was born. It was thick, rich, and smoother than any of its predecessors. Preziosi Postcards

Syrup Dispenser Progression

The evolution of the drugstore soda-fountain dispenser: from ceramic (center), to hand-drawn (right), to automatic (left). The beautiful porcelain fountain urn could be earned with a 35-gallon order of syrup, along with other premiums such as advertising clocks, prescription scales, and showcases. Courtesy of The Coca-Cola Company

continued from page 14

the installments on their vehicles. The every day rigors of life and the quest to make a living dominated the existence of the majority who owned and cherished an automobile.

Traveling great distances from their homes to do industrial work, a multitude of laborers was forced to consume meals far from the conveniences of home. Although lunch pails and sacks packed by the wife provided the noontime meal for many factory laborers, there were times when this practice born of school days proved impractical—not to mention boring. Isolated from the comforts of home with nothing but their vehicle for comfort, workers longed for a place where they could down a quick, inexpensive lunch with all the trimmings of hearth and home.

To fill the need, the "beanery" and other so-called "greasy spoons" appeared to serve the daily worker. Located in proximity to factories and in concentrated places of commerce, they became the first step in supplying food to the average Joe. Though not in the least bit reminiscent of home, they captured the ready audience with quickness, convenience, and fair prices.

Similar variations opened in big cities to serve the growing influx of commuters, shoppers, and employees arriving around the clock. It wasn't long before a panoply of coffee-shops, lunch counters, diners, cafeterias, taverns, luncheonettes, and other eateries began to fill the streets with the smell of bacon, eggs, and hot coffee. America's restaurant boom was on! In the two decades following 1910, the estimated number of dining spots exhibited an increase of almost forty percent.

The new restaurants continued to ignore the specific needs of car customers, however. Methods that could easily be adopted to serve vehicles efficiently were neither tried nor remembered. After all, Fortune's drugstore in downtown Memphis had been serving curbside customers within their carriages as early as the turn of the century. A crew of waiters delivered soda delights directly to the customers in the street! Yet, for some reason, the bulk of businesses along America's Main Streets chose to regard this service as an oddity. Efforts were concentrated in the various formats used for inside dining. To purchase a fast meal or drink, patrons would simply have to park their cars and walk inside a building to be served.

The problem: Owners of automobiles were growing accustomed to the speed and comforts of internal-combustion living. An increasing dissatisfaction with available restaurants and their supposed conveniences was growing. For those used to the wide open spaces of the road, city cafeterias were the worst. Endless lines had to be negotiated to select food; confining quarters and the habits of others had to be tolerated while waiting. Hand-carried trays were a standard, toted individually to a spot at a communal table. Packed from elbow to elbow with unmannered gourmands, lingering was frowned

Root Beer Stand
Root beer barrel roadside stand selling "toasted" sandwiches. Circa 1920. Culver Pictures

upon. But who would want to? Oblivious to the genteel sensibilities of others, fellow diners reduced mealtime to an unenjoyable experience. Vehicle owners accustomed to the comfort of their automobiles' seats bristled at the hurried atmosphere.

While the roadside lunch wagon allowed easier access with a more forgiving parking arrangement, patrons still had to forsake the seclusion of their conveyances to place an order. Once again, the cherished motorcar had to be left behind, temporarily abandoned. Even then, food would have to be consumed while standing. Those in search of sit-down succor would have to carry their victuals back to their car.

Then, it happened: Prohibition went nationwide with a constitutional amendment in 1919. With the sale of liquor officially banned, existing soda fountains, ice cream parlors, and candy shops enjoyed a sudden rise in popularity. As back-alley operators and bootleggers began to organize a clandestine network to sell liquor, non-alcoholic liquids were rediscovered for recreational relief. Ice cream sodas became the new favorite and root beer came to be known as the "national temperance drink."

At the same time, vehicle owners were discovering just how enjoyable driving and dining really were. With the freedom for consuming alcohol disallowed, Americans held dear the remaining liberties they still had, including the pleasures of the motorcoach. By 1920, there were 8 million cars jamming the roadways with recreational eating the newest kick. Comfortable seats, glove compartments, and other accoutrements joined roll-up windows, rear-view mirrors, and windshield wipers as standard equipment. The course was set for the automobile to become as comfortable, if not more so, than the suburban dining chamber of home. With the spartan era of the Model T in decline, the environment for taking meals on wheels was primed with excitement. "Ain't we

continued on page 24

Teapot Ice Cream Cone Stand
Los Angeles ice cream stand borrowing the shape of a teapot for its attention-getting architecture. Circa 1930. Culver Pictures

Betty's Shack With Coca-Cola Signs
Below, Betty's Shack in Texas was a typical example of the roadside business trying to attract the attention of the thirsty motorist in the early decades of this century. Coca-Cola, Dr Pepper, Royal Crown Cola, and even Seven-Up were available to wash down steaks and a quick lunch. From the collections of the Texas/ Dallas History and Archives Division, Dallas Public Library

IMMORAL SODAS TO SUNDAES

America's first ice cream soda fizzed to life in October of 1874. At the time, Robert Green was working as a soda fountain concessionaire at the Franklin Institute's exhibit in Philadelphia. Serving drinks from a three-foot square dispenser, he ran out of cream for a popular beverage. Plopping a large dollop of ice cream into a flagon of flavored seltzer, he created the ice cream soda.

After sneaking a tentative sip, Green was wowed. The resulting blend of soda, syrup, and frozen cream was delightful! Without hesitation, the innocent libation was added to the menu, and by the end of the exhibition, customers showed approval by cracking their money purse. Green was taking in over $600 dollars a day in ice cream soda sales alone.

As more and more customers sampled the creamy texture of the new drink, word of the frosty frappé spread among the locals—then to surrounding states. The phenomenon spread quickly and soon ice cream sodas were slurped in fountains from New York to California.

After two decades of unbridled consumption, a placated populace began to recognize Green's handiwork as "the national beverage." As the soda addiction took root, pious Midwestern clergymen were quick to observe that the lascivious consumption was becoming uncontrollable. Not only were some Americans practicing gluttony during the week, they were now neglecting the Sabbath day of worship. The hedonistic act of sipping what was soon referred to as "the immoral soda" became a pleasurable substitute.

It wasn't long before pulpits became platforms for heated sermons. Men of the cloth rallied against the loathsome drink and denounced the country's twisted devotion to the dogma of the ice cream parlour. God-fearing congregations took heed of the warnings, and before long, a throng of righteous citizens initiated a campaign to outlaw sales of the corrupt concoction.

The Ice Cream Sundae
By the 1920s, ice cream became the fastest growing industry in America. Hailed as "America's typical food," it was consumed at the annual rate of nine quarts per person. What's more, consumer's wanted their vanilla coated in chocolate! This desire for chocolate was instrumental in lifting the cocoa-dependent economy of Ecuador out of depression. That is, until America's own Depression made those nickels to buy ice cream harder to come by. Fred D. Jordan, Unicorn Stock Photos

During the 1890s, Evanston, Illinois, became the first principality to enact laws against the "Sunday Soda Menace." Two Rivers, Wisconsin, followed with their own legislation, and soon, the banning of Sunday ice cream sodas spread nationwide. Liberated Americans, who had finally discovered a legal substitute for alcohol, became the target of a new prohibition. To the disbelief of many, a simple mixture of carbonated water and ice cream entered illegal domain.

Incensed at the excommunication of one of the best products the confection business had, fountain proprietors began searching for the ice cream soda's savior. Another "forbidden treat" had to be found, one that would legally circumvent the Sunday blue laws.

The most believable account credits fountain owner Ed Berner of Two Rivers with the unassuming creation of the new dessert. As the story goes, George Hallauer came in for a dish of ice cream and desired chocolate syrup be poured over it. Berner sampled it himself, liked it, and began to sell "ice cream with syrup" for the same price as a regular dish.

After customers began demanding it, George Giffy was forced to sell the nickel a dish treat at his soda bar in nearby Manitowoc. Afraid he was losing money on the combination, he limited sales of "the Sunday" to the seventh day.

When Giffy realized its profitability, he started promoting the "Soda-less Soda" throughout the week. To disassociate the treat with Sunday-only sales and to satisfy the vigilant clergy, the spelling was eventually altered. While the ice cream soda was not entirely forgotten, Americans now had a new Sundae. ∎

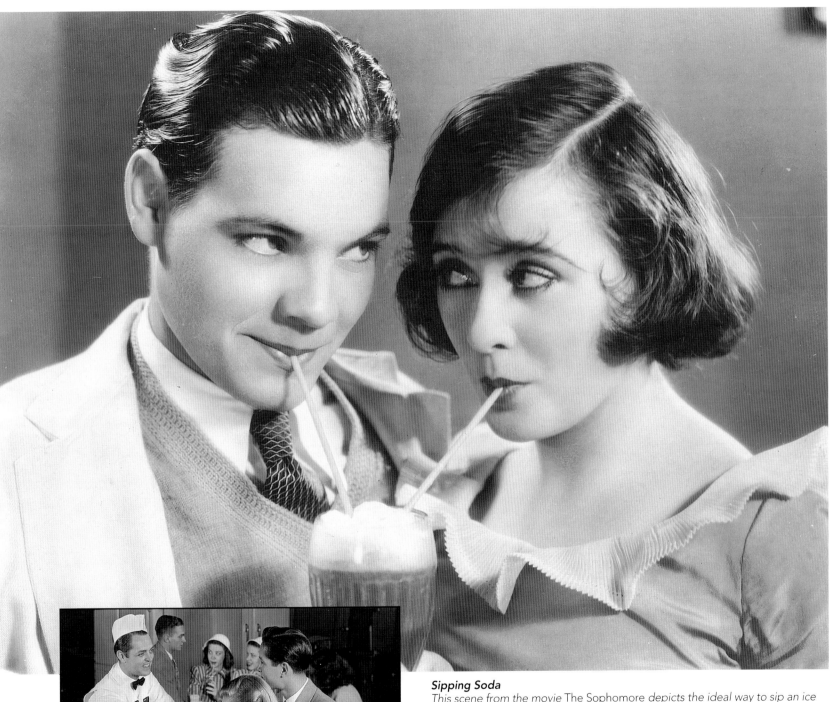

Sipping Soda
This scene from the movie The Sophomore *depicts the ideal way to sip an ice cream soda: using two straws while gazing into each others eyes. Aaaaaah, what could be sweeter?* Museum of Modern Art/Film Stills Archive

Walgreen Customers with Soda
Left, a Walgreen soda jerk combines generous supplies of whipped cream, syrup, and bubbling waters to create that frozen delight—the ice cream soda! Hedrich-Blessing photograph. Courtesy the Chicago Historical Society

THOSE DACHSHUND DOGS IN A BUN

Almost nine centuries before the birth of Christ, the Greek poet Homer made reference to the roasting of sausages in his epic writings. The Romans acquired a penchant for them, too, gorging their stomachs to the limit at bawdy parties. It wasn't long before Christians denounced the cased meat as lascivious, eventually influencing the emperor Constantine to ban them from his empire.

By the time the Middle Ages were in full swing and the population a bit more tolerant of new foods, minced meat packed within intestinal wrapping lost most of its pagan mystique. Suddenly, every butcher in Europe handy with a meat grinder and a carving knife was experimenting with, and eating, sausages.

Residents of Germany's Frankfurt am Main liked their "frankfurters" ground particularly coarse, with an ample amount of seasonings added to flavor the meats. In nearby Austria, the good people of Wien (or Vienna) preferred "wieners" of a much finer consistency, easy on the spices. But, regardless of the ingredient mixture or the name, both European localities served their sausages on a plate, accompanied by a healthy helping of sauerkraut or potato salad.

When German Charles Feltman immigrated to the United States, he unknowingly brought with him the essence of this legacy, one that would eventually propel him to local fame and fortune. But like everyone else who is raised with something familiar and eventually takes it for granted, he suppressed his appetite for sausage and settled for pushing a pie wagon up and down the beach at New York's Coney Island. It was a decent living, albeit a little discouraging: customers were always inquiring whether or not he had any hot sandwiches for sale.

Convinced that sandwich vending would entail an unmanageable amount of cooking and cutting, he resisted the requests until a hot dog popped into his imagination one day in 1867. In a flash of brilliance, remembrances of Old World eating habits assembled themselves into a radically new plan for seaside profits.

It was all too simple! He would keep a small pot of warmed sausages steaming in his pushcart and sell them to the persistent customers. Sliced milk rolls would provide the means to hold the heated links, enabling spur-of-the-moment diners to enjoy their quick lunches while standing up. Unlike some of the other restaurants opening nearby, table and chair arrangements wouldn't be required, making his service almost instantaneous, cleanup non-existent.

Excited with the possibilities, Feltman approached a local wheelright named Donovan and asked if he could fashion a small burner for his food cart. Donovan accepted the task, and soon a small pot heated with coals became the core of a Feltman's new enterprise. Two at a time, he began selling his tubular lunch to curious Coney Island visitors. Everyone loved the convenience, allowing him to expand his business beyond his wildest expectations. By the time sports cartoonist T. A. Dorgan coined the term "hot dog" in 1901, Feltman managed to parlay the meager pushcart operation into a full-scale restaurant, with 1,200 waiters.

Today, the hot dog persists as the last linchpin in the regional merry-go-round of American fast food. Dictated by local tastes, hot dogs are still prepared with limitless variety. And why not? Loved and eaten across all social classes, the unheralded frankfurter has jumped the chasm from ordinary fast food to culinary common denominator. ■

French's
Mustard Cream Salad
Francis French created the nation's largest mustard company with the development of a new formula that was light and creamy, and marketed as French's Cream Salad in this 1926 ad. Courtesy Reckitt and Coleman, Inc.

Easy Hot Dogs & Beer
What better combination than an easy hot dog and a beer, as advertised by this derelict drive-in sign near San Antonio, Texas? Great for stationary dining, but not so good when the time calls for motoring.

Hot Dog Heaven
In 1913, it was a widely held folk belief that hot dogs actually had dog meat in them. The Coney Island Chamber of Commerce banned the use of the term "hot dog" on any signs or menus. Instead, they referred to the popular boardwalk wieners as "Coney Islands!" ©1994 Michael Karl Witzel

Hot Dogs and World's Largest Drive-In
Nathan Handwerker worked slicing rolls at one of Charles Feltman's grills at Coney Island, New York. He saved $300 and leased the corner of a building on Surf Avenue in 1916. Undercutting Feltman's price, he began selling what were now being referred to as hot dogs (cartoonist T. A. Dorgan coined the term in 1901) for a nickel apiece. When the subway reached Coney Island, "Nathan's" continued to grow and became the largest hot dog emporium in the world. For the World's Largest Drive-In, the hot dog provided a potent symbol for advertising.
Preziosi Postcards

Dallas Pig Stand Number 2
A short while after the first Pig Stand was opened on Chalk Hill Road (the old Dallas-Fort Worth Highway) in 1921, J. G. Kirby and R. W. Jackson constructed a second stand in Dallas. Located on Zangs Boulevard, it followed the same design philosophy as the first: close proximity to the curbside, with "carhops" servicing the arriving automobiles. Courtesy of Texas Pig Stands, Inc.

"People with cars are so lazy they don't want to get out of them to eat!"

—Jessie G. Kirby,
Pig Stand founder

continued from page 19

got fun" became more than the lingo of the speakeasy, but the battle cry for the motorist as well.

Unfortunately, the simple connection between serving food to passengers within an automobile—though blatantly evident—remained to be made. Out along the expanding byways, the most hospitable sort of restaurant any traveler could hope to find was of the tea-room genre. Playing on the themes of home, these nostalgic eateries occupied buildings of historical character—namely old barns, grist mills, and vintage homes. Home-cooked meals were the specialty and alcohol never mentioned. A fair number were constructed along well-traveled tourist routes in New England, but eventually fell out of favor due to competition and amateurish management. (In the years to follow, slick operator Howard Johnson upgraded the tearoom concept with sound business practices and a visible image.)

For the time being, the most convenient choice for food pointed to the numerous "hot dog kennels" that proliferated along the motorways. At the time, anyone with a gimmick, frontage on a busy roadway, and enough scrap lumber to construct a shack could be in business. Attracting customers with a prodigious display of hand-painted signs, they capitalized on the hapless motorist "just passing through" and often became a legitimate outlet for Aunt Martha to sell her home-made sausages or Uncle Jed his hand-cranked ice cream. Despite the problems associated with quality and sanitation, reputable home-grown operations prospered.

Along with billboards and other signs, food and refreshment stand operators began to employ architecture itself to attract those passing. Bizarre constructions soon mimicked an eclectic assortment of animals and objects. Echoing the products they sold, many "programmatic" structures were erected along the established roadways during the twenties. Giant milk bottle buildings hawked malteds and three-story ice cream freezers promoted frozen desserts; oversized cranberry bottles became outlets for juice, while house-sized swines sold barbecued ribs.

Instead of using fantastic imagery as his hook, Dallas candy and tobacco magnate Jessie G. Kirby decided to exploit the habits of the average vehicle owner. "People with cars are so lazy they don't want to get out of them to eat!" was the sentiment he expressed to future partner Reuben W. Jackson when pitching the idea for a drive-by sandwich business. He believed that the time was right for an eatery geared specifically towards serving diners within their cars. A well-known Dallas physician, Jackson didn't know much about the food business but did understand the appeal of the motorcar. He was duly impressed with Kirby's practical idea of serving cars at

the curb and wasted no time providing the initial $10,000 financing needed for a corporation that would construct a prototype pork stand.

In the fall of 1921, the American automobile and the restaurant collided head on, forever altering the nature of dining along the roadways. That year, Kirby and Jackson's ambitious food enterprise dubbed the "Pig Stand" began offering its tasty sandwiches to the motorists of Texas, enticing automotive commuters to exit their speeding path on the bustling Dallas-Fort Worth Highway to "Eat a Pig Sandwich." One by one, car customers hungry for something new eased off the throttle to become part of the festive grand opening. On the busy cross street bordering the Pig Stand's lot, an assortment of motor vehicles awaited their turn in line.

Curiously enough, the scene was more reminiscent of a curbside traffic jam than a restaurant opening. But the problems of traffic

The Claude Neon Pig
Over seventy years old, the famous Pig Sandwich sign manufactured by the Claude Federal Neon Company still delights customers. Four additional pig signs remain, and owner Richard Hailey plans to display them at other Pig Stand locations. When an infringement lawsuit against the Hard Rock Cafe (a Pig Sandwich appeared on the their menu) went to court in the early 1990s, Hailey wheeled the large sign into the courtroom as evidence. Judgment for the plaintiff: the "Pig Sandwich" belongs exclusively to the Pig Stands restaurants! Broadway location dining room, San Antonio, Texas

control proved minimal: automobilists savvy to the latest fads picked right up on the concept. Attracted by the economical prices, Tin Lizzy owners comprised the majority of the first customers, with operators of refined vehicles such as the Packard Twin Six and the Cadillac Touring Sedan eventually vying for space at the junction.

As the first month of operation drew to a close, local residents and passing travelers were discovering for themselves the thrill of eating in your car. Rewarded within the privacy of their vehicles with savory pork sandwiches, bottled soda beverages, and courteous service, there were no surprises or disappointments. No longer would the casual motorist have to leave the privacy of his or her vehicle to suffer the perceived indignities of the typical roadside food operation. The family picnic could now be had within the motorcar itself,

effectively converting any automobile into a dining room on wheels. At long last, America had its "new motor lunch."

As both the famished and curious steered in for service, dapper young men accosted the speeding vehicles during their final moments of deceleration. Wasting no time with formalities, they jumped without hesitation right up onto machines moving along the curbside to gather food orders. Fortunately, most automotive models were equipped with running boards in those days: side-mounted strips of metal running under the length of each side door. Normally, these platforms were used by the driver or passenger to facilitate safe entry. When unused as a step, they held spare tires or the occasional suitcase.

To the lunchers' delight, the daring young servers of the Texas Pig Stands superseded both of these mundane applications. As customers became acquainted with the idea of waiters jumping up on their cars, many began to wonder if the thin sideboards had been designed just for them! In an age of idols and ballyhoo typified by pole-sitters and daredevils, it was just the type of brash exhibitionism needed to attract public interest and a write-up in the local newspaper.

In reality, the motivation was more basic for the jumping order takers: Those who got to the car first were the ones who made the best tips. Therefore, speed was of the utmost importance. By the time an automobile braked to a complete stop, one of the competitive curb boys would be hanging off its side, his

continued to page 30

Pig Stand Menu
The breakfast menu from the Number 2 stand, circa 1930.
Courtesy Chuck Sturm

PIG STANDS, INC.

Good Morning!

We respectfully suggest to You any one of these appetizing . . .

CLUB BREAKFASTS

No. 1
One Egg, Ham, Bacon or Brookfield Sausage, Toast, Jelly and Coffee
25c

No. 2
Half Grapefruit, One Egg, Ham, Bacon or Brookfield Sausage, Toast, Jelly and Coffee
35c

No. 3
Half Grapefruit, Two Eggs, Toast Jelly and Coffee
35c

No. 4
Cereal with Cream, Two Eggs, Ham Bacon or Brookfield Sausage, Toast Jelly, Coffee
45c

Our Eggs Are Scrambled in Pure Cream and Fried in Butter

PIG STANDS, INC.

Or . . .

if You prefer for Breakfast . . .

Orange Juice	.10
Tomato Juice	.10
Pineapple Juice	.10
Grapefruit Juice	.10
Half Grapefruit	.10
Ham and Eggs, Toast, Jelly and Coffee	.30
Bacon and Eggs, Toast, Jelly and Coffee	.30
Brookfield Sausage and Eggs, Toast Jelly and Coffee	.30
Ham or Bacon Omelette, Toast Jelly and Coffee	.35
Two Eggs, any style, Toast, Jelly and Coffee	.25
Plain Omelette, Toast, Jelly and Coffee	.25
One Egg, Toast, Jelly and Coffee	.20
Hot Cakes, Melted Butter and Maple Syrup	.15
Side Order of Ham, Bacon or Brookfield Sausage	.15
Cereals with Cream	.15

PIG STANDS, PIG STANDS, EVERYWHERE

Pioneering the Drive-Thru Window
The drive-thru window was an idea tried in 1931 at the California Pig Stand Number 21. Customers could drive-in, place their order, and exit. It was quick and convenient, the basic model for the way fast-food businesses operate today. The only difference was that the order taker was not a machine. Courtesy of Texas Pig Stands, Inc.

Crowd Loves Pig Stand Number 21
After California Pig Stand Number 21 was remodeled, crowds charged with Golden Bear Coffee posed happily for a photograph. Circa mid-1930s. Courtesy of Texas Pig Stands, Inc.

Royce Hailey With Pig Sign
Coca-Cola and the Pig Sandwich—a winning combination for Royce Hailey, ex-carhop turned chain owner. Today, son Richard Hailey continues the tradition of the sliced pork lunch and has taken over the reins from his dad. From the collections of the Texas/Dallas History and Archives Division, Dallas Public Library

Octagonal Los Angeles Stand
By 1930, more operators were entering the market with their own food stands. Basic Pig Stand designs were upgraded with colored tile and new signboards. But even those were not enough: a large "Sandwiches" sign lettered in neon now occupied a place of prominence, almost as large as the stand itself! Courtesy of Texas Pig Stands, Inc.

Beaumont Circular Pig Stand
Beaumont was the Texas town where Royce Hailey came up with his most famous invention: Texas Toast. Around 1941, he was working as the district manager and began experimenting with bread. One day, he asked the Rainbo Bakery to slice his loaves thicker and was presented with slabs that were simply too big to fit in the toaster. One of the cooks suggested that they butter them and toast both sides on the grill. It was a good idea: they turned out extremely moist with a flavor totally different from regular toast. Another cook suggested they call it "Texas Toast" and the rest is history. Unfortunately, Hailey failed to patent the invention. This circular Pig Stand was located on Calder Avenue. Circa 1941. Courtesy of Texas Pig Stands, Inc.

San Antonio Streamline Pig Stand
By 1939, the outdated buildings typical of the early locations was retired. Streamlined traffic-stoppers like this impressive San Antonio tower unit took the barbecued pork sandwich to a new level. Courtesy of Texas Pig Stands, Inc.

Broadway Pig Stand
The Texas Pig Stands are still alive and well and thriving in the Lone Star State. The Broadway location in San Antonio is reported to be one of the nation's oldest sit-down restaurants. San Antonio, Texas

A&W Stand

In 1921, the nation's first A&W Root Beer stand opened on the corner of K and 19th Streets in Sacramento. Pioneering fast-food franchising much like the Singer Company sold its sewing machines, A&W allowed investors to sell its popular refreshment products. After Mr. Wright's half of the partnership was bought out by Allen in 1924, a major push to franchise the root beer was undertaken. Color schemes were duplicated, along with architecture, signs, and trademarks. Allen's biggest transaction followed in 1927 when young J. Willard Marriott purchased the rights to sell the A&W brand in the Washington, D. C. market. Eventually, his fledgling hole-in-the-wall stand grew into the Hot Shoppes drive-in chain. A&W Restaurants, Inc.

A&W Root Beer Barrel Stand

Right, what better way to entice customers to purchase root beer than to construct a building like a giant root beer barrel? It was a concept that worked for many franchisees of the A&W brew during the twenties and thirties and continued well into the 1950s.
A&W Restaurants, Inc.

continued from page 27

face peering through the driver's side window. As fast as the operator behind the steering wheel could rattle off his or her order, the energetic order taker would be gone. With all the energy of youth, the boys snapped up food requests as fast as humanly possible. Leaping on and off the shifting line of auto

platforms with a practiced style, they dodged crazily between a dozen or more sputtering vehicles and were gone.

As the curb filled up, they ran back and forth to the small board-and-batten box that housed the kitchen, delivering their requests to the short-order man working his craft within the wooden structure. As the orders came up, efficient servers scooped up the entrees with one hand and snatched up a couple of frosty Coca-Cola bottles with the other. Sprinting a return to the ordering vehicle with food in hand, they were greeted by the vehicle occupants with child-like anticipation. As paper-wrapped meals were thrust through the customer's side window, coins and greenbacks were exchanged. Lightning speed and friendliness were rewarded generously by the mobile visitors; a bulging pocket full of tips was the only ballast that slowed the frenetic pace.

The nation's first automotive food servers quickly became a local phenomenon and the term "carhop" was coined to describe the flashy combination of waiter, busboy, cashier, and daredevil. Soon, other operations picked up on the style. It wasn't long before the car-hopping carboy of the Pig Stand pushed out the saddle-jumping cowboy of the rodeo as the new hero of the American West. As news of the new serving style spread beyond the expanse of Texas, motorists lauded the motoring waiter as just another benefit of automobile ownership. After all, the gasoline station had its service attendant and the lubritorium its grease monkey. Why should the roadside food stand be any different?

A number of operators were answering that question with their own car service, including those on the West Coast. Around the same time Kirby's car servers were thrilling Dallas customers, Roy W. Allen was training his own crew of "tray-boys" to work at his drive-in root beer stand in California. According to a May 1968 article in *Drive-In Restaurant*, it all started in 1918:

Roy W. Allen met a traveling chemist who boasted of a special formula he had concocted for draft root beer and explained how well it would sell for a nickel a glass. Allen was skeptical, but tried the drink anyway. That sip proved to be worth a fortune.

Mr. Allen was going about his business of purchasing old hotels and restaurants to remodel for resale when at one establishment in Flagstaff, Arizona, Allen met a traveling chemist who boasted of a special formula he had concocted for draft root beer. Raving about this brew's taste, he urged Allen to serve the frothy drink at the hotel and explained how well it would sell for a nickel a glass. Allen was skeptical, but tried the drink anyway. That first sip proved to be worth a small fortune.

Without delay, an agreement was made between the two men to produce and market the root beer concentrate. Armed with the confidence afforded by the tasty formula, Allen opened a small root beer stand in the small town of Lodi, California, and began selling icy refreshments to the public on a busy corner downtown. By the end of 1919, his

foaming beverage made from a secret mixture of herbs, spices, barks, and berries became a well-known thirst-quencher in the area. It was the height of Prohibition, and the small stand easily attracted an admirable volume of business. Encouraged by the success and profits of this first refreshment shack, he decided to construct a duplicate outlet in Stockton.

A&W Tray-Boys & Girls at Stand
Above, at this circa 1925 A&W stand in Salt Lake City, Utah, "tray-boys" and "tray-girls" line up with trays in hand. In the background, the heat of the day is already rising—root beer customers are on their way! A&W Restaurants, Inc.

A&W Round Stand
Left, a crude version of the streamlined drive-in structures to come, circa 1940s. Hot dogs, root beer, and popcorn were America's first automotive comfort foods. A&W Restaurants, Inc.

Forties A&W Tray-Boy With Cars
J. Willard Marriott employed the service of young men to cart what was known as "Food for the Whole Family" to motorists in cars. These "running boys" were an updated version of the car-serving prototype of the twenties, now sporting two-toned suit jacket, black tie, white shirt, and white brimmed hat. A round neon sign caught the look of the car server in full stride and soon became a beacon for those in the Washington, D. C. area. Courtesy Library of Congress

In 1920, an employee from the Lodi location, Frank Wright, officially joined the drink enterprise and the search for a new name was undertaken. Utilizing the first initials of their names—"A" for Allen and "W" for Wright—the team opted for simplicity and formally christened their temperance beverage A&W Root Beer.

With a brand identifier established, the pioneering refreshment stands (operating without a defined brand) in Stockton and Lodi were leased to other operators. The newly

formed soft drink pair had more ambitious plans: an entirely different operation would be built in Sacramento, with more to follow. Featuring the delivery of frosty mugs right out to the customer, they would become California's first drive-ins.

In 1921, the nation's first root beer stand using the A&W name opened on the corner of K and 19th Streets in Sacramento. Like their Texas cousins, the peppy tray-boys (and later, tray-girls) introduced Californians to the magic of car service and developed their own unique serving style. But unlike the Pig Stand's free-wheeling acrobatics, A&W's curb service was more subdued: workers toted multiple mugs of brew atop sturdy trays within a defined parking area. Presented in a mug made of characteristically heavy glass, root beer was a refreshment that required ginger handling during delivery. Unlike bottles of soda pop that were bandied about with little care, fluted decanters had to be carried with more thought. They required retrieval to a central washing area where they were cleaned for the next batch of customers. As a result, cars weren't allowed to zip up to the curb and drive away at their own leisure. Waiting in a patient and orderly fashion was a required practice.

In the end, however, the diverse styles Roy Allen and J. G. Kirby presented to serve food and drink to patrons waiting within their automobiles were inconsequential. What mattered most was the ultimate digression from established patterns of food service had finally been initiated. Now, two major markets were experimenting with a natural symbiosis: recreational dining and the gasoline-powered automobile.

With only a minimal investment in structure and virtually none in advertising, the Pig Stands fixed the notion that customers really did like to eat inside their cars and would gladly patronize restaurants that subscribed to that mode. Similarly, the A&W Root Beer stands made a point for refreshment: Motorists speeding by in an auto would—and actually preferred to—drive in for something as simple as a cold beverage. No longer were the normal styles enough to satisfy; the bustling city cafeteria was destined to become the "carfeteria" and the cramped luncheonette a full-blown drive-in with all the room of the great outdoors.

Although both of these operations became the nation's first models for the coming glut of roadside eateries and the transition to eating-on-the-go, their potential was somewhat hampered by their adherence to established menus. While barbecue was a big favorite in many regions of the country, it was not as highly esteemed in others. Similarly, while root beer was loved in Utah, other states remained loyal to soft drinks such as Coca-Cola, Dr Pepper, or Moxie. One person's milkshake was another's malted. In an age preceding the dominant influence of national advertising, many people were slow to try new things—especially tastes that they were not accustomed to.

As a departure from what appeared to be an inevitable sequence of events, the union of barbecue sandwich and root beer drink would not become the combination to push the drive-in phenomenon into the future. A new food was required, an entree that could become nationally popular. Even then, it would have to be simple, made with readily available materials, by a variety of operators. To become a universal standard for quick dining, it would have to possess an inbred appeal that evoked, "I am the food for automotive dining." Coincidentally, there was one comestible already being flipped and fried on griddles throughout America that fit these criteria. The only qualities it lacked to become the hand-held meal of the motorist were notoriety, respect, and promotion. Something plump, juicy, and covered with sesame seeds was almost visible over the horizon. For all those who loved to eat within their automobiles and acknowledged that the future of dining along the roadways was the drive-in restaurant, the best was yet to come. ■

A&W Ad
A year's income in six months? How could an adventurous entrepreneur refuse? A&W ad circa 1940.

McDonald's Had Some Carhops

*"Situated across the street from Monrovia's municipal airport,
they called their stand the 'Airdrome' and began attracting motorists
upon their arrival and departure."*

The brothers McDonald left New Hampshire to avoid the fate that had befallen their father: sudden unemployment. After toiling forty-two years as a shoe factory foreman, his job was eliminated along with thousands of others working New England's cotton mills and textile plants. To escape the depressed conditions and to find their own financial independence, Richard and Maurice headed to California in search of a more promising future.

By 1928, they managed to find work in the movie business transporting sets and driving trucks for Columbia Studios. The pay was adequate and within a few years, their "careers" in show business afforded the opportunity to lease a movie theater in the town of Glendora. They renamed it the Beacon, but never managed to pack in the large crowds they had anticipated. Short of funds at the end of the month, they had no choice but to consider other alternatives.

With eyes bent to finding a money-maker, they were soon inspired by two occurrences that shaped their economic destiny. It all started when they took notice of the steady line of customers wolfing frankfurters and guzzling root beer at Walt Wiley's local refreshment shack. With little overhead and minimal stock, he was handling quite a respectable volume of clientele. After they learned that a local Sunkist packing plant was discarding perfectly good fruit, the answer to their problems began to gel: buy the fallen fruit for a steal, squeeze it into juice, and sell it along with hot dogs from a roadside food stand!

In 1937, a deal was made to purchase the oranges at twenty-dozen for a quarter. With more enthusiasm than actual restaurant experience, the McDonalds borrowed some lumber and constructed a tiny octagonal building on Huntington Drive, in nearby Arcadia. A close neighbor to Monrovia's municipal airport, they called their stand the "Airdrome" and began attracting motorists upon their arrival and departure. Being less than two miles from the Santa Anita racetrack didn't hurt, either: jockeys and horse trainers became loyal regulars. To satisfy the following, ushers were recycled from the Beacon to serve as carhops.

According to "Skeeter" Kobzeff, one of the original car girls, "everything was citrus back then…and orange juice was everywhere!" The demand was so great that they soon decided to open another stand—a separate structure—right across the street. Shaped as what Richard McDonald described as "a beautiful orange," it was manned by one lone attendant during the months of summer. In 1939, fresh-squeezed orange juice was served from the hut. Hundreds of motorists stopped in daily to be refreshed while others just stared or took snapshots. The great orange was a magnet for cars.

By this time, Mac and Maurice were devout believers of drive-in dining. They obtained financing for a larger operation and by 1940, sold the juice stand and closed down their airport unit. After finding a promising location in San Bernardino, they sliced the Airdrome in two pieces and had it transported to the new site at Fourteenth and E Streets. As curious students from a nearby high school watched, workmen remodeled, enlarged, then carefully reassembled the faceted building.

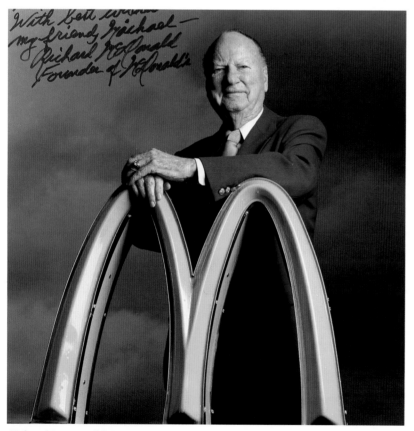

Richard McDonald Portrait
Richard and brother "Mac" Maurice McDonald were the originators of the roadside dining system now referred to as "fast food." In every sense, their story is a true Horatio Alger tale, rich with intrigue, humor, and excitement. The next time you bite into a burger, take a moment and think of the McDonalds…they started it all. ©1994 Steven Lewis

The McDonald Brothers Drive-In

In 1940, the McDonald brothers sliced their Airdrome orange juice stand in two pieces and transported it to a new site at Fourteenth and E Streets in San Bernardino, California. It was remodeled, and twenty carhops in satin uniforms hired. On weekend nights, 125 cars touched fenders in the parking lot
Courtesy Richard McDonald

Richard McDonald sketched "Speedy" as a new hamburger-faced mascot and installed a neon sign featuring the blinking chef roadside. Having a similar effect on the passing traffic as the colorful fruit stand, his engaging burger face pulled in diners with a friendly smile—the kids loved him! Twenty carhops in satin uniforms handled the onslaught to come: on weekend nights, 125 cars touched fenders in the parking lot! By 1948, revenues from the wonder topped $200,000. Mac and Maurice had their plates piled with American dream.

Despite the success, the McDonald brothers grew restless. After World War II, they could sense customers were becoming impatient with the service and speed of the hops. Invisible to the layman, the "faults" in their operation were growing evident. Shortly, they would decide to close the drive-in, fire the carhops, cool the barbecue pit, dump the silverware, and reduce the menu. America's prototype of the fast-food stand that served "hamburgers, Cokes, and French fries" was on its way. ■

MILDRED "SKEETER" KOBZEFF, THE AIRDROME

In 1937, Richard and Maurice McDonald opened the Airdrome in Arcadia, California. At the time, they also managed the Beacon Theater in Glendora and recruited the usherettes for car service. Mildred "Skeeter" Kobzeff became one of their first carhops and served auto patrons with burgers, dogs, orange juice, coffee, and beer (although Skeeter's mom didn't really approve of alcohol). During her first hours of employment, Skeeter found out that the roadside refreshment biz was more than just taking car orders: she also had to cook, cashier, and clean!

Skeeter often borrowed her parents' car to get to work and one day her father discovered a pair of men's boxer shorts lying in the backseat. He wasn't happy about the discovery and Skeeter had quite a time explaining where the mysterious underwear came from. Although she was determined to uncover the prankster, she never found out who owned them! Fortunately, the dubious incident had a happy ending: her mom washed the shorts and they eventually became part of her dad's wardrobe.

By the time the Airdrome was moved to San Bernardino and the McDonalds gained notoriety with their fast-food system, Kobzeff left the carhopping business for good. The demands of three children replaced the wants of car customers, later augmented by four grandchildren. Currently, she is regarded by the locals as the "Unofficial Glendora Historian" and participates as an active member of local clubs and historical organizations. She has been a staff writer on the *Glendoran Magazine* since it started in 1982 and still finds time in her schedule for a part-time job. ∎

SEATTLE'S ROADSIDE IGLOO

*"The engaging little Eskimo that smiled upon the passing traffic
and shone its colorful palette of neon onto the roadway was silenced forever,
demolished by the thoughtless forces of change."*

When Seattle's Igloo Drive-In opened during the forties, the American roadside was still a magical place. Numerous commercial buildings typified by out-of-scale hot dogs, gigantic root beer barrels, house-sized milk bottles, colossal vegetables, and overgrown animals dotted the highways coast to coast. The increase in motoring brought on by better roads and the automobile's proliferation provided a surge of prospective customers. With a corresponding rise in advertising stimulus competing for attention, ordinary signs and billboards lost much of their impact.

Creative refreshment stand operators learned that in order to stand out among the cacophony of images, this new class of visual excitement had to be employed. Inducing motorists to pilot vehicles from the roadbed called for a hint of the spectacular. Strong symbolism and eye-popping themes employed by "programmatic" architecture proved the hook

Igloo Drive-In Menu Courtesy Ralph Grossman

required to lure those passing to stop and spend.

The whimsical appeal of these mimetic styles proved to be what Ralph Grossman and Ernie Hughes were looking for when planning their proposed Seattle drive-in. With a long list of prospective building designs ruled out by both as "ordinary," Hughes suggested the eatery be shaped in the form of an igloo. Acknowledged by both as a stroke of genius, the partners soon raised the extra capital required to commence construction. On what seemed like an appropriate date to begin work on a building planning to masquerade, construction crews broke ground on Halloween day, 1940.

Enticed by the promise of generous tips and salary, Seattle's most attractive girls were persuaded to try their luck as tray-girls. A bevy of beautiful women clad in abbreviated skirts and high boots proved to be the perfect magnet to interrupt the flow of traffic on Denny Way. Aggressively recruited from the pool of underpaid usherettes employed at local movie theaters, the majority welcomed the change to serving car customers. Wages were better and they could become part of the real-life movie as seen through the motorists' windshield.

Every night, a new featurette played out in the Igloo's parking lot. Music piped to speakers provided the opening soundtrack for the production, as bright spotlights illuminated the domes. Directed by the commotion to drive on in, cars of all makes and models lined up for a front row seat. Right on cue, food orders were delivered in perfect time. Carhops had the right moves and the right lines.

A close-up revealed young lovers of the day enjoying fast food and passionate kisses in the front seat. Dissolving to the rear bench, youngsters were showcased slurping up milkshakes, a drip-drop lost here and there. Panning left, a cameo from mom and dad…married couples renewing vows over a double-malted and sack of onion rings. Zooming in on a serving tray attached to a car window, deluxe cheeseburgers could be seen stacked high with all the trimmings. Wonderful sights, sounds, and smells—all part of the Igloo's script, written specifically for the customer's satisfaction.

Unfortunately, the Igloo's sparkling domes ended up being cut from the closing reel. Years ago, their final fate was sealed by the business of economics and perceived aesthetics. In the quest for profits, they succumbed swiftly to the wrecker's ball with nary a complaint from the public. The engaging little Eskimo that smiled upon the passing traffic and shone its colorful palette of neon onto the roadway was silenced forever, demolished by the thoughtless forces of change.

Revamped, regraded, resurfaced, and ultimately resold, the small patch of land once bustling with short-skirted carhops, chromed automobiles, and hamburger-hungry motorists was redesignated for more significant usage. Within a few years, an uncontrolled glut of franchised burger factories took up

Igloo Tetons
Seattle's Igloo Drive-In was a well-known attraction during the 1940s. Inside seating for seventy customers made the dual-domed wonder attractive to those who occasionally liked to eat in a dining room. Outside, wintertime carhops wore ski-togs from Nordstrom with high white boots; in summertime, they sported short skirts. Owners Ralph Grossman and Ernie Hughes recruited most of the good-looking girls from local theaters to work as carhops. Ralph and Ernie also had the same taste in convertibles. Like their twin-domed Igloo Drive-In, they liked their automobiles to match. Courtesy Ralph Grossman

positions all over Seattle. The days of Ralph and Ernie's grilled "Husky Burgers" and ice-cold "Boeing Bombers" had ended abruptly. Progress, in the form of an automobile repair shop catering to motor vehicles imported from overseas, had usurped the Igloo's rightful place along the American roadside. ■

BLACKIE'S DRIVE-IN IS RELISHED

"Nel Flavin still makes hot-pepper relish the same way she did when Blackie's first opened—and customers can still have as much as they like on their hot dogs!"

As the sun falls below the tree line and the sky floods with the sienna hues of dusk, Blackie's Drive-In begins an incredible transformation. At just the right moment, a bank of switches are flipped from within. Electrical impulses race through wiring and into transformer coils, energizing electrodes designed to stimulate rare gases trapped within glass tubing.

Milliseconds later, the red-hot outline of the rooftop marquee momentarily blinks, then stabilizes, branding an indelible image into the darkness. In accompaniment to the neon buzz, colorful crests mounted at each side of the structure flash to life, proclaiming its glory to the night. No golden arch can match the effect, nor passing car resist the sight.

Drawn from the roadbed to this light-filled oasis, a continuous flow of traffic pours into the warm circle of light bathing the parking lot. Families, singles, seniors, and truck drivers—anyone and everyone enters through the open breezeway with one thing on their mind: a piping hot tubesteak topped with the delicious home-made relish that has made Blackie's a local legend. Comfortably perched upon the row of counter stools chomping their dogs,

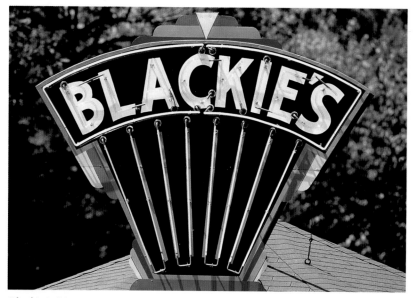

Blackie's Marquee
Mounted on each of Blackie's dual octagonal towers, multi-colored crests illuminate the parking lot during the evening hours.

customers tentatively exchange glances—then smiles of approval as depleted containers are refilled with the popular mash.

Not a word is spoken as utensils are thrust into the mix from all directions, copious amounts of zesty condiment spooned up and ingested. At Blackie's, there's no time for idle talk or pleasantries; the obsessive hunger for a home-style frankfurter smothered in hot-pepper relish reigns as the unabashed ruler of all thought and action. This singularity of mind is plainly echoed by the limited food menu and abbreviated ordering language customers use to make their food requests. In contrast with the soda jerk or lunch counter waitress of yesteryear (who developed their own jargon to facilitate quick orders), the accepted syntax at Blackie's calls for simplified, one-word commands. Protocol dictates that diners desiring a hot dog call out their order directly to the counter girl, where it's rebroadcast verbatim to the cook in charge of assembling franks.

Experienced alumni properly schooled in Blackie's succinct ordering vocabulary call out "one, two, or three," depending on their appetite and ability to digest large amounts of peppers. Since first timers invariably make requests with complete sentences, it's easy to distinguish the neophyte from a regular! Regardless of the method used, drive-in car customers make it clear by the shear quantities consumed that the enticing flavor of Blackie's homemade relish is what cements their loyalty to this established roadside eatery.

To this day, owner Nel Flavin persists in maintaining that customer devotion, insisting that the flavorful concoction responsible for the success be made from scratch. Ensuring that the secret family recipe used for the past sixty-five years is still followed religiously, she fiercely defends all attempts to downgrade the quality of her ingredients. She still makes the relish the same way she did when Blackie's first opened—and customers can still have as much as they like on their hot dogs!

In the creative atmosphere of her kitchen, ordinary pots and pans take on the identity of artisan's tools. Fresh-from-the-farm vegetables and a palette of natural spices become her medium. In her grasp, a wooden cooking spoon becomes a precision utensil. Her stove serves as the easel on which she works her special cookery. Like an Old World master, she becomes lost in her craft, chopping, dicing, slicing—transforming otherwise unexceptional ingredients into a culinary labor of love.

Ultimately, when her refined mixture is ladled upon the cylindrical canvas of a steaming dog and bun, the combination becomes a new entity. Existing in the temporal realm of what the eye can see and nose can smell momentarily, Flavin's hot-pepper relish makes the final transition to personal memory by way of the tastebuds. There, it becomes edible art. For the devotees eager to take a taste of what the real roadside has to offer, Blackie's Drive-In will always be a true masterpiece of pleasurable roadside dining. ■

Blackie's Drive-In

Blackie's still serves up hot dogs with homemade relish to motoring customers. It's tucked away in Cheshire, Connecticut—off the beaten path and a welcome find for the hungry traveler not afraid of leaving the interstate. Taking the

architectural cues from the food stands that proliferated in California during the thirties, Blackie's features two octagonal structures. At the center, a double-door garage setup opens to welcome customers.

FROM PAPER BAGS TO WINDOW TRAYS

When the first drive-in restaurants began serving customers in their automobiles during the twenties, it was novelty enough just to have food delivered by carhop. At most operations, sandwiches were simply wrapped in waxed paper and drinks served out of the bottle. Car servers clutched entrees in their hands and delivered large food orders with the aid of paper sacks.

As the number of eateries featuring car service multiplied, simply tossing a barbecue sandwich through an open car window became unacceptable. While car customers loved the independent ambiance afforded by the new gimmick of in-car dining, they didn't discourage improvements in the areas of added convenience and service. All attempts to further civilize the drive-in dining procedure were welcomed.

Taking their cues from interior "sit-down" restaurants and their waitresses, drive-in eateries adopted standard serving trays for parking lot use. After a short stint in customers' laps, they were upgraded for automotive service by the simple addition of window clips permanently attached to one side. Before long, an extended support leg was grafted onto the tray's underside, allowing larger food orders—complete with heavy serving china, silverware, and glasses—to be safely balanced carside.

With the window-mounted serving tray an accepted accessory of the carhop, the pleasure of eating within an automobile increased dramatically. Food and beverages were now at arm's length, and the chance for accidental spillage within the passenger compartment reduced. Best of all, when the meal was finished, greasy dishes and napkins could be removed from the car and placed on the exterior platform. Carhops would bus the load, trash the garbage, and pocket the pile of change left beneath.

Of course, the use of car trays had its share of drawbacks during periods of inclement weather. Wind caused many of the flats to become airborne, resulting in a sticky mess of flipped-over food. When it rained, trays became impromptu catch-basins for water, reducing already-greasy French fries to a soggy mess. To allow customers the enjoyment of meals shielded from the elements, radical improvements were necessary.

Fortunately, the drive-in industry's wish list was promptly filled when companies introduced a new line of platforms. Available in a range of sizes, models like the "TraCo" number 26 were

TraCo Serving Trays
Serving trays were not confined to the outside of the vehicle. Many models were available to clip to the steering wheel or occupy the space in front of the passenger.

For DRIVE-IN SERVICE

SERV-A-CAR
Trays and Accessories

*W*ith the window-mounted serving tray an accepted accessory of the carhop, the pleasure of eating within an automobile increased dramatically. When the meal was finished, greasy dishes and napkins could be removed from the car and placed on the exterior platform.

Trays Available In Two Sizes - No. 300 Standard 10" x 14" and No. 500 Large 12" x 17".

No. A 100 Napkin & Straw Holder. Attaches instantly to the side of either tray. For tray or counter use.

No. A 200 Ice Cream Cup Holder. Holds up to 6 cups. May be used in conjunction with either tray or individually.

Go Modern . . .

• SEE YOUR DEALER OR WRITE FOR FULL INFORMATION •

Serv-A-Car Trays and Accessories
Serving trays came in all shapes and sizes. Wire-rack types were all the rage for some time, complete with special holders that organized napkins, salt and pepper, and cradled multiple ice cream cones.

specifically designed for use within a car's interior. Attached to the steering wheel with two molded brackets, an extra arm hooked up to the vent window to stabilize. Another version was designed just for passengers, aided by an assembly that braced against the dash. Some were even made from wire mesh.

Henry Boos shook it all up in 1929 when he crafted a long serving board that stretched from door-to-door inside the car. He field tested the thin wooden "table" at the Roberts Brothers Drive-Ins in Los Angeles and found a receptive audience with his brother-in-law's regular customers. The interior tray unit caught on quickly, and soon, manufacturers were mass producing it.

Upgraded with pressed aluminum, two fully loaded 6 by 46 inch trays could be installed for diners in the front and backseat and adjusted to fit across virtually any car.

As drive-ins were edged out by coffee-shops, walkup fast food stands, and the drive-thru franchise, serving trays lost favor with the motorist. Waiting for a carhop to serve a meal and remove the dishes became a luxury of another era. The hand-held window clip tray, interior steering wheel mount, and long buckboard contraption were now too impractical. Once again, American motorists were content to eat their automotive meals from paper bags. ■

Carhop at Wagner's Drive-In
No bagged meal from a fast-food restaurant will ever compare with the style of service provided by the classic drive-in. Food is presented with style, hung on the window for all to see, admire…and consume. At drive-ins across America— such as Wagner's in St. Louis Park, Minnesota—this is still the way food is served today. Michael Dregni

Kings-X Drive-In Meal on a Tray

When competing hamburger outlets came to Wichita, Kansas, during the sixties, they brought with them simple menus consisting of only a few items. In contrast, the Kings-X restaurants had an elaborate selection. To reduce confusion for the customer and to allow for easier identification of food when delivered, color-coded packaging was implemented. Every burger selection had its own unique color. Courtesy Kings-X Inc.

CHAPTER TWO

THE CIRCULAR MECCA OF NEON

Traveling fry cook Walter Anderson settled down in the heartland of America and opened up a small lunch wagon in 1916. It was a spartan affair, without the luxuries of Wichita's fancy restaurants—but it did feature a serving counter, three stools, and a flat-iron fry griddle. That simple trio was enough for An-derson. His determination to elevate the much-maligned hamburger from its lowly position to one of prominence was more important.

By the early 1900s, the hamburger had gained a rather inauspicious reputation. Like the hot dog, the true composition of cooked burger was difficult to determine by mere

continued on page 52

White Castle Crenelated Tower
Walter Anderson teamed up with Wichita, Kansas, real estate and insurance man Edgar Waldo "Billy" Ingram in 1921 to enlarge his burger operation. With a $700 loan and a lot of optimism, Anderson constructed his fourth, and most memorable, burger emporium from rusticated concrete block. It was the beginning of the White Castle chain and the nationwide standardization of the hamburger. Today, Wichita, Kansas, is a magnet for fast-food restaurants. Courtesy of Kings-X Inc.

Bart's Drive-In
Previous pages, this circular drive-in (located in Portland, Oregon) was called Bart's during the forties and was later changed over to The Speck during the fifties. In close proximity to Franklin High School, it was a favorite destination for cruisers. Today, a Burger King operates from this location, dedicating its decor to the memory of the past tenants: metal-flake vinyl covers the seats and images of classic cars dominate the interior walls. Oregon Historical Society

BIRTHPLACE OF THE HAMBURGER

Sure, history books tell of the Tartar's fondness for raw meat and how sailors from Germany loved to order Hamburg Style Steak upon their arrival in the New World. The real question is: Who created America's first all-beef patty, ancestral prototype of today's Quarter Pounder, Big Mac, and Whopper?

Pinpointing the origination of the hamburger to one particular person has proven more difficult to substantiate than the introduction of buttered toast. From localities across the nation, a roster of colorful characters have all staked their claim to the honor, forever obscuring the faint lines of fast-food lineage.

Popular food folklore—peppered with a light sprinkling of facts—often gives the top billing to "Hamburger" Charlie Nagreen, an inventive resident of Seymour, Wisconsin. Seems it all started somewhere around 1885, when fifteen-year-old Charlie began peddling his chopped beef to the throng of hungry visitors attending the Outgamie County Fair.

Worried about soiling their hands with grease, a few genteel patrons asked if Nagreen could supply a more sanitary way of toting the snack meat. Responding with a sizzling stroke of genius, he slapped one of his cooked patties between two slices of bread—and presto! The first truly portable combination of ground beef and bread became a reality.

Five states to the south, the burger-loving denizens of Athens, Texas, have posted a plaque promoting their own history. For them, the original father of the blessed burger has been and always will be legendary lunch counter owner, operator, cook, and chief bottle washer Uncle "Fletch" Davis.

By the latter part of the 1890s, old Dave gained a notable reputation locally for his fried patties of steer. He decorated his first hand-held version with a healthy dose of hot mustard, crowned it with a slice of Bermuda onion, and nestled the stackup between dual slabs of home-made bread. *Voilà*, pardner—the hamburger was born!

The state of Ohio throws its own entry onto the griddle with the exploits of Akronite Frank Menches. Seems that in 1892, he tapped into the mother load of grease at the Summit County Fair with his own creation. When a pork delivery failed to materialize one busy morning, the Menches brothers were left lacking the main ingredient for their famous sausage sandwiches. Snorting their noses at the adversity, they substituted ground beef. With zeal, circular hunks were flavored, formed, and fired. In the spirit of saving the day in the "last minute" (all too prevalent in food folklore), Frank Menches began slapping patties between the two halves of buns and proceeded to canonize himself as the "inventor" of the hamburger.

Even more colorful is the "just in the nick of time story" handed down to descendants of Louis Lassen, once famed burgermeister of Louis' Lunch in New Haven, Connecticut. According to Ken Lassen, current owner and grandson of the founder, an unidentified man came waltzing in at the turn of the century and requested a "quick" sandwich. Ever ready to please, his grandfather mashed a handful of sliced meat trimmings into a single patty, cooked it in a vertical broiler, and slipped it in between—you guessed it—two slices of bread!

Is there really one birthplace of the hamburger? No one will ever know for certain. In all probability, the hamburger sandwich invented itself—created simultaneously by a melting pot of individuals who happened to tune into the universal consciousness of human inventiveness, imagination, and hunger. ∎

"Hamburger" Charlie Nagreen
Seymour, Wisconsin, resident Charlie Nagreen is one of many claimants to the right of "hamburger inventor." Seems it all started somewhere around 1885, when 15-year-old Charlie began peddling chopped beef to the throng of hungry visitors attending the Outgamie County Fair. Courtesy Tom Duffey, Home of the Hamburger, Inc.

The All-American Hamburger
Served, as usual, with a side of French fries and dill pickle. Martin R. Jones, Unicorn Stock Photos

Takhoma-Burger
Right, "We didn't invent the hamburger, we just perfected it!" Another claim from a mom-and-pop operation in Wichita, Kansas, that still manages to capture the public's interest. "Takhoma-Burger" is a derivative of the Steak n Shake catch-word "Takhomasak," first popularized in the Midwest during the late thirties to describe the chain's convenient, "four-way service."

Louis' Lunch

Louis' Lunch in New Haven, Connecticut, is one of the American establishments that claims to have originated the hamburger. Reportedly, an unidentified man came in and requested a "quick" sandwich at the turn of the century. Burgermeister Louis Lassen formed a lump of meat trimmings into a patty, cooked it on a broiler, and slipped it between bread! The burger was born.

DAILY NEWS, Los Angeles II
FRIDAY, OCT. 5, 1951

Hamburger inventor dies

AKRON, O., Oct. 5. - (U.P.) - Concessionaire Frank Menches, who is credited with "inventing" the hamburger, died here today at the age of 86.

Menches ended his active life as concessionaire for county fairs here in 1938, but not until after he had left his mark on the gastronomic habits of the nation.

Before the turn of the century, Menches entered the concession business. At the Summit County (Akron) fair in 1892, Menches nearly ran out of sausage. In an effort to please his customers, he ground up a sausage and sold it as a cooked, meat patty.

It was unexplainably named "hamburger" about two years later.

That concoction, plus his introduction and manufacture of ice cream cones here from the world's fair of 1903, brought Menches a small fortune.

By the early 1900s, the hamburger had gained a rather inauspicious reputation. Like the hot dog, the true composition of cooked burger was difficult to determine by mere sight or bite.

continued from page 48

sight or bite. Claims for purity were rarely made, the description on signs and chalkboards merely reading "hamburg." Gristle, bone, scraps of fat, and even horse meat became the backroom filler for the most disreputable grill men. Public suspicion deterred

sales and focused on the short-order cook with his secret cabinet of "hamburger helpers."

Of course not all of America's burger stands resorted to padding their ground beef; there were many reputable operations in business. Even so, while some excelled by using quality ingredients and sanitary methods, they

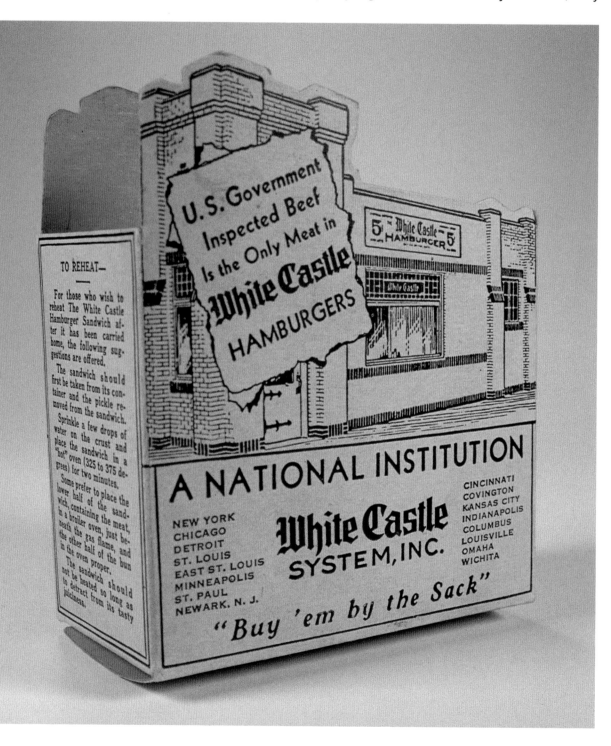

White Castle Hamburger Holder
White Castle hamburgers were small, often cradled in a paper container for easy hand-holding. From the Chuck Sturm Collection

failed in the most basic culinary arts. Self-taught operators often cooked their flattened meatballs too long, resulting in a grilled patty that lacked any flavor or moistness. Unskilled cooking procedures rendered even the finest ground chuck into a tasteless mass of meat. The result was a dried-out patty that required a prodigious amount of ketchup to lubricate its journey through the esophagus.

Fortunately, Anderson was handy with a spatula and griddle. Before his arrival in Kansas, he fine-tuned his short-order shtick in numerous hash houses across the land. Through a combination of hard work and experience, he learned how to get the most out of a lump of ground beef. To the ordinary observer, his method appeared as a simple manipulation of materials: instead of forming thick wads of minced meat and forcing them to fruition upon hot metal, he fashioned his patties thin. With high heat on the griddle, he

Building a White Castle
During their heyday in the thirties, White Castle hamburger buildings were constructed on location. Simple in design, they were completed almost as fast as you could slice a pickle for garnish. Courtesy of Kings-X Inc.

Retired White Castle
Left, by the fifties, the porcelain-covered White Castle stand became a fixture on many American street corners. This stand was retired from hamburger service in Minneapolis in the eighties and replaced by a new, back-lit-panel stand—but the old stand was moved to a new lot and continues to do business as an office. Michael Dregni

seared them quickly on both sides, sealing in flavor. At the same time, a small amount of shredded onions was mashed into the sizzle. Two halves of a bun followed, coming to rest over the steaming meat as it finished cooking. As grease dripped over the side of his grill (it didn't have edges to trap the fat), the bread assimilated the aromatic meat and onion vapors, capturing flavors usually lost to the air.

The public responded favorably to Anderson's burger methodology and within months, his flavorful hamburgers became the lunchtime feed for Kansas workers. The remodeled streetcar quickly became too cramped to serve the crowds and a much larger shop was opened in the summer of 1920. Soon, a third Anderson burger outlet followed. Apparently, he was doing something

right; his little nickel-apiece hamburgers were disappearing as fast as he could have the fresh meat and buns delivered.

Finally, Anderson decided that it was time to expand the horizons of his steamed onion burger and make a name for it in the marketplace. He was short on funds, and teamed up with local real estate and insurance man Edgar Waldo "Billy" Ingram to enlarge the operation. With a $700 loan and a lot of optimism, Anderson constructed his fourth, and most memorable, burger emporium in March of 1921.

Following the design of his third stand, the new building was constructed completely from rusticated concrete block. But instead of forming a simple rectangle with concrete stones and leaving it at that, he decided to edge the roofline with a crenelated arrangement. The results were attention-getting: the small building instantly recalled images of a castle. However, the imperial design didn't stop there. At one corner of the roof, a tiny tower was erected of the same material. Reminiscent of the medieval days of knights and chivalry, it provided the diminutive building the visual wallop required to stand out. The exterior was painted a bright white and above the single door and window combination were painted the words "White Castle Hamburgers," with the five-cent price. Coined by Ingram, the majestic title lent a heightened level of respectability to the hamburger, one that conjured up associations of purity, uniformity, and strength.

As White Castle spread to cities throughout the country, "Buy 'em by the Sack" soon became the slogan for the burgerization of America. Although it was a long battle, the tainted image of yesterday's dubious burgers began to fade, replaced by scenes of bright white porcelain, gleaming countertops, polished metal, and freshly scrubbed employees. By 1931, 115 units from Wichita to New York City provided customers friendly service within the same spic and span surroundings. Now, identical juicy onion burgers were served on identical counters and consumed on identical stools, regardless of the location.

The success didn't go unnoticed for long. Imitators copied the format right down to the

continued on page 59

"*Buy 'em by the Sack" soon became the slogan for the burgerization of America. It was a long battle but the tainted image of yesterday's dubious burgers faded— replaced by scenes of bright white porcelain, gleaming countertops, polished metal, and freshly scrubbed employees.*

Hamburgers and Coca-Cola
Always available at the sign of the White Castle. Michael Dregni

HAMBURGER ARCHITECTURE

Hamburgers made their debut on the food scene as irregular lumps of chopped beef, hand shaped according to the improvisational jazz of lunch counter short order. During the early years, long before the cookie-cutter aesthetics of the Big Mac came into vogue, concerns over circular uniformity and ingredients were minimal.

When fry-by-the-seat-of-your-pants legends Charlie Nagreen and Frank Menches formed ground round for the griddle, personal artistry ensured that every burger was a unique one. Irregularly molded perimeters of meat—with one piece more or less hanging out at one side or the other—didn't affect taste. At the time, it was all part of their appeal.

Redeemed of their dubious reputation by the mid-1930s, the individuality of America's beef patties slowly waned. Suddenly, the proprietors of roadside food businesses followed the preparatory parameters of the White Castle outlets. Mixing in just the right amount of fat became a major concern, the quality of meat of utmost importance. Approved by the public, the unvarying look of the "assembly line" became the credo for hamburger standardization.

Aiding this quest for a perfect burger blob, manufacturers of restaurant equipment soon introduced a useful arsenal of kitchen gadgetry. The Sanitary Hamburger Press Company marketed a hand-operated device capable of producing meat cakes possessing identical specifications. With the speed and accuracy of three hyperactive butchers, eleven precise "patties" of meat could now be extracted from just one pound of grind.

For even the most addle-minded burgermeister, creating an exacting

Sanitary Hamburger Press
As the ad promised, "Makes all hamburger cakes of uniform size."

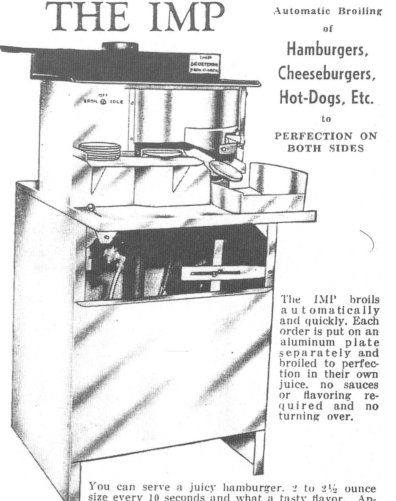

The Imp Broil-O-Matic
Labor-saving devices like this Broil-O-Matic were just the thing for the small-time operator of roadside refreshment stands. In one, compact unit, hamburgers and hot dogs, etc., could be cooked up without a lot of equipment.

*T*he visual aspects of the hamburger were re-energized when restauranteur Bob Wian created his famous double-decker creation in 1937.
By simply adding a center slice of bun, what had fast become a mundane marriage of beef and bread was elevated to a new level.

The Famous Double-Decked Delight
The famous Big Boy double-deck burger circa 1970 taken at the Sepulveda Boulevard Bob's in San Fernando, a California drive-in now part of street history. After Bob Wian created his Big Boy hamburger in 1937, the craze for double-decker hamburgers galvanized the nation. Soon, there were "Boy" theme burger bars everywhere. Imitators followed, introducing sandwiches named the Beefy Boy, Fat Boy, Chubby Boy, Bun Boy, Country Boy, Husky Boy, Brawny Boy, Lucky Boy, Super Boy, Hi Boy, and a long list of others. ©1994 Kent Bash

succession of identical "hamburger sandwiches" was now second nature. Anybody could do it: a minced batch of meat was loaded into one end and a crank was turned. Extruded wheels of beef, 3 1/2 inches in diameter by 1/4 inch thick plopped out from its bottom—untouched by human hands! The age of burger boredom had officially arrived.

Fortunately, the visual aspects of the hamburger were re-energized when restauranteur Bob Wian created his famous double-decker creation in 1937. By simply adding a center slice of bun, what had fast become a mundane marriage of beef and bread was elevated to a new level. In a perfect example of art imitating life—or in this case food mimicking architecture—multiple stories of beef, lettuce, cheese, relish, and sesame seed bun resulted in what would become the motoring crowd's ultimate Dagwood.

Reincarnated as a fast-food representation of the streamlined designs typical of Simon's, Herbert's, Carpenter's, and a long list of structures being erected to serve customers within their chariots, the once-disreputable hamburger attained an aura all its own. All grown up and dressed to the hilt, it was a "Big Boy" now—a hand-held monument to American ingenuity and culinary pluck.

By the 1950s, hundreds of millions of hamburgers were being sold each year. Coming as no surprise, the popularity of hot dogs, barbecue, grilled cheese, chili con carne, steak sandwiches, and even the chipped beef platter fell quickly to a position at the bottom of the menu. The culture born of the motorcar finally had a food it could hold in one hand and still eat while driving the strip.

Portable, palatable packages perfectly suited for eating-on-the-go, hamburger sandwiches are now solidly established for all forms of bench-seat snacking. To this day, they continue to sizzle as the quintessential staple of the American road. ■

Hamburger Heaven
Wimpy would have swooned at the sight of this hot, neon hamburger. It smells so good one can almost see it.

buns and soon there were all kinds of eateries adhering to similar methods of standardization. The proprietors of America's car-oriented eateries were paying close attention; those with foresight borrowed what features they could and nominated the cooked wafer of beef nestled between two fluffs of bread to become the new candidate for "roadfood most likely to succeed."

The Central States, California, and Texas were now well on their way to serving the hungry within their cars. But, the East Coast regions lagged behind in accommodating four-wheeled diners. That was understandable; since a brief warm season limited most outdoor activity to a few short months, it just

made better sense to remain with the established norm of indoor eating. More important,

continued on page 64

Kings-X Canvas and Ribbed Tower

In 1938, the White Castle hamburger chain decided to close down all of its restaurants west of the Mississippi. Andrew James King was employed by the square burger maker at the time, ten years under his belt as head of research and development. As principle "idea-man" for the company, it was his responsibility to develop new products and devise advertising promotions. When Billy Ingram announced he was moving the Castle's headquarters to Columbus, Ohio, King declined. He bought out the three Wichita White Castle locations and decided to try his own luck in the burger business. Later he expanded his holdings to other locations, opening Kings-X Drive-Ins and coffee-shop restaurants. Jimmie King's son Wayne used to work as a Kings-X carhop when he was a kid and often reminisces about the good times. Fridays are particularly memorable: Catholics couldn't eat the burgers, so cars began to pile into the lot by 9pm and proceeded to order a glass of water or a Coke. Straight up at midnight, car headlamps began to flash and horns would honk. Suddenly, everyone wanted a hamburger! For the Kings-X curb server, Fridays were rough. This unit built during the late fifties is still standing at Kellogg and Oliver in Wichita. Today, it is known as Livingston's. Courtesy of Kings-X Inc.

Kings-X Chicken Meal Box

Left, during the fifties, Kings-X manager Jack Bowman came up with an idea for a "chicken special." Wichita customers loved the special so much that they couldn't keep up with the demand. People were waiting in line until they closed, all there for the chicken meal. Courtesy Kings-X Inc., Hal Pottorf photographer

BOB'S BIG BOY BURGER

*"Wian plopped on some relish, and began stacking up
a ridiculous caricature of the hamburger—a double-decked delight
pushing burger creativity to the outer limits!"*

Robert Wian learned the restaurant business the hard way. When his father's furniture business in California faltered during the early thirties, he took a job washing dishes at the White Log Tavern to help out. Although fresh from high school, it didn't take long for him to become manager. His experience was soon rolled over into a better job at the Rite Spot, a Glendale eatery favored by Angelinos. There, he learned all the rules of the eating-out game—realizing along the way that he had a growing desire to become his own boss.

When two elderly ladies considered selling out their ten-stool lunch counter on Colorado Boulevard, Wian saw his opportunity. Still, he had to make a painful decision: sell his prized 1933 DeSoto roadster to get the bulk of the $350 asking price or pass over the deal. It was a clear choice. The car found a new owner and Wian got the money he needed. The eatery was his! He renamed it Bob's Pantry and began to work the counter alone.

Members of Chuck Foster's Orchestra adopted the Pantry as a late-night hangout and stopped in after gigs. High school pals of Wian's felt comfortable there, filling up with numerous hamburgers, gallons of Hires root beer, and packets of cigarettes. One frosty night in February of 1937, bass musician Stewie Strange became bored with the usual midnight snack and uttered the historic question, now ensconced in legend: "How about something different for a change, Bob?"

In a teasing mood, Wian was quick to accommodate. He proceeded to cut a sesame seed bun into three slices and flipped two burgers onto the griddle. While the meat sizzled, the band watched in fascination as leaves of lettuce and slices of cheese were readied on the sideboard. Finally, the cooked patties were lifted from the hot plate. Wian plopped on some relish, and began stacking up a ridiculous caricature of the hamburger—a double-decked delight pushing burger creativity to the outer limits. The band loved it!

A few days later, chunky Richard Woodruff wandered in through the front door. He lived down the street and often came in to sweep the floor and perform other busy work for Wian. Only six years old, he was already exhibiting a "Wimpy"-sized appetite for hamburgers—with a stomach to match. He figured out his own way to get them and charmed both the lunchtime customers and Wian with his plump physique and droopy overalls. It came as no surprise to the regulars why Bob Wian christened his unique sandwich the "Big Boy!"

After a local cartoonist sketched a rendition of the urchin on a napkin, the tousled hair and chubby cheeks became a trademark adorning the front facade. News of the great-tasting "double-deck" cheeseburger spread and within three years, Wian opened a second eatery in Los Angeles. By 1949, he was franchising his sandwich (and its youthful mascot) to operators in a half-dozen states. Meanwhile, a trio of his own Big Boy dinettes prospered. Featuring "snappy service" drive-in lanes and inside seating, their transitional design bridged the carhop era with the coming age of coffee-shops. In 1964, Wian's built his last open-air unit.

A few years later, McDonald's franchisee Jim Delligatti wanted to bring out a "new" idea for a sandwich when he remembered Wian's tasty double.

Bob Wian Behind Counter
Robert C. Wian was the brains and brawn behind the counter of a ten-stool hamburger stand he purchased from two little old ladies in 1936. To raise the money he needed to buy this Glendale, California, eatery, he sold his prized possession, a 1933 DeSoto. Unfortunately, the sale only netted him $300—the women were asking $350! He scraped up the balance, consummated the deal, and ventured forth into hamburger history. The burger bar was promptly renamed "Bob's Pantry." Courtesy Richard McLay

Bob's Pantry Exterior

When local bass player Stewie Strange asked for something different one night in 1937, Bob Wian created a new burger sensation at the spur of the moment. The double-deck cheeseburger was an immediate sensation and was later dubbed the "Big Boy," inspired by local lad and burger biter Richard Woodruff. A local cartoonist sketched the portly kid on a napkin and forever immortalized the image of Wian's stacked delight. Courtesy Richard McLay

Bob's Big Boy Carhops and Interior

Right, the carhops at Bob Wian's first drive-in wore a number of different uniforms before settling on one style. The western-style outfit with hat was one of the earliest variations. The setup men behind the counter, or "Boyfriends" as they were later referred to, stuck with the established norm of black tie and disposable paper wedge-cap. Courtesy of June Wian

Toluca Lake Bob's Neon Sign
The Bob's Big Boy restaurant in Toluca Lake, California, has managed to elude the wrecking ball. When a building in Los Angeles survives for more than forty years, it's a remarkable accomplishment. During the early 1990s, the state designated the 43-year-old restaurant as an official "California Point of Historical Interest." ©1994 Kent Bash

Bob's Big Boy Menu
Right, updated version of the early cut-out menu, circa early 1940s. The Big Boy was slowly becoming more refined. Courtesy Richard McLay

HOME OF THE
BIG BOY HAMBURGERS

Bob's

Famous for
HAMBURGERS
CHILI • STEAKS
THICK MALTS
THIN PANCAKES

2 Locations

900 E. COLORADO
GLENDALE

624 S. SAN FERNANDO RD.
BURBANK

The Big Boy Combo

At highway dining facilities such as those on the Garden State Turnpike in New Jersey, the Big Boy can still be found. There, plastic banks are sold as souvenirs. Elias Brothers is a chain of Big Boy hamburger franchisees operating in Michigan. From the Chuck Sturm collection

During the fifties, he managed a West Coast drive-in and was impressed by the numerous imitators of the twin burger. Whether influenced by nostalgia or imagination remains unclear. What's certain is that he developed a close copy of the bi-level Big Boy. Later, he admitted that the conception of this burger clone "wasn't like discovering the light bulb—the bulb was already there…all I did was screw it in the socket."

This Big "Mac" was introduced nationwide at McDonald s outlets in 1968. It was an immediate hit, soon accounting for 19 percent of sales! But, that was no surprise for Robert C. Wian, Jr. His double-decked sandwich—created at the spur of the moment to satisfy the desire for something different—had already built a food empire. Another variation on the theme couldn't hurt. He—and everyone else acquainted with hamburger history—would always know the Big Boy was Bob's. ■

Bob's Big Boy Drive-In

Robert Wian opened this California drive-in around 1947. Bob's Home of the Big Boy really hit the big time, complete with interior coffee-shop and separate curb-service facilities. Courtesy of June Wian

The Chuc Wagun
The Chuc Wagun was an early predecessor to the Arby's chain. Wheel-Burgers and Hub-Burgers could be had for a mere 15¢ during the forties. Was axle grease used as a topping? Courtesy of Kings-X Inc.

continued from page 59

the diverse range of popular foods available in the Atlantic States proved a difficult menu to breach with plain ol' burgers and barbecue. Fried clams, pizza pies, gyros, and an assortment of other delights often relegated beef—whether fried, boiled, steamed, or baked—to last choice.

All of that was about to change.

In the summer of 1927, J. Willard Marriott was on his way from Utah to Washington, D.C. on a quest to make his own fortune in the food business. A young Mormon elder with a cowboy background and college education, he figured the nation's capitol was an ideal place to start—since it was "big and hot" and receptive to root beer. Fortunately, a friend

from Utah who was currently studying law in the Capitol City agreed. He matched Marriott's three-grand investment and a root beer stand partnership was formed.

By this time, the name A&W had already gained a measure of brand recognition. The aggressive franchising of its flavorful concentrate to independent operators created a quick expansion in Northern California, Utah, and Texas. Hundreds of operators had already built substantial businesses on the nickel mug of root beer; by 1933, there were 171 A&Ws doing business nationwide. Marriott and his partner were well aware of the success, as A&W refreshment stands were among the first

to appear in their home state. Although A&W was not yet established in the competitive East Coast markets, they surmised it would be a worthwhile investment.

The optimistic pair became the first to obtain the rights to sell A&W in the Washington area and opened a hole-in-the-wall operation on Fourteenth Street NW and Park Road. As anticipated, business proved to be excellent during the tepid months of summer. However, when autumn breezes turned to brisk winds, the appeal of ice cold soft drinks plummeted. Concerned about her husband's livelihood, Marriott's wife Alice suggested that the men

continued on page 72

Chicken in the Rough
Chicken in the Rough was invented in 1936 by Mr. and Mrs. Beverly Osborne. They ran a small Oklahoma City drive-in and franchised their tasty poultry dish to operators throughout the nation. Consisting of one-half of a golden brown chicken served with shoestring potatoes, hot buttered biscuits, and a jug o' honey, it was a meal served without silverware. In 1958, Chicken in the Rough could be purchased for $1.40 Tuesday through Sunday, reduced to $1.00 on the Monday "family night." Courtesy Chuck Sturm

STORY OF THE COCA-COLA CLASSIC

On the Spring afternoon of May 8, 1886, inventor Dr. John Styth Pemberton toiled over a three-legged brass cauldron in the backyard of his ante-bellum house on Atlanta's Marietta Street. Gingerly stirring a thick, syrupy mixture of sugar and flavorings over an open fire, he was on the verge of a breakthrough that would one day awaken the taste-buds of an entire nation and receive accolades from around the globe.

The experimental brew was originally intended to improve "French Wine of Coca," a bitter nostrum for headaches that Pemberton previously developed for drugstores. To his surprise, the reformulated ingredients exceeded the best taste expectations he could imagine. With great enthusiasm, he hastened to share the delicious news with his other business partners.

Upon tasting the creation and inquiring of its ingredients, Pemberton's partner, bookkeeper Frank Robinson, sat down and penned today's ubiquitous "Coca-Cola" trademark in flowing Spencerian script. Armed with a catchy new name, a striking trademark, and a gallon jug topped off with the sweet mixture, Pemberton headed east towards Jacobs' Pharmacy to begin marketing his product.

Hoisting the jug upon the counter, he offered proprietor Venable and landlord Jacobs a sample of his new concoction. Three glasses were taken down from the back bar and filled with the syrup, then chilled water, in careful proportions of one to five. As tumblers emptied, three faces beamed with unanimous satisfaction as all proceeded to sing praises for this wonderful new delight!

As the legend goes, a second round of drinks was called for, with Venable absent-mindedly shooting carbonated water into the glasses. But whether by accident or design, the fizzy combination unquestionably produced a far superior drink. According to Pemberton, it was just the catalyst required to pull the full flavor from his sublime kola nut blend.

Despite the success, Pemberton's failing health continued to worsen, forcing him to sell out two-thirds of his rights to Willis Venable and George S. Lowndes. Forthwith, all equipment and ingredients required to manufacture the syrup were trucked from his home to the pharmacy's basement. Eventually, local businessman Asa Candler sampled the formula and bought up all the rights to the process for a mere $2,300. In 1892, he incorporated the Coca-Cola Company.

The new entity instituted an aggressive plan for marketing, canvassing the South with colorful fountain signs and free sample tickets. By 1899, decorative advertising clocks, porcelain fountain urns, posters, calendars, and even serving trays became visible marketing tools. Bell-shaped glasses imprinted with the Coca-Cola logo were added to the list of premiums and within a few years, salesmen had soda fountains and restaurants

Jacobs' Pharmacy circa 1900s
Jacobs' Pharmacy as it appeared during the soda fountain's prime when the first glass of Coca-Cola was sold in 1886. The ornate fountain area was usually situated in the center of the drugstore, capturing the attention of all who entered. Courtesy of The Coca-Cola Company

Pretty Girl Tray
From 1894 to 1904, the Massengale Advertising Agency of Atlanta handled advertising for Coca-Cola. While the lithographic posters, calendars, and intricately detailed serving trays of the era were considered works of art, they appeared somewhat dated by the "modern" 1900s. In 1904, the D'Arcy agency took over Coca-Cola advertising and revamped the "pretty girl" image. Still elegantly dressed in her long frocks, she began appearing in more casual surroundings including scenes at the beach, playing tennis, riding in a horse and buggy, and floating in a rowboat. This 1897 "Victorian Girl" Coca-Cola serving tray is the oldest example known to exist. Courtesy of The Coca-Cola Company

displaying all variations of the mark.

With the popularization of the "Ritz Boy" billboard in 1925 and a variety of catchy ad campaigns, Coca-Cola became a highly recognized brand at virtually every drugstore, gas station, and luncheonette. When the distinctive fluted bottle became a registered trademark in 1960, the bubbly formulation it held was already an established favorite of customers patronizing drive-ins and

the raft of walk-ups spreading nationwide.

For the modern-day motorist, Coca-Cola's curvaceous container became permanently linked with the pleasure of grabbing a burger and a bag of fries. Along most of America's main streets, country roads, and two-lane highways, the familiar cursive lettering gracing green-tinted decanters now stood for just one thing: Coke…the pause that refreshes! ∎

Coke Bottle Development

When soft drink bottling was in its infancy, beer bottles and cork stoppers were the only materials available. As demand for specialty bottles grew, W. H. Hutchinson & Son of Chicago dominated the field. Initially, internal ball stoppers replaced cork. To break the seal, one pushed on the ball and with a "pop" it would drop to the bottom of the bottle. Hutchinson improved on this version with a patented spring stopper, featuring a wire-loop permanently attached to a flat metal disk. A gentle push downward released the bottle's contents. The automatic resealing feature preserved the fizz of any leftovers. From left to right: (1) 1894, the first acknowledged Coca-Cola bottler was a Vicksburg, Mississippi, man named Joseph A. Biedenharn. *"Blob-top" Hutchinson bottles embossed with "Coca-Cola" are extremely rare, since it was not customary to imprint contents on early soda bottles. (2) 1899–1902, another Hutchinson-style bottle used briefly by early bottlers (note the wire-loop stopper). (6) 1915, the first glass package using the classic contour desigi Bottle patented in 1915 and introduced to the public in 1916. This classic contour design is still in use today. (10) 1975, experimental plastic bottle, never marketed. (11) 1961 to present, the no-return glass bottle. Courtesy of The Coca-Cola Company*

Baird Coca-Cola Premium Clock
This clock, offered as a premium, reflects the ambivalence of early advertising associated with Coca-Cola. On the one hand it proclaims a "refreshing beverage" while on the other extolling its virtues as a "headache and nerve tonic"; this ambiguity was probably due to the syrup's early association with the pharmaceutical business. Around 1904, Coca-Cola's advertising finally broke free from the "medicinal" claims and concentrated exclusively on refreshment. This Chicago-era Baird Clock premium with eight day movement was manufactured between 1896–1900. Courtesy of The Coca-Cola Company

*O*n May 8, 1886, inventor Dr. John Styth Pemberton toiled over a three-legged brass cauldron in the backyard of his ante-bellum house in Atlanta. This experimental brew was originally intended to improve "French Wine of Coca," a bitter nostrum for headaches that Styth previously developed for drugstores.

Two Kids With Coke and Food Tray
Clean-cut all-American kids at the drive-in, circa 1969. Courtesy of The Coca-Cola Company

LORRAINE MAGOWAN, SIMON'S DRIVE-IN

In 1938, Lorraine Magowan went down to Wiggin's Trade School in Los Angeles to enroll. That day, a man hiring for Simon's Drive-In was out at the school recruiting workers. Already experienced as a waitress, Lorraine hooked an interview that later culminated in a job. She would become part of the Simon's Drive-In team at the new Wilshire and Santa Monica location. While Lorraine always dreamed of waitressing at the Brown Derby (a movie-star haven), she soon discovered a job at Simon's was the next best thing.

Back then, Simon's posted two carhops at each side of the parking lot and instructed the girls to call out "CI" ("car in") whenever a customer pulled up on their side. Lorraine spied a black sportscar approaching and made the call to claim her first outside customer. To her delight, screen star George Raft was in the driver's seat—Betty Grable his passenger! She remembers thinking, "I hope they don't want an inside tray" and fortunately, the pair opted for a chocolate malt. It was served unspilled by an excited Lorraine.

Another night, an elderly couple wheeled in and decided that they wanted to dine in the backseat of their car. Trays of food were delivered and the couple began eating when suddenly the sedan began rolling backwards! Before they could swallow a bite, Lorraine hopped into the front seat and slammed on the brakes! For a carhop, it was a heroic effort, garnering her a 50¢ tip for her efforts (that was a big one in those days). Today, Lorraine channels that early energy by volunteering at the local hospital and remaining active through her mid-seventies. Her early days at Simon's Drive-In have proven invaluable; she's indisputable proof that former carhops only get better with age. ∎

Paul's Bowls
Located at California and K in Bakersfield, California, Paul's Drive-In (run by Clif and Eddie) provided many souvenirs. Because of the acquisitive nature of the car diner, a few good examples exist today. From the Chuck Sturm Collection

Early Hot Shoppe
Lower right, while the tamales sold at J. Willard Marriott's original "hole-in-the-wall" stand on Fourteenth Street NW and Park Road in Washington, D. C. were eventually replaced with more popular entrees, the name somehow stuck. Later, when his chain of drive-ins was in full swing, running boys and waitresses cried out the imaginary order "Big Tamale!" whenever Mr. Marriott appeared. For the staff, it was a humorous way of acknowledging and honoring his presence—at the same time alerting others to look sharp. Courtesy Marriott International, Inc.

continued from page 65

add a small selection of sandwiches to their menu, along with some homemade chili and hot tamales. A small hot plate was put in the front window so pedestrians could see and smell the array of goodies.

Passersby were intrigued with the heavenly aroma and showed little resistance to stopping in for a bite. One day, an inquisitive customer asked when the Marriotts were going to open their "hot shop." Unknowingly, he presented the partners with a new name for their enterprise. The A&W logo on the front facade was soon joined by the words "The Hot Shoppe," painted in cursive lettering on the front window and overhead awning.

Marriott manned the counter area while his wife cooked tamales and ran the register. The combination of warm foods and cold root beer clicked: in the first year, their modest operation took in an admirable $16,000. The

business prospered and in less than two years, Marriott opened the first drive-in restaurant in the East. "Food For The Whole Family" served in your car caught on fast and by 1930 Marriott had three drive-in Hot Shoppes operating at full tilt. Visitors in automobiles loved the huge parking lots, the friendly "running boys," and the classy dessert called the hot fudge ice cream cake. Before long, Marriott's combination of orange roof tiles and familiar A&W logo became synonymous with East Coast car service.

Meanwhile, the hamburger, hot dog, and barbecue kings operating in California were making plans to inject new life into their own car-stands. Los Angeles was a city made by the automobile, with plenty of restauranteurs eager to capitalize on the year-round sunshine and general acceptance of new

ideas. As development changed the face of the roadside in the car's own image, the simple structures erected almost a decade ago were becoming increasingly boring. The wide, endless boulevards and extensive network of surface streets now sprawling in every direction demanded something better: a new style, a new look—one to match the glamour of this starstruck city.

When Mr. Harry Carpenter, a brilliant operator from Texas, arrived in Los Angeles during the Depression years, he was impressed by the expansive boulevards and took note of the vacant lots available at busy corners. There were already a number of Pig Stands doing business in the area, albeit with modest structures of octagonal design a bit larger than a couple of Model As parked bumper to bumper. Despite their modest architecture, they were doing an admirable business—

Hot Shoppe and Polar Bear
When the sale of alcohol was repealed in 1933, the Hot Shoppes became outlets for liquor. At one particular unit, the police got a call about a riot when a man insisted on dropping empty glasses to the pavement. The curb manager pulled him from the car and knocked him sprawling—soon to be joined by fifty curb boys and customers, all swinging. Later, when a carhop was handed money for some limeades used by a car full of men as chasers, one tipsy passenger asked, "Does that take care of everything?" "Yes, everything but something for the boy," replied the carhop. "We gotta take care of the boy!" said one of the men. He climbed out of the car and proceeded to smash a whisky bottle over the carhop's head! Courtesy Library of Congress

something Carpenter was quick to point out to his brother Charles. The observation was duly noted and the pair continued scouting locations for a series of eateries that would extrapolate the curb service idea further than ever before.

The Carpenters' most memorable sandwich stand opened at the cross-streets of Sunset and Vine in the early thirties, causing quite a stir for locals accustomed to the spartan accoutrements of the current haunts. As later reported in a 1946 issue of *The Diner*, Carpenter "dressed up this basic idea [of in-car dining] with typical Hollywood glitter. He paved his lot, put up a building that looked like a cross between the Taj Mahal and Mary Pickford's swimming pool bath-house and found a batch of would-be stars starving to death while waiting for the big chance." Carpenter's became the car-dining derivation of the Yucca-Vine Market, a well-known Los Angeles landmark designed in 1928 by architect Lloyd Wright, son of Frank Lloyd Wright.

Glorifying the subdued design of the Pig Stands, the Carpenter brothers took the format of drive-in dining into the fast lane. The carhops even had their own training films! Featuring an octagonal floorplan with stepped layers, the car-accommodating kiosk became a feeding trough for harried motorists hankering for a quick fifteen-cent hamburger. Not one inch was spared for advertising: a profusion of signs inset into the stepped layers broadcast the availability of "sit 'n eat" sandwiches, chili con carne, barbecued beef, fruit pies, and an assortment of beverages.

At the same time, Bill Simon was running a small chain of dairy lunch counters in Los Angeles. Bill happened to be poker buddies with Harry Carpenter and "Rusty" McDonnell (another local restauranteur, no relation to the McDonald brothers). As the story goes, the group had gathered for one of their late-night games when talk turned to the restaurant business and high overhead costs. Simon, who

As development changed the face of the roadside in the car's own image, the simple structures erected almost a decade ago were becoming increasingly boring. The wide, endless boulevards and extensive network of surface streets now sprawling in every direction demanded something better: a new style, a new look.

Octangular Carpenter's
During the early part of the thirties, Harry Carpenter constructed a more decorative version of the Pig Stand at the corner of Sunset and Vine in Los Angeles. With an octagonal layout and stepped design, it was the foreshadowing of more streamlined forms to come. Eventually, the sharp corners would be dropped in favor of the circular motif, a completely round design that was accessible from all angles and offered little visual resistance. Henry E. Huntington Library and Art Gallery

Carpenter's at Night
Harry Carpenter followed the lead of the other operators by the end of the thirties and constructed small circular units of his own. Los Angeles Dairy Lunch counter owner Bill Simon started the trend when he boasted he could build a small unit for under $6500. "Rusty" McDonnell wagered he couldn't do it—but with the help of architect Wayne McAllister, Simon came in under that goal. The rush for small, efficient units was on! Courtesy Library of Congress

Sunset Boulevard Pig Stand
Opposite page, the Pig Stands were one of the first drive-in restaurants to show the Californians just how Texans cooked up delicious barbecue. At night, crowds of cars packed this Sunset and Vine stand to maximum capacity during the thirties. When Harry Carpenter and his brother arrived (also from Texas), they added a little bit of style to the formula. Carpenter's octagonal stand (and neon sign) can be seen in the background. From the collections of the Texas/Dallas History and Archives Division, Dallas Public Library

Circular Drive-In Design

Lower right,
Circular Drive-In Roof Plan

Roberts at Night
Opposite page, to circumvent local sign ordinances and rules against erecting large illuminated signs on the tops of buildings, many drive-ins incorporated rooftop towers, or pylons as part of their integral structure. Whether adorned with neon lettering, flashing lights, atomic balls, or twisted spirals of light, they attracted the attention of the motorist more readily than any billboard could ever have hoped. "The Burbank" Roberts Brothers drive-in located on Victory and Olive Boulevards featured a twisted flash of what appeared to be electricity at the top of its pylon. With circular design, modern equipment, and air conditioning for inside diners, it was a mecca for motorists in the San Fernando Valley. Courtesy Burbank Historical Society

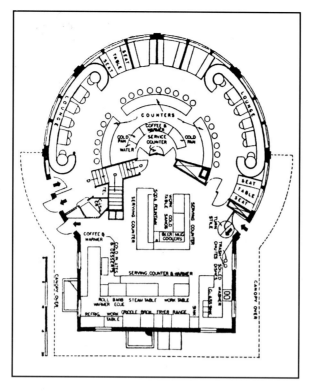

had a few ideas of his own, began bragging that he could open a carhop eatery for only $6,500. His gambling buddies saw a sure bet and wagered it couldn't be done!

Simon accepted the challenge and contracted local architect Wayne McAllister to develop a simple, economical, and eye-catching design. By planning the eatery with small "taxpayer" lots in mind (under 150 feet square), he developed a compact, concentrated version of existing service structures. To utilize every inch of available space, the building followed a circular layout, allowing full utilization without the inefficiencies of a rectangle. The kitchen and rotary barbecue oven were located directly within the center, allowing the carhops and customers to be served from multiple angles. Only twelve stools were provided for the sit-down customers. Even with a "layer cake" roof stepping up to a centrally

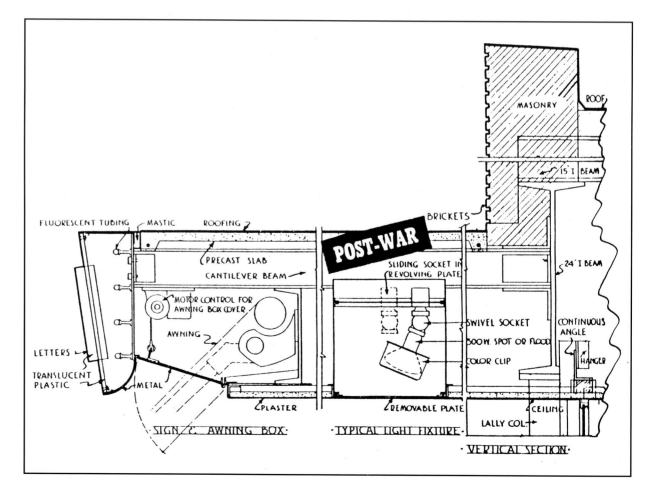

mounted tower, the total cost for the plan came in a little under the goal—an unbelievable victory for Simon! Of course, McAllister helped win Simon's bet—and the confidence of the entire California curb-stand clique.

One by one, the major players switched over to a more softened style, the angular ziggurats of the Art Deco era yielding to purely circular motifs. McAllister's practice thrived and he was soon inundated with work, drawing up similar floor plans for the proprietors of Herbert's, McDonnell's, Roberts', Bob's Big Boy, and even Van de Kamp's. Suddenly, every major intersection in the city of Los Angeles was accented by a circular landmark!

continued on page 86

LIGHTING WITH LUMINOUS NEON

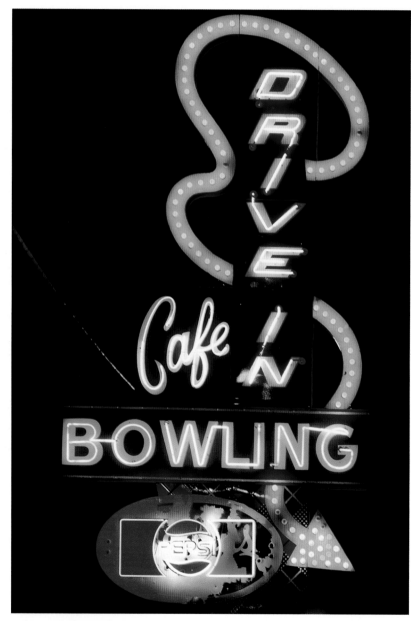

Drive-In Cafe Bowling
Neon hung above a drive-in bowling alley and snack bar in Wichita, Kansas.

Heinrich Geissler devised one of the first genuine prototypes of the non-filament lamp in 1856. Employing high voltage alternating current, he excited carbon dioxide gas trapped within a glass tube to create light. Unknowingly, a magic genie was released from a bottle, one that would eventually become part of the art and architecture of the American road.

Although Geissler's first lamp was an efficient source of illumination, it had one major drawback: The energized gas had a tendency to react chemically with the power electrodes, causing their eventual deterioration. Pressure dropped and the depleted tubes began to sputter.

Fortunately, former Edison employee D. McFarland Moore solved the pressure problem. A device designed to replenish gas lost as electrodes broke down became part of his improved light tubes. Confident of their extended lifespan, he sold his first commercial sign installation to a Newark, New Jersey, hardware store in 1904. Filled with atmospheric gas, it became the precursor of the "neon" sign.

Georges Claude continued experimenting with Moore's tubes in France. Rare distillations like neon and argon gas were substituted for carbon dioxide. When electrically excited with high voltage, neon was found to glow fiery red, argon a grayish blue. Eventually, he introduced a corrosion resistant electrode, registering the revolutionary design patent in 1915. Now, neon-filled tubing could hold its pressure indefinitely, paving the way for practical applications.

Eight years later, neon officially arrived in the United States. West Coast car dealer Earle Anthony became enlightened to the fragile creations produced by the Claude Neon Factory in Paris and decided to exploit the colorful signage at his Los Angeles auto dealership. Installed high where passing cars could see, two blue-bordered beauties spelled out the word "Packard" in searing orange script. Enraptured by the ethereal glow of the illuminated tubing, passing vehicles jammed the boulevard.

By 1932, the key patent to the non-corroding electrode expired, clearing the way for neon's proliferation. Free from restrictions, sign shops multiplied—and soon roadside commerce adopted the attention-getting hues of the new light form. By the end of the thirties, the majority of gasoline stations, drugstores, and hamburger drive-ins were bedecked in a kaleidoscope of electrified color.

As its popularity grew, neon lighting was often incorporated into the design scheme of streetside architecture itself. The rounded corners of the Streamline Moderne soon played host to racy rows of glowing glass. Mimicking the speed and movement of passing cars, colored tubes of plasma swooped, swirled, and danced, reinforcing the architectural illusion of forward momentum.

With their car-accommodating designs, drive-in eateries became roadside beacons for dine-in-your-car service. From their structural epicenter, dramatic pylons ribbed in neon bands poked skyward. Vertically arranged lettering cut a message into the night, proclaiming the availability of "Hamburgers" to a procession of vehicles on the strip.

At streetside, advertising signs attained a new boldness. Hand-painted boards became substantial constructions of porcelain-enameled metal and hollow glass pipe. As animated carhops toted idealized renditions of the perfect hamburger, swirling arrows pointed the way to food and fun. America's drive-ins flickered to life, a bold palette of visual excitement lighting the way with a hot, neon buzz. ∎

Sill's Drive-In With Neon

To the casual observer, there could be no disputing the location of Sill's spectacular drive-in: Las Vegas, Nevada. Like some of its gaming counterparts on the Strip, it was packed with as much neon tubing as it could hold and had its own towering carhop at the roadside. When the sun went down, many motorists decided they better not gamble with their appetites—it was Sill's Drive-In for the best food in town. Courtesy Brian Butko

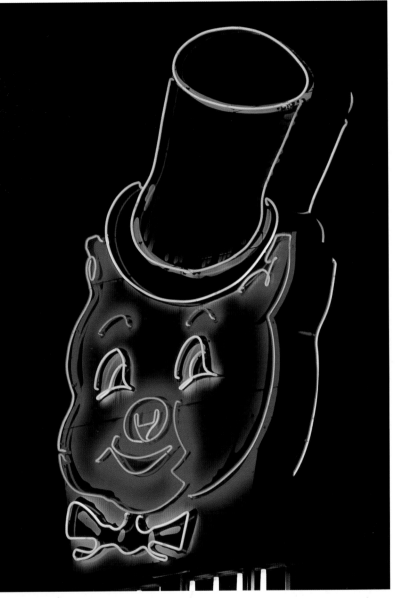

Porky's Drive-In
The pert Porky's pig is a sculpture in neon lighting the night above the famous drive-in in St. Paul, Minnesota. Michael Dregni

Van de Kamp's at Night
Left, the shimmering Van de Kamp's flagship building constructed on Fletcher and San Fernando in Glendale was architect Wayne McAllister's masterpiece. A massive, neon-trimmed delight, it was as much a nighttime confection for the eyes as the ice cream cone was for the lips. Miles of neon tubing outlined virtually every corner and crevice, including the vanes of the life-sized windmill that became the chain's trademark. Because the coffee-shop and bakery were such a success, a pure drive-in was later added on the same lot. With double-kitchens and service outlets, it could accommodate two separate flows of traffic. Later, this same design became the model for Robert Wian's first Big Boy drive-in. Security Pacific National Bank Photograph Collection/Los Angeles Public Library

continued from page 79

From the viewpoint out on the roadway, it appeared that these sculpted structures of chromium, glass, and stainless steel were carefully balanced illusions. Virtually all appeared to defy the laws of gravity with their free-floating overhangs. Many of the front entry areas were actually constructed without doors (Simon's was open twenty-four hours and never closed). Visually, the unified look offered by the circular arrangement transformed what was once a mundane box into a space station for cars. Now, the drive-in dining stand was a circular mecca of neon—conceived, constructed, and operated exclusively for the motorist.

Still, there was more substance to the circular design than just aesthetics. Ever since the days of the original curbside stand, problems with traffic flow and the logistics of serv-

Melody Lanes

The Starlite Room of the Melody Lane drive-in (once a landmark structure located at Wilshire and Western in Los Angeles) served cocktails to (inside) car-customers after the nationwide repeal of Prohibition. For those in need of a Coca-Cola or ham sandwich, an adjoining drive-in provided all the amenities for in-car dining. Security Pacific National Bank Photograph Collection/Los Angeles Public Library

Herbert's Circular by Day

Right, many drive-in restaurants located on the busy cross streets of Los Angeles were considered "taxpayers." Never intended to become permanent landmarks, they typically operated for a short lifespan of ten years or less. As real estate values of these prominent plots rose, the buildings that occupied the space could no longer support the value of the land. Well-known Los Angeles restauranteur Sydney Hoedemaker opened Herbert's Drive-In during the early thirties. Circa 1940, located at Beverly and Fairfax, Los Angeles. Seaver Center for Western History Research, Natural History Museum of Los Angeles County

ing numerous cars were a concern. A completely round design was perfectly suited for the roadside: drivers could easily pull into the parking lot, cruise around the building's periphery, and find a parking space that suited their fancy. Like petals on a flower, automobiles could park around the structure along its entire circumference. Because every space was an equal distance from the kitchen and the curb servers, all were desirable spots (in theory). The "inner circle" eventually assumed a higher status, even though one might have to signal the cars parked behind to leave.

As the restaurants specializing in car food achieved a visual and functional unity by the close of the thirties, the imagery of America's tray toters was also being restyled. As men went off to fight in the war, the pool of

FRONTIER DRIVE IN — 24 HOUR SERVICE
MISSOULA, MONTANA

Frontier Drive In
The Frontier in Missoula, Montana, featured a circular facade combined with a rectangular building and kitchen area circa 1940s. Courtesy Chuck Sturm

Stan's Serve Area with Neon Ceiling
Left, bright neon lighting pulled the customer's eyes right into the front service area of Stan's Fresno drive-in. Beneath the lights, everything was positioned for easy access, including trays, cigarette machines, napkins, and dining utensils. Cooks, or "wheelmen" as they were often referred to, handed food orders directly through small portals to the carhops. At each side, a door allowed customers to enter two separate dining areas. Courtesy Martin Cable, Edwin Schober photographer

Sill's Drive-in Restaurant
5th St. at Charleston Blvd., Las Vegas, Nevada
"Good Food Need Not Be Expensive"

Sill's Drive-In
The Russian launch of the Sputnik on October 4, 1957, triggered more than simply a race for space. Suddenly, American drive-ins mounted satellites, atomic balls, and other futuristic forms atop their rooftop towers. The images of the future held much promise, ideal for the sales of fast-paced foodstuffs such as hamburgers, French fries, and shakes. Sill's Drive-In was ahead of its time with this Las Vegas location, circa late 1940s. Courtesy Chuck Sturm

Gorro Drive Inn
Right, along with the El Sombrero Motel, this border town Tijuana drive-in was perhaps the only circular drive-in ever fashioned in the shape of a sombrero. Circa late 1940s. Courtesy Chuck Sturm

The Gorro Drive Inn and El Sombrero Motel

available workers shifted from male to female. Male carhops became the minority as women took their place at almost every curb-stand, refreshment shack, lunch counter, and burger bar that needed help.

Managers discovered that more hamburgers were sold when served by a pretty face, and before long, the bow-ties and black slacks that typified America's first carhops were replaced by women's service uniforms. At the finest car feeders, carefully assembled outfits became the rage, taking the attire worn by usherettes at the local cinema or hotel bellboy as the standard model. A short waist jacket

became de rigeur, along with coordinating trousers adorned with wide military stripes. At one point, Stanley Burke's California hops donned contrasting uniforms of purple and green, the "Stan's" moniker embroidered right on the shoulder. If portraying a unified image worked well for the petroleum companies, it couldn't hurt the food industry.

The wave of style crested in 1940 when the cover of *Life* magazine featured a full-length cover photograph of Sivils' Drive-Inn girl Josephine Powell, in full-service dress. Taking the showmanship begun at Harry Carpen

continued on page 96

Mark's In & Out Beefburgers
Established in 1954, Mark's has provided a steady supply of 'burgers to hungry drive-in customers in Livingston, Montana—and was still going strong into the 1990s. The large neon sign above the front face of the building promised Montana cattle ranchers that there was no ham in their "beefburgers."
Michael Dregni

THE FABLE OF THE GOLDEN ARCHES

Richard and Maurice McDonald were planning to franchise their successful burger system in 1952. To stand above the visual noise created by miles of drive-ins, motels, car washes, bowling alleys, service stations, and coffee-shops, they decided a new structural style was needed. Without a unique design, nationwide recognition for their walk-up stand was an impossibility.

With this simple aim in the forefront, professional architects in Southern California were approached. A few interesting concepts were drafted for the brothers' review, but unfortunately met with immediate rejection. Later described by Richard McDonald as "squatty looking" boxes, they exhibited a blatant lack of memorable charm or character.

Undaunted, the drawings were taken home for further contemplation. Then, while Richard McDonald pored over the plans in his office one rainy night, the arrow of inspiration found its mark. He had an idea. With limited talents as an artist but unbounded intuition about what a roadside stand should look like, he began to sketch some tentative plans.

First, the height of the building had to be lifted. Tapping into personal preferences, Richard penciled in a slanted roof, sloping gradually from the front to rear. Influenced by Colonial columns dominating his twenty-five-room house, he included a few variations. Though imposing, they weren't the elusive element he desired in a fast-food restaurant.

Next, he oriented a large semi-circle parallel to the front of the square building. It looked a little funny, so he discarded the idea and proceeded to draw two arches, positioning one of them at each side of the structure. This time, he arranged them perpendicular to where the road might be. As soon as he lifted his writing instrument from the paper at the bottom of the second arch, McDonald realized he had found the answer!

Swelled with the post-invention confidence typical of any vanguard, he presented Fontana architect Stanley Meston with the idea. Unprepared for the abstract incarnation of Coffee-Shop Modern, Stan posed his question: "Dick, did you have a bad dream last night?" The garish arches assaulted his design sensibilities! He wanted no part of them, detailing their obvious impracticality to the brothers. (Amazingly, he would lay claim to the arch idea—decades later.)

Unfazed by the response, McDonald stuck to his vision. He wanted those arches and would have them! If Meston wouldn't work with the idea, then they would get someone else. Predictably, Meston eventually caught the "vision" and cooperated with sign maker George Dexter to amplify the golden wings with neon.

After further refinements were made, an eye-grabbing rendering was drawn up. Now, curved circles became taught parabolas, flaring gradually at their base. The upper portions of the dual yellow bands, along with the edges of the flying wedge roof, were rimmed with tubes of neon. Walls, striped with dramatic red and white tiles, jazzed the exterior.

Businessman Neil Fox and associates took the hook and became the first McDonald's franchisee in America to construct the arched design. In May of 1953, the illuminated arches born on a scrap of paper finally came to life in Phoenix, Arizona. As they brightened the opening night with their futuristic energy, lines of customers were dazzled by the sight. To many, it was obvious that the age of the carhop was over. The amazing success story of Richard McDonald's golden arches was just beginning. ∎

© McDonald's System, Inc.

McDonald's Golden Arches
As the slogan went, "Look for the Golden Arches." Preziosi Postcards

LOOK FOR THE GOLDEN ARCHES® McDonald's®

McDonald's Golden Arch Building

According to Richard McDonald (co-founder of the original McDonald's chain), pilots in private planes flying during the 1950s reported that they routinely spied McDonald's neon arches from the air. When they were lost or disoriented, it was easy to find the airport; a McDonald's fast-food stand was almost always located nearby. Royal Photo Company Collection, Photographic Archives, University of Louisville

STAN'S SNEAKS ANOTHER ONE

*"Tumblers chilled in the deep freeze provided an icy reception
for extra-thick milkshakes—the kind you could actually
turn upside-down without spilling!"*

Stanley Burke's newest Fresno drive-in was pulling a sneak opening at 8 o'clock! Word spread quickly through the grapevine and within hours, the local network of cruisers mobilized to claim their share of the action. Around town, family sedans were appropriated from astonished parents as lead-sleds and flaming hot rods rumbled to action. Spilling from sidestreets onto the main drag, a phalanx of car customers convened on the virgin drive-in…simultaneously.

In the instant it took to slap the cheddar on a cheeseburger, the parking lot of Burke's newest eatery overflowed with chromed steel and lacquered

Stan's First Round Drive-In
Drive-in legend Stanley Burke was raised in a Cincinnati orphanage and came to Sacramento, California, during his teenage years. He started in the food business with money raised from odd jobs and purchased used equipment. In 1933, he opened a small shack on Stockton Boulevard across the street from a cannery. When he began selling beer, cannery workers made his place a regular stop. Beer suppliers, however, insisted he sold the brew too cold, a fact relished by the overheated workers. Eventually, Burke's small stand became a drive-in and the beginning of a chain. With a bank loan, his first circular unit was constructed on 16th and K Streets for a price of $20,000 in 1941. Its center spire, ribbed rooftop parapet, and Stan's sign were lined with neon tubing. Courtesy Martin Cable

sheet metal. Sixty minutes later, the grills were fired up for the first time as a legion of carhops sharpened their pencils in anticipation of the melee to come. As the inaugural patty of ground beef hit the hotplate, another circular construction of plate glass and neon tubing sizzled to life—the burger and shake at the very heart of its soul.

For ardent drive-in fans, the overwhelming crowd of cars present at that sneak opening in 1949 was no surprise. Burke's showy operation served what front-seat diners liked—within the privacy of their vehicles. His curbside canteens capitalized on two basic elements required for success: superior carhop service and lip-smacking food. Stan's circular creations set the standard for all California watering holes paying homage to car culture.

Immortalized in lights on Stan's streetside marquee, the quintessential image of a sprightly tray-girl set expectations high. Those drawn in by the fantasy weren't disappointed: Stan's hops were some of the best tray-toters working the West Coast. All nine of them talked the talk and walked the walk, creating the standard by which all others were judged. Rushing orders, substituting sides, or running for extra pickles—it didn't matter. Stan's girls knew how to treat customers like humans—earning tips with pleasing personalities and customer-is-always-right attitude.

But without the type of food that ensures repeat business no amount of carhop hospitality could create a loyal following. First and foremost, a drive-in had to have an appetizing menu—Stan's did. Based on the stacked creation popularized by burgermaster Bob Wian, Burke's crowd-pleasing "Double-Burger" possessed flavor characteristics all its own. All of the trimmings befitting the classic hamburger sandwich were stacked between the buns, including garden-fresh lettuce, tomatoes, pickles, and onions. There was no need for special sauce; freshness made the taste.

For dessert, mountains of home-made whipped cream were shot from specialized guns onto myriad fountain favorites. Oversized banana splits satisfied the most discerning customer. Tumblers chilled in the deep freeze provided an icy reception for extra-thick milkshakes—the kind you could actually turn upside-down without spilling!

Unfortunately, management problems and the shifting values of youth thawed the ice. One by one, the plug was pulled on the energetic neon of Stan's Drive-In restaurants. Today, most of Burke's circular structures have been demolished—victims of spiraling real estate values and the climate of cut-throat franchising. All of the carhops have long since retired, former burger flippers forced to take positions in coffee-shop kitchens. Nowadays, the roar of T-bucket hot rods and the laughing cackle of customers enjoying their food out in the parking lots up and down Highway 99 are but distant echoes.

Is the concept of the drive-in restaurant dead? Hardly! The sights, sounds, smells, and flavors that forged Stan's eateries into landmarks of memory live on in the minds of the California motorists lucky enough to have experienced

Stan's Circular At Night

Stanley Burke's first circular unit located at 16th and K Streets in Sacramento, California lit up the boulevard after dusk. During the 1940s, "Legs" the carhop was one of the main attractions, flashing her tray treats to motorists speeding past. Burke knew what the customer wanted and gave it to them. Circa 1941. H. Sweet Collection, City of Sacramento, History and Science Division, Sacramento Archives and Museum Collection Center

them. For anyone with wheels who has ever eaten at a carhop drive-in and fallen in love there, Stanley Burke's concept of the roadside eatery was—and always will be—the uncoronated king of automotive dining. Anyone who has ever taken a few loops "'round the Main" knows that. Long live the burger, the French fry, and carhop-service. Long live Stan's! ■

Stan's Carhop and Cadillac
Bakersfield Carhop Nita Howard was a favorite of car-customers at Stan's famous California eatery. Donning a snappy uniform reminiscent of the finest military service garb, she was a living, breathing icon of roadside service and a perfect example of the drive-in's friendliness, personal service, and the customer-is-always-right attitude. Courtesy Martin Cable

Stan's at Night
Left, the sign company that constructed the famous carhop neon for Stan's California Drive-Ins won an award for the effort. The colorful attention-grabber was inspired by "Legs," one of Stanley Burke's earliest carhops. Given free rein to take the essence of the curb server and immortalize her in neon, sign artisans created one of the most memorable marquees in drive-in history. This circa 1950s example once stationed at the Fresno Stan's is now a memory. Courtesy Martin Cable, Edwin Schober photographer

Sivils' Beauty Queen Pose Promo
Curb-girl Johnny McNeely poses at the left wearing another variation of the Sivils satin uniform. This version followed the lead of the more risqué cigarette girl oufits used at Sivils: satin shorts and a bare midriff top. The boots were custom-made, adorned with the Sivils name in leather. The young lady on the right is Margie Neal, one of those energetic cigarette sellers. Posing for this image wearing her tiara, she was fresh from an appearance in a local beauty contest. From the collections of the Texas/Dallas History and Archives Division, Dallas Public Library

Chesterfield Cigarette Girl
Opposite page, right, when Louise and husband J. D. Sivils opened their historic "drive-inn" restaurant in Houston, Texas, "curb-girls" were outfitted with colorful majorette uniforms made of satin. Louise Sivils explained that the idea for eye-catching service garb came to her after she saw this Chesterfield cigarette ad in the late 1930s. After Life magazine featured an article on the Sivils curb-girls in 1940, the majority of American drive-ins joined the stylized uniform parade. Before too long, carhops donning pert pillbox hats, satin jackets, short skirts, and polished boots were a common sight along the American roadway. Courtesy Liggett & Myers Tobacco Company

Decked Out Sivils' Carhop
Opposite page, far right, Louise Sivils came out with a new curb-girl outfit almost every year. Buna "Johnnie" Van Hekken models one of the classic satin majorette-type designs in this circa 1940s publicity photograph. This particular entry was made of bright red satin, trimmed with white sleeves and piping. The plumed hat followed the same color scheme, all the way to the white-feathered crest. Johnnie worked the south side cash register (the drive-in had two curb service ends) at the Houston location, taking care of inside customers with a style equal to the outdoor curb servers. From the collections of the Texas/Dallas History and Archives Division, Dallas Public Library

continued from page 89
ter's stands to an entirely new extreme, she legitimized the car service restaurant nationwide for anyone and everyone who owned a car. With white satin majorette gear featuring fringed epaulets, a plumed hat, decorative wrist cuffs, cowboy boots, and all the gold braid and piping possible, she stood proudly with her tray carefully balanced on one hand—while walking a full gait! When it came to satisfying hunger on the go, she became the nation's ideal curb-girl: rosy-cheeked, well-dressed, and just as polite. The girl next door with a Texas smile (and drawl to match), she was about as American as apple pie can get.

Both J. D. and Louise Sivils came from families with experience in the restaurant business. When they married in the thirties, they continued the family tradition by opening a restaurant of their own in Houston. It was a typical sit-down eatery with interior service,

worlds apart from the myriad stands setting up shop on street corners and vacant lots all over the city. Despite the differences, Louise was taken by the proliferation of these streetside hamburger businesses and began to consider the possibilities. Her intuition told her that the future was going to be car service, if only a few changes were implemented. There had to be a way to combine the excitement of the stands with the more dignified amenities of sit-down dining.

Louise discussed these views with her husband, explaining her notion for creating a grand restaurant to serve motorists, incorporating all the convenience of curb quickness. She would call it a "drive-inn," promoting the double letter combination to pique the interest of the customer and to bring a little more class to the operation. When J. D. balked, she countered with the comment, "Well, that's what people will do there…drive in!" While on the surface it seemed like a simplistic idea, it was actually pure genius. Until that time, no car service operation had used the term in combination with their name.

The Sivils opened their first Drive-Inn on the outskirts of Houston in 1938 and showed the rest of the nation how to run a world-class dining park. The differences were evident almost immediately! For starters, Mrs. Sivils dismissed the term "carhop" as too undignified. Jumping up and down on running boards was not going to be the way her girls greeted customers. They would do it with style, grace, and dignity. At her roadside palace, the window waitresses would be referred to as "curb-girls." The new title demanded a first-class uniform treatment, and fortunately, Mrs. Sivils was prepared. She had already dreamed up the ultimate image for the carhop years ago, long before America's restaurants even thought of stylizing their carhops. Inspired by an advertising drawing depicting a Chesterfield cigarette girl, it was an idea available for the taking. Luckily, Louise Sivils saw the connection first, had the uniforms made up, and brought the fantasy to reality.

The *Life* magazine article of 1940 summed it all up with the headline: "Houston Drive-In Trade gets Girl Show with its Hamburgers." But, this was much more than journalistic hyperbole; Louise Sivils' curb-girls really did put on an extravaganza! At each shift change, what equated to a live floor show-on-a-parking-lot commenced like clockwork. Practiced until perfect, the girls leaving their assigned posts would file into the building as a new team of workers made their debut on the lot. To the beat of music blaring out over external loudspeakers, Sivils' girls fanned out like players in a musical revue. Neatly lined up at each side of the parking lot in shimmering rows, it was time for inspection. Only then were they released to serve cars.

Patrons watching from the five-hundred-space parking lot were thrilled with the flamboyant floor show! Not only were they getting an appetizing meal with the best service in town, but entertainment as well. Visitors soon arrived from all parts of the state to witness the spectacle and taste the trout sandwich.

With a new standard of service to live up to, drive-in restaurants throughout the United States adopted similar styles for their car girls. Endless variations in costumes and serving

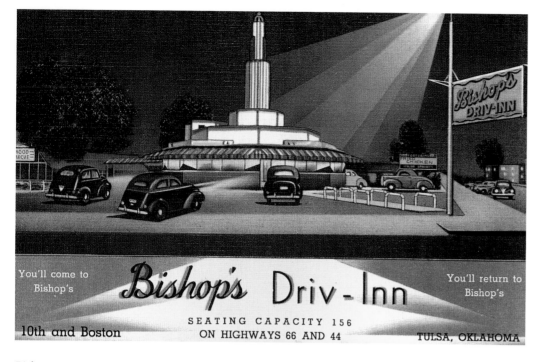

Bishop's Drive-Inn
Above, octagonal design with massive pylon. Located on Highways 66 and 44 in Tulsa, Oklahoma, circa 1940s. Courtesy Chuck Sturm

Arctic Circle Drive-In Mascot
Left, "Acey" the chicken is the animal mascot used by the Arctic Circle drive-ins. From the Chuck Sturm Collection

styles proliferated. By the mid-forties, almost every motorized dining den in America featured some iteration of Louise Sivils' flashy satin garments. Even smaller drive-ins adopted the skirted style, including one modest operation located in San Bernardino, California, run by the two brothers named McDonald.

As more curbside restaurants became generally known as drive-ins, the carhop that started the legend in the early twenties with his athletic abilities and derring-do was replaced by the curb-girl. With running boards now fading to memory, the carhop became part service attendant and part showgirl. Undeniably, she was pure pizzazz—a dignified, hard-working gal gaining recognition as the undisputed queen bee of all America's drive-ins.

Now, the unparalleled act of eating in one's automobile was no longer a novelty in itself. It was a right shared by all those who owned an automobile. The actual restaurants that served those hungry folks sitting behind the wheel and riding in the backseat shifted into the spotlight. Now, the all-girl revue revolved around sparkling structures that lit up the night and set fire to the imagination. All

across the country, on busy intersections and along commercial approach routes, these beacons of light became the new focal point for captivated motorists.

The golden age of the American drive-in restaurant had begun. From here, it would only get better. New advancements were on the way to increase service and productivity—along with profits. Tired methods and inefficient processes would be abandoned for more reliable techniques. New advancements in food handling, refrigeration, and freezing would simplify preparation. The carhop would be aided by a new electrical device that could speed service and simplify tasks. Architectural embellishments would increase customer comfort. It all sounded promising as industry publications like *Drive-In Restaurant* and *Highway Cafe* debuted the latest ideas to come. Sure, conditions would improve, but from whose perspective? Only time would tell. ■

SIVILS' HAMBURGER REVUE

"As imitators nationwide copied the style, legions of young women soon clamored for the available carhop jobs. It was an idea that appealed to many with sights set on careers in motion-pictures."

J. D. Sivils and his wife opened their first car service restaurant on the outskirts of Houston in 1938. They dubbed their operation a "drive-inn" and hired five "curly-haired cuties" to serve car patrons. With uniforms reminiscent of a Busby Berkeley musical, their satin-skirted carhops soon became the main attraction—much more appealing than the burgers, steaks, and trout sandwiches sold there.

While people in their cars waited for their food to be prepared, a small movie screen located on the rooftop provided further entertainment with cartoons and other featurettes. Automotive air-conditioning units with flexible hoses cooled vehicles and became a popular feature during the 100 degree days of summer.

A few years later a second restaurant was opened in the Dallas suburb of Oak Cliff, complete with north and south curb service and its own bevy of satin-clad beauties. A 500 car parking lot kept the girls busy: while curb servers hoofed it in boots, cigarette girls sped around on motor scooters. A "caller" positioned at the top of the building's central tower directed the gals quickly to new arrivals. As customers drove to their parking position, their precise location was relayed by intercom. Before the automobile stopped, a server was there, ready to take the order!

As imitators nationwide copied the style, legions of young women soon clamored for the available carhop jobs. It was an idea that appealed to many with sights set on careers in motion-pictures. In fact, winners of the state's top beauty pageants secured many of the Sivils' positions—some using their car-serve stint as a stepping stone to Hollywood. One-time Sivils' carhop Kay Williams did exactly that, taking her own shortcut to fame and fortune by marrying screen star Clark Gable.

However, it wasn't always all fun and glamour. Louise Sivils ran the Houston operation like a drill team. It was her responsibility to cull the best prospects from the applicants, eliminating all of those who weren't between the ages of eighteen and twenty-five from the running. To even be considered, carhop hopefuls had to be smart; high school diploma and health card were an absolute must. Even then, brains didn't insure employment. All of the Sivils' parking lot girls had to have good figures and exhibit "come hither" personalities to boot.

Mrs. Sivils ran a well-oiled production, often coaching the girls in speech and diction and why it was important to laugh at customers' jokes. More serious rules dealt with serving procedures, dictating that trays be balanced at ear level and held with one hand at all times. Touching the customer's car was not allowed and chewing gum while on duty was prohibited. Change had to be placed on the tray, not in the patron's hand. Actually entering a patron's vehicle was a mortal sin! A major rule infraction ended employment, a minor one resulted in punishment. Folding stacks of napkins often served as penance.

Sivils' Drive-In Card

At Sivils Drive In
Dallas, Texas

Sivils Dallas Drive-In
Life *magazine's only drive-in cover girl was a Sivils curb-girl. Louise Sivils originated the idea of dressing curb-girls in satin shorts and majorette uniforms, beginning a trend that the rest of America's drive-ins would follow. When the*

"caller" was perched high atop his central tower and the curb-girls were lined up at attention, Sivils Drive-In was a sight to see. In an age before theme parks, video games, and cyberspace, virtual reality was what one experienced from the front seat of an automobile. Preziosi Postcards

When the Oak Cliff area went dry in the late sixties and beer sales ended, Sivils' business began to decline. The usual reasons added to the demise: the busy intersection became too clogged for traffic flow, fast food stands offered quicker service, and customers changed. By then, a sinister box known as television provided more exciting imagery than a real drive-in ever could, frozen dinners wrapped within foil more convenience. By the time the Dallas landmark was closed, sold, and finally demolished in 1970, the nights at Sivils' seemed like a dream....

Satin shorts and shapely thighs...painted lips, golden hair, burgers and

fries. Eyes peer out over a dash dappled with light—rows of motorists duplicate the sight. Look! Pillbox hats and majorette jackets, cigarette girls sell little white packets! Summer's first lightning bugs signal the call as lamps flash on and off, tires at rest. White boots on blacktop, numbers picked up, orders are served. Trays hook to windows—no papers, nor wrappers, real glassware, true style. Dollar bills go for food as smiles turn to laughs. Thanks very much. Did he tip? The smell of spilled beer and auto exhaust, songs for the feed blast out from the jukebox. Ya'll come back now! Oh, you racy Sivils carhop girls, how we wish we could. ■

I. D. Sivils and his wife opened their first car service restaurant on the outskirts of Houston in 1938 with five "curly-haired cuties" to serve car patrons. With uniforms reminiscent of a Busby Berkeley musical, their satin-skirted carhops soon became the main attraction—much more appealing than the burgers, steaks, and trout sandwiches sold there.

Sivils' Cowboy and Uniformed Carhops
After Life magazine published an article about the Sivils' Drive-In location in Houston, Texas, shoulder patches embroidered with "Enjoy LIFE at Sivils" became part of the working outfit. During the forties, working as a Sivils curb-girl was considered by many young women to be the ultimate employment. Like the airline stewardess, toting trays to cars had a status all its own. The next best thing to being in show business, servicing hungry car-customers allowed many girls the chance to meet local celebrities, big-time movie stars, statesmen, and the occasional cowboy singer. From the collections of the Texas/Dallas History and Archives Division, Dallas Public Library

MEET ME AT THE VARSITY

*"By combining quality ingredients, friendly employees,
and assembly-line production, restaurant visionary Frank Gordy crystallized
his dreams of childhood into a world-famous landmark."*

When Frank Gordy was a small boy growing up in Thomaston, Georgia, most of his schoolmates fantasized about becoming baseball players, firemen, aviators, cowboys, or railroad engineers. At the turn of the century, those romantic careers were the standard stuff of children's dreams.

Yet, despite the worlds of fantasy these professions sparked in the imaginations of undeveloped minds, they held little interest for the enterprising Gordy. Even then, his sights were squarely set on owning his own business. Other aspirations paled in comparison. Throughout his schooling, he followed avenues compatible with his dream to bolster his original inspiration. After graduation from Oglethorpe University, shrewd investments coupled with the boom in Florida real estate paid-off. A nest-egg of $1,200 staked his first operation.

At age twenty-one, Gordy opened his first restaurant in Atlanta at the crossroads of Luckie Street and North Avenue in 1928. Christened the Yellow-Jacket, it offered the collegiate crowd and passing motorists a convenient bill of fare. Soon after, Gordy wanted to expand his eatery's appeal to surrounding college communities, so a space large enough to serve extra customers was secured. The original moniker was dropped and the more general Varsity name adopted. Within a few years, the once-tiny hot-doggery had expanded to cover almost two city blocks.

Today, The Varsity Drive-In's food operation is unequaled, conducting business as the largest fast-food operation of its class on the entire planet. Every day of the week, a loyal following of Atlanta regulars descend upon the "V's" expansive ordering counter in hungry anticipation. In overall sales, the shear volume of automotive eats assembled, sold, and eaten staggers the imagination. On football Saturdays alone, 30,000 hungry Georgia-Tech fans jam the dining areas for their pre-game fill up. Even on the most routine days, well over two miles of hot dogs are gobbled up—along with 2,500 pounds of French fries, 5,000 fried pies, 7,000 hamburgers, and 300 gallons of chili! A torrent of Varsity Orange and chocolate milk flow freely, eclipsed only by enough Coca-Cola gallonage to float a battleship.

Prepared from the same tried-and-true family recipes Gordy perfected with his "million-dollar tastebuds," crispy fries are still made from the freshest potatoes—not frozen. Chili dogs, or "Heavy Weights" as they are known by customers, are world renowned for their flavor and imposing size. Fried to a golden hue and stuffed with flavorful filling, hand-pressed peach pies are a fitting showcase for Georgia's famous fruit. Of course, there's the hot and juicy "glorified steak" to consider, a fitting tribute to the institution of the American burger. Topped with lettuce, tomato, and mayo, it's the perfect companion to a piping hot order of batter-dipped onion rings.

Much to the customer's approval, the food served at The Varsity is only one small facet of its success. Out on the front lines, red-shirted employees never fail to greet customers with a smile and an excited, "What'll Ya Have?" The entire operation is galvanized by a spirit of cooperation and teamwork. Sandwich makers, burger flippers, hot dog cooks, singing curb-men—even members of the cleanup crew—are driven by one engine: pleasing the walk-up and drive-in diner with an unparalleled level of service and fabulous food.

By combining quality, friendliness, and assembly-line serving techniques, restaurant visionary Frank Gordy proved that even the most simplistic of childhood dreams can be worthwhile. Today, Atlanta's premier drive-in exists as an example of free enterprise at work, a living tribute to the man who once exclaimed, "The Varsity is my life and I love it!"

So, the next time you're in Georgia, motor on into the V and have them "walk a dog sideways" for you with a "bag of rags." Try a Mary Brown Steak or a Yellow Dog and be sure to ask about Flossie and his crazy hats. Check out the hot dog conveyor belt, have fun, eat well, and be sure to tell all of your friends. Frank Gordy would have wanted it that way. ∎

The Early Varsity
At age twenty-one in 1928, Frank Gordy opened his first restaurant in Atlanta at the crossroads of Luckie Street and North Avenue. Christened the Yellow-Jacket, it offered the collegiate crowd and passing motorists a convenient bill of fare. Today, his dream has expanded to become the world's largest drive-in eatery. Approaching motorists, pedestrians, and bus riders can smell the food from blocks away! Photo circa 1930. Courtesy of The Varsity, Inc.

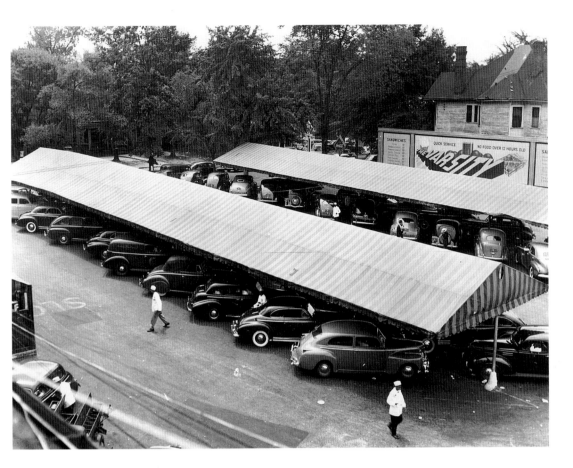

Forties Varsity from Above
Atlanta's Varsity Drive-In has always provided numerous places to park. Two double canopies create ample shade during the hot summers and protection from the elements in the winter. With the amount of cars requesting food, it's enough to keep even the best curb-men busy. Courtesy of The Varsity, Inc.

The Varsity Park Lot, circa 1950s
Unlike the majority of drive-ins that chose to employ female carhops, the tradition at The Varsity has favored "curb-men." Nipsy Russell worked as an energetic server (he was number 46) years ago, long before his rhyming rise to notoriety on television and film. Flossie (another curb service veteran), gained his notoriety by singing the menu to customers! Courtesy of The Varsity, Inc.

Sixties Varsity and Street Scene
The Varsity is a patchwork of curb service spaces, awnings, and asphalt surrounding the famous fast food Mecca. Five television viewing rooms, inside seating for over 800 customers, and a continuously moving conveyor belt are only a few of the wonders. Inside, a 150ft stainless steel ordering counter is manned by dozens of employees, all eager to ask "What'll Ya Have," making sure you get your order quick. Courtesy of The Varsity, Inc.

THE TROUBLE WITH FRENCH FRIES

Served as a chip with clam dip, the sliced potato is classified by law as a fruit. When it accompanies a cut of steak, it suddenly becomes a vegetable. So, what happens when the starchy tuber is cut into small strips, fried in a vat of boiling oil, showered with salt, and teamed with a patty of chopped beef? Quite simply, the ordinary potato is transformed into a bag of French fries—a fast food drive-in meal maintaining a class all by itself.

French fries exist today as the perfect motoring finger food. Their size, shape, and packaging make them ideal for quick, easy consumption within the automobile. Indeed, they can be said to promote deep psychological satisfaction as well, for the very act of devouring them constitutes a re-enactment of behavior long forgotten, of times when our ancestors enjoyed dining without the benefit of "modern" utensils.

Despite this undeniable link to the past, French-fried potato sticks started life in America as an uninspired foodstuff, a plate filler to be chomped down between bites of burger and sips of soda. When the enterprising McDonald brothers finally began to lavish them with the attention they deserved during the forties, the once greasy potato strips at long last began their slow rise to the top of the fry basket.

For the McDonalds team, only the best Idaho Russets would do justice to this fast food side-order. Stored in small wire-mesh bins at the back of their warehouse, continuously circulating air moved among the containers, slowly aging the potatoes in the dry air of California. Only when they reached the peak of perfection were they ready to be peeled.

By the quarter sack full, the fry man tumbled potatoes into the hopper of a mechanized potato peeler. As an 18-inch abrasive wheel spun around, the spuds ambled about in every direction, efficiently stripped of their coverings. With just the right timing, they would emerge flecked with traces of skin, affording the most flavorful and visually pleasing fries in the free world. If left in too long, a robust bunch of potatoes were reduced to what Richard McDonald described as a handful of "little marbles."

As sack upon sack of potatoes were peeled and processed, the accumulated starch began its slow buildup. Eventually, it started overflowing from a drain vent pipe on the roof top! Using their proven "trial and error method" for finding solutions, the McDonalds hit upon the idea of eliminating the pesky starch with a soak in ice water.

Lucky for the customer, the age-old problems addressing taste were also rectified. Unlike many unscrupulous operators who used the same oil they deep-fried their fish and chicken in, Richard and Maurice decided at the start to use only the best, unadulterated cooking oil. When the French fries emerged—spattering all golden brown and a-burstin' with flavor—patrons begged for more.

Packed with labor and love, the three-ounce sacks of French fries sold for only ten cents—truly a rare bargain! Car customers were quick to recognize the value available at the McDonald's French fry window and soon it became the busiest portal for food in all of San Bernardino. Hundreds of future aficionados of the French fry lined up to order the crispy delights, readily acquainting themselves with the oversized aluminum salt shaker supplied at the walk-up serving window.

Today, it can be said that a little bag of French fries built an empire. After all, they were precisely what folks in a hurry wanted—a quick, hot, and cheap food, a fried variation of the ordinary potato that the McDonald brothers had lifted from its humble beginnings to a recognized form of American road food. ∎

First In French Fries
Circa 1950s advertising postcard from McDonald's depicting the candy-striped golden arches building.
Courtesy Chuck Sturm

Chrome And Fries
French fries have become the modern-day staple for the hurried motorist. New Haven, Connecticut

Plate of French Fries
Preziosi Postcards

CHAPTER THREE

NEWER VISIONS FOR ROADFOOD

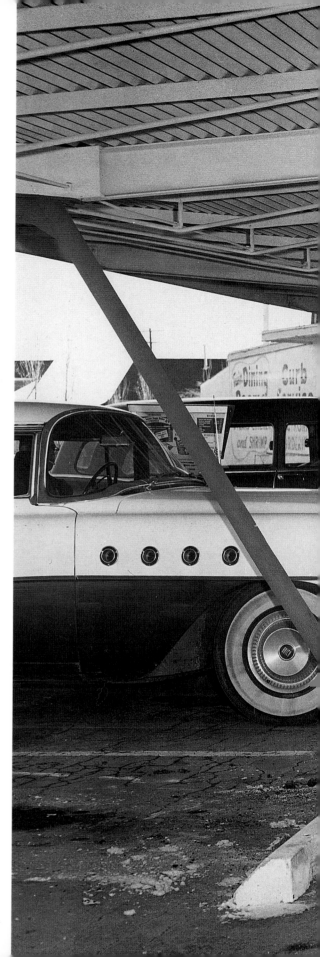

Carhop Under The Canopy
Opposite, the 1960s brought unforeseen changes to the Wichita drive-in market. Griff's planned to locate four "fast-food" eateries in the area and Sandy's four of their own. To make matters worse, the McDonald's chain proposed construction of their own quartet. Kings-X drive-in owner Jimmie King took the incursion seriously, well aware that the sight of Golden Arches foretold an increased level of competition. Soon, overhead canopies and Western wear would not be enough to draw customers to his East Kellogg Street curb-server. A large Pontiac dealership now occupies the lot. Courtesy of Kings-X Inc.

Porky's Drive-In
Previous pages, the last of the famous Porky's Drive-Ins that once ruled Minneapolis and St. Paul. Founder and owner Ray Truelson began in the 1940s with the Adobe root beer stand situated at Hiawatha and 35th in Minneapolis. Around 1950, he opened the Flat Top Drive-In at 58th and Lyndale with a full line of drinks and food. The Flat Top was soon renamed Porky's, and a second Porky's was built in 1953 on Univeristy Avenue in St. Paul. Two additional Porky's were added in the late fifties at opposite ends of Minneapolis' Lake Street. The pictured Porky's in St. Paul closed its drive-thru window in 1979 and remained derelict throughout the 1980s, as did many of America's drive-ins. Faced with an ultimatum from the city to renovate or demolish, Truelson restored Porky's to its former glory in 1990. Today, the parking lot is packed with classic cars and hot rods on most summer nights, a flashback in time to the days when the classic drive-in first turned on its porcine neon sign. Michael Dregni

At the close of the 1940s, Richard and Maurice McDonald began formulating some innovative ideas to improve drive-in service. Although their San Bernardino, California, operation was lucrative, they perceived some basic flaws in the system and wanted to eliminate them. With an eye towards efficiency, they began an in-depth examination of their drive-in's strengths and weaknesses.

First, they noticed that postwar patrons were growing increasingly restless with carhop service. It wasn't anything obvious; only a feeling that car-diners wanted something more convenient. Richard McDonald observed that "the customer would come in and the carhop would go out. She would give them a menu, and go back into the drive-in again. When she returned, the customer might not be ready to make an order and she'd probably go back and forth four or five more times. Sometimes it was taking twenty-five to thirty minutes before people actually got their food served!" A service speed once considered an acceptable norm became noticeably sluggish.

Besides the sometimes slow rate of delivery, carhops posed other problems as well. Boyfriends regularly stopped by for prolonged chats, diverting them from their work. Because of the stand's proximity to a local high school, there was never a lack of eager males vying for attention. Every weekend, they descended upon the parking lot with their hopped-up roadsters and jalopies. The hours after dusk were filled with loud bragging, flirting, and the usual displays of male bravado that accompany adolescent mating rituals. Even more disturbing, carhops often quit at a moment's notice, leaving the McDonald brothers short of staff and long on disgruntled motorists blowing horns for service.

In perspective, most of these situations could be worked around when the occasion called for it. But what couldn't be justified was the monetary loss due to missing trays and

THE WORLD'S FAIR CORNUCOPIA

Despite the mysterious parentage of the ice cream cone, most historians agree on its birthplace: the St. Louis World's Fair. Although Italo Marchiony's patent on a split-cone mold was applied for prior to this event, he did not achieve the distinction of introducing the hand-held holder to the public. That achievement was shared among a group of vendors who were working the exposition in 1904.

That year, over fifty ice cream booths and waffle shops were operating within the sprawling fair grounds. Among the roster of concessionaires, three individuals staked their claim as original instigator of the consumable ice cream cone. While logic indicates that all three may have stumbled upon the concept simultaneously, subsequent obituaries and accounts in print claim otherwise.

Abe Doumar (Albert Doumar's uncle), now recognized by the Smithsonian Institution as the most likely originator, was employed by the City of Jerusalem Show during the day. After closing, he gathered with friends at a nearby waffle shop to chat. As crowds thinned, he got the notion to roll up a French waffle into an inverted spire. After filling it with a scoop of ice cream from next door, he suggested the waffle vendor sell the unusual combo to increase sales. To show his appreciation for the crowds, the ecstatic waffler presented Abe with one of his prized irons at season's end.

Another account relates how Ernest Hamwi sold Persian pastries from his concession stand. Baked on a flat waffle iron, he topped the latticed "zalabia" with sugar and other sweet toppings. When a nearby ice cream seller exhausted his supply of clean dishes, the inventive Hamwi rushed to his aid. Within seconds, a rolled up wafer became the receptacle for a dollop of frozen delight. The "World's Fair Cornucopia" made its momentous debut.

The last third in the infamous trilogy of cone creators was fair vendor David Avayou. As an observant visitor from Turkey, he claimed to have imported the ice cream cone idea from France, where he witnessed small frozen confections served in pointed paper receptacles. He applied the concept to his own wares and soon created an edible version to hold his frosty desserts.

Despite these conflicting origins, the popularity of the cone quickly gained momentum. Before the close of the Fair, several local foundries were scrambling to produce baking molds for the World's Fair Cornucopia. Eventually, everyone who had a hand in the development of the cone went on to profit from its meteoric rise to fame.

By the thirties, competition among cone manufacturers intensified, each attempting to outsmart the other with innovation. Marvels of edible engineering, "Dripless" models featured elaborate trough systems to trap melt. Others sported clever side-pockets for extra scoops. Exaggerated versions assumed the shape of spirals, space ships, and bathtubs.

As the cone became less of a novelty, the aggressive competition among manufacturers began to wane. Major bakeries began to dominate the field, eliminating creative offerings with functional cones. Soon, uncomplicated cake and sugar models triumphed. No longer a culinary work of art, the World's Fair Cornucopia was reduced to the status of ancillary food item with simple utility.

Eventually, the waffle-making legends of Doumar, Hamwi, and Avayou were forgotten. The ice cream cone became a separate entity, whole-heartedly accepted into the fold of American confections. Cones, and the frozen dessert they held, were now part of roadside food. ■

George Doumar and Waffle Maker
All the Doumar children learn to make cones when they are sixteen. Young George Doumar (shown here at age sixteen in 1983) represents the next generation of ice cream cone makers. Once learned, it's an easy process: Pull one of the four irons out on their tracks, open it, and ladle on a couple of ounces of batter. The filled griddle is slid over the gas flame and allowed to bake. Up and down the flame, the process is repeated, the irons flipped midway through the cooking process. As the first waffle becomes ready, the iron is pulled out, the top lifted, and the soft waffle wrapped around a tapered form made of wood. Then, the completed cone is placed into a cooling rack. Courtesy of Albert Doumar

flatware. Everyday, a plate or a knife or a fork would somehow leave the parking lot, never to be seen again. The dishes that escaped pilferage were dropped, lost, or accidentally thrown in the trash. Replacements were constantly cycled in from stock, only to be replaced again the following month. While the loss didn't bankrupt the business, it contributed to overhead costs. With a frugal New England ethic for thrift, the McDonalds couldn't tolerate the waste.

In the fall of 1948, they shut down the octagonal drive-in at Fourteenth and E Streets for three complete months. It was time to reshape the drive-in formula into a totally new entity, one that would operate on speed, efficiency, and self-service. The first order of business was the immediate dismissal of all twenty carhops. Next, windows used for pick-up were converted to self-serve portals where customers could place food orders. Then, the entire kitchen facility was gutted and reworked to accommodate two custom six-foot grills. Finally, the remaining stock of china, forks, knives, and spoons was phased out. From now on, edibles would be served in paper wrappers and soft drinks in disposable cups. This made the dishwasher's job redundant, so he was sacked, too.

The final stages included an entire rework of the menu. Because receipts showed that 80 percent of sales was from hamburgers, the hickory chip barbecue pit was dumped. The advertising money used to promote barbecue on the radio could now be saved. But there were even more changes to come: the twenty-five food selections currently offered were decimated to nine. The abbreviated menu was planned solely around hamburgers and cheeseburgers—all prepared the same way with ketchup, mustard, onion, and two pickles!

continued on page 116

It was time to reshape the drive-in formula into a totally new entity, one that would operate on speed, efficiency, and self-service. The first order of business was the immediate dismissal of all twenty carhops. Next, windows used for pick-up were converted to self-serve portals where customers could place their own food orders.

McDonald's After the Carhops Were Fired
In the fall of 1948, the McDonald brothers closed down their San Bernardino drive-in and fired all of the carhops. A new plan based on what they called the "Speedy Service System" was implemented. Its main features were self-service, minimal choice, and fast turnover. The 15¢ hamburger stand was born.
Courtesy Richard McDonald

DOLORES DRIVE-IN HOLLYWOOD

*"Screenwriters, producers, agents, stuntmen—
everyone involved with the creation of American celluloid—
would take their meals beneath the neon lights."*

Martin Cable had trouble finding a job when he returned home from the Marine Corps in 1946. Fortunately, drive-in dining spots occupied almost every street corner in Los Angeles, providing numerous opportunities for employment. When he heard that Ralph and Amanda Stephens were opening their second eatery at Wilshire and La Cienega and that they needed new carhops, his interest piqued. With only three dollars in his pocket, Cable hoofed it double-time over to Beverly Hills to join up.

His timing was perfect. That year, the male carhop crew working at the first Dolores location on Sunset Strip garnered a rather dubious reputation. Hiring strapping soldiers fresh from the military ranks was thought to be the perfect solution for upgrading the image. As a result, Cable was hired on the spot. There was only one obstacle: a white shirt, black bow-tie, and brown slacks had to be provided by the applicant. Cable's current wardrobe included only the green slacks he was wearing.

That night, he purchased a small box of dye for one buck and picked up a cheap bow-tie for another. He returned home and proceeded to dye his military trousers brown while wondering just how he would fare as a parking-lot waiter. By the close of the next day, his worries disappeared with his last car customer. A full shift of carhopping left his pockets bulging with tips and stained with dye! Wearing a grin wider than two slices of apple pie, he went home and confidently told his wife "not to worry…we've got it made!"

Four months later, Cable assumed the role of manager and began his drive-in education. From the outer parking lot to the kitchen, there was a lot to learn. First, he discovered that Amanda Stephens was an accomplished chef. She showed by example how important it was to have tasty recipes, illustrating the point with her famous onion soup and homemade pies. Under her wing, Cable found out just how much time and labor a profitable drive-in restaurant involved.

Making some discoveries of his own, Cable realized that ex-service folk weren't always the best candidates for outdoor food work. Aspiring actors fit the bill more appropriately and were soon applying for the jobs. As employee turnover changed the faces each year, he began noticing that some former hops were returning in snazzy cars. Having found fame and fortune in pictures, they returned to their old alma mater to hang out and flaunt their accomplishments on the silver screen.

Eventually, every movie actor or actress that came out to the Golden State got the tip to drive down to Dolores, and "try the pecan pie." The Beverly Hills location soon became a local landmark, the place to see—and be seen. During its heyday in the late forties, it became the restaurant of choice for the image-conscious Hollywood crowd. Screenwriters, producers, agents, stuntmen—everyone involved with the creation of American celluloid—would take their meals beneath the neon lights. The unassuming act of eating a hamburger often became an impromptu publicity event.

Gregory Peck was one of Dolores' best customers, as were many stars who drove in for a bite on their way to and from the studios. To avoid the prying eyes of gossip columnists, Tyrone Power rubbed fenders with Linda Christian in the most remote region of the lot. Vivian Leigh and her husband, Robert Walker, were also regulars. Susan Hayward motored in for car service often. Even character actor Ward Bond stopped in daily for hot coffee.

The expansive parking area beneath the striped awnings became the asphalt stage for displaying Hollywood's portable symbol of wealth: the automobile. Where else could a rising film star properly show off his or her luxury Packard or two-tone convertible? Cable recalls the day Bing Crosby stopped in to have his afternoon salad and flaunt his newest eight-cylinder acquisition. "Marty, guess what…just bought me a new Cadillac for $5500," he crooned. Despite the trappings of wealth and fame, Crosby's face revealed a man pained by the price. In those days, that could buy a lot of burgers! ■

Dolores Drive-In Wilshire

When the carhops at California's Dolores Drive-In were handed a dime for their tip, they tossed the coin on top of the roof in disgust. For some, this proved a lucrative habit. When times were tough during the winter months, it wasn't unusual to see one of the capped car servers scrambling atop the building, scouring the roof for some extra pocket money! During the heyday of the drive-ins, dining out in a motorcar meant only one thing: Dolores. This drive-in was the Wilshire and West La Cienega location, circa 1956. Bison Archives

Franchising Speedy Service
An executive from Southern California Edison and the brothers Richard (right) and Mac (center) McDonald discuss a new neon sign for their revamped drive-in. Richard specialized in marketing while Mac headed up operations. Courtesy Richard McDonald

continued from page 113

Meat patties were made smaller; now they would be ten to the pound instead of eight. This allowed for a "minor" price reduction and the usual thirty-cent sandwich swooped down to a low fifteen! The extra money saved by customers could be spent on three types of soft drinks, coffee, milk, fries, or a thick milkshake. The McDonalds' plan to create a volume operation through speedy preparation and self-service was ready for the ultimate test: the fickle public.

In December, the new walk-up stand re-opened to a rather lackluster reception. From the start, the McDonalds' improved "Speedy Service System" didn't produce the volume anticipated. The customers hated it! They wanted the carhops back, they wanted the car service, they wanted the barbecue pit, they

wanted the big menu. The once-bustling parking lot was reduced to three cars—and two of those belonged to employees! In the meantime, former carhops heckled, "We have our uniforms all ready—just call us!"

Apparently, the McDonalds changed the image of their stand too much. "We thought this was really going to knock 'em loose," recalls Richard McDonald. "Well, the only ones that it knocked loose were the McDonald brothers." Doubting the makeover, Maurice "Mac" McDonald said, "You know Dick...this looks like a dumb idea. What do you think...should we write this off and call back the carhops?" Although their pride was hurt, they decided to tough it out for a few more months. Three months later, their patience proved a profitable virtue.

Slowly, a more diverse segment of the market began showing up at the self-serve windows: taxi drivers, construction workers, salesmen, and motorists on their way to and from work. As the hangout image waned, even families began to frequent the stand. Small children soon joined in the melee, placing their orders independently as parents looked on proudly from the Buick.

During busy periods, lines were twenty deep at each service window. Inside, a crack assembly line of workers cranked out the food. With spotless stainless steel as backdrop, a "grill man" prepared the hamburgers, a dedicated "shake man" mixed up the milkshakes, and a separate "fry man" prepared the potatoes. "Dressers" added toppings and assembled the burgers, while the front "countermen" specifically concentrated on their tasks, wrapping food and taking care of customers. What was once an impromptu enterprise was now a smooth-running machine. The Speedy Service System worked!

News of the McDonalds' prototype spread fast and within the year, curious drive-in proprietors traveled from all over the country to see what made the unit work. The brothers

continued on page 120

DRIVE-INS ACROSS AMERICA

The Tik-Tok Restaurant
Left, the Tik-Tok was one of Portland, Oregon's, premier restaurants during the forties. While teenagers generally hung out at Bart's, a slightly older clientele sipped coffee at the Tik-Tok. Today, a parking lot occupies the former site. Oregon Historical Society

Yaw's Long Drive-In
Below, teenagers in Portland, Oregon, followed a complete "circuit" when they cruised during the fifties. First it was the Speck, followed by a trip downtown on Broadway. Coming back on the other side of town, Yaw's Drive-In became the next destination, along with 82nd Street. Back then, numerous curb service eateries jammed the strip. A McDonald's fast food outlet now occupies the site once designated to Yaw's. Oregon Historical Society

54 Drive-Inn Cafe
Left, today, the Highway 54 that passes through Kansas is nothing like the one that played host to drive-ins like the "54." The Kansas Turnpike now shoulders much of the traffic, along with the multi-laned interstate. Time and progress have passed by many of the old haunts...but fortunately, some may still be discovered. Courtesy Chuck Sturm

Harry Lewis Triple XXX
Below, Triple XXX Root Beer was a popular brand that assumed high visibility during the thirties and forties. Many of the drive-ins that sold the drink incorporated a root beer barrel into their design. Harry Lewis operated one such stand in Waco, Texas, featuring famous foods that garnered the approval of Duncan Hines. For early restaurateurs, earning the Duncan Hines seal of approval equated to guaranteed success. Hines started out in the restaurant review business by a fortunate stroke of fate. A well-traveled salesman, he had compiled a list of favorite eateries for his friends and family. The public's interest prompted Hines to expand the list and publish it as a book, entitled Adventures in Good Eating. By 1939, it was selling at a steady clip of 100,000 per year! Courtesy Chuck Sturm

Tiny Naylors
Above, William Wallace "Tiny" Naylor (he weighed 320lb at 6ft, 4in tall) started in the restaurant business around 1927. Waffle shops were his first foray into the world of roadside food. He slept in his first unit at night, alternating with a partner a schedule of rest and sleep. The single store grew into a chain of twenty-one, pleasing customers from Redding to San Diego, California. By 1949, he opened a Hollywood drive-in called Tiny Naylors and made his mark in the curb server walk-of-fame. On opening night, Humphrey Bogart commented that it looked like "a huge bird about to take off." That it did, satisfying customers with carhops on roller skates (for a few years) and copper heating pipes in the canopy. Despite protests, it closed in 1984 and was later demolished. Courtesy Dick Whittington Collection Dept. of Special Collections, University of Southern California Library

Merle's Drive-In & Barbecue
Left, the barbecue pit at Merle's was always fired and fried chicken was at the ready. Courtesy Chuck Sturm

continued from page 116
proudly revealed the entire operation, generously sharing the fast-food know-how they had developed. The intricacies of the stand were ravenously assimilated by all, and soon a number of similar burger bars popped up all across America. The McDonald brothers were definitely on to something big.

When a representative for Prince Castle Sales Division named Ray Kroc noticed that the McDonalds ordered more Multimixers than any of his other clients, he became curious. Why would anyone need ten of these multi-spindle mixers? More important, how could they possibly use all those machines at one time? During a sales trip in 1954, the puzzled Kroc decided to pay the San Bernardino hamburger stand a little visit.

What Kroc found captivated him. He couldn't believe the hundreds of customers driving up for hamburgers and was astonished at the lines. At first sight, he knew this busy operation had all the elements of great success—and he wanted to become part of it. The opportunity presented itself shortly: the McDonald brothers (who had already begun

World's First Fly-in-Drive-In
Below, Elwood, Indiana, was the town where Ruth and Charles Sullivan opened the world's first "Fly-in" drive-in. Known from coast to coast and located on Highways 13 and 37, it was a popular stopover for flyers looking for a quick lunch served in the cockpit. Preziosi Postcards

WORLD'S FIRST
Fly-In - Drive-In
ELWOOD, INDIANA

SULLIVAN'S

Track Service Drive-In
One of the most progressive enhancements to drive-in service was the "Motormat." Making its debut in 1949, this Los Angeles innovation promised the total elimination of carhops. At a new drive-in called "The Track," it attracted customers from as far as Santa Monica with its unique mode of service. Like horses at a watering trough, cars ringed around a central building, forming a circular pattern. Food rode the rails within carrying bins. Interestingly enough, each compartment was assigned its own name, much like horses at a real racetrack. "Ponder" is the unit depicted. National Archives

Sanders Court and Cafe
In Corbin, Kentucky, "Colonel" Harland Sanders got his start in the chicken business with a motel court he owned and operated during the forties and fifties. When a highway bypass around his original roadside restaurant caused business to plummet in 1955, he began selling his secret recipe chicken wherever he could. Kentucky Fried Chicken eventually became one of the giants in the fast-food industry. Unfortunately, mass-production methods made it impossible to re-create his tasty gravy. Courtesy Chuck Sturm

Multicolored Metal Drive-In Canopy
Lower right, in 1931, what is believed to be America's first drive-in canopy was installed at the Zangs Boulevard Pig Stand (Number 2) in Dallas, Texas. A brown canvas affair, it was the simple predecessor of the elaborate constructions installed during the fifties. Top Hat Drive-In operator Troy Smith followed in 1953 by installing Oklahoma's first drive-in canopy. By the start of the sixties, the canopy of multicolored sheet metal or corrugated tin was a common sight along the roadsides. Courtesy Brian Butko

SANDERS COURT & CAFE

CORBIN ——— KENTUCKY

Corbin, Ky.
Junct. U. S. 25, 25E and 25W
32 Rooms — 32 Baths
At Asheville, N. C.
5 Miles North
At Junct. U. S. 25, 70, 19 and 23

franchising the concept to operators out West) suddenly found themselves without a franchising agent. Kroc became the perfect candidate to fill the position and readily took over the duties. With new zeal, the job of transforming the McDonald's name and its streamline system into a household word was begun. "Fast food" was on its way to becoming a dominant force in roadside dining.

In the meantime, America's drive-in restaurants were holding their own. Despite the incursion of self-serve burger walk-ups and soft-serve ice cream stands (such as Dairy Queen and Tastee-Freez), they continued to satisfy the expanding pool of motorists swelling the roads. But realistically, this new competition could not be ignored. Drive-in proprietors recognized that they had to act swiftly to keep stride with these low-overhead operations. To ensure the popularity of carhop service into the 1950s, changes were in order. Like every other consumer entity interested in appearance, functionality, and profits, the dri-

Richard's Drive-In
Richard's Drive-In of Cambridge, Massachusetts, featured a large weather-shielding roof to protect its in-car diners circa 1957. Richard's promoted "Car-feteria" service at its East Coast and Midwest dining operations. Extrapolating the theme of the young boy holding a hamburger (originally developed by Robert Wian with the double-deck "Big Boy"), Richard's utilized a male and female duo of similarly dressed youngsters, each holding their own hamburger. Cambridge Historical Commission

THE STORY OF CARBONATED WATER

The Transcendent Puffer Fountain

The Transcendent was featured on page 108 of A. D. Puffer and Sons' 1889 catalog. This elaborate structure was sold at the height of the soda fountain's Golden Age. The marble exterior housed a tank of carbonated liquid encased in ice beneath the counter. On each side were spigots that dispensed chilled syrup. Initially, these were called "fountains," but later, the name came to imply the complete counter area where sodas and ice cream were served. However, the dispensing fountain is still located under the serving counter in most of today's establishments. Landauer Collection, New-York Historical Society

When English scientist Joseph Priestley charged a glass of water with carbonic acid gas in 1767, it barely made a fizz in the chemistry community. Unlike his more astounding discovery of oxygen, the curious creation was largely ignored, treated by peers as a laboratory oddity.

About forty years later, Yale University professor Benjamin Silliman began experimenting with the idea of marketing the bubbling waters. Stopper bottles held the liquid, and exclusive shops in New York City sold them to thirsty patrons. Later, Philip Physick tried his own luck at the carbonation game by blending in a secret mixture of minerals. Sold widely as a cure for obesity, it helped to accelerate public awareness and desire for effervescent beverages.

When young Englishman John Matthews arrived in New York in 1832, he saw this yearning for fizzy drinks as an opportunity for fortune. By exploiting his unique skill for producing carbonic acid gas, he almost singlehandedly popped the top on the soda water market. Incorporating his ideas into a portable, doghouse-sized carbonating apparatus, he revolutionized the soda water business with his practical "fountain."

Store owners were amazed by the new device, even if they did not understand the scientific principles that made it work: when proper proportions of sulfuric acid, carbonic acid, and water were filtered through marble dust, carbon dioxide gas was liberated. The resulting liquid became a modified sort of water—highly saturated with myriad harmless bubbles, all eager for simultaneous release.

As Matthews secured rights to gather the scrap marble (enough to carbonate 25 million gallons) from the construction site of St. Patrick's Cathedral, established manufacturers began to take notice. Soon, aggressive corporations like Boston's A.D. Puffer and Philadelphia's John Lippincott debuted elaborate versions of their own fountains.

In the competition to follow, an incongruous hodge podge of decorative styles soon found their way into new fountain designs. Ostentatious motifs were typified by bare-breasted nymphs, decorative orbs, beaded strings, and spear-toting centurions. Still, the era's drugstores and sweet shops adored the haughty designs and purchased them without restraint. Aficionados of American soda now had the freedom to order a tumbler of unadulterated seltzer water whenever and wherever they pleased.

At first, inhibited converts to the bubbly liquid imbibed it totally straight, slightly chilled. Fortunately, attitudes about additives began to soften when perfume dealer Eugène Roussel arrived in Philadelphia from France.

A short while after he opened a bustling perfume emporium, he began to offer the sparkling water to his clients. No stranger to experimentation, he put aside his fragrances and began dabbling with flavors around 1838. Like magnet to steel, soda and syrup joined and a tasty new drink sensation was born: the flavored soda.

Not surprisingly, the tingling taste treat was an immediate hit with the socializers of Philadelphia's soda parlour scene! Re-energized by news of the phenomenon, fountain operators city wide began the scramble to produce their own custom made beverages.

Within a few years, no reputable soda fountain would be caught without a vast stock of vanilla, cherry, pepsin, birch beer, kola, champagne, or claret flavored syrups under the counter. Tickling the taste buds and soothing the palate was the new domain of carbonated waters. ■

The most progressive enhancement was the "Motormat," which debuted in 1949 in Los Angeles and promised the total elimination of carhops. Twenty semi-circular parking spaces bridged a center hub kitchen by means of metal tracks. Food and condiments rode the rails within carrying bins, each compartment powered by a small 1 1/2hp motor.

ve-in segment of the restaurant industry welcomed all improvements.

One of the most progressive enhancements was the "Motormat." Debuted in 1949, this Los Angeles innovation promised the total elimination of carhops. At a new drive-in called "The Track," it attracted customers from as far as Santa Monica with its unique mode of service. Like a group of horses at a watering trough, cars ringed around a central building, forming a circular pattern. Twenty semi-circular parking spaces bridged a center hub kitchen by means of metal tracks. Food and condiments rode the rails within carrying bins, each compartment powered by a small 1 1/2 horsepower motor.

The mechanical setup was reminiscent of the wackiest Rube Goldberg device. Positioned in a pre-determined parking space, the customer rolled down the car window and was greeted by a stainless-steel bin that could be pulled flush with the door. Inside the box were plastic cups, a water bottle, menu, order pad, and change tray. It was large, too. Food for six people could be ferried back and forth on the elevated platforms. Patrons would jot down their orders and with the push of a button, the unit scooted a return into the kitchen.

When the empty bin arrived at the kitchen, an attendant put through the order and added up the bill. As hamburgers and other entrees were prepared, the rail box made its second journey to the automobile to collect the money. By the time it returned to the preparation area, the food was ready to go— loaded into the compartment along with condiments and the customer's change. According to inventor Kenneth C. Purdy, the spoke-wheel-track arrangement sped service 20–25 percent. Best of all, it reduced labor costs, making the large staff of carhops normally required to run a drive-in unnecessary. And, there were benefits for the customer,

continued on page 128

AIR-COOLED COMFORT DINING

Drive-in restaurant dining often had distinct advantages. Automobile owners could enjoy the great outdoors while consuming their food—without the hassles of a roadside picnic. As the sun's rays shone through the front windshield, frosty milkshakes and steaming cheeseburgers could be eaten without a care.

Of course, this idyllic scene was only indicative of the milder times of year. Taking lunch at a curb-service restaurant during the summer months often posed discomfort. In extremely humid cities like Houston, Texas, the metal surfaces of an automobile often created an oven-like environment when heated by the sun. As more and more indoor eateries featured "air-cooled by

Marquee Drive-In
Combining a circular layout with an overhead canopy parking area was a natural progression for drive-in restaurants operating in extreme climate conditions. Located at 216 East Main in Mesa, Arizona, the Marquee was a welcome watering hole when the summer temperatures edged over the century mark. Inside diners had it even better: "refrigerated" air cooled the overheated brow. Circa 1960. Courtesy Karl Korzeniewski

refrigeration," drive-in operators were literally left in the dust—and the hot air that held it.

Houston drive-in proprietor and visionary R. E. "Sonny" Stuart decided to fight fire with fire—or in this case hot air with cold—during the Texas summer of 1955. By employing the latest in modern technology, he offered his own version of air-conditioning to a public prostrated by the heat. America's "most air-conditioned city" became the proving grounds for a revolutionary new kind of drive-in climate control.

As the mysterious installation was in its last stages of completion, curious customers drove into Stuart's to see what all the rumors were about. Before they could engage their parking brake under the canopy, a smiling carhop greeted them with two flexible hoses in hand. To the uninitiated, it seemed like a scene from a science-fiction serial: tubes ribbed with accordion-like folds were thrust into the front vent window and instructions given to roll up all others. Just what was happening here?

Surprise quickly turned to delight as overheated passengers literally breathed a deep sigh of approval. As a refrigerated column of air began pouring into the vehicle's interior, interior metal cooled. By means of simple convection, hot air was forced out through the second exhaust tubing, jammed in above the first.

Suddenly, the temperature inside the automobile dropped! In the short time that it took for the car server to return with an order, the car became as cool as a mountain cabin. For the next fifteen minutes, drinking and dining was virtually perspiration-free. Parked side by side under the glowering heat island of the city, automobiles became miniature oasis for comfort dining.

A few feet above under the canopy, advanced air-conditioning facilitated the transformation. Designed and manufactured especially for this unique application, Stuart's refrigeration units were the first full-scale trial of practical drive-in air-conditioning. Since seventeen were installed, the project wasn't cheap: the specialized three-quarter ton coolers served two customers at a cost of almost $500 each!

Still, the investment proved worthwhile for the enterprising Stuart. After the installation, drive-in business increased over 20 percent. Customers that ordinarily just pulled in to buy a cold beverage were now requesting food. Since normal business averaged 1,000 cars per day at each of his two locations, it didn't take long to recoup startup costs.

As the last pieces of burger were swallowed, customers signaled to the carhop their readiness to leave. Tubings were removed from the window, retracted by long springs. Transformed like a Cinderella carriage, hot air replaced cold in one gulp. The refreshing trip to Sonny Stuart's amazing drive-in was over. ∎

A smiling carhop would greet you with two flexible hoses in hand, which were thrust into the front vent window. As a refrigerated column of air began pouring into the vehicle's interior, interior metal cooled. By means of simple convection, hot air was forced out through the second exhaust tubing, jammed in above the first.

Drive-In Air Conditioning
Air conditioning was a novelty tried by many drive-in operators during the fifties. R. E. "Sonny" Stuart used the radical system at his Houston drive-in, as did J. D. and Louise Sivils.

*T*he ultimate canopy was finally produced, which "served as flower gardens filled with color and life, but without the time-consuming necessity for taking care of flowers." It kept customers out of the rain, provided visual enjoyment, and replaced the natural flora of the American roadside. Who needed parks with grass and real trees? The drive-in had it all.

Canopy Styles
Council manufacturing of Fort Smith, Arkansas, introduced a wide range of canopy styles during the fifties and sixties. Forward-thinking operators could choose from models like the curved, lazy boomerang, pitched, canted, and folding plate. © 1994 Gabriele Witzel

continued from page 125

too: a large "No Tipping" sign hung on the building facade.

Despite its labor-saving features and promise of thrift, the impersonal track system never caught on. Even so, the frenzy for other mechanical contrivances continued. In Hammond, Indiana, the "Driv-O-Matic" Drive-In relied on a conveyor belt to deliver food out to its carhops. By using a continuous belt over 62 feet long, co-owner and inventor Mrs. Edwin Bennett side-stepped the need for girls to run "helter-skelter around the parking lot." When the food appeared at the end of the outgoing belt, the girls would deliver the trays to the appropriate vehicle and return the soiled dishes to the conveyor.

Eventually, systems like these were regarded as curiosities—unique, but certainly not a threat to conventional carhop service. During the early 1950s, the majority of car-dining patrons still preferred personal interaction with a carhop. It was an accepted form of service that had characterized the industry for over three decades. Like the lunch counter waitress and the service station attendant, she was an integral part of roadside culture that couldn't be replaced so easily. At first, the acceptance of minimal carhop service would be slow, but once the idea took root there would be no turning back.

*A*s the consumers of American convenience foods continued to gulp milkshakes

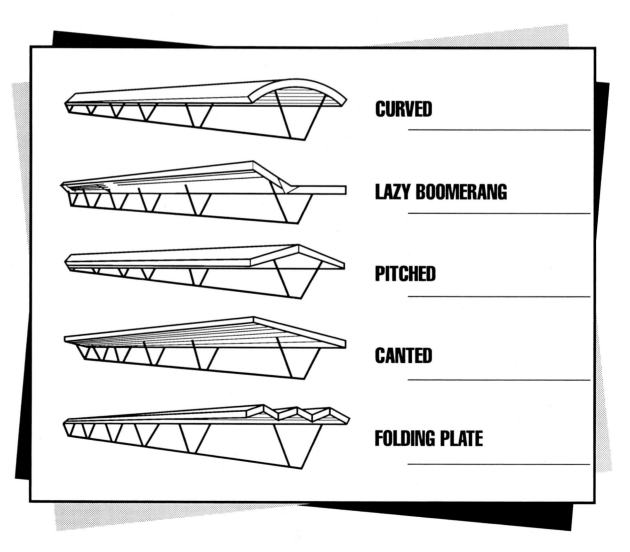

CURVED

LAZY BOOMERANG

PITCHED

CANTED

FOLDING PLATE

and cheeseburgers in the open-air dining rooms, the restaurant industry continued dreaming up new ways to attract customers and increase comfort. One method was the utilization of overhead canopies to provide an oasis of shade, particularly in the hot summer sun of the Southern and Southwestern states. In 1931, Dallas Pig Stand number 2 became America's first curb server to install an elevated canopy of brown canvas. Although business was good during morning hours, it diminished in the afternoon when the sun's heat permeated the parking lot. With this unique covering, the Pig Stand promoted business during the hottest hours, providing customers with luxurious shade.

Surprisingly, it took other drive-in operators almost thirty years to recognize the canopy! By the late fifties, interest picked up and most curb operations were installing some type of raised protection. With a minimal investment in time and materials, any modest refreshment shack could sport an updated appearance with the installation of a suspended overhead roof. The benefits were numerous: not only were canopies instrumental in providing customer comfort, they also improved employee morale. Now, carhops could enjoy the fringe benefit of working under protected coverings in a cool and dry comfort zone. Customers loved the shady parking lots and business improved.

As new materials were developed, the canopy matured. Canvas sheeting was soon replaced by lightweight nylon, laminated with vinyl. Ideal for use in harsh climates, this pliable fabric proved extremely colorfast, wear resistant, and durable. Next, flexible metal panels made their debut, providing manufacturers the perfect material to produce pre-fabricated canopies. Easily assembled on site, drive-in owners could now create stunning structures with minimal effort and investment.

Soon, the reasons for installing a canopy became more than just functional: they were a great decorative element and caught the at-

NOVELTY OF ORDERING BY PHONE INTRIGUES PATRONS

ALL PATRONS RECEIVE EQUAL ATTENTION

CUTS TRIPS IN HALF — 50% FEWER CAR HOPS REQUIRED

FREE MUSIC BUILDS GOOD WILL AND INCREASES PATRONAGE

PATRONS APPRECIATE THE FASTER SERVICE

As carhops were supplanted by vacuum tubes, the radically new format of car service inspired the slogan "Service With the Speed of Sound."

Order Phone Advantages
Remote ordering units at the drive-in offered many advantages—including the elimination of carhops. Motiograph, Inc., of Chicago manufactured the Servus-Fone, an advanced unit promising to "improve your service with half the help."

Teletray Ordering Unit
The Teletray electronic ordering system was a popular model used to speed ordering efficiency at the drive-in of the fifties. Unlike the belt-mounted ordering communicators used today, talking with customers within their cars often required a central operator manning a large, interior switchboard. National Archives

ing and falling plates running its entire length. But none could compare with the "Rock and Roll," a sine-wave copy that featured contrasting colors above and below its crests.

The so called "doodad frame" was another curious addition to the lineup with steel frames 6 by 4 feet, supporting a number of irregularly shaped pieces of metal tensioned by springs. As reported by *Drive-In* magazine in April of 1958, the doodad frames "served as flower gardens filled with color and life, but without the time-consuming necessity for taking care of flowers." The ultimate canopy was finally produced: one that kept customers out of the rain, provided visual enjoyment, and replaced the natural flora of the American roadside. Who needed parks with grass and real trees? The drive-in had it all.

Canopy aesthetics were soon overshadowed by a greater development. In 1955, Buddie's Food 'n Fun opened a new car service outpost in Brooklyn, New York. The gala event featured "Captain Video" who blasted off from the rocket ship "Galaxy" and handed out space cannons and other valuable prizes to the kids. It proved to be a timely promotion, since a number of manufacturers were already introducing futuristic communications equipment to a receptive drive-in market. That year, the Fone-A-Chef Company debuted a thoroughly modern intercom cast of aluminum and finished in "high luster automobile enamel." Borrowing the best features of Detroit's latest cars, Fone-A-Chef's new units featured gleaming tray-bars of chrome and high-fidelity speakers. Car service was entering a new stage.

This Space Age technology—with its promise to keep costs down, send sales soaring, and speed up service—probably originated during the onset of the fifties. More than likely, an enterprising drive-in theater operator got the notion to make his window speakers work both ways. Why not allow the customer to talk into the speaker head instead of just listening to it? With the addition of a few off-

tention of the motorist with the same ease as a large billboard. First implemented by the Illinois-based Dogs 'n Suds chain in 1953, the "Butterfly" canopy featured uplifted "wings" that served as visual magnets. Other assemblies like the "Flying Saucer," a gigantic 40-foot-diameter behemoth, incorporated both nylon sheeting and steel framing. With their grandiose attitude and sparkling colors, these structures were difficult for passing customers to ignore.

During the sixties, Ohio canopy manufacturer Selby Industries took these elaborate creations even further. Selby's "High 'n Hailing" model was the height of modernism: 20-foot parabolas stretched skyward above a flat overhead at intervals of 20 feet. Beneath the arcs, suspended geometrics provided decoration. The "Mountain Range" was a more subdued style, providing angular effects with ris-

the-shelf electrical components, food orders from the snack bar could now be taken directly from cars. At first, a minority of perceptive drive-in owners picked up on the innovation and began to install their own kitchen-based public address amplifiers. It didn't take long for the rest to follow.

When drive-in owner Troy N. Smith stopped at a Louisiana car joint for lunch in 1954, he encountered the cable talk-back system for the first time. He returned to Shawnee, Oklahoma, and enlisted the expertise of a local radio repairman to install one of the parking lot communication systems at his own drive-in. As carhops were supplanted by vacuum tubes, the Top Hat Drive-In became the first Oklahoma eatery to go totally elec

continued on page 136

Placing Order at a Speaker Box
The remote-order speaker box was an advancement that promised to improve the bottom line at America's drive-ins. While this may have been true for the operators, carhops didn't fare so well. As technology replaced footwork, curb-girls were relieved of their duties in large numbers.
National Archives

NOBODY HOPS LIKE SONIC

*"Electrified by the latest in modern gadgetry, curious teens
took to the inventive ordering devices and jumped at the chance to play
fast-food disc jockey within their vehicular cocoons."*

On the outskirts of Shawnee, Oklahoma, where North Harrison Road turns into Highway 18 and the neon turns to woods, Troy Smith purchased a small root beer stand in 1953. He liked the log house that came with the deal and figured he could utilize the soda pop business to finance his ultimate plans of building a family restaurant. In his mind, the cabin out back would become the real goldmine…once he converted it into a full-service eatery.

Smith borrowed the capital needed to improve the stand and wasted no time transforming it. He named it the Top Hat and installed Oklahoma's first drive-in canopies, visually upgrading the structure. Steel supports held the

wooden coverings aloft, offering car customers increased protection from the weather. Next, a series of neatly organized parking stalls were established to improve traffic flow and end congestion, one row on each side of the building. Finally, the shack was modified to allow carhops to pick up their food orders inside.

Convinced he could streamline the process of ordering food, Smith called on a television man to construct an electronic intercom system for the reorganized car lanes. Hot vacuum tubes, mechanical relays, clunky switches, carbon microphones, and thick wiring soon became part of a practical intercom system. Speaker housings much like those used at the drive-in theater contained the bulky components. Cables coiled from each communicator to an upright post. Each parking position had its own ordering unit, every customer a hand-held line to the kitchen. It was another historic first for Oklahoma car customers.

While the new ordering apparatus proved to perform flawlessly, Smith worried that the new technology might not be accepted. To calm his anxiety and ensure the success of his investment, he decided a catchy slogan was needed to generate excitement prior to grand opening. But how could he convey the ideas of speedy delivery and customer service with one simple phrase? He was confident his carhops could outdo the tray-boys at the A&W across town, but he was unsure how to express it. Suddenly, he realized his high-speed ordering boxes held the answer: "Service with the Speed of Sound!" Smith was ready to welcome the public.

Within a matter of weeks, the once inconspicuous root beer stand on the edge of town became the buzz of Shawnee's drive-in restaurant crowd. Suddenly, every curious citizen with a driver's license in their wallet and a gallon of gasoline in their automobile wanted to check out the town's newest carhop eatery. As the fledgling sounds of rock'n'roll tapped out a steady beat, a crowd of motorized youth queued up for the best parking positions. Families followed, station wagons brimming with children. Toddlers pressed inquisitive noses to the glass as their elders shook heads in disbelief. Just what was this futuristic setup?

Electrified by the latest in modern gadgetry, curious teens took to the inventive ordering devices and jumped at the chance to play fast food disc jockey within their vehicular cocoons. For a while, even the car radio took a backseat to the unique ordering gimmick. "Favorite station buttons" introduced by Detroit on the latest models were quickly ignored as the novel telephones were favored.

News of the excitement spread and Smith soon fielded inquiries from dozens of interested entrepreneurs. Former supermarket manager Charlie Pappe was one of the first, anxious to learn how the revolutionary operation worked. A partnership was formed and soon a second Top Hat opened. Two

Top Hat Aristocrat Hamburgers
The Dachshund dog was not only a symbol of the hot dog, but Troy Smith's early drive-in restaurant, the Top Hat. He opened the curb service restaurant during the early fifties and installed electronic speaker boxes to assist customer ordering. Sonic Drive-Ins originated from that first little stand. Courtesy Sonic Industries Inc.

Early Sonic Speed of Sound
During the late fifties, Sonic provided "Service With the Speed of Sound" to its drive-in customers. Signboards depicted all the energy of the atom and its idealized electrical discharge. Scientifically, it may not have been totally correct—although it was fanciful enough to sell hot hamburgers and onion rings. Basically a small rectangular building straddled by two canopies, the first Sonic outlets were simple affairs that offered tasty food. Every car stall had an ordering unit, each customer a "direct line" to the kitchen. Courtesy Sonic Industries Inc.

more units followed, as did plans to franchise the success of the expanding operation in 1959.

The drive-in business begun by Troy Smith with one root beer stand and an idea to speed up service was at the crossroads. Since "Top Hat" was already registered as a trademark, Smith checked the dictionary and discovered his catchy motto could be represented by just one word: Sonic. As America left the age of propellers and entered the jet age, the future of drive-in restaurants was secure. For the next three decades, automotive diners could—and would—get their "Service With the Speed of Sound!" ∎

Electrified by the latest in modern gadgetry, curious teens took to the inventive ordering devices and jumped at the chance to play fast food disc jockey within their vehicular cocoons. The high-speed ordering boxes were truly "Service with the Speed of Sound!"

Sonic Drive-In
By the time C. Stephen Lynn became President and Chief Executive Officer in 1983, Sonic's number had grown to over 900 units. When Lynn and key management completed a leveraged buyout in 1986, Smith's original philosophy that "owners make better managers" helped rocket the organization to prominence. By 1994, Sonic became America's number one drive-in with over 1,300 units in operation. At America's Sonic Drive-Ins, the window-mounted serving tray has been re-incarnated as a one-piece plastic model. The automotive machines of yesteryear sported windows made of flat glass; today, curved glass dictates that the tray mount "hooks" provide extra clearance to keep the tray rigid while installed. Stopping for a 'burger are Clare Patterson and his 1955 Chevrolet and Dan Daniels and his 1939 Cadillac at this East Central, Wichita, Kansas, location.

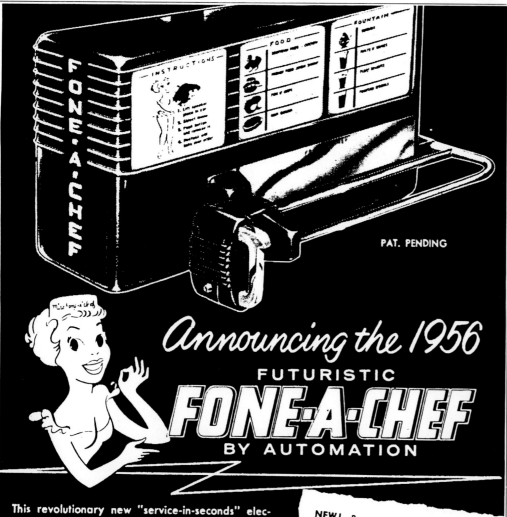

FONE-A-CHEF

INSTRUCTIONS

PAT. PENDING

Announcing the 1956

FUTURISTIC

FONE·A·CHEF

BY AUTOMATION

This revolutionary new "service-in-seconds" electronic ordering and music system for DRIVE-INS, engineered by automation specialists and designed by Detroit automobile stylists, will . . .

⭐ **SEND YOUR SALES SOARING!**

⭐ **KEEP YOUR COSTS DOWN!**

⭐ **SPEED YOUR SERVICE!**

NEW! Styled for '56, a streamlined *Automation* TWO-CAR SERVING STATION . . . of cast aluminum finished in high-lustre automobile enamel . . . with smart-looking, high fidelity, two-way speakers and brilliantly direct-lighted MENU AREAS . . . and with gleaming, all-chrome tray bars.

NEW! Portable *Automation* REMOTE CONTROL ORDER-TAKER that's easier to operate than home telephone (no special switchboard operator training)! This revolutionary unit can be plugged in at chef's or cashier's station when traffic is light. You use as many of these units and operators as you need. Built with the same precision and quality as "Automation Controls," used widely in automobile industry.

- Competitively Priced—Delivery in 4 to 6 weeks!
- Distributors: A few choice territories still available!

ACT TODAY!
WRITE, WIRE
OR PHONE . . .

FONE·A·CHEF Division of Automation Products Corp.
• 109 East Nine Mile Road •
Ferndale 20, Michigan • LIncoln 7-0515

Designers and Manufacturers of Automation Controls for the Automobile Industry

continued from page 131

tronic. The radically new format of car service inspired the slogan "Service With the Speed of Sound" and the name for a new chain. It was the beginning of the Sonic Drive-Ins and a new dimension in curbside service.

With its practicality proven, the rush to install electronic ordering networks was on. From 1951 until the end of the fifties, a wide assortment of models was introduced. All the industry publications featured articles on the two-ways, introducing the modern restauranteur to an engaging roster of brands with names that exuded speed and convenience: the Aut-O-Hop, Ordaphone, Fon-A-Chef, Servus-Fone, Teletray, Dine-A-Mike, TelAutograph, Dine-a-Com, Auto-Dine, and Electro-Hop. Each boasted myriad features that included internally illuminated menus, record changers, dual-speech amplifiers, an ability to play music, and spring-mounted posts that bounced back when hit by an automobile!

With the acceptance of the hard-wired communications systems, surplus wireless equipment found its way onto the asphalt, too. Portable "walkie-talkies" proven during World War II were soon utilized by drive-ins looking for a memorable gimmick. Serving customers on Kentucky's Dixie Highway, Schilling's Drive-In chose the "Wireless Expeditor" for its carhop-to-kitchen communiqués. Customers were impressed with the hand-held devices toted to their cars and showed inter-

Auto-Dine
ELECTRONIC CARHOP
SPEAK CLEARLY

est by spending more money on hamburgers.

Milwaukee's Ace Foods followed the radio trend with portable, eight-pound transceivers of their own. Operating on a short-wave radio band and licensed by the Federal Communications Commission with their own call letters, three roving radio girls relayed food tickets from a 136-car lot to a central control dispatcher based in the kitchen. Over 950 customers could be served nightly with the shoulder-strap devices, with more efficiency than five carhops on the run. This was definitely the stuff science fiction was made of, well received by a public ravenous for images of the future and the latest in labor-saving devices. Now, customers had an instant way to make their requests known. The carhops had electronic allies—or did they?

Planning their strategy for the future, the owners of America's drive-ins had an ulterior motive: improve the bottom line. High labor costs, training, turnover, and other problems concerning employee relations were becoming more of a deterrent for using real, live waitresses. For many, it became evident that an inanimate machine offered a lot less trouble for a one-time investment. More important, radio speaker boxes were never late for work and didn't talk back when they were told to do something. Taking the lead followed by the McDonald brothers more than ten years earlier, drive-ins "upgraded" by methodically eliminating their surplus parking lot personnel.

By the 1960s, multiple trips back and forth to the automobile became a tired custom of the past. With the aid of electrical impulses, the curb-girl now had only one complete circuit to make: one trip to deliver the food and drinks, the other to retrieve a tray full of dishes...and her tip.

During the extra time freed up by the speedy ordering practice, the remaining curb-girls had pause to consider their pole-mounted helpers. Sure, intercoms made their work more efficient, but how long would it take be-

fore the last of the carhops were replaced? Those with any sense could see that the entire concept of the carhop was in danger. The unseen specter of remote menus and the drive-thru window were already being refined for tomorrow's restaurant designs.

What should have been a positive force for improvement slowly turned into a negative contribution to the drive-in's denigration. The once-elegant concept of bringing food and drink out to people parked curbside was being improved...right out of existence.

In the end, the advent of technological aids would prove to be the first nudge toward a more impersonal roadside. One particularly outspoken manager summed up the attitude in an industry magazine: "we don't have to take a lot of time selecting people with an education. If she can smile, if she can talk, and if she is nice, she doesn't have to be a salesman anymore...because we can do that from the switchboard." The quest for faster service, more customers, larger food sales, higher

continued on page 141

Only Aut-O-Hop Has AMG!
Intercom manufacturers employed every gimmick they could think of to sell their new units. Special circuitry, noise canceling microphones, and pre-recorded messages were the latest improvements. The carhop was suddenly outmoded—or was she?

Fone-A-Chef
Opposite, far left, the 1956 Fone-A-Chef was the future incarnate. As this magazine ad promised, "This revolutionary new 'service-in-seconds' electronic ordering and music system for Drive-Ins engineered by automation specialists and designed by Detroit automobile stylists, will send your sales soaring!"

Auto Radio Rock 'n' Roll

Electric Push-Button Tuning
Soon after there was a radio in every car, push-button tuning was invented to allow instant access to your favorite station.

With their 100-watt transmitter broadcasting returns of the Harding-Cox election of 1920, Pittsburgh's KDKA became America's first commercial radio station. Imitators soon followed, and within a couple of years, almost two-dozen stations were sending radio waves into the ether. By 1923, the kilocycle band became crowded: the number of licensed stations jumped from just sixty to 573!

As hooking radio transmissions from the sky became a popular pastime for home hobbyists, motorists became intrigued with the possibilities. Radio magazines anticipated the interest and began detailing do-it-yourself plans for mobile radio-receivers.

The Automobile Radio Corporation sidestepped the craze for kits with their "Transitone," designed to fit behind the instrument panel of almost any vehicle. While its large cabinet housed vacuum tubes, batteries were installed under the floorboards. A rather cumbersome horn mounted above the windshield served as a loudspeaker.

By the close of the thirties, a range of models featuring remote control tuning were introduced. Soon, decorative speaker grills emulated the grandiose chrome of the jukebox. Overly embellished with thick, gleaming chrome, the parallel ribs of the automotive speaker compartment comprised a substantial part of the dash. The car radio had arrived—in style!

As automatic transmissions came into use, improved radios that tuned themselves followed, mimicking the ease of their powertrain cousins. Zenith debuted its "Radionic" unit, featuring foot control, in 1946. One year later, Delco chose to continue the trend with its steering-column-controlled "Signal Seeking" model. Consumers liked the improvements—and within a few years, over 7 million motorists were snapping their fingers to the sounds.

It wasn't long before young listeners availed themselves of the convenience and discovered a new reason to borrow the family car: music! By the time most amplifying tubes and components were miniaturized in 1951, WJW disc jockey Allen "Moon Dog" Freed began spinning a new type of music in Cleveland. As the phenomenon spread, push-button tuners with improved circuitry were just the thing to capture the new sounds of "rock'n'roll."

Suddenly, dashboards came alive with an electrified beat, galvanizing a new generation of drive-in car customers together with its hypnotic rhythms. While carhops stepped in time to the thumping backbeat of the bass, listeners were mesmerized by the raucous sounds.

Future teenage idols sang of drag racing, dancing, and romance, one of the radical new Fender electric guitars twanging out the battle cry for changes to come. From chromed slits in the dashboard, the music of a new generation made its way into the hearts and minds of youthful car culture.

Now inseparable, the drive-in eatery, the automobile, and the car radio became one. The act of parking under the muted circle of drive-in neon with your date—a cheeseburger in one hand, the other around your girl—was now a complete ritual. For couples huddled together at drive-ins all across America, the warm glow emanating from the tuning dial became a new communal campfire.

More than just a novelty, the car radio was now an electronic bridge to a new era. A point of connection between the vanguards waiting for their moment to come—one with time for new ideas, new morals, and new music. "One, two, three o'clock, four o'clock rock ...." ∎

Crosley Roamio Car Radio
Once the radio receiver became a permanent feature of the American motorcar, the public began to view the luxury as a basic right. When rock'n'roll music began energizing the airwaves during the fifties, there was no turning back—the car radio became a vital link to the car culture of youth. Living without one was tough.

5144·27

Wolfman Jack Doing His Stuff
The howling, prowling Wolfman Jack was the behind-the-scenes alter-ego for the teenagers in the movie American Graffiti of 1973. Without him, rock'n'roll would not have been the same. Frozen Popsicle anyone? Museum of Modern Art/Film Stills Archive, Copyright © by Universal City Studios, Inc. Courtesy of MCA Publishing Rights, a Division of MCA Inc.

continued from page 137

profit margins, and fewer hassles with employees brought the drive-in industry to the edge.

While tiny transistors replaced vacuum tubes, America's perceptions about everyday life were changing. Postwar prosperity became equated with faster cars, faster shopping, faster working, faster living, faster eating, and finally, faster dying. Flickering images flashing on the television screen became a substitute for real life, re-formatting the way people thought about authority, automobiles, and the food they consumed while cruising through the roadside carnival.

As society began its self-inflicted launch towards a higher speed, new ideas and dreams and frustrations were slowly taking root in the youth of the nation. In the new environment of automation, respect for the establishment was eroding as social misfits known as juvenile delinquents, or JDs, made their presence known. Trouble was just around the corner for the outdoor car eatery in the form of rowdy behavior, vandalism, and endless loitering. As heat lamps were switched on in franchised fast-food kitchens all across America, the infrared glow above the stack of pre-made hamburgers was a signal that the nation's drive-in restaurants would never be the same. The heyday was about to end. ∎

Dari-ette Drive-In Speaker Box
During the 1950s, manufacturers developed a variety of drive-in communications gear. The hand-held speaker box and microphone combination was one of the most widely used designs, taking the nation's drive-in customers into the electronic age. This pole-mounted speaker box continues to offer radio-relayed orders to the kitchen at the Dari-ette Drive-In in St. Paul, Minnesota. Michael Dregni

Dari-ette Drive-In
Left, the Dari-ette on St. Paul, Minnesota's, east side began life as a simple ice cream stand in the 1950s, adding on drive-in parking, speaker boxes, and a small inside dining area in later years—all built around that original building. Dari-ette is famous for its Italian spaghetti sauce, and is probably the only drive-in ever to offer spaghetti as a side dish with a hamburger. The rich, spicy sauce is also available for take out by the pint, quart, or gallon. Michael Dregni

Hicks Drive-In Restaurant
Hick's Kentucky drive-in specialized in steaks, chops, and chicken dinners. At one time, it was a major food stop for motorists making their way down the Dixie Highway. Caufield and Shook Collection, Photographic Archives, University of Louisville

Hicks Drive-In Interior
Right, the interior of Hick's Drive-In featured many of the futuristic building materials of the 1940s and 1950s. Glass block comprised the dining counter. Caufield and Shook Collection, Photographic Archives, University of Louisville

A HEAVEN FOR HOT RODS

During the time of postwar prosperity, America's love affair with the motorcar turned to obsession. Automotive manufacturers turned out a parade of new models and soon, the desire for bigger, flashier, more comfortable vehicles turned to nationwide lust. Unofficially, the timeworn styles were dead: rocketlike tailfins, massive grills, acres of chrome, and a cushioned ride were in.

For Detroit's auto companies, 1955 proved to be a banner year; all records were exceeded as production reached 9 million vehicles! As the consumer frenzy for new models reached its peak, a surplus of outmoded flivvers were soon retired. Former favorites were sold as used cars to new owners or eventually handed down to children coming of age. Those exceeding their limit of usefulness were unceremoniously dumped.

In road-dense cities such as Los Angeles, New York, and Detroit—where cars and culture mixed—suburban neighborhoods were often littered with discarded vehicles. Backyards, driveways, and vacant lots became the final resting grounds for many abandoned jalopies. Parked among weeds, they were left to rust—or to wait for their day of revitalization.

Fortunately, their time away from the fast-track was limited. A steady supply of teenagers reaching the age of eligibility for a driver's license took immediate advantage of the surplus. Eager to join the fast lane of motoring in the most economical way possible, a majority of unused car parts and bodies were efficiently recycled by enthusiastic teens.

Promptly, Ford flathead engines were removed, transmission casings cannibalized, steering wheels pulled, fenders appropriated, radiators revived, and tires unbolted. During the afterhours sessions at the corner gas station that followed, an unrelated conglomeration of auto parts were carefully united. With a tentative spark of loose ignition wires, a new form of motorized folk art rumbled to life: the American "hot rod."

With a little imagination and a lot of sweat, the burned-out shells of Fords and Chevrolets were transformed into perky T-bucket roadsters, hi-boys, low-boys, lead sleds, and customs. Family sedans junked during the days of the Depression were chopped and channeled, Frenched and flamed, until they bore no resemblance to their original identity. Fenders were removed and bumpers replaced by nerf bars. Even hubcaps became reflective bowls of chrome.

While painted flames became the street rod's ultimate trademark, gray primer assumed dominance as the every man's paint. In the unfinished reality of homemade car construction, perfection was not that important. Missing a few dashboard knobs or door panels didn't make a hot rod any less cool. Searching for elusive parts, working with friends, and taking a show-off cruise thru the local drive-in restaurant was really the most. Unfortunately, the flamboyant displays of speed and the accidents that followed cast a negative light on the hot rod. Ever vigilant for traffic safety and excessive noise, the cops made a living out of harassing the homebuilt carboys—even when they reserved their high-speed sprints for the quarter-mile strip. For the establishment, the hot rodder and juvenile delinquent became one.

Sure, there were a lot of incidents where souped-up vehicles screamed out of the drive-in with trays still attached—milkshake glasses and silverware trailing behind in a cloud of dust. So what? It was only a small part of growing up, a brief moment in the timeline of the road when the drive-in restaurant really was the heaven for hot rods. ■

Cruise Night
A deuce coupe (1932 Ford) with a chopped top sits proudly at a California Bob's Big Boy —once a popular haven for hot rods in Southern California. ©1994 Kent Bash

RUTH FORKE, TEXAS PIG STAND

Ruth Forke began her job as a carhop when she was only sixteen years old. It all started back in 1939 when a downstairs neighbor was working as a curb server at the Flores Street Pig Stand in San Antonio. Dressed in a fetching ensemble consisting of a blue jacket with four pockets, gray slacks adorned with a dark blue stripe, and a gray "air cadet" hat trimmed in blue, she was a sight that conjured up all the images of patriotism and service at a time when many young boys were going off to war.

When the neighbor left for work, Ruth caught sight of her snappy uniform, shifting her own imagination into overdrive. Suddenly, Ruth wanted to be a carhop too. A short while later, Ruth joined the Pig Stand ranks. She commuted to work on the bus and frequently fielded questions from passengers curious about her uniform (everyone thought she was an Air Force girl). For a teenager, this public notoriety was a lot of fun. Eventually, the military-style uniforms were replaced by more feminine styles, including a motif comprised of a satin dress and white boots.

Fortunately, there was more to the Pig Stands than just fancy uniforms: Working a double-shift, Ruth could often pull in $80–$90 in one night! While the wages of 10¢ per hour were minimal pay, the tips were phenomenal. Of course, it was a lot of hard work—labor that eventually paid off in a management position. Ultimately, illness cut Ruth's career short in the mid-eighties, forcing her to leave the drive-in business for good. "If I could, I would still be working there today," she says. Working as a Pig Stands carhop was very, very good for Ruth Forke. ■

DOUMAR'S CONES AND BARBECUE

*"Amidst the growing atmosphere of fast food banality,
Al Doumar rediscovered his hook—a bonafide skill and culinary folk talent
that none of the modern burger shacks could ever hope to replicate."*

Today, Norfolk, Virgina's, Monticello Avenue is paved over with a dizzying procession of fast-food restaurants. Illuminated marquees vie for the attention of passing traffic, obscuring the view of the roadside. In an unceasing battle for the motorist's dollar, franchised giants wage an unending war. Burger King, McDonald's, Kentucky Fried Chicken, Hardee's, and Wendy's all fight for dominance with meal deals and price combo strategies.

Right there, smack dab in the middle of it all, Albert Doumar sells North Carolina-style barbecue (made with vinegar) and ice cream cones, content to take on all the competition. He's been holding his own for the past sixty years now, ever since his father George's ice cream concession at Virginia's Ocean View Park was obliterated by the hurricane in 1933. Back then, his dad had exclusive rights to sell frozen desserts at the seaside resort. When the winds of change literally destroyed his operation, all that remained were the machinery and fixtures used to make his living.

Albert Doumar and Doumar's Drive-In
Albert Doumar's Virginia drive-in is straddled by two of today's largest fast-food chains: Wendy's and Taco Bell. In fact, almost the entire stretch of Norfolk's Monticello Avenue is paved over with fast-food outlets! Hardees, Burger King, and a trio of McDonald's restaurants dominate the strip. To make matters worse, another fast-food chain is planning to build a structure right across the street. Does all the competition worry Doumar? Not in the least! He is a true survivor in the competitive arena of drive-in food. © 1994, W. S. McIntosh

Among the debris sat what would one day become the saving grace of a new enterprise: a small, four-iron waffle machine made of cast iron and brass. To the unknowing, it may have appeared to be another piece of junk to be cleared away, but to Doumar it was much more. This was, after all, the very machine inspired by the waffle iron Uncle Abe used to create the World's Fair Cornucopia in 1904. With it came the power to produce the best cones ever tasted by man! The only requirements to reap a bounty of 200 cones an hour were hand-eye coordination and a knack for old-fashioned showmanship.

In short order, the small machine joined the rest of the salvageable equipment and was moved farther inland to Norfolk's Monticello Avenue. The family operation reopened in 1934 as a drive-in restaurant with carhop service and offered barbecue pork sandwiches, limeades, and soda fountain treats to the local patrons. As curb-serving competitors such as Bill's, Frank's, and Bobby's catered to beer-drinking clientele, Doumar's favored the family crowd by featuring delicious waffle cones filled with frosty chocolate, vanilla, strawberry, and butter pecan ice cream.

At the time, the legendary waffle maker that set the Doumar legacy into motion was put into retirement. A much larger, electrically operated unit boasting eighteen irons and forced gas circulation was used to crank out the tasty ice cream holders. Eventually, the cone-spewing behemoth disintegrated and a succession of smaller machines were recruited to manufacture the latticed forms. Meanwhile, the art and style of cone-making passed down so many years ago—Al learned how to make his first cone when he was fourteen—was beginning to be taken for granted.

As franchise after franchise began to set up shop along the boulevard, the climate of competition began to change. Suddenly, all of the barbecue stands began dying out, leaving Doumar's as the last remaining outlet. When the golden arches materialized in 1958, the interest in pork sandwiches faded and business experienced a drop. As the purveyors of convenience foods became absorbed with the flashy promise of a quick hamburger, Al Doumar realized that something had to be done—fast!

Promptly, the "old number one" waffle gizmo was taken out of mothballs and set up on the sidewalk in front of the drive-in. Doumar began pouring batter, flipping irons, and forming cones as he fielded questions from curious customers. The gimmick worked, and soon both young and old were taken in by the unpretentious show. With no artificial flavors, colorings, or preservatives added, mouth-watering cones rolled easily off the seasoned waffle iron (Al calls it "Grandma's Teflon") into the hands of a pleased audience.

Amidst the growing atmosphere of fast food banality, Al Doumar rediscovered his hook—a bonafide skill and culinary folk talent that none of the modern burger shacks could ever hope to replicate. With that talent intact, Doumar's Cones and Barbecue is poised to enter the next century—confident to base a drive-in business on one simple metal machine. ∎

Doumar's Other Drive-In
The enterprising Doumar family expanded operations into Detroit and the Florida area. These drive-ins unfortunately did not survive when the fast-food giants moved into their territory. Preziosi Postcards

Wanda Morris Holding Two Trays
Left, carhop Wanda Morris has worked at Albert Doumar's Norfolk drive-in for over twenty years. She's proven that a carhop can beat an electronic ordering menu and drive-thru window any day of the week. For her, toting two trays filled with the tasty barbecue and ice cream cones that made Doumar's a local legend has become second-nature. © 1994, John Witt, Richmond Newspapers, Inc.

CHAPTER FOUR

DRIVE-IN DEMISE AND RE-RISE

During the twilight of the fifties, youngsters coming of age in America desperately desired a place they could call their own—an up-to-date hangout where they could act freely, make their own choices, listen to their kind of music, and gather with others of like mind. Increasingly disillusioned with the lifestyles of their elders, teenagers began to break free from societal constraints to seek a measure of personal autonomy.

Social pressures peaked when planned communities modeled after Levittown transformed farmland into middle-class conformity. To make the dream of a home with white picket fence affordable for returning veterans, room designs were small—only large enough for studying and sleeping. As a result, entertaining friends was difficult. Besides, adults screened visitors and dictated dinner time. As mother toiled over her new electric range defrosting peas for supper, father switched on "The Texaco Star Theater" and reclined in his easy chair with paper and pipe. The same scenario was repeated in row after row of identical homes on carbon-copy streets. While this model of postwar life was ideal for adults, it was not so idyllic for teenagers.

Fortunately, there was one outlet where the young citizens of suburbia could exercise their freedom. At any time, day or night, one could escape the stifling confines of the tract-house lifestyle and find fulfillment with a sack of hot French fries and a cheeseburger. The only requirements: the ownership of a car or the ability to borrow one. Within minutes, one could motor down to the local milkshake watering hole and enter a new world: slap the car into park, kill the engine, order some food, flirt with the carhops, smoke some cigarettes, fiddle with the radio, or cuddle with a sweetheart...free from parental control. For the teen, the drive-in restaurant became a home away from home.

Congregating at the local tray food retreat soon became an obsession of the adolescent.

Steak 'n Shake Kids and Shakes
Right, hunger, a station wagon full of kids, and a busy mom meant only one thing during the 1960s: a trip to Steak 'n Shake! With window trays stacked to the hilt with Tru-Flavor milkshakes and all sorts of food delights, it was a time a child would remember for the rest of his life. Courtesy Steak 'n Shake, Inc.

Sonic Drive-In
Previous pages, cruising down to the local drive-in restaurant was a popular pastime of youth during the 1950s and 1960s. On almost any night of the week, teenagers could be found there in great numbers—socializing, eating hamburgers, and tinkering with their cars. Back then, spying a shiny 1955 Chevrolet (Clare Patterson, owner) or a classic 1939 Cadillac (Dan Daniels, owner) would not have been at all unusual. East Central, Wichita, Kansas.

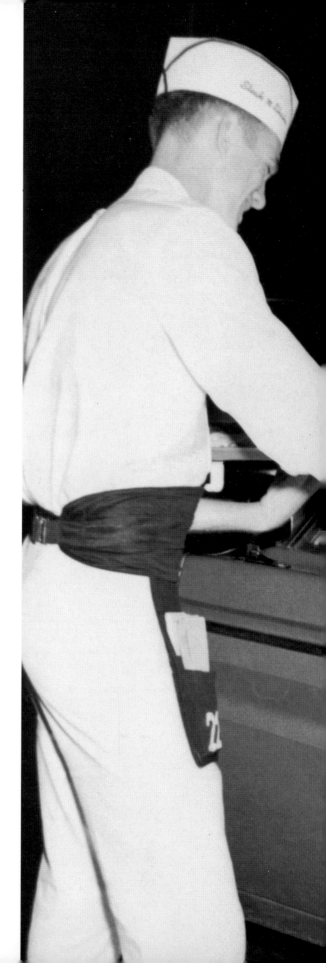

Along with pep rallies, football games, and the high school hop, this open-air gathering place run on liquid cola and ground beef was an appropriate venue for teenage socialization. After the final school bell, it became a popular destination to rendezvous with peers, find romantic interests, and come fender to fender with rivals. Without the constant scrutiny found at indoor eateries, kids could relax. Best of all, one wasn't required to leave the security of the car. If desired, the entire visit to the drive-in could be experienced from the comfort of the automotive shell. Automotive prowess now defined one's social status.

As America entered the sixties, the teenage takeover of the nation's drive-ins began to degrade the atmosphere for others. Now, the family trade was avoiding the carhop domain entirely—and who could blame them? In the most extreme situations, cars remained parked for long periods as boisterous teenagers blasted loud rock'n'roll music on their car radios. Amidst the din of yelling and all manner of carrying on, many kids drank beer and engaged in fist fights. When guitarist Chuck Berry released "No Particular Place to Go" in 1964, it sounded like he had the drive-ins in mind. Finally, the nation's restless rabble of teenagers had an anthem for their nightly ritual of "cruisin' and playin' the radio."

By 1966, over 78 million cars packed America's corridors of asphalt, making the inner circle at the drive-in eatery a crowded place. With nothing to do and no place to do it, food businesses along the strip became waypoints for gasoline-guzzling adolescents.

Rowdyism replaced relaxation. To park and enjoy a meal became almost impossible, as cars stalled for hours in the lots, their occupants "hanging out" until something eventful happened—while food and drink orders were kept to a minimum. Cars never left and paying customers were hindered from using the drive-ins at all. Revenues began to suffer.

Ironically, the drive-ins themselves were partly to blame: with circular layouts providing ease of access and traffic flow, they invited habitual cruising. As a result, a continuous train

CRUISIN' THE MAIN STREET STRIP

During the 1950s, it seemed that all of America's commerce had suddenly become an extension of the automobile. Society mobilized, taking entertainment at drive-in theaters and eating meals from behind the

Lovers At Doumar's Drive-In
Gloria Harper of Oscar Smith High School and Tommy Bland, all-state full-back of Maury High School, dine at Doumar's Drive-In in 1956. This favorite high school hangout was paid full tribute in the 1956 Oscar Smith High School Yearbook. The fifties—we remember them well: the boy, the girl, the car, and of course, the drive-in! Courtesy of Albert Doumar

dashboard. Shopping centers, gas stations, supermarkets, car dealerships, and drive-in food stands became the new crossroads for social connection.

So dominant was the influence of the motorcar that even ordinary routes of passage became part of the action. Without any stimulating activities to call their own, the commercial "strip" became the playground for adolescent youth. Hypnotized by the prosperous imagery and inebriated with the freedom of the automobile, teens clogged the major business corridors more than ever before.

For the postwar generation weaned on personal mobility, the act of "cruising" quickly became a national pastime. Since gasoline was cheap and egress over the public roads free, recreational driving reached a new level of popularity. "Motorvating" down bustling Main Street to see the sights, meet members of the opposite sex, and show off one's car was elevated to a defined social activity. The horseless carriage had evolved into a portable amusement compartment.

In towns small and large, Saturday nights were reluctantly relinquished for the motorized rituals of youth. As the sun gave way to the electric hum of neon, the asphalt stage came alive with the sounds of tuned headers and dashboard radios. One carload at a time, the main "drag" welcomed four-wheel contestants onto the playing field. By 10 o'clock, the divided blacktop was packed from curb to curb with music and motion.

As the aroma of cheeseburgers punctuated each block, all manner of motor vehicle took to the streets to see and be seen. Donning ducktail doos, "low riders" moved along pavement in white-walled lead sleds. Garage mechanics who knew how to mate three deuces with a flathead rode herd in custom hot rods. Jocks and the so-called social elite joined the frenzy, piloting classy Corvettes and other stock vehicles. For the unfortunate few without wheels, the family station wagon proved a dismal contender.

Regardless of the vehicle type used, the basic parameters of cruising quickly crystallized: guide a car down the strip at slow speed, wave at friends, and attempt to make new ones. For the boys, looking cool was a high priority. Racking the pipes and laying a little rubber at the green became part of the show. Amused by the boulevard strut of the motorized male, carloads of girls engaged in "Chinese fire drills" and preened to capture their share of the attention.

If the action reached a level of boredom for either group, any number of local eateries could be frequented for a change of atmosphere. To avoid spending a lot of money and being kicked out, only one of the car occupants would order French fries and Coke. At each drive-in to follow, the restrained ordering procedure was repeated, until ultimately all passengers had eaten. For a minimal expenditure, a carload of teenagers could cruise the town and do "the loop."

By the end of the fifties, the car-crazed high school crowd had established important tenets of motorized culture. Riding the Main continued to root itself as an established tradition of American youth. Van Nuys Boulevard, Sunset Strip, or the countless other roads across the nation—it didn't matter. A full tank of gas, a warm evening, and a carload of friends would always mean one thing: cruising the Main Street strip. ∎

of unwanted automobiles streamed unhindered from the main road. Kids rolled their tires at an excruciatingly slow clip—scanning the stalls for boyfriends, girlfriends, and acquaintances. When they reached the end of the lot and exited to the street, a loop of the block was made and the circuit repeated until the night ended or they were chased down by a police cruiser. Locked in by the heavy traffic, those already positioned in the service lanes remained there. Congestion, confusion, and arguments resulted.

Although only one-fourth of the nation's drive-ins reported problems with youthful customers, the situation appeared out of control to many. With over 2,000 drive-in eateries, California experienced the brunt of the problems, followed by Texas and the Great Lakes regions. Isolated incidents cast a bad light on them all, including those that employed techniques to control exuberant customers.

During the mid-1960s, the establishment's negative view of the drive-in was exacerbated

AN AMERICAN INTERNATIONAL PICTURE

by a chilling report from Camarillo, California. From the first day he purchased The Bullet Drive-In, owner Violney Robison could tell he was going to have problems with his business.

continued on page 158

Hot-Rod Girl and Hot Rod Gang
Hot rods powered a new breed of youngsters to cruise Main Street and hang out at the drive-ins. Called juvenile delinquents, or JDs, they were personified by James Dean in Rebel Without A Cause, as well as the slew of B-budget exploitation films that ran in a never-ending chase across the screens of America's drive-in theaters. Ron Main/Main Attractions

Second Life for a Drive-In
Left, Minneapolis' two Nora's restaurants were once hopping Porky's Drive-Ins located at both ends of the Lake Street strip like magnetic poles for hot-rod cruisers. Both Porky's turned off their neon in the 1970s. In the 1980s, the car stalls were walled in and the drive-ins reopened as indoor sitdown restaurants.

DINING AT THE DRIVE-IN THEATER

Drive-In Theater Brochure
As the brochure promised, "Romance by Moonlight." Courtesy Chuck Sturm

In the early thirties, Richard Hollingshead had a grand idea. Why not show moving pictures in the great outdoors where people could watch from their cars? After all, the drive-in restaurant was a popular gathering spot. Extending this in-your-car convenience to include the silver screen seemed only natural.

Tentatively, he proceeded to position a projector on the hood of his car. Nailed to a nearby tree, a makeshift screen became the beam's focus. Hollingshead like what he saw, and three years later, the basic elements of his outdoor theater concept were refined and patented. In June of 1933, the first outdoor theater in America where "people could enjoy talkies in their car" opened for business in Camden, New Jersey.

As the novelty of viewing moving pictures within a motorcar slowly gained popularity, car customers realized something was missing: they were hungry! Claudette Colbert's hitchhiking scene in *It Happened One Night* was no time to drive off to the neighborhood Pig Stand. Fortunately, operators were already one frame ahead. "Dining room" was already being added to the varied list of convenient automotive attributes.

By the late forties, most food concessions at the "Ozoners" were basic stands. Positioned at one or two serving stations, counter girls took the orders, made food, and returned change. Inefficient and slow, it was a frustrating process for those anxious to return to their vehicles. During intermission, conditions only worsened. A throng of customers converged on the ill-equipped shacks, turning off eager film fans in the process.

Further investigation revealed much of the snack bar patronage was lost by people not wanting to leave their cars. Often, a long walk to the stand was necessary. Carrying food by hand proved limiting since only a finite amount of burgers and beverages could be hand-held.

Bringing food out to the customers was a much better method. By the mid-1940s, vendors toting shoulder-carried snack-packs loudly hawked their wares among the sea of rubber and chrome. At many theaters, tricycles were introduced to cover long distances. These were soon superseded by elaborate pushcarts capable of holding all sorts of food. Summoned by cards placed on the windshield, these "Buffeterias" roamed the lot in search of hungry customers.

Still, there were problems: as the diminutive casters of these mobile vending carts forged a path through the gravel, patrons nearby would be disturbed by the noise. The shear weight of the 100-pound supply of hot dogs, soft drinks, and popcorn made them difficult to maneuver. Artificial viewing burms in the viewing lot did not help matters.

At the dawn of the fifties, a solution arrived in the form of the "talk-back system." Hungry movie watchers at the Park Drive-In in Greensboro, North Carolina, could now depress a button on the side of their speaker, instantly summoning a central switchboard operator. Carhops would pick up the orders and deliver, while pleased car customers eased back into the vinyl and enjoyed the film, without missing a single scene.

Eventually, the impracticality of in-car service lost out at the rampatoriums. Dimly illuminated lots were dangerous, a tangle of speaker cords and trash a detriment. The centrally located snack-bar, or "profiteria," became the safest choice. No longer commercially viable, carhops were out; cafeteria-style was in. Drive-in movie dining entered headlong into the netherworld of self-serve. ∎

Drive-In THEATRE
REFRESHMENTS

*Delightful and Tasty Refreshments served in
Your Car while You enjoy the Picture*

**IF YOU DESIRE REFRESHMENTS DURING
THE SHOW PLACE THIS CARD UNDER
YOUR WINDSHIELD WIPER
UNIFORMED ATTENDANT WILL SERVE YOU**

PRICE LIST

How
Many?

Coca-Cola (Ice cold in bottles)   .10c

ALL OTHER SOFT DRINKS.....

HAMBURGERS—Jumbo Si

RED HOTS .....

MALTED MILKS—

MILK SHAKES ...

BLACK COWS ...

ICE CREAM CUPS

CHOCOLATE ICE C

COFFEE (with pure

FRESH HOT POPCOR

SALTED PEANUTS ..

POTATO CHIPS ......

CIGARETTES ....

**RESTAURANT IS LOCATED IN THE
CENTER OF AISLE 5**

"Another Drive-In Service"

FREE!   FREE!

ADMITS

CAR and DRIVER

Golden Spike DRIVE-IN
THEATRE

114th and Dodge Sts. — TE. 2211

Courtesy of . . . . .

GOOD ANY DAY EXCEPT Saturday, Sunday, Holidays

*W*hy not show moving pictures in the great outdoors where people could watch from their cars? After all, the drive-in restaurant was a popular gathering spot. In June of 1933, the first outdoor theater in America where "people could enjoy talkies in their car" opened for business in Camden, New Jersey.

Drive-In Theater Card
For service, you simply placed the card underneath your windshield wiper and the uniformed attendant was at your beck and call. Courtesy Chuck Sturm

Abandoned Drive-In
Today, most of the drive-in restaurants adored during the fifties have disappeared from the roadside landscape, such as this relic in Fort Worth, Texas. While car service relics are hard to come by, some decaying survivors can be found in regions where the real estate prices have not exceeded common sense.

continued from page 155
Right away, youths drove in after school and began to plug up his driveways. They double-parked all over the lot and refused to move their vehicles when asked nicely. What's worse, they ignored the rules of deportment, substituting disrespect and anarchy.

When Robison went out to the lot one night to ask the kids to leave, bedlam broke out as they shouted him down and refused to budge. He returned to the store room to gain his composure and fell to a heart attack. Meanwhile, the delinquents in the parking lot

were carrying on and laughing about how they had won out. Robison's unfortunate death pointed to a system that needed rethinking given the type of "patrons" now ruining it for the majority.

When neighborhoods adjacent to America's drive-ins began complaining to local government about the mayhem, municipal ordinances were introduced to curb the unrestrained curb servers. Laws outlawed the act of cruising around in an automobile simply "for the thrill of it" and even banned loitering in parking lots. Curfews cut back afterhours traffic. Some regulations dictated that litter be cleared regularly, while others called for fences to enclose the ruckus. When shielding the public from the commotion proved ineffective, a handful of ordinances attempted to eliminate carhop service completely. As if they didn't have enough problems, drive-in owners were being held legally accountable for what happened on, and even near, their lots.

For many establishments, the ordinances alone were not enough to stem the growing tide of teenagers. Many went on to contract the services of police officers and posted patrols to preclude fights and other rambunctious behavior. Entry gates were also installed. As silent sentinels, they effectively controlled exit by way of a token or quarter. If a customer drove in and ordered food, a free exit coin was given. When a teen attempted to slink through with the express purpose of checking out the scene, he was required to pay for the liberty. Unfortunately, this controlling attempt

Coffee-Shop Sign of the Times
California led the nation with coffee-shops during the sixties, popularizing the idea that interior seating served more customers with less hassle. It didn't take long for the notion to spread nationwide, decimating the drive-ins. Broadway Pig Stand, San Antonio, Texas

Decayed Drive-In Sign Pointing Back in Time
Left, another sign of the times.... By the end of the 1960s, many of the classic drive-ins were boarded up and ready for the bulldozer. This old drive-in sign along the Berlin Turnpike in Connecticut is a streetside survivor.

Classic Sign
Right, Speedy points the way to the Downey, California, McDonald's. David Fetherston

Classic McDonald's
Below, one of the last of the early McDonald's still standing, this classic restaurant in Downey, California, was slated for demolition in 1994. David Fetherston

to curtail the craving for cruising only aggravated the situation. It annoyed the responsible customers, eliminating two reasons why the drive-ins became so popular in the first place: convenience and easy access.

The government put in their two cents worth during the White House Conference on Natural Beauty in 1965. Spearheaded by civic activist Ladybird Johnson, legislation was proposed to eliminate "endless corridors walled in by neon, junk, and ruined landscape." The meeting culminated in two bills that complicated the drive-in owner's job. Suddenly, businesses that served motorists were responsible for upgrading the nation's roadscape! Junkyards, gas stations, hot dog stands, billboards, and finally, drive-in restaurants were put on the list as potential "eyesores." Once a loud

continued on page 166

STEAK 'N SHAKE TAKHOMASAK

*"Belt's first 'Steak 'n Shake Drive-In opened in
Normal, Illinois, and proved anything but. Unlike other curb-stands,
his outfit catered to the individual mood of customers."*

While California restauranteurs were restyling the drive-in as circular monument, A. H. "Gus" Belt was working on something more important: improving the hamburger. In 1934, his efforts culminated in the "Steakburger," a seared sandwich of ground beef fortified by fine cuts of T-bone, strip, and sirloin. When he teamed it with a hand-dipped shake, it became an irresistible meal.

Belt's first "Steak 'n Shake" Drive-In opened in Normal, Illinois, and proved anything but. Unlike other curb-stands, his outfit catered to the individual mood of customers. If someone wanted to dine within their car, that was fine. When inclement weather called for dinner inside, it was available. Patrons with itchy feet were accommodated, too: sacks could be packed to go or meals eaten at a counter.

It didn't take long for this innovative "four-way service" to seize the interest of those who liked to dine-in-a-hurry. By 1948, the first drive-in had grown into many and motorfood fans in St. Louis were introduced to the versatility of "Takhomasak." Indiana was next, the tasty reputation of the mouth-watering steakburger spreading throughout the state.

Numerous outposts followed with white-tiled buildings edged in black. On their rooftops, painted signboards featured the words "Steak 'n Shake" in bold lettering. Out along the overhang, smaller signs reminded the hungry of the "Genuine Chili" and "Tru-Flavor" shakes, teasing tastebuds with aplomb.

Best of all, every part of the cooking process was visible to customers. Spotless kitchens draped in stainless steel were designed in such a manner so that those in the dining room could see grill men frying and shake men mixing. Strategically placed windows allowed customers parked in their cars to view the preparations. For the patron tired of inferior quality, it was a confidence builder. "In Sight, It Must Be Right" became a popular slogan.

Unfortunately, Steak 'n Shake founder Gus Belt died in 1954. But by then, his admirable program to improve the flavor of the hamburger was firmly established. Today, that legacy is continued as modern Steak 'n Shake eateries continue the tradition. Although carhop service is no longer offered, current owner Consolidated Products, Inc., has managed to inject a measure of fifties ambiance into its new structures. Nostalgic components are used throughout: glass brick adorns entry vestibules and nostalgic awnings decorate the facades. On each corner, rounded "wings" adorned in neon anchor the design to the roadway, rekindling the era of Art Moderne.

Inside, the flavor-packed steakburgers formulated by Gus Belt sixty years ago are still made the same way. At over 135 modern Steak 'n Shake outlets located throughout Missouri, Indiana, Illinois, Georgia, Florida, Ohio, Kentucky, Iowa, and Kansas, food is served using real glassware and china. Every entree is prepared to customer order and pre-cooking abhorred.

With burger boredom now an unfortunate byproduct of motoring's modern age, it's encouraging to see that certain recipes remain cherished. After all, the American hamburger is just a hamburger. The Steak 'n Shake steakburger is much more. "It's a Meal!" ∎

Steak 'n Shake Drive-In
Built on the concept of a Steakburger and hand-dipped milkshake, Steak 'n Shake is one of America's original drive-in restaurants. This drive-in is located on old Route 66, on the outskirts of St. Louis, Missouri. ©1994 Craig Curtin

Steak 'n Shake Balloons and Beetle
Balloons for the kids (and adults) were an effective way to excite customers and develop loyal clientele. For Steak 'n Shake, it was a visible way to attract attention when opening new outlets. Still, the food garnered the most attention; the delicious Steakburger was often reward enough for the hungry motorist. Courtesy Steak 'n Shake, Inc.

Steak 'n Shake
Left, by the 1960s, the Steak 'n Shake chain of drive-in restaurants was well known throughout the Midwest. Gus Belt's original formula for serving up a complete meal of Steakburger and hand-dipped milkshake became a roadside standard. "It's a Meal" was the company's popular slogan. Because the customer could see the order being prepared, "In Sight It Must Be Right" joined it as car-dining catch-phrase. Courtesy Steak 'n Shake, Inc.

Steak 'n Shake Carhops
By the 1950s, drive-in restaurants had developed quite a list of do's and don'ts. Standing erect while taking the order without resting the checkbook on the car was standard procedure. At Steak 'n Shake Drive-Ins throughout the Midwest, carhops adopted the styles pioneered by the early service station attendant: black bow-tie, slacks, and white shirt. Courtesy Steak 'n Shake, Inc.

FROM FISH BRINE TO KETCHUP

Ahhh…that tangy, thick, and sticky condiment known as ketchup. Where would American roadfood be without it? Certainly, drive-ins, diners, coffee-shops, and in many cases, fine restaurants, wouldn't be the same. Burgers would be bland, fries embarrassed by nakedness, and hot dogs robbed of their bite. In a world devoid of the red sauce, Archie Bunker would have starved.

Historians trace the ancestry of the zesty mixture as far back as the Roman Empire. Ancient cooks created a sauce from the entrails of dried fish they called "garum," a highly prized addition to the dinner table. The more familiar word "ketchup" however, probably had its origins in the 1690s, from what the Chinese called "kôechiap" or "kê-tsiap." Created from the brine of pickled fish or shellfish, it was the Orient's answer to a flavor-enhancing food additive.

After the East India Company opened trade with the Far East during the sixteenth century, the port markets of Singapore became a favorite place for sailors. There, exotic dishes accompanied by a tasty hot sauce dubbed "kechap" were hyped by Malaysian vendors. The dressing became an immediate favorite and promptly exported when the seafarers returned home (the Dutch renamed it Ketjap). Before too long, frazzled housewives began experimenting with the recipe, attempting to recreate the tantalizing concoction their well-traveled mates were raving about.

It came as no surprise that *Mrs. Harrison's Housekeeper's Pocketbook* and *Mrs. Glasse's Cookery Book* began featuring recipes during the 1700s to aid the creative cook in her adventures. But since the exotic ingredients in the Indonesian mixture were not available in England, a variety of other staples were cleverly substituted. Ketchups made of mushrooms became the first choice, followed by purees based on tomatoes, walnuts, anchovies, and even oysters.

Despite the variety, the idea of ketchup as a food enhancer began to grow in popularity. Sailors returning to America eventually brought the sauce across the Atlantic, adding tomatoes gathered during expeditions to Mexico or the West Indies to the sauce. Their families loved it, and soon tomato seeds were planted so that they might have a ready supply of the prime ingredient.

Now, women had to add the task of mixing up large batches of condiment to their wifely duties. It was a laborious job, requiring an entire day of stirring just to ensure that the pulp didn't stick to the bottom of the pot. Henry J. Heinz saw his opportunity in this work and wasted no time adding ketchup to the line of condiments he was producing for sale. In 1876, he began to manufacture and bottle America's first commercially processed tomato ketchup.

Since then, ketchup has risen to its place of prominence as the supreme condiment for the masses. The distinctive multi-faceted bottle has established itself as an icon of the fast food table-top, taking its rightful place along with salt and pepper shakers and rectangular napkin dispensers. For the frenzied aficionados who thump, shake, and pour the piquant sauce upon every conceivable foodstuff known to man, there is no other substance like it.

Move over, mayonnaise, mustard, and secret sauce—tomato ketchup reigns unchallenged as the primo junk food compliment from coast to coast. Call it ketchup, catsup, or catchup—nobody really cares. Just be sure there is a full bottle on the table, an ample supply in the squeeze pump, and at least a half dozen of those little plastic packets in the bag. ∎

Heinz Ketchup ad, 1925
In today's world of roadside dining, it's becoming difficult to find an actual ketchup bottle or mustard pot residing at the table arrangement of any fast-food restaurant. To properly dress a quick roadside meal with the right quantity required to satisfy, a small fistful of impregnable packets must be carefully opened without splattering their contents. The frivolous days when streams of ketchup flowed freely from bottles have passed. Courtesy Heinz, Inc.

During the twilight of the fifties, youngsters coming of age in America desperately desired a place they could call their own—an up-to-date hangout where they could act freely. Fortunately, there was one outlet. At any time, day or night, one could escape the stifling confines of the tract-house lifestyle and find fulfillment with a sack of hot French fries and cheeseburger.

continued from page 160

attention-getter, America's carhop eatery had no choice but to conform—to be seen but not heard! In fear of litigation and strangulation by red tape, curb operators kowtowed to the whims of lawmakers and scrambled to improve their appearance.

Waco, Texas, gained notoriety for its beautification efforts when Jim Kimbell, vice-president of Kim's Drive-In, implemented a few simple changes in landscaping. "Let's put up a building that belongs to its surroundings…one that improves the neighborhood but doesn't embarrass it. Not a neon palace, but something subtle and attractive that will blend with its neighbors," he proclaimed. Kim's proceeded to do just that, softening their service building and canopy by facing them with cedar shake shingles. The colorful geometric doo-dads that adorned the drive-ins only a few years ago were out of style. Now, shrubs with thorns—strategically placed wherever teenagers might congregate—were all the rage. It was all part of blending into the environment.

Sadly, the carhop could no longer blend with her surroundings either. When compared to counter servers at the fast-food burger stand and the well-coifed waitress at the indoor eatery, she appeared out of place. To make matters worse, the image of the carhop as a wholesome girl was fading. As early as the fifties, the once-eminent carhop was showing some tarnish. The abbreviated skirts and revealing uniforms once regarded as advantageous for business were now blamed for attracting the wrong element. When Big Boy hamburger king Robert Wian ventured forth into the Dallas market to open a new franchise, he experienced trouble recruiting local girls. Was the drive-in theater's tawdry reputation as a "passion pit" rubbing off on its road-food cousin? Probably; Wian had to fly a team of twenty carhops in from California.

While the drive-in industry battled these problems, the value of real estate spiraled up.

In dense cities such as Los Angeles, modest units like Simon's and Herbert's could no longer generate enough revenues to sustain the land they occupied and both operations were defunct by the sixties. The answer was maximum customer turnover, a program perfectly suited to indoor coffee-shops. In 1961, *Drive-In* magazine reported that of the 209 restaurants built over the last ten years, 191 were of the "sit-down" type, the majority being coffee-shops. Though the Midwest was largely unaffected, motor canteens began dominating California, relegating carhop service to an accessory. The trend was understandable, since an indoor format offered more advantages to the modern restauranteur.

In the same *Drive-In* article, Matt Shipman (founder of Ship's coffee-shops) related one of the main reasons for the disappearance of the drive-in format: some people regard eating in their car as uncomfortable. Shipman remembers the time comedian Bob Hope ordered a drink and a sandwich at Tiny Naylor's Drive-In. When the carhop delivered the order, she pinned him behind the wheel with an oversized serving tray. With the food only inches away, Hope politely inquired if he could have a "short fork!"

More seriously, coffee-shops reduced business fluctuation due to the weather. Even in sunny Southern California, an overcast day could cause revenues to vary from $800 to $900. The contrast between a drive-in's summer volume and winter business was often as much as 60 percent. What's more, the average check for each coffee-shop visit was higher. Pleasant surroundings encouraged more food ordering and less rush. As a bridge to the modern age (where casual wear could be worn for all occasions), the coffee-shops were as comfortable for the well-dressed businessman as they were for the sportsman right off the golf course.

On a Los Angeles drive during the fifties, Douglas Haskell, a writer for *House and*

continued on page 174

Mike's Drive-In Table Service
The well-stacked hamburger meal served with a plate of French fries and extra large Coca-Cola has achieved legendary status in the annals of American roadfood. When teamed with a full bottle of ketchup, salt and pepper, stack of napkins, and rock'n'roll music blaring from a tabletop jukebox, it's a combination that can't be beat. Jukebox control units like this model were standard issue at most of America's diners, coffee-shops, family restaurants, truck stops, greasy spoons, and drive-ins during the 1950s. Forget Muzak piped in from a central speaker— nothing compares to punching up your own musical selections while downing a mouthful of fries. This Crosley Select-o-Matic jukebox is a replica of the original units. Jukebox Courtesy Red Horse Museum

WACO'S DR PEPPER DRINK

Down at The Old Corner Drugstore fountain in Waco, Texas, an imaginative medical school graduate named Charles Alderton formulated the "King of Beverages" in the year 1885.

Alderton was highly fascinated with the soda fountain and observed that patrons often had a difficult time choosing which flavoring to add to their carbonated water. He started to experiment, mixing available flavorings in countless combinations. After eliminating a host of formulations, he succeeded in creating a particularly palatable syrup.

Delighted with the tasty results, drugstore owner Wade Morrison foresaw its great profit potential. Further refinements were made in the formula and within a short time, it was offered to local soda-sippers for judicious sampling.

News of the charismatic blend spread fast, and soon more and more customers were asking for it. Alderton's engaging beverage was soon a jewel in The Old Corner Drugstore's crown. Eventually, it became so popular that nearby

Dr Pepper Vintage Logo
Courtesy Dr Pepper Company

drugstore operators inquired about dispensing it. "Shoot me a Waco" became one of the most popular orders at soda counters throughout Central Texas.

To satisfy the demand, Morrison and Alderton teamed up to mix the syrup by themselves until its phenomenal growth rendered the task impossible. As the number of drugstores and soda parlours interested in the syrup grew, they could no longer keep up with the volume.

Luckily, Texas bottler R. S. Lazenby came to the duo's rescue. After some initial experimentation, he confirmed that the "Waco" mixture was a prime candidate for large-scale bottling. To exclusively package the soda drink and capitalize on its success in the marketplace, he formed a new company.

By 1891, The Artesian Manufacturing & Bottling Company had taken what was once just a soda fountain flavor experiment and turned it into a commercially viable product. The familiar Waco nickname was abandoned and an engaging logo designed to enhance recognition of the popular drink. Repackaged for a mass market, the unique beverage became "Dr. Pepper's Phos-Ferrates."

Conflicting stories detailing the original inspiration of the name eventually surfaced, with a host of players throwing their stories into the pot. Unfortunately, the only one with any truth tells of Morrison's early work at Dr. Charles Pepper's pharmacy in Rural Retreat, Virginia. Apparently, he thought well of the good doctor and adopted his "spicy" surname for the beverage.

Further extrapolation of Morrison's younger days enters the realm of fable: supposedly, he fell in love with the Virginia pharmacist's teenage daughter. According to legend, Pepper wasn't thrilled with this and discouraged the romance. Dejected, Morrison said farewell to both and sought his fortune out West. Years later, he decided Alderton's drink should be called Dr. Pepper—as a tribute.

Regardless of the name's mysterious beginnings, the popularity of Dr Pepper continued to spread nationwide. Wherever the public welcomed a new flavor, it flourished. By the time the first drive-in restaurants were capturing the

Dr Pepper 1891 Logo
Courtesy Dr Pepper Company

Down at The Old Corner Drugstore fountain in Waco, Texas, an imaginative medical school graduate named Charles Alderton formulated the "King of Beverages" in the year 1885.

Dr. Charles Alderton Portrait
In 1885, Dr. Charles Alderton developed the "King of Beverages." Alderton's engaging drink was soon the jewel in The Old Corner Drugstore's crown. Eventually, it grew so popular that nearby drugstore operators inquired about dispensing it. "Shoot me a Waco" became one of the most popular orders at soda counters throughout Central Texas. By 1891, the familiar nickname was abandoned and the first official bottle of "Dr. Pepper's Phos-Ferrates" was produced. Courtesy of the Dr Pepper Museum, Waco, Texas

fancy of motorists, the sweet-tasting liquid was already a staple drink of roadside stands.

Assuming its rightful place among the emerging roster of carbonated beverages, Dr Pepper has gone on to become one of the soft drink world's distinct flavors. Whether at 10, 2, or 4 o'clock, it's always in demand by thirsty pilots and passengers of America's automobiles. ■

THE DOCTOR'S FAVORITE CASE
.......HOME TREATMENT FOR FATIGUE

1926

1926

Dr Pepper Logos With Doc
In 1926, Southwestern Advertising designed its first logo for Dr Pepper in the form of this genial, chubby "doc." Dressed in top hat and sporting a monocle, he was to convey the very essence of the soft drink's qualities to the public. But alas! After just a few years of service, "Old Doc" was retired prematurely, his jovial face no longer required. Seems he evoked a certain "medicinal" connotation. Courtesy Dr Pepper Company

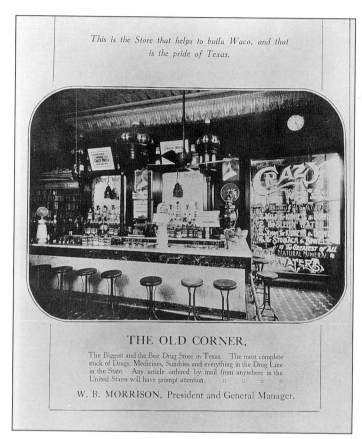

This is the Store that helps to build Waco, and that is the pride of Texas.

THE OLD CORNER,
The Biggest and the Best Drug Store in Texas. The most complete stock of Drugs, Medicines, Sundries and everything in the Drug Line in the State. Any article ordered by mail from anywhere in the United States will have prompt attention. :: :: :: :: ::

W. B. MORRISON, President and General Manager.

The Old Corner Drugstore
The Old Corner Drugstore was located on Fourth and Austin in the midst of bustling Waco, Texas. Owned and operated by W. B. Morrison, it dominated the social scene. The elaborate soda fountain area was the main attraction, serving numerous concoctions of the day. Town doctors, travelers, and cowboys mingled within its roomy interior, sharing stories, jokes, and refreshments. In November 1897, it became the site of a shoot-out between Judge G. B. Gerald and two newspapermen, apparently the result of a long time feud. But more important, The Old Corner Drugstore's historical status was secured when pharmacist Alderton developed the Dr Pepper formula. This photograph was taken when bottled "Crazy Water" was at the height of its popularity. The Texas Collection, Baylor University, Waco, Texas

*A*ssuming its rightful place among the emerging roster of carbonated beverages, Dr Pepper has gone on to become one of the soft drink world's distinct flavors. Whether at 10, 2, or 4 o'clock, it's always in demand by thirsty pilots and passengers of America's automobiles.

Dr Pepper Neon Clock
The numerals 10, 2, and 4 reflect one of Dr Pepper's most successful advertising slogans. Research conducted at Columbia University revealed that these were the precise hours that an average person's energy level dropped. Because Dr Pepper contained inverted sugars readily absorbed by the bloodstream, it produced an immediate energy lift that counteracted this cycle. The slogan "Drink a Bite to Eat at 10, 2, and 4 o'clock" was introduced in 1926 and survived in one form or another for thirty years. Courtesy of the Dr Pepper Museum, Waco, Texas

ROEN'S A&W ROOT BEER

"A scaled-down mug was produced by the Indiana Glass Company during the early twenties. Designed exclusively for children, it held a 3 1/2 ounce squirt of root beer."

Miniature root beer mugs hardly seem like something substantial enough to build a business upon. Yet America's A&W Drive-Ins have managed to do just that, continuing today with their free flagon of drink for the toddlers. The curious tradition began during the early twenties, a few thousand gulps after chain founders Allen and Wright first teamed up to sell their sweet brew to California motorists.

Ted Roen's Ravenna, Ohio, Stand
Ted Roen fooled around with automobiles most of his life. Trouble was, his trio of A&W Drive-Ins took up so much of his time that he didn't have the opportunity to enjoy his hobby. For purely selfish reasons, he decided to start a regular "cruise-nite" at his Ravenna, Ohio, A&W stand in 1979. "If I couldn't be out with my friends, I decided to bring them to me." Now, he sees "a lot of gray hair" out there on the parking lot—along with flashy hot rods and souped-up vehicles. Every Wednesday night, automobile aficionados from fifteen county areas come to show-off their pride and joy. At Ted Roen's Ohio A&W, they still make food the way customers want it, use real carhops instead of electronic ordering boxes, and never serve root beer without a frosty mug. What's more, they don't take American Express.... Courtesy Ted Roen

From the start, serving youngsters with root beer was a daunting task. While kids loved the tasty drink, stealing swigs from a parent's tankard added nothing to their enjoyment. Still, what else could be done? Standard-sized mugs were simply too large for tiny hands. They were heavy, imposing, and prone to accidental spillage. What's more, the volume of liquid they contained was usually too great for the little ones. A smaller copy of the adult decanter was needed, one young moppets could polish off without parental assistance.

To the delight of juveniles and approval of parents, a scaled-down mug was produced by the Indiana Glass Company during the early twenties. Designed exclusively for children, it held a 3 1/2 ounce squirt of root beer—plenty for all those under six. Featuring a petit handle, fluted base, round dimples, and the familiar A&W logo embossed into the glass, it possessed all the characteristics of the larger version. Finally, tikes clamoring for refreshment in the backseat had their own container.

By the time young Lila Roen secured employment as an A&W carhop in Marshfield, Wisconsin, in 1942, the so-called "kiddy mug" promotion was already a long-established tradition. Eventually though, she married and left her work as a car server, but never forgot the friendly faces and happy times experienced in the business of roadside root beer.

When husband Vernon announced in the early fifties that he wanted more out of life than just a sales position for the Sears Company, they began their search for a profitable and enjoyable business venture. At the time, mutual friends already ran their own A&W franchise. Lila's fond memories of her early job experience were rekindled and their choice became clear. Is there doubt that she remembered the cute little mugs and cracked a smile?

In May of 1956, the Roens picked out three locations in the Ravenna, Ohio, area and proceeded to build their own network of A&W outlets. When all were completed in 1957, they became typical examples of the automobile drive-in, serving a simple menu of regular and foot-long hot dogs, root beer floats, barbecued beef, milkshakes, orange drinks, and popcorn. When son Ted and his wife Elma took over the operation in 1971, burgers became the favorite—but the little mugs were never forgotten. He continued the established traditions, his primary consideration to recruit an entirely new generation of root beer lovers.

Yet a measure of dedication was required for Roen to keep his liquid treat in the limelight. With only half the carbonation of the average soft drink, root beer must be served in a frigid container to maintain its fizz and froth; lukewarm glassware just won't do. A thick mug chilled in a deep freeze is the only container for the job. When served up properly, there's nothing that compares. "The kids know Coca-Cola and Pepsi," says Roen, "but they don't know root beer. When they finally do get a taste of it, they really like it!"

However, the simple secret behind Ted Roen's successful string of A&W

A&W Root Beer Patch
When Roy Allen and Frank Wright teamed up to sell root beer in the early twenties, they decided to combine their initials and form a new company name. A&W was the result, incorporated into a graphic symbol featuring the now-familiar "pointing arrow." From the Chuck Sturm Collection

A&W Kiddy Mug
Left, to the delight of juveniles and approval of parents, a scaled-down A&W mug was first produced by the Indiana Glass Company during the early twenties. Designed exclusively for children, it held a 3 1/2 ounce squirt of root beer, plenty for all those under six.

Drive-Ins lies not only in his zeal for developing new customers, but in his personal philosophy as well. "When it's done right, there is still room in the marketplace for the old-fashioned operator who wants to take care of his customers and give them good value," he suggests. "Not everything can come back again—but quality and taking care of the customer never dies."

In effect, that credo sums up the whole idea behind the notion of the little children's mug: making doubly sure that everyone, including the youngest members of every carload, exit the parking lot grinning from ear to ear, bellies filled with freshly brewed, delicious, ice-cold root beer. Ted Roen can be proud of his reputation for quality, because somewhere, somehow, Allen & Wright are smiling, too. ∎

continued from page 166

Home, spied an extremely unusual coffee-shop called Googie's. Impressed by the design, he used the term in an article to classify the architectural forms of Coffee-shop Modern. Typified by gravity-defying abstracts, the Googie style combined multiple structural systems made up of materials like glass block, plastic, asbestos, cement, and plywood. Re-energized with these new components, the eye-popping arrangements that comprised the programmatic buildings of the twenties were retrofitted for the modern boulevard.

The coffee-shop became a dramatic roadside form: steel channel decking, neon tubing, delta wings, glass louvers, exposed support beams, terrazzo tile, and integrated billboards (sign as part of building) became a few of its hallmarks. As a consequence, drive-ins could no longer compete visually with extraordinary structures exemplified by Ship's, Biff's, Burke's, Coffee Dan's, Carolina Pines, Romeo's Times Square, or the Clock. On the West Coast, the future had arrived in the form of a coffee-shop, re-classifying dine-in-your-car curb service as a vestige of old.

Despite their impact on the drive-in trade, the modern coffee-shops had little effect on the monumental growth of the fast-food franchising industry. The reasons were obvious: by replicating established food and service systems already proven for their profitability, entrepreneurs could establish a suc-

Hart's Neon Burger Sign
Hart's 19¢ hamburger price started a price war with the Sacramento Stan's (visible in the background). Eventually, most of the burger joints throughout the states raised their prices, relegating the 15¢ hamburger to history. H. Sweet Collection, City of Sacramento, History and Science Division, Sacramento Archives and Museum Collection Center

When McDonald's announced in 1967 that it was going to increase the price of its hamburgers to eighteen cents, shock waves rocked the entire franchise industry; the average price of a burger had remained at fifteen cents for years. Labeled by the press as "Black Wednesday," the stage was set for the eventual elimination of many of the smaller hamburger chains.

Porky's Drive-In
St. Paul, Minnesota's famous Porky's Drive-In was shut down for many years in the 1980s, with broken neon glass covering the parking area and grass growing between cracks in the pavement. Owner Ray Truelson revived the classic drive-in in 1990 with drive-thru and walk-in service for the cars parking under the canopy. On any weekend night in the summer, owners of classic cars, hot rods, customs, and motorcycles make their pilgrimage to Porky's, overflowing from the parking lot to line both sides of University Avenue for a block in either direction. The action doesn't let up until the neon turns off after midnight.
Michael Dregni

cessful food enterprise quickly. As a bonus, advertising campaigns like those employed to market soap powder or aspirin ensured franchisees a steady supply of burger biters. The statistics didn't lie: by 1956, Ray Kroc had only thirteen McDonald's units in operation. Three years later, he boosted that figure to 100 franchise outlets nationwide. In 1959 alone, 67 new pairs of the bold yellow arches would light up strips across America.

Capitalizing on menu simplicity and task streamlining, a rash of imitators cloned their own versions of the McDonald's formula. A spontaneous race to spread the verisimilitude of the hamburger had begun. Originating in 1956 in Gary, Indiana, a new chain named after its founder's daughter attempted to mirror Kroc's success. Substituting turquoise boomerangs for the arches and promising "A serving a second," the Carrol's chain grew to over 163 units by the seventies. Sandy's, yet another McDonald's look-alike from Illinois, multiplied into a string of 250 during that same period. Proclaiming "Thrift and Swift Service," the chain's plaid-kilted Sandy proved that a little lass could sell a lot of hamburgers. In 1953, George E. Read's patented "Insta-Burger Broiler" also inspired Keith Cramer to open a walk-up based on the McDonald's model. When Hawaii hosted Cramer's 2,000th Burger King in 1977, the flame-broiled "Whopper" was already a mainland staple.

Suddenly, it seemed as if every splatter of grease on the grill was turning to gold. To the amazement of the food industry, even more self-serve copy cats decided to capitalize on the "cash cow," including Frank Thomas with Burger Chef restaurants and William Hardee with his Hardee's chain. A stampeding herd of competitors kept on a comin', including Biff's, Jiffy, Golden Point, Kelly's, Burger Queen, Henry's, Steer-In, Wetson's, Carter's, Burgerville USA, Mr. Fifteen, and Burger Boy Food-O-Rama. The roadsides became thick with cheap meat sandwiches in the round.

continued on page 183

Mels Drive-In
Today, a drive-in revival is bringing back former drive-ins and building new ones. Delighting visitors with their fantastic attractions, the Universal Studios theme parks in Hollywood, California and Orlando, Florida pay homage to the drive-in legacy begun by restauranteur Mel Weiss. Both locations feature an idealized re-creation of the now legendary Mels Drive-In. ©1992 Universal Studios Florida

Mels American Graffiti

"With the drive-in as backdrop, customers related their early years of love and romance—how they first met at Mels— dated, and ultimately got married!"

Tourists are generally unaware that along with the Golden Gate Bridge and its trolleys, San Francisco is famous for drive-ins. Mel Weiss and Harold Dobbs started it all back in 1947 when they built their first carhop eatery, inspired by similar restaurants serving motorists in Los Angeles. With a staff of fourteen carhops covering a 30,000 square foot parking lot, they lured the hungry with a local radio personality broadcasting a live remote. As music reverberated through car radios in the drive-ups, the curb-stepping gals of 140 South Van Ness became a new paradigm for service.

At all hours of the day and night, crowds of patrons that fancied dining-in-your-car came early and often. It didn't take long for the first unit to multiply into eleven! Six Mels became landmarks in the Bay Area with an additional cluster achieving their own notoriety in Stockton and Sacramento. They reigned for almost twenty years, until a parade of franchised fast food outlets finally outpaced their service. As the new philosophy of "serve yourself" began to reprogram attitudes about dining, Mels began its gradual decline.

By 1972, a New York restaurant conglomerate purchased most of the faltering units and changed their names. As colorful marquees were scheduled for removal, it appeared to many local enthusiasts that Mel's success story was about to end. They were only partly right. Around the same time, filmmaker George Lucas was scouting out locations to serve as centerpiece for his rock'n'roll fable about life, love, and coming of age in postwar America. The original Mels burger spot came to his attention and was leased prior to its demolition. Crews descended on the site and soon it was lights…camera…action…all over again. Mels was back in business, immortalized in 35mm.

Out on the parking lot, Ron Howard, Candy Clark, Richard Dreyfuss, Mackenzie Phillips, Harrison Ford, Cindy Williams, Paul LeMat, Suzanne Somers, and Charlie Martin Smith took their first steps to future stardom. As the bulldozers razed the last remnants of the historic drive-in and trucks carted off the debris, *American Graffiti* opened in theaters.

Thirteen years later, Mel's son Steven began to grow increasingly nostalgic about his father's defunct dream. As memories of the fifties dominated his imagination like a jukebox replaying the same old record, he tried to dismiss the thoughts. A lifetime of experience in the restaurant business told him that any attempt to resurrect the Mels idea wouldn't be easy. His father agreed, actively discouraging the idea. Fortunately, Steven persisted. When partner Donald Wagstaff confirmed interest with his own commitment, the path to reclaim a Northern California legend was clear.

At the grand re-opening in 1985, Steven's fondest wishes were realized: former teenagers who once dined at the first Mels were now re-visiting with their families. Weary of tasteless road food, they wanted to show their kids a glimpse of what the "good times" were really like—long before the age of video games and compact disc players. With the drive-in as backdrop, customers related their early years of love and romance—how they first met at Mels—dated, and ultimately got married! Mels was back on the charts with new locations on Frisco's Lombard and Gary Street. Two more opened in Los Angeles—joined by full-scale replicas (complete with food service) at the Universal Studios theme parks in Florida and California. Weiss had the Mels name officially trademarked in 1985 and now, it continues to take on a life of its own. Rightly so!

After all, Mels Drive-In is the burger, the French fry, and the milkshake. It's playing a joke on friends by unscrewing the top of the salt shaker and ketchup cap. Mels is the howlin', prowlin', Wolfman Jack…the phase-shift echo heard when walking past a row of roadsters tuned to the same raucous station. It's the haunting sound of an electric guitar banging out the "chunka-chunka" rhythm of "Green Onions" while cruisin' the circuit in a little deuce coupe, hair slicked back in a ducktail. Mels is the generic haven for the automobile, the youthful hangouts fondly remembered, along with one's first car, first date…and first kiss. ■

Mels Drive-In on South Van Ness

"Didn't we meet at Mels?" has become the popular slogan for the new chain of Mels restaurants operated by Steven Weiss and partner Donald Wagstaff in California. The original Mels Drive-In located at 140 South Van Ness in San Francisco was started in 1947 by Steven's father, Mel. After the movie American Graffiti was filmed there during the early seventies, it was demolished. Fortunately, the film re-awakened interest in the idea of hanging out at the drive-in and the Mels concept was reborn for a new generation of diners. Courtesy Steven Weiss

Mels Drive-In San Francisco
In 1985, Steven Weiss and partner Donald Wagstaff re-opened Mels Drive-In. Two new locations on Frisco's Lombard Street and Geary Boulevard attracted crowds, and classic cars. The fifties were back, complete with neon, hamburgers, chrome, and the milkshake! ©1994 Annabelle Breakey

Mels Salinas Drive-In

During the fifties, Mel Weiss operated a string of successful drive-in restaurants throughout California. His flagship San Francisco eatery was made famous by its appearance in the movie American Graffiti. The curb server classic depicted in this rare color image gained notoriety simply by supplying burgers and fries to the residents of Salinas. Most remembered by the high school crowd (it was only two blocks away) for its multi-colored curb-girl sign and distinctive "winged" architecture, it was eventually replaced by a Burger King. ©1955 Andy Southard, Jr.

Mels Drive-In Burger Pin

Left, Mels Drive-In restaurant and the classic sesame-seed bun hamburger: two inseparable institutions that have made this country worth fighting for. Pin Courtesy of Steven Weiss

continued from page 177

When the McDonald's Corporation announced in 1967 that it was going to increase the price of its hamburgers to eighteen cents, shock waves rocked the entire franchise industry; the average price of a burger had remained at fifteen cents for years. Blamed on rising beef costs and spiraling operating expenses, the meat hike was an ominous precursor to the great burger battles soon to come. Labeled by the press as "Black Wednesday," the stage was set for the eventual elimination of many of the smaller hamburger chains. After a period of unprecedented growth, the wild proliferation of the McDonald hamburger clones was over.

But what about the drive-ins? By the early eighties, the eat-in-the-front-seat format featuring carhops and serving trays was hardly mentioned! Sadly, the entire concept was regarded as impotent, unfit as a contender. When the Jack in the Box clown (who was part of a drive-thru intercom system) was detonated on national television, the pure form of the drive-in restaurant had already mutated into something unrecognizable. The unforgettable curb service eateries that captivated the imagination of an entire nation slipped into obscurity along with the services and features that made them great. With life quickening, motorists imagined themselves in too much of a hurry even to stop! Drive-thru windows (a method first tried in 1931 by the Pig Stands) and electronic menus became the norm.

Now, even the need to turn off the car motor was eliminated.

Fortunately, a few of the mom-and-pop operations continued to slog through the slush of burgers. Family-run landmarks like Atlanta's Varsity and Norfolk's Doumar's made a defiant stand against the franchising pods threatening to take away their souls.

Troy Smith managed to perpetuate his original drive-in chain and took the company to the operators in 1973. Sonic Industries was formed and true to name, they streaked towards success—indicated by the fact that 130 units were still operating! By the time C. Stephen Lynn became President and Chief Executive Officer in 1983, Sonic's number had grown to over 900 units. When Lynn and key management completed a leveraged buyout in 1986, Smith's original philosophy that "owners make better managers" helped rocket the organization to prominence. By 1994, Sonic became America's number one drive-in with over 1,300 units in operation.

With the introduction of their "Beach Burger '50s Combo" meal during the summer of 1990, Sonic helped fuel the nation's growing interest in nostalgia and the fifties. In thirty-second television ads, teen idol and *Beach Blanket Bingo* star Frankie Avalon pitched the new hamburger meal deal with assistance from Sue Phillips (winner of the company's 1989–1990 Carhop of the Year contest). In the spot, Avalon sat in a sandpile at one of Sonic's automotive stalls and entertained a daydream about the perfect day at the beach. Of course, his ultimate fantasy included the Beach Burger Combo.

For the millions of car-crazy Americans enamored of the drive-in restaurant's glory days, the timing of the commercial couldn't have been more appropriate. Classic car organizations and cruising clubs had begun seeing a marked increase in membership. As more and more baby boomers realized that the car could serve as a time machine, restoring the beautiful machines of yesteryear grew into a popular hobby. And naturally, this swelling body of street rodders required appropriate locations to display their pride and joy. Car shows were nice, but nothing equaled the drive-in as the ultimate location to park, cruise, and show off. To the delight of the few drive-ins remaining, the generation that fell in love with carhop service as teens had come full circle, rediscovering dining in your car by way of the internal-combustion engine.

continued on page 187

To the delight of the few drive-ins remaining, the generation that fell in love with carhop service as teens had come full circle, rediscovering dining in your car by way of the internal-combustion engine.

ROLLER SKATES ECHO THE AUTO

Joseph Merlin, a Belgian musical instrument craftsman and inventor, fashioned the world's first pair of roller skates around 1760. His enthusiasm for the gadget was demonstrated during a masquerade at Carlisle House (in the Soho Square district of London), where he glided among revelers, playing violin. Unfortunately, he misjudged his forward momentum and crashed headlong into a mirror, shattering interest in his wheels.

By the time Merlin recuperated from his injuries, a number of tinkers began improving his design. In 1819, Frenchman Monsieur Petitbled introduced the predecessor of today's inline blades by lining up a quartet of ivory wheels in a single row. Further refinement in 1823 by London fruit merchant Robert John Tyers resulted in skates that featured five aligned wheels—one of larger diameter in the center, employed as a turning pivot.

In a precursor of events to come, the proprietor of a Berlin beer tavern known as the Corse Halle encouraged its barmaids to strap on the wheeled contraptions in 1840. Laden with steins, buxom table servers soon scuttled about on roller skates, delivering their brew to thirsty customers. Service improved dramatically, albeit with mishaps: dodging tipsy customers proved difficult with rollers that tended to go straight.

Fortunately, that problem was somewhat alleviated in 1849, when Frenchman Louis Legrange split the inline wheels into two pairs. Fourteen years later, American James Plimpton contributed the missing link needed for ultimate maneuverability: a springy rubber mount. Now, by "rocking" the angle of the foot while in motion, two parallel sets of rollers could be influenced to execute a smooth skating curve.

With most of the bugs worked out, roller skating fell in and out of favor over the next seven decades, until the third major revival hit the nation during the thirties. In 1932, Olympic star Sonja Henie inspired movie-goers with her ice-skating prowess, further stimulating interest in the hobby. Suddenly, everyone who could afford inexpensive skate rental laced up, experiencing for themselves the wonders of roller skating.

Inspired by the growing interest, American industry saw the potential and outfitted employees with wheels. United Airlines experimented with strap-on rollers for their ticket agents and terminal workers. Western Union supplied skates to their message matrons, as did American Telephone and Telegraph. Operators skated through their work day, delivering messages, connecting customers.

It wasn't long before drive-in restaurants began experimenting with free-wheeling car service—pushing the idea of mobility to the extreme. Speed suddenly became an important factor of service, directly affecting customer satisfaction and turnover. To accommodate the pace, carhops had to cover ground as effortlessly as the vehicles on the boulevard. Miniaturized re-creations of tires, axles, and shock absorbers—mounted underfoot—became the ultimate means to mimic the movement of the motorcar.

Ultimately, the act of waitressing with tiny wheels strapped to one's feet proved too impractical. To become as graceful as one of Gloria Nord's Skating Vanities while balancing a loaded tray called for a marked level of skill and coordination. Even the most experienced skaters had problems, especially when they hit the gravel at the parking lot edge.

Though connected forever in the public's mind as standard equipment of the car server, roller skates were to be reserved exclusively for special promotions and publicity events. Served tray-top—shakes, burgers, and dogs were extremely popular with American car customers—but lost most of their appeal when abruptly deposited in one's lap. ∎

Courtesy Metro ImageBase

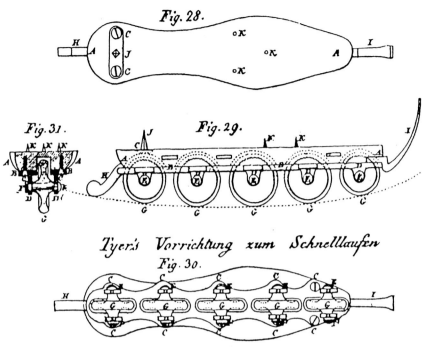

Roller Skate Patent Drawing

In 1823, London fruit merchant Robert John Tyers improved the roller skate with his own version. He called his model the "Volito" and fashioned the pair with a lineup of five wheels, the center roller having a larger diameter than the rest. The two wheels at the front and back were used for normal skating and the center spinner employed when turning. Today's "inline skates" are really nothing new—they have been around for centuries, predecessor to the carhop's working footwear.

American Graffiti Album

Left, roller-skate-riding carhops was more an image of drive-in folklore and myth than of reality and history. The image was made popular in the film American Graffiti, which played at movie theaters during the early 1970s. Later, it became a cult classic and is now replayed frequently on television. Ron Howard, Candy Clark, Richard Dreyfuss, Mackenzie Phillips, Harrison Ford, Cindy Williams, Paul LeMat, Suzanne Somers, and Charlie Martin Smith all took their first steps to future stardom in this drive-in classic. Album soundtrack circa 1973. David Willardson, cover artist. Copyright © by Universal City Studios, Inc. Courtesy of MCA Publishing Rights, a Division of MCA Inc.

RAMONA LONGPRÉ, MELS DRIVE-IN

Ramona Longpré was employed as a carhop at a number of California drive-in restaurants during the fifties and sixties. Her most memorable assignment: curb-girl at the Berkeley Mels. Although she never wore roller skates like the gals portrayed in the motion picture *American Graffiti*, she donned the smart service uniform and signature jacket that became the standard for West Coast car culture during the golden age of the drive-ins.

Sometimes, she would fill in for girls at a few of the other Mels locations, including the auto eatery many hops referred to as the "big stand" in San Francisco. But regardless of the particular locality, those nights spent serving the denizens of the roadways were pretty much the same: Fun food served up fast and furious in an atmosphere that reeked of pure excitement.

While toting trays at Mels, there was never a dull moment. She met lifelong friends there and wouldn't trade her experiences for anything. "Being a carhop at Mels was the best job I ever had," she proclaims proudly. "If I could do it again, I would!" When questioned further about the boundless energy most of today's retired curb-girls seem to exude, Ramona quickly explains why her associates seem so sprightly: "We have to be energetic…after all, we didn't save any of our money during our youth!" Today, Ramona operates a bar out in Point Richmond, California, and has permanently retired her window tray and ordering pad. ∎

continued from page 183

Now, as our nation heads towards the second millennium, "cruise nights" have become a common occurrence at remaining curb servers all across the country. In California, automobile clubs like the Auto Butchers, L.A. Roadsters, Over the Hill Gang, Road Kings, Rodfathers, West Coast Kustoms, and the Yakety-Yaks convene regularly at Bob's Big Boy in Toluca Lake (as of this writing, a landmark spared demolition). Sometimes, it's *American Graffiti* all over again when the clubs cruise Mels Drive-Ins. To everyone's approval, owner Steven Weiss has lovingly resurrected the fifties food bar with a quartet of outlets in Los Angeles, San Francisco, Sherman Oaks, and Woodland Hills. On special occasions, carhops return to duty as roadsters, woodies, and coupes rule the lot.

In the state where it all began, the same rituals are repeated. At the Pig Stand in Beaumont, Texas—perhaps the nation's oldest circular drive-in—"Eat a Pig Sandwich" continues as the popular slogan. Today, a new crowd of visitors eyeball the crazy rock and roll canopy and marvel at the neon pylons that wowed diners during the forties. Owner Richard Hailey hosts nostalgic festivities at the Broadway Pig Stand in San Antonio, including cruise nights frequented by the Best Little Ford Club in Texas, the Falcon Club, the Mopar Club, the Packard Club, and the T-Bird Club. At a recent event, local radio station KJ-97 staged a remote broadcast. A chauffeured ride in Elvis' black 1971 Caddy was a contest prize, and a dinner of Pig Sandwiches with all the trimmings was served to the winning couple.

In the Midwest, A&W Root Beer operator Ted Roen continues his own traditions in Ravenna, Ohio. Every Wednesday night during the summer months, his cooling refreshments are reserved for the local cruisers. Car organizations like the Nostalgic Cruisers and the Coachman Street Rod Club take over the grocery and drugstore's adjoining parking lots. A disc jockey spins stacks of wax from the fifties as revelers participate in a dance contest ("Come on baby, let's do the twist") and an entertaining trivia quiz. It's a blast from the past, fueled with mugs of frosty root beer.

Regardless of locality, the force that once contributed to the demise of the drive-in is now influencing its revival. While the unchanneled energies of youth may have caused trouble during the sixties, that exuberance has grown into experience and a respect for the way things were. Police patrols and entry gates are no longer needed. Ordinances have been discarded. Now, the baby-boom car crowd congregates to gather with friends, show off restored automobiles, and relive a few of the memories from the "good ol'days." Despite the passing years and changes, it's still a real "gas" to hop in a convertible, put the top down, and cruise to the nearest hamburger stand.

Fast food, step aside. The American drive-in restaurant—it's still as good as you remember! ■

BIBLIOGRAPHY

"Add Sparkle…Add Profits…to Your Drive-In With Council Canopies!" *Drive-In Restaurant* (November-December 1961): 24.

"Air-Conditioned Drive-In Service." *American Restaurant* (July 1957): 69.

Allen, Jane E. "White Tower Eatery Becomes Museum Piece." *Sunday News Journal*, Wilmington, Delaware (January 3, 1988): B7.

Anderson, Warren H. *Vanishing Roadside America*. Tucson: The University of Arizona Press, 1981.

Anderson, Will. *Mid-Atlantic Roadside Delights*. Portland, Maine: Anderson & Sons Publishing Co., 1991.

Anderson, Will. *New England Roadside Delights*. Portland, Maine: Anderson & Sons Publishing Co., 1989.

"Announcing the Exciting Childers New Look For Drive-Ins." *Drive-In Restaurant* (February 1964): 29-33.

Anson, Mike. "Drive-In Ettiquette." *Motor Trend* (March 1989): 8.

Armour, Richard. *Drug Store Days: My Youth Among the Pills and Potions*. New York: McGraw-Hill Book Company, Inc., 1959

"A&W Shows New Designs." *Drive-In Restaurant* 32 (July 1968): 42-43.

"A Blast From the Past—Cafe an Explosion of Things '50s." *Identity* (Winter 1990): 28-31, 78.

"Always Beckoning Customers…the ABC's of Good Design." *American Restaurant Magazine* 40 (May 1957): 214-216.

"Aut-O-Hop Electronic Carhop Systems." *Drive-In* (June 1955): 14-15.

"Automobile Air Conditioners Send Sales Up 20%." *Fountain & Fast Food* (July 1955): 30-31.

Baeder, John. *Gas, Food, and Lodging: A Postcard Odyssey Through the Great American Roadside*. New York: Abbeville Press, 1982.

Baraban, Regina. "The Amazing Evolution of Fast Food." *Restaurant Design* (Winter 1981): 30-37.

Bailey, K.V. "The Silent Salesman." *The Diner* 7 (September 1948): 14.

"Better Drive-In Service with Functional Planning." *American Restaurant* 33 (September 1951): 59, 79.

"Big Business with Small Menu." *American Restaurant* 38 (July 1955): 86, 89.

Bigelow, John. "The Detroit Study of Drive-In Problems." *Drive-In Restaurant* (August 1964): 12-15.

"Bloomington Gets Beautiful Restaurant Theatre—The Phil-Kron." *American Restaurant Magazine* (October 1947):62-63, 96.

Boas, Max and Steve Chain. *Big Mac: The Unauthorized Story of McDonald's*. New York: E.P. Dutton and Co., Inc., 1976.

Bongiorno, Bill. "Cruising Nick's." *Hot Rod* (March 1989): 112.

Bottles, Scott L. *Los Angeles and the Automobile: The Making of a Modern City*. Los Angeles: University of California Press, 1987.

Boyne, Walter J. *Power Behind the Wheel: Creativity and Evolution of the Automobile*. New York: Stewart, Tabori & Chang, 1988.

Brown, William R. "The 'Teen' Problem." *Drive-In and Carryout* (August 1970): 27-30; (September 1970): 28-29, 49.

"Brooklawn Serves Cars At Fountain." *Fountain Service* (November 1947): 26-27.

"The Burger Queen." *Drive-In Restaurant* 27 (September 1963): 16-19.

Burroughs, A. D. "First Impressions Are Lasting Impressions…." *Drive-In Restaurant and Highway Cafe Magazine* 20 (March 1956): 8.

"The Butterfly." *Drive-In Restaurant and Highway Cafe Magazine* 19 (July 1955): 15.

Caldwell, Bruce; Editor. *Petersen's The Best of Hot Rod*. Los Angeles, California: Petersen Magazine Network, 1986.

Califano, Alfred N. "A Study of Curb Service Drive-In Restaurants." *Drive-In Restaurant* (July 1964): 13-15.

Campbell, Dana Adkins. "Yesterday's Sodas and Shakes." *Southern Living* 27 (February 1992): 130.

"Canopies: What's Behind an old Standby's New Appeal." *National Petroleum News* 50 (November 1958): 99-104.

"Carhop Orders Speeded By Walkie-Talkie." *Popular Mechanics*. (November 1951): 227.

Carlino, Bill. "Beach Blanket Burgers' Welcome Summer at Sonic." *Nation's Restaurant News* 24 (June 1990): 12.

"The Carvel Story." *Ice Cream Trade Journal* (March 1954): 26 and 28, 119-120.

Cass, Lionel E. "Drive-Ins Coming For British Highways." *Drive-In Restaurant and Highway Cafe* (January 1957): 10.

Cather, Eddie. "Thanks, Eddie." *Car and Driver* 37 (October 1991): 22.

Cawthorne, Nigel. *Sixties Sourcebook, A Visual Reference to the Style of a New Generation*. Secaucus, New Jersey: Chartwell Books, 1989.

Chazanov, Mathis. "A Burger To Go and a Landmark Drive-In Is Gone." *Los Angeles Times* (March 12, 1984): Metro, 1.

"Chicken In the Rough." *American Restaurant* (June 1958): 60-61.

Childs, Leslie. "Hot Dog Kennels' as Nuisances to Adjoining Property Owners." *American City* 63 (February 1928): 137.

"Circular Drive-In Includes Commissary." *Architectural Record* (September 1946): 101.

Claudy, C. H. "Organizing the Wayside Tea House." *Country Life in America* 29 (June 1916): 54.

"Clean-Ups Every Hour At Starlite Drive-In." *Fountain Service* (October 1947): 32-33.

"Clowns On Roller Skates—Carhops With Extra Appeal." *American Restaurant* (September 1954): 63.

Cody, Larch. "Are Drive-Ins Being Driven Out?" *Los Angeles Herald-Examiner* (March 4, 1973) California Living: 9-10.

"Coffee Drinking In Public Declines 22 Per Cent." *Drive-In Restaurant and Highway Cafe* (July 1955): 14.

Coleman, Brent. "Designing an Image, Businesses Want Competitive Distinction." *The Sacramento Union* (August 25, 1987) Business Tuesday: 1, 4-5.

"Colossal Drive-In For Super Scenery." *Architectural Record* (September 1946): 104.

Corwin, Miles and Lorna Fernandes. "They Voted to Preserve 43-Year Old Restaurant." *Los Angeles Times* (March 15, 1992): Section R.

Coyle, Patrick L. *The World Encyclopedia of Food*. New York: Facts on File, Inc., 1981.

Dawson, Jim and Steve Propes. *What Was the First Rock'n'Roll Record*? Boston: Faber and Faber, 1992.

"Designed to Stop Both Eye and Car." *Drive-In Restaurant* 25 (July 1961): 8-9.

"Delores Drive-In." *Nation's Restaurant News* (October 20, 1980): 18.

"A Detour for Roadside America." *Business Week* (February 16, 1974): 44.

"The Detroit Study of Drive-In Problems." *Drive-In Restaurant* (August 1964): 12.

Dettelbach, Cynthia Golomb. *In the Driver's Seat: The Automobile in American Literature and Popular Culture*. Westport, Connecticut: Greenwood Press, 1976.

DeWolf, Rose. "Ice Cream Sun Days, The Treat That Says Summer Drips With Delicious Memories." *New Choices For the Best Years* 30 (July 1990): 96.

Dickson, Paul. *The Great American Ice Cream Book*. New York: Atheneum, 1972.

"Dina-A-Mike." *Drive-In Restaurant* (November-December 1961): 25.

"Dogs and Suds." *American Restaurant* (June 1958): 63.

Dolan, Carrie. "If You Really Cut the Mustard, You Will Relish This Job." *The Wall Street Journal* (July 7, 1992): A1, A8.

"Doumar's Cones and Barbecue." *The Virginian* (August 1985).

"Drive-In Closes Curb Because of Rowdyism." *Drive-In Restaurant* (January 1964): 27.

"The Drive-In Ordinance and You." *Drive-In Restaurant* (February 1965): 26-27.

"Drive-In Ordinance Roundup." Drive-In Restaurant (November 1965): 22-23, 26; (August 1967): 39-41; (June 1967): 59.

"Drive-In Patios." *Drive-In Restaurant* (August 1963): 20-21.

"Drive-In Restaurant." *The Architectural Forum* (November 1945): 162-163.

"Drive-In Restaurant Near Jantzen Beach, Oregon." *Progressive Architecture* (June 1947): 61-63.

"Drive-In Restaurants and Luncheonettes." *Architectural Record* (September 1946): 99-106.

"Drive-In Restaurant Telephones." *Fountain Service* (July 1950): 28-29.

"Drive-In Service Goes Automatic." *American Restaurant* (September 1953): 89.

"The 'Drive-Thru.'" *Drive-In Restaurant and Highway Cafe* 21 (January 1957): 11.

Duffy, Tom. "Home of the Hamburger." *Celebration* Booklet; Seymour, Wisconsin (August 5, 1989): 1-7.

Dunne, Mike. "Can the Fab Fifties Rock 'n' Roll?" *The Sacramento Bee* Final (September 3, 1987) Scene and Style: 1, 6-7.

"Eating Goes On Assembly Line at California Drive-In." *Business Week* (July 23, 1949): 22-23.

"The Eccentric." *Drive-In Restaurant* 27 (November 1963): 31.

Eiss, Albert. "Carhop Service—Yes Or No?" *Restaurant Management* (June 1960): 32, 130, 132.

"1,800 Meals Is Daily Average at Steak n Shake, St. Louis, Mo." *Fountain and Fast Food* (September 1953): 50-51.

"The Electronic Ordering Systems Manufacturers Speak." *Drive-In* (April 1957): 5-15.

"Elevating the Standing of the 'Hot Dog Kennel'." *American City* 38 (May 1928): 99-100.

Ellis, Harry E. *Dr Pepper, King of Beverages*. Dallas, Texas: Taylor Publishing Company, 1979.

Emerson, Robert L. *Fast Food: The Endless Shakeout*. New York: Lebhar-Friedman, Inc., 1979.

"Everything is Automated But the Carhop." *Science Digest* (November 1966): 32.

Fair, Ernest W. "Denver…Where Business is Averaging $650,000 a Month For Restaurants." *American Restaurants* (August 1947): 24.

Fair, Ernest W. "Salt Lake City, A Great City for Eating Out and Keen Competition." *American Restaurant* (September 1947): 26-28, 66.

Fair, Ernest W. "Tulsa, One of the Best Restaurant Towns In The Nation…Where Drive-Ins Are Numerous and Sumptuous Dining Rooms Are the Rule." *American Restaurant* (May 1948): 30-32.

Fair, Ernest W. "Atlanta, Restaurants Are Doing a $20,000,000 Business in This Southern Metropolis." *American Restaurant* (May 1947): 22, 26, 52-53.

Fanald, Lon. "A Robot Takes the Car Hop Out of the Track's Service." *Fountain Service* (November 1950): 30.

Farragher, Marcella. "Graphics Splash Color Into Bland Buildings, Dunlavey Studio Pulls 3D Building Into Sharp Focus." *The Sacramento Union* (July 9, 1989) Home & Real Estate: 27, 29.

Farb, Peter and George Armelagos. *Consuming Passions: The Anthropology of Eating*. New York: Houghton Mifflin Company, 1980.

Ferguson, Frank L. *Efficient Drug Store Management*. New York: Fairchild Publications, Inc., 1969.

"50 Ideas For Drive-Ins." *American Restaurant* 42 (July 1959): 52-53, 86.

Finch, Christopher. *Highways to Heaven: The Auto Biography of America*. New York: HarperCollins Publishers, Inc., 1992.

"41 In Florida." *Drive-In Restaurant and Highway Cafe* (June 1955): 19, 26.

Fling, Ray. "Is the Public Turning Away From 'Established' Restaurants?" *Restaurant Management* (March 1929): 43-44.

Flink, James J. *The Automobile Age*. Cambridge, Massachusetts: The M.I.T. Press, 1988.

"Foods Made Fast Sell Fast." *American Restaurant* (February 1955): 70.

Franks, Julia. "California Dreaming." *Restaurant/Hotel Design International* (November 1989): 69, 71.

Frazer, Elizabeth. "The Destruction of Rural America: Game, Fish and Flower Hogs." *The Saturday Evening Post* (9 May, 1929): 39, 193-194, 197-198.

Friddel, Guy. "The Smithsonian Agrees: Doumar's Ice Cream Cone Was the First." *The Virginia Pilot* (March 18, 1994).

Furniss, Ruth MacFarland. "The Ways of the Tea House." *Tea Room Management* 1 (August 1922): 5.

Gaines, Jerry. "How We Handled the Kansas City Problem." *Drive-In Restaurant* (March 1965): 27.

Gebhard, David, and Harriette Von Breton. *L.A. in the Thirties*. New York: Peregrine Smith, Inc., 1975.

Gelderman, Carol. *Henry Ford, The Wayward Capilist*. New York: St. Martin's Press, 1981.

"Goodbye Carhops." *Fast Food* (November 1963): 18-21.

"Good Mormons Don't Go Broke." *Saturday Evening Post* (June 10, 1950): 48-49, 157-160.

Gordy, Wilbur Fisk. *History of the United States*. New York: Charles Scribner's Sons, 1922.

Goydon, Raymond. "Custard's Last Stand." *Forbes Magazine* (July 1, 1985).

Gutman, Richard J. S.; Kauffman, Elliot; and David Slovic. *American Diner*. New York: Harper & Row, 1979.

Gutman, Richard J. S. *American Diner, Then and Now*. New York: HarperCollins Publishers, Inc., 1993.

Hayes, Jack. "Drive-thrus Get Into the Fast Lane: Upstart 'Burger Boxes' Challenge Fast-Food Giants." *Nation's Restaurant News* 23 (November 1989): 1, 70.

Hastings, Charles Warren. "Roadtown, The Linear City." *Architects and Builders Magazine* 10 (August 1910): 445.

Heat Moon, William Least. *Blue Highways: A Journey Into America*. Boston: Atlantic Monthly Press, 1982.

Heimann, Jim and Rip Georges. *California Crazy, Roadside Vernacular Architecture*. San Francisco: Chronicle Books, 1980.

Helen Christine Bennett, "'Pinkie's Pantry' Took The Cake." *American Magazine* (June 1928): 65-66.

Hellemans, Alexander and Bryan Bunch. *The Timetables of Science*. New York: Simon and Schuster, 1988.

"Here's How Ott's Picks Good Dispensers." *Fountain Service* (January 1950): 32-33.

Hempt, Grace Elizabeth. "Old Grist Mill is Now a Tea Room." *Tea Room and Gift Shop* 2 (March 1923): 7.

Hess, Alan. *Googie, Fifties Coffee Shop Architecture*. San Francisco: Chronicle Books, 1985.

Hicks, Clifford B. "Computerburger Hit the Assembly Line." *Popular Mechanics* (September 1966): 81-85.

"Highway Restaurants" *Architectural Record* (October 1954): 163, 167-169.

Higdon, Edna. "Customers Phone the Orders At Bill's Seattle Drive-In." *Fountain Service* (November 1950): 31.

Hill, Debra Goldstein. *Price Guide to Coca-Cola Collectibles*. Lombard, Illinois: Wallace-Homestead Book Company, 1984.

Hirschman, Bill. "Confrontation Outside Drive-through Window Cost Man His Life." *The Wichita Eagle* (April 15, 1993) 1D, 3D.

Hirshorn, Paul and Stephen Izenour. *White Towers*. Cambridge, Massachusetts: The MIT Press, 1979.

Hoopes, Lydia Clawson. "From Root Beer Stand to Millions." *American Restaurant* 31 (May 1948): 39-42, 117-122.

"Houston's Drive-In Trade Gets Girl Show With Its Hamburgers." *Life* (February 26, 1940): 84-87.

"The Howard Johnson's Restaurants." *Fortune* 22 (September 1940): 82-87, 94, 96.

"How Drive-Ins Compare With Other Restaurants." *Drive-In Restaurant* 32 (April 1968): 40.

"How Pig Stands Started the Drive-In Restaurant." *Drive-In Management* (September 1961): 22-30.

Hungerford, Edward. "America Awheel." *Everybody's Magazine* 36 (June 1917): 678.

Hunt, Gordon. "Call the Mayor, They're Cruising Again!" *Drive-In Restaurant* (November 1965): 18-22.

Hunt, Mary. "Good-by To Everett's." *Ann Arbor Observer* 3-10 (June 1979): 27-28, 50.

Huxtable, Ada Louise. "Architecture for a Fast Food Culture." *New York Times Magazine* (February 12 1978): 23-25.

"Improve Your Service With Half The Help." *American Restaurant Magazine* (May 1955): 39.

"In Atlanta, All Roads Lead to the Varsity." *Business Week* 8 (October 1966): 132-133.

"In-Car 'Hopless' Service is Big Boy's Answer." *Fountain & Fast Food Service* (February 1952): 34.

Ingram, E.W., Sr. *All This From a 5-cent Hamburger! The Story of the White Castle System.* New York: The Newcomen Society in North America, 1964.

Jackson, Howard E. "It Pays to Pay Employees for Putting Forth Extra Effort." *American Restaurant* (June 1950): 35, 121.

Jarvis, Jack. "Tombstones To 'Burgers." *Seattle Post Intelligencer* (August 31, 1965).

Johnson, Robert. "Frozen Custard Is Soft Ice Cream But Hard To Find." *The Wall Street Journal* (June 19, 1986).

Jones, Dwayne and Roni Morales. "Pig Stands, The Beginning of the Drive-In Restaurant." *SCA NewJournal* 12 (Winter 1991-92): 2-5.

Jones, W.E. "A Million $ A Year, Allen's Drive-In Does It by Specializing, by Service, by Food Control, by Quality." *Fountain & Fast Food Service* (December 1951): 18.

Joy, Dena. "At the Car Hop, Drive-In Has Disappeared But Memories Remain for the Girls From Stan's." *The Bakersfield Californian* (March 11, 1986) Accent: 1-2.

Keegan, Peter O. "Video Drive-Thrus Speed Fast-Food Service." *Nation's Restaurant News* 24 (November 1990): 3, 110.

Keller, Ulrich. *The Highway as Habitat: A Roy Stryker Documentation, 1943-1955.* Santa Barbara, California: University Art Museum, 1986.

Kimball, Jim. "How Kim's Design Discourages Litterbugs." *Drive-In Restaurant* (November 1965): 27-29.

King, Marsha. "Cruising In the Past Lane." *Seattle Post Intelligencer* (June 14, 1992): Section K1-2.

Kendall, Elaine. "The Most Famous Boring Food In America." *Vogue* (October 1, 1969): 258, 260-261, 265.

"Kitchen Layout and Equipment Design Gives Fast Service at Hardee's." *Drive-In Restaurant* 26 (August 1962): 10-12.

Knutson, L.W. "Ideas From 20 Years in Drive-Ins." *Drive-In Restaurant* 30 (April 1966): 37-38, 67.

Kowinski, William Severini. "Suburbia: End of the Golden Age." *The New York Times Magazine* (16 March, 1980): 16-19, 106.

Kroc, Ray. *Grinding It Out: The Making of McDonald's.* Chicago, Illinois: Henry Regnery Company, 1977.

Kurtz, Stephen A. *Wasteland: Building the American Dream.* New York: Praeger Publishers, 1973.

Langdon, Philip. *Orange Roofs, Golden Arches: The Architecture of American Chain Restaurants.* New York: Alfred A. Knopf, 1986.

Lay, Charles Downing. "New Towns for High-Speed Roads." *Architectural Record* 78 (November 1935): 352-354.

Lewis, David L. and Lawrence Goldstein. *The Automobile and American Culture.* Ann Arbor: The University of Michigan Press, 1980.

Liebs, Chester. *Main Street to Miracle Mile: American Roadside Architecture.* Boston: Little, Brown & Co., 1985.

"Life After Death Along Gasoline Alley." *Fortune* (November 5, 1979): 86-89.

Linder, Robert. "Parking Comments." *Drive-In Restaurant* (March 1963): 20-22.

"Los Angeles Lowdown." *The Diner* (September 1946): 8-9.

Louis, David. *2201 Fascinating Facts.* New York: Wings Books, 1983.

Love, John F. *McDonald's: Behind the Arches.* New York: Bantam Books, 1986.

"Lunch Wagons Streamline—Customers Stream In." *Nation's Business* 25 (September 1937): 74.

Luxenberg, Stan. *Roadside Empires: How the Chains Franchised America.* New York: Viking Penguin, Inc., 1985.

Mackaye, Benton, and Lewis Mumford. "Townless Highways for the Motorist." *Harper's* 163 (August 1931): 347-356.

"Main Street 1910." *Fast Service* 39 (October 1980): 34-36, 61.

"Making Big Money For Owners!" *Fountain Service* (May 1948): 3.

Mariani, John. *America Eats Out.* New York: William Morrow and Company, Inc., 1991.

Marken, Cal. "How Big Are You?" *Drive-In Restaurant* (September 1965): 10.

Marks, David. "'A Dessert No Less Curious,' A Short History of Ice Cream in America." *Early American Life* 22 (June 1991): 64.

Markstein, David. "The Frostop Story." *Fountain and Fast Food* (September 1956): 56 and 58.

Marling, Karal Ann. *The Colossus of Roads: Myth and Symbol Along the American Highway.* Minneapolis: Univ. of Minnesota Press, 1984.

Martin, Richard. "Marriott Brings Car Hop Service to Bob's Big Boy." *Nation's Restaurant News* 24 (October 1990): 4.

Marvel, Bill. "Savoring the Classic Sizzle." *Dallas Times Herald* (August 26, 1984): 1E and 8E.

Matteson, Donald W. *The Auto Radio, A Romantic Genealogy.* Jackson, Michigan: Thornridge Publishing, 1987.

McCall, Bruce. "Los Angeles, Once Upon a Time." *The New Yorker* 67 (June 1991): 36.

"Mexican Foods—Family Style." *Drive-In & Carry-Out* (April 1969): 46-47.

"The Moderne." *Drive-In Restaurant and Highway Cafe Magazine* (October 1956): 19.

Montagne, Prosper. *Larousse Gastronomique.* New York: Crown Publishers, 1961.

"More Than a Shade of Difference." *Drive-In Restaurant* (November 1965): 16-17.

Morrison, Tom. *Root Beer Advertising and Collectibles.* West Chester, Pennsylvania: Schiffer Publishing, Ltd., 1992.

"Motormat 'Magic' a Revolutionary Method of Food Service For Drive-Ins." *American Restaurant* (September 1949): 48, 62.

"**T**he New Outlet—Roadside Refreshment Stands." *Printer's Ink* 135 (22 April 1926): 127.

"New Profit Boom In Electronic Service." *Drive-In Restaurant and Highway Cafe* (November 1955): 12-14, 17.

"The Newspaper Said...Bill Ihlenfeldt Replied." *Drive-In Restaurant* (March 1965):26-27.

"Now! Only Aut-O-Hop Has AMG!" *Drive-In* (May 1958): 9.

"**O**K, Who Ordered the Burger With 500 Pickles?" *Life* (August 27, 1971): 68.

Oliver, Thomas. *The Real Coke, the Real Story.* New York, New York: Random House, 1986.

O'Meara, John B. "Drive-In Service Do's and Don'ts." *American Restaurant* 39 (July 1956): 70-71, 110-111.

O'Meara, John B. "Do's and Don'ts for Better Drive-In Service." *American Restaurant* 39 (July 1957): 82-85.

"122 Ideas For Drive-Ins." *American Restaurant* (June 1955): 65.

"One Million Hamburgers and 160 Tons of French Fries a Year." *American Restaurant* (July 1952): 44-45.

Oppel, Frank. *Motoring In America: The Early Years.* Secaucus, New Jersey: Castle Books, 1989.

Orth, Fred A. "Neon Gas Signs—What Are They?" *The American Restaurant* (April 1928): 53, 87-91.

Paul, John R. and Paul W. Parmalee. *Soft Drink Bottling, A History With Special Reference to Illinois.* Springfield: Illinois State Museum Society, 1973.

"Palaces of the Hot Doges." *Architectural Forum* 63 (August 1935): 30-31.

Patton, Phil. *Open Road: A Celebration of the American Highway.* New York: Simon & Schuster, 1986.

Pearce, Christopher. *Fifties Sourcebook, A Visual Guide to the Style of a Decade.* Secaucus, New Jersey: Chartwell Books, 1990.

Petretti, Allan. *Petretti's Coca-Cola Collectibles Price Guide.* Radner, Pennsylvania: Wallace Homestead, 1992.

"Pick a Good Location." *American Restaurant Magazine* (October 1954): 71-73.

"Pizza Burger—New Idea In Sandwiches." *American Restaurant* (September 1954): 59.

"Prizes Mark Gala Opening." *Drive-In Restaurant and Highway Cafe* (August 1955): 5.

Poling-Kempes, Lesley. *The Harvey Girls, Women Who Opened the West.* New York: Paragon House, 1991.

Pollexfen, Jack. "Don't Get Out." *Collier's* (March 19, 1938): 18, 52-54.

Pomeroy, Ralph. *The Ice Cream Connection.* New York: Paddington Press, Ltd., 1975.

"Ptomaine Joe's Place." *Collier's* 102 (1 October 1938): 54.

"Puritan Maid Drive-Ins Feature Bird-In-Hand." *American Restaurant* (July 1940): 22.

Rapoport, Roger. "Restored Soda Fountains of Yesterday." *Americana* 19 (July-August 1991): 60-61, 64.

"Rectangular Drive-In With Non-Glare Front." *The Architectural Record* (September 1946): 103.

Reddin, John J. "Dag's Keeps Frying With Imagination." *Seattle Times* (April 15, 1962).

Reinhart, Dorothy. "Laughter, Tears Mark the Final Closing of Henry's, 41-Year Glendale Landmark." *The Legder*, Glendale-Burbank (November 2, 1977): Section 3, 11.

Richmond, Ray. "Going, Going, Gone—It's Over For Tiny Naylor's" *Los Angeles Daily News* (March 14, 1984): L.A. Life, 7.

Riley, Robert M. "The Big Boom Out West: Coffee Shops." *Drive-In* (November 1961): 44-48.

"Roadside Diners." *The Architectural Record* (July 1934): 56-57.

"The Roadside Stand Grows Up—Ultra Modern, Magnificent." *Drive-In Restaurant and Highway Cafe Magazine* (November 1955): 21, 27.

"Robert C. Wian, Jr." *American Restaurant* (June 1952): 148.

Roberts-Dominguez, Jan. *The Mustard Book*. New York: Macmillan Publishing Company, 1993.

Rodd, W.C. "One Building For Two Types of Clientele." *American Restaurant Magazine* (August 1948): 35-37, 131.

"Roy W. Allen, Drive-In Pioneer, Dies at 85." *Drive-In Restaurant* (May 1968): 58-59.

Rubin, Charles J., David Rollert, John Farago, and Jonathan Etra. *Junk Food*. New York: Dell Publishing Co., Inc., 1980.

"Rutherford's Pioneer Drive-In Marks Thirty Years As Renton Institution." *Renton News Record* (April 11, 1960).

Sacharow, Stanley. *Symbols of Trade*. New York, New York: Art Direction Book Company, 1982.

"San Bernadino's New Drive-In Ordinance." *Drive-In Restaurant* (November 1964): 20-21.

Sare, John. "Unique Drive-In Recalled, Owner J.D. Sivils Has Died at Age 78." *Dallas Morning News* (June 24, 1986): 14A.

Schuman, Michael A. "A Trip Into the McPast." *The Seattle Times* (June 20, 1989): D6-7.

Segrave, Kerry. *Drive-in Theaters, A History From Their Inception In 1933*. Jefferson, North Carolina: McFarland & Company, Inc., Publishers, 1992.

"Selby Industries, Inc." *Drive-In Restaurant* (October 1963): 12.

Selby, John. "Prefab Canopies, The New Look in Drive-Ins." *Drive-In* (April 1958): 16-17.

"Service Fone Equipment." *Drive-In Restaurant* (February 1966): 51.

"Serving 3,000 Cars Daily." *American Restaurant Magazine* (August 1951): 42-43, 72.

"$64 Answers." *Drive-In Restaurant and Highway Cafe* (June 1955): 24, 27.

Skellenger, Gordon. "We Thought Everything Would Be All Right." *Drive-In Restaurant* (June 1965): 12.

Skenazy, Lenore. "The King Had a Love Affair With Food." *The Arizona Daily Star* (August 8, 1993): Section D, 11.

Short, Robert. "Delay Costs Man His Life at Restaurant." *Wichita Eagle* (April 14, 1993).

"Shrine To the Hamburger." *Popular Mechanics* (January 1949): 101-103.

Silk, Gerald, Angelo Anselmi, Henry Robert, Jr., and Strother MacMinn. *Automobile and Culture*. New York: Harry N. Abrams, Inc., 1984.

Snow, Richard F. "King Cone." *Invention & Technology* 9 (Fall 1993): 4-5.

Snyder, James. "Roadside Beauty and YOU." *Drive-In Restaurant* (November 1965): 24-26.

Society for Commercial Archeology. *The Automobile in Design and Culture*. Edited by Jan Jennings. Ames: Iowa State University Press, 1990.

Squire, Latham C., and Howard M. Bassett. "A New Type of Thoroughfare: The 'Freeway.'" *American City* 47 (November 1932): 64-66.

Steingarten, Jeffrey. "Simply Red." *Vogue* 182 (August 1992): 244, 298-300.

Stern, Jane and Michael Stern. *A Taste of America*. New York: Andrews and McMeel, 1988.

Stern, Jane and Michael Stern. *Encyclopedia of Pop Culture*. New York: HarperCollins Publishers, Inc., 1992.

Stern, Jane and Michael Stern. *RoadFood*. New York: HarperCollins Publishers, Inc., 1992.

Stern, Rudi. *Let There Be Neon*. New York: Harry N. Abrams, Inc., 1979.

Stuckey, Lillie and Avanelle Day. *The Spice Cook Book*. New York: David White Company, 1964.

"The Sweep Inn." *Drive-In Restaurant and Highway Cafe* (September 1955): 15.

Tackett, John. "Restaurant Wins Pig Sandwich Case." *The San Antonio Light* (February 16, 1990).

"Take Home Takes Up Slack In Volume." *American Restaurant Magazine* (April 1955): 92

Teague, Walter Dorwin. *Design This Day: The Technique of Order in the Machine Age*. New York: Harcourt, Brace & Co., 1940.

"A $10 Million Drive-In." *Drive-In Restaurant* (May 1964): 12-16.

Tennyson, Jeffrey. *Hamburger Heaven, The Illustrated History of the Hamburger*. New York: Hyperion, 1993.

"That's The Important Word—Thank You!" *Drive-In Restaurant* (October 1963): 12-13.

Thomas, Frank B. "Parking Comments." *Drive-In Restaurant* (March 1963): 21.

Thurow, Roger. "Frankly, Viennese Eschew Verbal Link to Their Weiners." *The Wall Street Journal* (February 15, 1994): A1, col. 4.

"Tomorrow's Secret of Faster Food Service." *American Restaurant Hospitality* (April 1963): 58.

Trap, Jack. *Roller Skating Start to Finish*. New York: Penguin, 1980.

"Tray on a Trestle Serves at Drive-In." *Popular Mechanics* 72 (September 1949): 127.

"2,500,000 gallons of Mix For Soft-Serve Products Sold By Tastee-Freeze in 1952." *Ice Cream Trade Journal* (July 1953): 38 and 79.

"2 'Catchy' Items…33 Busy Drive-Ins." *American Restaurant* (July 1958): 51.

"Two Roadside Drive-Ins Use Light Framing and Lots of Glass." *The Architectural Forum* (October 1946): 144.

"Unique Building Attracts Customers." *Soda Fountain* (September 1941): 58.

"Visual Attraction of Canopy Can Draw More Customers." *Drive-In* (April 1959): 34.

"Walkie-Talkie Drive-In." *Restaurant Management* (September 1951): 40-41, 103.

"Washington, D.C.: Curb-Service Dictates A New Form." *Architectural Record* (March 1938): 70-71.

Watters, Pat. *Coca-Cola, An Illustrated History*. New York: Doubleday & Company, Inc., 1978.

"Wayside Stands, Billboards, Curb Pumps, Lunch Wagons, Junk Yards, and Their Ilk." *American City* 44 (April 1931): 104-108.

Weinstein, Jeff. "Four Time-Worn Chains Plot Course For Recovery." *Restaurants & Institutions* 101 (November 1991): 39.

Welch, Dr. John M. "Is Experience and Asset of a Liability?" *Drive-In Restaurant* (April 1966): 39-40.

"Where the Drive-Ins Are." *Drive-In Restaurant* 28 (April 1964): 16.

"Who'll Get Helped or Hurt by Auto Freeways." *U.S. News and World Report* (21 December 1956):90-92.

Wilkins, Mike; Ken Smith and Doug Kirby. *The New Updated and Expanded Roadside America*. New York: Simon & Schuster, 1986.

William Poundstone. *Big Secrets, The Uncensored Truth About All Sorts of Stuff You Are Never Supposed to Know*. New York: William Morrow & Company, Inc., 1983.

Willis, Lyn. "J.A. Rutherford, Who Came West To Ranch, Eventually Struck Gold In the Northwest's First Drive-In Root Beer Stands." *Montana* 13 (Winter 1963): 8-17.

Wilson, Richard Guy; Dianne H. Pilgrim and Dickran Tashjian. *The Machine Age in America 1918-1941*. New York: Harry N. Abrams, Inc., 1986.

Witzel, Michael Karl. *The American Gas Station: History and Folklore of the Gas Station In American Car Culture*. Osceola, Wisconsin: Motorbooks International, 1992.

Woodson, LeRoy. *Roadside Food*. New York: Stewart, Tabori & Chang, Inc., 1986.

Wynne, Robert. "Hamming It Up, Pig Stands Mark 68th Year With '50s-Style Sock Hop." *The San Antonio Light* (October 12, 1989):F1, F17.

The World Book Encyclopedia. Chicago: Field Enterprises Educational Corporation, 1969.

"Your Curb is Your Atmosphere." *Drive-In Magazine* 24 (March 1960): 32-35.

MILKSHAKES *counter service*

INDEX